Henry C Lockwood

Constitutional History of France

Henry C Lockwood

Constitutional History of France

ISBN/EAN: 9783337326579

Printed in Europe, USA, Canada, Australia, Japan

Cover: Foto ©ninafisch / pixelio.de

More available books at **www.hansebooks.com**

Napoleon Bonaparte, as First Consul.
(From a Drawing by L. C. David.)

CONSTITUTIONAL
HISTORY OF FRANCE.

BY

HENRY C. LOCKWOOD,

AUTHOR OF "ABOLITION OF THE PRESIDENCY," ETC.

SUPPLEMENTED BY

FULL AND PRECISE TRANSLATIONS OF THE TEXT OF THE
VARIOUS CONSTITUTIONS AND CONSTITUTIONAL
LAWS IN OPERATION AT DIFFERENT
TIMES, FROM 1789 TO 1889.

substantially a reproduction of the Constitution of the year VIII, and the Constitutional laws which now govern France were never adopted by a constituent assembly.

The *senatus consultum* of the 16th *Thermidor*, year X, creating the consulship for life; of the 28th *Floreal*, year XII, making Napoleon I. Emperor; and of August 19, 1807, suppressing the Tribunate, were but modifications of Napoleon's Constitution of 22d *Frimaire*, year VIII.

Napoleon III. governed France for seventeen years by virtue of his Constitution of January 14, 1852, as modified by the *senatus consultum* of November 7, which established the hereditary empire; of December 25, 1852, which completed the imperial structure; of November 24, 1860, which permitted the Senate and Legislative Body to reply by the "Address" to the Crown's message; of January 19, 1867, which acknowledged the right of interpellation; of September 8, 1869, declaring the ministers responsible; and of April 23, 1870, claiming to enact a new Constitution, and to assure the future of the Napoleonic dynasty.

The Constitutions which are set forth in the appendix of this book were translated from the text as published in the "Histoire Constitutionnelle des Français. Textes et Commentaires," par F. E. Planteau, translator for the Court of Appeal in Paris. In making the translation of the Constitutions of 1793, 1795, and 1799, the author was assisted by the work of Bernard Roelker on "The Constitutions of France," as he was also largely aided by the translations of the Constitutions of 1814, 1830, 1848, and 1852, made by Francis Lieber, LL.D., in his work on "Civil Liberty."

Scarcely a page of this book could have been written without reference to the following works, among others, which have been consulted, quoted, or mentioned, and from whose pages expressions, and even sentences, have been made use of by the author. The works referred to are: The works of Thiers, Taine, Lamartine, Blanc, Mignet, Capefigue, Michelet, Guizot, Morley, Scherer, Lockroy, Hugo, De Tocqueville, and Sir Erskine May. "Histoire de la Civilisation Contemporaine en France," par Alfred Rambaud; "La France du Centenaire," par Edouard Goamy; "Journal Officiel;" "Les Constitutions de la France," par Faustin Hélie; "Les Orateurs de la Constituante, de la Législative, de la Convention," par Aulard; "Histoire Parlementaire de la Revolution," par Buchez et Roux; "La France en 1789," par Pezard; "Le Centenaire de 1789," par E. D'Argill; "The Code Napoleon;" "Les Constitutions Européennes," par Demomlynes; "Les Constitutions Françaises," par Plouard; "La Constitution Française de 1875," par M. M. Bard et Robiquet; "Codes et Lois," par Roger et Sorel; "Droit Administratif," par Aucoc, and "Etudes Administratives," par Vivien.

In the preparation of Chapters V, VI, and VII, the author has, in his statement of the historic facts, drawn freely from the work of M. Planteau, but in such a manner as not to make that writer in any way responsible for the opinions of others that may have been added, or for the arguments or reflections that are expressed in that portion of this work.

On September 22, 1889, the quadrennial elections for deputies took place, under the provisions of the law of July 17, and resulted in a victory for the Government. The re-balloting which occurred October 6 further strengthened the party that favors the continuance of the Parliamentary Republic.

CONSTITUTIONAL HISTORY OF FRANCE.

I.

THE REVOLUTION AND THE FIRST REPUBLIC.

Whenever an advance in governmental evolution has been suggested, or advocated, by great parties springing from the people, the events of French history, from the time of the encyclopedists to the present day, have generally been distorted by the reactionary forces which usually constitute the opposition to reform; and when, in the last 100 years, it was proposed to do away with the remnants of feudalism, abolish slavery, extend the popular suffrage, and establish parliamentary government, by some strange paradox in reasoning, the experiences and struggles of this brave people, in their march from absolutism to democracy, have been paraded as furnishing a dreadful example against any attempt for the betterment of mankind.

When it was suggested in England to abolish the slave trade, and repeal the Test Act, ghastly references were made to noyades, fusillades, and guillotines; and Sir Robert Peel was warned, in his effort to reform the corn laws, that he was bringing about a catastrophe like that of 1789, while Cobden and Bright were likened to Babœuf,

Chaumette, and Anacharsis Clootz. Robespierre, Danton, and Marat were trotted forth in their sanguinary winding-sheets, and treated as the counterparts and precursors of "modern worthies," and an innocent meeting of voters has recalled to some well-known writers lurid visions of the Cordeliers and Jacobin Clubs.

Mr. John Morley has been described as the Saint Just of the English revolution of the present day. "It would have been just as well," says Morley, "to call me Nero, Torquemada, Iago, or Bluebeard." The course pursued toward this publicist illustrates the general treatment of French politics and governmental reform by the English-speaking people. The idea underlying what is known as conservative thought is, that if the French had never had a revolution of their own, and had never been compelled to resort to extreme measures to overthrow bad government in their country, that good government would have grown faster in the rest of the world.

Nothing could be a greater perversion of fact than this position, which has been assumed by so many influential writers and prominent political leaders, for a careful examination of historic facts will show that the effect of the French Revolution was most beneficial upon the structural mechanism of the governments of the world.

It is perfectly true that there is a continuity in history; that it is quite impossible to comprehend the affairs of one country in their general form without knowing the historic facts which precede them; that history opens the mind to generous impulses, quickens the political imagination, instructs the mass in the experiences of government, allows the thinker to make analogies, and, in fine, to profit by that force which lies back of the growth and development in government. This force, however, must be treated in its general spirit and essence, and, above all, one must be careful to avoid strained comparisons and unnatural attempts to bring dissimilar events into juxtaposition. If the greatest care is not practiced, positions will be assumed that are both fictitious and unreal, and precedent, which is ever sought for by the human mind, will be used to forge new chains for humanity.

Beyond doubt, as a philosophical abstraction, it is true that the Cromwellian hastened the American, and the American the French Revolution; still, the environments of these three epochs are quite dissimilar, and can not strictly be compared with each other. It would be unscientific to claim that there was a semblance between Cromwell and Washington. Such an attempt would possibly result in a straining after an antithesis for literary effect.

The practical question is: What influence have the events of French history exerted, for the last 100 years, upon the people of the world, as manifested through their governments? If a general lesson is given to the world by this nation, what is it? To examine this question properly, it will be necessary to discover what the French people have done in the development of constitutional and statute law.

Italy, Switzerland, and the Netherlands had made rapid strides in the art of self-government before democracy had taken any outward form in France, but after it had been once organized and put in action in that country, its movement was most rapid and vigorous; it was necessary for it to be vigorous, for it was compelled to meet a condition of things created by one of the most infamous of all systems of absolutism, and rapid because it assumed the form of revolution. Reform, which is slow revolution, would not suit the conditions; only active, merciless revolution could strike the blow that was required to clean the Augean stables. There is no history which so brilliantly illustrates the social and political causes which led to democracy; none which exemplifies its force, power, and efficiency so thoroughly as the experiences of the French people in the last 100 years.

To comprehend the condition of things that immediately preceded the eventful revolution which occurred in France, it must be remembered that a combination between State and Church existed there for the purpose of enslaving the people through feudal laws, ignorance, suppression of personal rights, taxation, and every device that could be suggested by priest or courtier. If a parliament, or a semblance of one, as in 1771, showed any signs of independence, as it did at this time, it was abolished by Louis XV.

Louis XIV. silenced his parliament by the creation of *lits de justice;* if his subjects—and citizens were then called subjects—raised their voices in remonstrance, they were imprisoned by *lettres de cachet;* if they were offensive, they were banished by *lettres d'exil.* The Edict of Nantes was revoked. The *conseil du Roi* assumed and exercised all administrative, legislative, and judicial power. A condition of personal power existed known only to a system of most pronounced and complete absolutism.

Whatever truth there is in the saying that Paris is France—one of the favorite aphorisms of English-speaking people—it is certainly true that at one time the votaries of monarchy did much to give that great city an undue political influence. One would think, from the usual way of discussing French affairs, that all the so-called socialists, red republicans, atheists, revolutionists, proletariats, and the offscourings of creation had come to Paris for the purpose of destroying the pure-lived priests and nobles, overthrowing the best government the world had ever been blessed with, and thus giving a check, in the name of liberty, to actual liberty among all nations.

The fact is, that the population which eventually constituted the revolutionary class was brought to the city of Paris by monarchy itself. It was once the policy of State to make Paris the center of art, literature, and particularly of manufactures. It was quite impossible successfully to carry on manufacturing interests outside of Paris. The consequence was that vast numbers of skilled workmen concentrated in that city.

But it was not only these classes that sought the capital, for it became fashionable for country gentlemen to abandon their positions as magistrates at home, and in many cases princes in power repaired to Paris and became little less than servants to the king, while they abandoned their estates to decay, and to the ravages of the usurer. Then, suicidal as this policy was, they also consented that the peasantry be taxed and robbed by Church and State, or dragged from their homes involuntarily to serve in the army or navy. The natural consequence of this condition of things was that the healthy middle and agricultural class was destroyed. At last famine stalked abroad, forcing men to become robbers, poachers, and thieves.

Practically there could be no appeal to the fundamental law, for the general law took its rise in the will and purpose of the sovereign, and there could be no enforcement of personal rights in the courts. Under such circumstances it is no wonder that the people's minds turned to thoughts of violent interference with such a travesty of justice, even though masked under all the solemn forms of judicial dignity.

This condition of things produced a class of reformers and theorists. They were thoroughly iconoclastic in their antagonism to the religious and political systems of that day. They were so regarded. They existed by sufferance— hanging on the verge of society, at times; then driven into exile, and from country to country, suffering obloquy and imprisonment.

Voltaire, who stood foremost in the rank of the destroyers of everything that belonged to the past, scoffed at the priests, whom he regarded as the enemies of mankind, and hurled his cynical invective at theology. In this crusade he employed verse and prose, tragedy and burlesque, history and fiction. Restless activity and versatility, untiring vivacity of wit and humor, with felicity of style, characterized his work. Love of labor led him to produce a vast variety of voluminous works. His correspondence alone, including letters from d'Alembert, and Frederick of Prussia, constitutes fifteen volumes. He produced the "Philosophical Dictionary," and contributed largely to the "Encyclopédie," in which he advocated common sense and humanity. Although Voltaire showed much indulgence to kings, and even to the Church, still his writings undoubtedly contributed to the revolution which followed.

Rousseau was more original than Voltaire in his methods, and all his writings were revolutionary in their essence and character. He wrote to illustrate his favorite theory of the superiority of the savage state. His "La Nouvelle Héloise" and "Emile" were condemned; still, it was the "Contrat Social," which appeared in 1762, that did more to hasten the great Revolution than any other work of one man. The "Contrat Social" bases all government on the consent, direct or implied, of the governed. It was thoroughly anti-

Voltaire.
(From the Statue by Houdon.)

monarchical, and Rousseau, therefore, was compelled to
flee from France to the territory of Berne, thence to
Moitiers, in Neuchâtel, when it belonged to Prussia.
He then migrated to the Ile St. Pierre, in the Lake of
Bienne; the Bernese government ordered him to quit the
territory. David Hume offered him an asylum in England,
but he went back to Paris and became a wanderer, and,
at last, returned to copy music for support. Such was,
in brief, the life that was sacrificed for the idea that all
government should exist by the consent of the governed.

Diderot conceived the stupendous design of the " Encyclopédie." He was a writer on physics, geometry, meta-
physics, ethics, and *belles-lettres*. He was assisted in this
work by many others. He compiled a description of the
arts and trades, and aimed to make his work a compre-
hensive review of all human knowledge. But he passed
his life under suspicion of king, noble, and priest. He was
ill paid, and if it had not been for the kind offices of the
Empress of Russia, he would have lost the few books he
had collected. He was openly charged with atheistical
and anarchical designs. Still, this work of his life let in
a light upon the minds of the masses, showed them the
power of knowledge, and taught them the doctrine of
humanity. Whatever may have been his intention, the
result of his labor was an incentive to the great revolutions that followed. Philosophers and men of letters
increased on every side, and the new intellectual movement even reached the lower classes. The Church
stubbornly fought these movements, and, so far as in its
power, repressed public opinion.

Of this group of thinkers and heralds of '89, none is
more illustrious than the Marquis d'Argenson. His
great work consists of his " Reflections on the Government
of France." Within its pages may be found the germ

of the democracy which has again and again asserted
itself in France; the basis of the local administrations;
the system of departments which replace the ancient
provinces; the repudiation of the privileges of nobility;
the condemnation of local restrictions in trade; "and the
dream of a new France, where personal equality should
reign, and where the cultivator of the soil should be lord
of the land he tilled." A statement of the reforms which
Turgot advocated, from the time he was appointed
intendant of Limoges, in 1761, until the fall of Necker's
ministry, in 1781, embodies most of the practical results
of the Revolution.

"To recall Turgot," says Frederic Harrison, "is to
recall Condorcet, the equal of Turgot as thinker, if
inferior to Turgot as statesman. Around the mind
and nature of Condorcet there lingers a halo of a
special grace. Sprung from an old baronial family, with
bigoted prejudices of feudal right, the young noble, from
his youth, broke through the opposition of his order to
devote himself to a life of thought. He who would understand what men mean by the ideas of '89, should mark,
learn, and inwardly digest those two small books of Condorcet, 'The Life of Turgot,' 1787, and 'The Historical
Sketch of the Progress of the Human Mind,' 1795."

On the accession of Louis XVI. to the throne, in 1774,
he found the people already turbulent and discontented.
The King was only absolute in theory, for monarchy was
encompassed by a suppressed democracy that had
imbibed the progressive ideas of the age, and digested
the doctrines of the philosophers and encyclopedists.
The King was compelled to favor the democratic and
revolutionary movement in America. Many nobles,
among whom were Mirabeau and Abbé Siéyès, cast their
lot with the commons, which body assumed the title of

the National Assembly. This political event constituted one of the first overt acts in the commencement of the great upheaval of society that was destined to shake every throne in Europe to its center. Spirits had been invoked that could not be controlled. There are few bad revolutions, and the French Revolution was not an exception to the rule. Ancient orders were to be demolished and new forms were to be established. The people defied the King, who virtually lost his sovereignty.

The Parisians rushed to arms. The Bastile was captured. This prison was razed to the ground, because it was a symbol of tyranny and monarchy. The King was compelled to wear the revolutionary "cockade." In the provinces, nobles and tax-gatherers were murdered. Agrarian anarchy ensued.

Talleyrand was in sympathy with the people. Lafayette, who had just returned from America, proclaimed the rights of man. D'Orléans was an enemy to the Court. Robespierre was conspicuous. There was a general uprising. Feudal rights and personal servitude were abolished. The nobles and the Church renounced privileges. The Paris clubs were centers of agitation. The mayor's army of 30,000 men took the place of the King's. There were great numbers of proletariats; workmen were out of work. Democratic newspapers aroused the people, who held meetings in the Palais Royal. Public workshops were started. The State had to rescue the multitude from starvation. Wages were instituted for nominal work.

The speculative character of the clubs now gave force to the Revolution by political action. The Jacobins were powerful, but they were not radical enough for Danton, and he organized the Cordeliers. Lafayette essayed a counter and conservative movement in the organization of the Feuillants. The King, from 1789, was completely under the control of the people.

Revolutions are not made; they make themselves. The people do not revolt against existing law through mere fancy or pique. In fact, the tendency is decidedly too strong in the other direction—a proneness to suffer the ills they have rather than fly to those they know not of. In this attempt to glance at the constitutional development of France the statute law will also briefly be referred to as exemplifying and explaining the more condensed and concise fundamental law.

Wrongs existed on all sides, permeated society, and saturated the body-politic. Special privileges were granted to individuals, classes, towns, provinces, and even to trades. Shackles of every description were placed upon industry and upon the very genius of man. These violations of human rights had to be swept away; the future had to be provided with guarantees. The Revolution at first seemed to be merely smoldering, but at last it broke forth brilliantly and startlingly.

It is not historically correct to say that a revolution commenced at any particular date; still, the legislation about to be referred to marks one of the most significant events in the tragedy that was soon to be enacted.

As early as May, 1788, a deliberate movement was made against the power of the French King, when the parliament of Paris resolved that France was a monarchy governed by a king, according to the laws; and while it confirmed the right of the reigning house to the throne, from male to male, in the order of primogeniture, it asserted the right of the nation to grant subsidies freely through the organ of the "States-general," regularly convoked and composed; the irremovability of the magistrates; the right of the courts to verify in each province

the edicts of the King, and not to order the registration
of them, unless they were conformable to the constituent
laws of the province as well as to the fundamental law
of the State; the right of each citizen to be tried by his
natural judges, who were appointed by law; and that all
citizens should have a speedy trial.

The States-general met at Versailles, May 5, 1789.
The *tiers état* numbered 661, the nobles 285, and the
clergy 308. On June 20 the hail was found to be shut
up, under the pretext that preparations were necessary
for the presence of the King. The deputies of the *tiers
état*, who were a majority of the whole body, felt themselves outraged by the conduct of their colleagues. Some
proposed to hold a meeting under the windows of the King;
others proposed the Tennis Court, where they repaired.
The Tennis Court was spacious, but the walls were dark
and bare. There were no seats. The President refused
to take a chair brought to him, and chose to stand with
the Assembly. A bench served as a desk. An oath was
then taken never to separate until the Constitution of the
kingdom was founded on a permanent basis. On the adjourned day the deputies found the princes playing in the
Tennis Court. They then held their sitting in the Church
of St. Louis.

When the royal sitting of the States-general took place,
the deputies were kept waiting outside in the rain. When
they at last entered, they found the seats occupied by the
two higher orders—the clergy and the nobles—with soldiery everywhere.

It is interesting to know what ideas of sovereignty the
King entertained at this time. He launched reproaches;
issued commands; enjoined separation into orders; annulled the preceding resolutions of the *tiers état;* maintained all feudal rights as inviolable property; constituted

the nobles and clergy judges of what concerned them; and declared that he considered himself the sole representative of the people.

The King then withdrew, followed by the clergy and the nobles. The deputies remained. Mirabeau said to them: "Gentlemen, I admit that what you have just heard might be the salvation of the country, if the gifts of despotism were not always dangerous. * * * * Adhere religiously to your oath; it forbids you to separate before you have framed the Constitution."

The *tiers état*, on June 17, 1789, declared the Constituent Assembly the only legal one representing the people; that all existing taxes were illegal; denied the veto power to the King; proclaimed the rights of man, and abolished the feudal system.

The citizens of France refused to treat or compromise with anybody representing the King until the battle of liberty was fought; for the fiat went forth that justice only comes at the price of battles. The aristocracy were put to flight; the Court was encompassed by the Assembly, the people, and the militia.

Until this epoch in the history of the world, the crime of treason against kings and potentates had been familiar; but it remained for the French formally to proclaim that there could be such a crime as high treason against the nation, and the Assembly, after recognizing this fact, conferred its cognizance upon the tribunal of the Châtelet. This action was a masterpiece in legislation.

From November, 1789, until September, 1791, the following may be mentioned as the most important acts of the Constituent Assembly: It declared all ecclesiastical property national property; abolished monastic vows; suppressed religious orders; abolished *lettres de cachet* and the salt tax; established free trade in corn; instituted the jury;

denied the right to the King of declaring war and making peace with the declaration that that right belonged to the nation; abolished titles of nobility; restored to the heirs of dissenters, expelled by the revocation of the Edict of Nantes, their confiscated property; established the Tribunal of Cassation, and the Institution of Patents for inventors; abolished the monopoly in the cultivation of tobacco; admitted free people of color to an equality to political rights; took away the right of pardon of criminals from the King; established institutions for the deaf and dumb; suppressed decorations and orders of knighthood; ordered emigrants to return to France, and prepared and presented the Constitution of 1791 to Louis XVI., who was compelled to accept it.

"The French Revolution began to attract attention in different parts of Europe; its language was so lofty, so firm, and it had a character of such generality that foreign nations could not but be alarmed at it. Up to this time it might have been taken for a temporary agitation; but the success of the Assembly, its firmness, its unexpected constancy, and, above all, the prospects it held out to France and to all nations, could not fail to draw upon it both respect and hatred, and to engage the notice of cabinets."

The flight of the King to, and his return from, Varennes, occurred June 21-25, 1791. The attempt to escape was made in an eight-horse lumbering Berlin—a kind of chariot coach. He seemed to think that he must join his regal friends with all the pomp and circumstance that generally attend the movements of a king. His arrest was fatal; a guard was placed over him. He had been advised to join the enemies of the Revolution, and to link his fortunes with those who wanted to crush it. His course united all classes against him except the nobles and the clergy, prepared men's minds to do without him, and also excited a wish for a republic. On the morning of his arrival the Assembly had provided for everything by a decree. Louis XVI. was suspended from his functions, a guard was placed over his person, and that of the Queen and the Dauphin. Although the Assembly conducted itself with decorum, still it was evident that the King was, for the time being, dethroned.

Evolution in government had been making rapid strides in France, and the nation was now ready to adopt its first written constitution, which was formally accepted by the King on September 14, 1791. The principal features of it were the change of the divisions of the kingdom from thirty-four equal provinces into eighty-three departments, each department being again divided into districts, and each district into cantons. The legislative National Assembly consisted of only one chamber, and its sessions were continual. The unicameral characteristic of the legislature was purely democratic in its form, and to this day it is only the conservative and reactionary political forces that demand two chambers in the formation of constitutional law.

The number of representatives was fixed at 745, exclusive of those granted to the colonies; they were distributed on the basis of territory, population, and direct taxes. Of the 745, 247 were assigned for the territory, each department choosing three members, but Paris only one. To the population 249 representatives were given; the whole population of the kingdom being divided into 249 parts, and each department choosing as many representatives as it had such parts of population. For direct taxation, 249 representatives were chosen; the main sum of the direct taxes of the kingdom being divided into 249 parts

Mirabeau.

and each department choosing as many representatives as it paid such parts of the whole contribution.

The representatives were chosen for two years. Primary assemblies chose electors, and these the representatives. The qualifications of a voter were, to be a Frenchman, twenty-five years of age, paying a tax in value of three days' labor, a domicile in the canton for at least one year, being registered on the list of citizens, and not being a servant for wages in a household.

An alien might be naturalized after an uninterrupted domicile of five years in the kingdom, if he besides held real estate, or had married a French woman, or established a trade, or taken the oath of a citizen.

The King was made the chief executive, and his person was declared to be both sacred and inviolable. In this respect this constitution was monarchical. The French people had not yet learned that a king was not a necessary function in a government, but they fully comprehended that the source of all power could place limitations upon the exercise of personal power, and they proceeded to formulate the requisite constitutional provision.

The King exercised his power by the aid of ministers. All acts were signed by the King and countersigned by the ministers, who were named and dismissed by the King. Deputies were forbidden to become ministers throughout their terms of service and for two years thereafter. This last provision was based upon the fear that they might be corrupted by the Court. The minister could only come before the Assembly when requested, to be interrogated. The minister was sequestered in his bureau, as the King was secluded in his palace. The King was not personally responsible. The ministers were, therefore, held and could be tried before the High Court. Certain powers

were taken from the King. He could neither declare war
nor conclude peace. The King proposed war, but the
Assembly declared it; the King signed treaties, but the
Assembly ratified them; the King could not nominate
judges, nor could he pardon criminals. The administrative departments — judicial, financial, military,
ecclesiastic -depended upon the elective system. The
King could give no directions to the legislative branch of
the government. He could neither select nor replace
municipal officers. The King was stripped of all power
except warning and persuasion.

It must be borne in mind that prior to 1789 France was
divided administratively into thirty-two general governments. They were called *généralités*, and the affairs of
each were directed by an officer of the king called an
intendant. The power of these officers varied in different
regions. Taxes were levied directly by the King and
distributed by the *intendants* under the orders of the
King. These officers had judicial, police, commercial,
military, fiscal, and municipal powers. This was one of
the abuses that the Assembly wished to put an end to.
In fact, the idea of 1789 is as much that of decentralization as centralization—the latter being a legacy from the
old monarchy, and is not the work of the Revolution. The
excessive power in the hands of a prefect is an ancient
tradition of France. The aim of d'Argenson, of Turgot,
of Mabli, of Malesherbes was to create a local energy,
and restrain the abuses of bureaucracy. The great problem of to-day is, how to combine the unity of sovereignty
with local government.

The Constitution of 1791 divided the territory of France
into eighty-three departments of nearly equal extent,
without regard to the boundaries of the ancient provinces.
This arrangement broke up the inequalities and traditions

of the Middle Ages. The names of the departments were largely taken from the natural features of the country — its mountains, rivers, and coasts. The departments were in their turn divided into districts, and the districts into cantons. From this division of the provinces and the mixture of the population came the idea of national unity.

A superior administration for each department and a subordinate administration for each district are confided to agents elected by the people, says the Constitution, when, in point of fact, they were chosen indirectly by electors. In this way the people named the local administrators; the legislative body determined their duties, and the King gave them their orders. These officers were essentially charged with the distribution of taxes and the superintendence of the collection of the public moneys in their territory.

The application of the separation of powers, as developed in the Constitution of 1791, was borrowed from Montesquieu, Blackstone, and the Constitution of the United States; but the spirit of liberty breathed into this instrument was derived from the writings of Rousseau.

The King was denied the right to march his troops within 30,000 yards of the Assembly. This body assumed the power to educate the King's son. There were five causes for dethronement, eight causes for constraint of ministers, eight for condemnation to death.

Between the lines of this Constitution is written the fear that any kind of personal executive power is inimical to the public welfare. The principle disclosed is that the legislative body alone must possess the confidence of the people; that the executive is always tempted to commit abuses or to engage in conspiracies; that every independent act of the King is regarded as rebellion against his superior, which is the Assembly— which is the people.

It was declared that "men are born and remain free and equal in rights common to all. * * * All citizens have the right to take part, in person, or through their representatives, in the formation of law." There was no longer any recognition of hereditary right to any public office; it was, therefore, proclaimed that hereditary royalty was illegitimate: that the living law should abolish the written law.

The last sitting of the Constituent and the first sitting of the Legislative Assembly took place October 1, 1791. The Constituent Assembly was characterized by noble courage and perfect equity. It was hated on the one side as revolutionary, and on the other as aristocratic. It was composed of the enlightened men of the nation.

"Threatened by the aristocracy, by the Court, and by an army; not yet foreseeing the popular commotions that were to take place, it declared itself inviolable, and forbade power to touch it. Convinced of its rights, it addressed itself to enemies who were not convinced of theirs, and, by the mere expression of its determination, gained the ascendency over a power of several centuries, and an army of 30,000 men. Such was the Revolution. Such was its first and noblest act. It was just, it was heroic, for never did nation act with greater propriety or amid greater dangers.

The Constituent Assembly had been patient, and hesitated in the deposition of Louis XVI., who seemed to gain courage because he was allowed to exercise personal power, under the Constitution of 1791, and he now even became aggressive. He refused to sanction an act against emigrants, and vetoed a bill relative to priests. But great events were to transpire, and he was to be awakened from his dream. Chabot abruptly enters the presence of the King with his hat on, and the Legislative

Assembly abolishes the ceremony of New Year's Day, because it had been the custom to pay great homage to the King on this day. Even Dumouriez, who afterward became a traitor to France, said to the Queen: "This is not a transient popular movement, as you seem to think It is an almost unanimous insurrection of a mighty nation against inveterate abuses. Great factions fan the flame."

The nations of Europe were growing restless, and a treaty was formed between Austria and Prussia to quell what they were pleased to call "a disturbance in France." In July, 1792, 40,000 Prussians and as many Austrians and Sardinians were approaching the frontiers. The Court acted in concert with the enemy, and in every way possible in its power thwarted the measures of the Legislative Assembly, while General Dumouriez stood ready to deliver up France by uniting with the emigrants.

The Legislative Assembly now declared: "That the country was in danger." Preceding this declaration, Vergniaud made his eloquent speech. "It is in the name of the King," said he, "that the French princes have endeavored to raise Europe against us. It is to avenge the dignity of the King that the Treaty of Pilnitz has been concluded. It is to come to the aid of the King that the sovereign of Hungary and Bohemia makes war upon us, that Prussia is marching toward our frontiers." This orator then argues that, under the Constitution of 1791, the King ought to be considered as having abdicated the throne of France.

The city of Marseilles presented an address to the Assembly, asking "the abolition of royalty in the reigning branch, and to substitute in its stead a merely elective royalty, without the power of veto, that is to say: a purely executive magistracy, as in republics."

In August of this year the Tuileries was attacked, stormed, and carried by the populace, and the following day the King was suspended in his powers, and an executive council was formed. The King and royal family were then imprisoned in the Temple, and the foreign ambassadors took their leave of Paris.

These events constitute most prominent landmarks in the causeway of liberty. The dethronement and imprisonment of a monocrat and the establishment of an executive council in his stead, strengthened the hearts of all lovers of good government. But this council did not have parliamentary powers, which had already been developed in the cabinet government of England.

Lafayette, after trying to induce the army to rise in favor of Louis XVI., fled from France.

The Legislative Assembly closed November 19, 1792, after having passed, between that date and October 1, 1791, 2,140 decrees.

The opening of the National Convention then followed.

Among the most important acts of the Legislative Assembly, it may be mentioned that it sequestered the property of emigrants; suppressed religious communities; prohibited ecclesiastical costumes; declared war against Austria; formed a camp of 20,000 men, near Paris, to oppose the army of the King; abolished the title of sire and majesty, usually given to the King; and directed the sale of the property of emigrants.

The Jacobins now rallied around Robespierre, while the Girondins and the more moderate leaders clustered around Petion.

Barbaroux, of Marseilles, accused Robespierre of intending to make himself a dictator. Barbaroux said the people of Marseilles would never bow their heads to a king or a dictator.

Marat wished to destroy all enemies of the Revolution. He said he had wandered from cellar to cellar, and preached truth from wood-piles.

Louis XVI. was now separated from his family.

"The monarchy, the aristocracy, in short, all the past, against which the Revolution was struggling, was personified, as it were, in the unfortunate Louis XVI. The manner in which each person should henceforth treat him was to be the test of his hatred to the counter-revolution. The Constituent Assembly declared the King inviolable, and did not venture to decide upon his fate; it had suspended and shut him up in the Temple; it had not even abolished royalty, and had bequeathed to the Convention, through the Legislative Assembly, the duty of judging all that belonged to the old monarchy, whether material or personal."

It was now held that there could be no tranquillity until Louis should be sacrificed.

The success of the armies of France, the capture of Frankford, the occupation of Savoy and Nice, the revulsion of opinion throughout Europe, caused many to fancy that they could hear the crash of monarchies, and that all nations were about to overturn thrones, and to form themselves into republics or democracies. It was believed that nations were awakening to avenge the world for all the crimes of crowned heads, and that there was about to be established a grand confederation of the peoples of the world to maintain the rights of man and the freedom of commerce.

The fallacy has always existed and now exists in most governments, that one generation has the right to make the laws for succeeding ones, and by the contrivance of a written constitution establish systems that are next to an impossibility to eradicate or change—a sort of an original sin arrangement. The Constitution of the United States is a living example of the fact, for it is so decreed in the fundamental law that its mode of amendment is so difficult that there have never been any amendments in any true sense to that instrument. This same question came up in the French Revolution, and the Convention had to settle the issue as to whether any law could be inviolable.

"But these new constituents assembled under the name of the Convention, and did not conceive themselves to be more bound by the institutions of their predecessors than these latter imagined themselves to be by the old institutions of feudalism._ Men's minds had been hurried along with such rapidity that the laws of 1791 appeared as absurd to the men of 1792 as those of the thirteenth century had appeared to the generation of 1789. The conventionalists, therefore, did not deem themselves bound by a law which they regarded as absurd, and they declared themselves in insurrection against it as the States-general did against that of the three orders."

The idea of inviolability of a law was rejected. However, there were those who argued that the Constitution of 1791 guaranteed certain rights to the monarch, and that the Assembly could not dispossess him without violating a national engagement or contract.

"In the first place," said the adversaries of inviolability, "in order that an engagement shall be binding, it is requisite that the party contracting such engagement shall have the right to bind himself. Now the national sovereignty is inalienable, and can not bind itself for the time to come. * * * * The nation, therefore, can not have bound itself in regard to Louis XVI., and it can not be met with an engagement which it had not the power to make.

Louis XVI.

"Secondly, even supposing the engagement possible, it would be requisite that it be reciprocal. Now, it has never been so on the part of Louis XVI. The Constitution, on which he now wishes to support himself, he never liked; he always protested against it; he has continually labored to destroy it, not only by internal conspiracies, but by the sword of enemies. What right has he then to avail himself of it?

"But here is the sovereign nation, which unites in itself all powers; that of executing, as well as that of enacting laws, and of making peace and war; here it is with its omnipotence, with its universality, and there is no function but it is capable of fulfilling. The nation is the Convention, which represents it, commissioned to do everything in its behalf; to avenge, to constitute, and to save it. The Convention, then, is competent to try Louis XVI. * * * * The nation can do no wrong, and the deputies who represent it partake of its inviolability and its powers."

Many ingenious arguments followed. St. Just claimed that the King was not a citizen– that the question was one of war, not of law.

The Convention summoned Louis before it for trial. The King made a defense by counsel. He was convicted and notified of the sentence of death; an appeal to the people was denied him. He was allowed a last interview with his family on January 20, 1793, and on the following day he was executed.

The concrete facts have been stated merely for the purpose of showing more distinctly the more important abstract questions that were involved in the debate before, and decided by the Convention. For the first time the relations that existed between citizen, King, and government, and the rights, duties and powers of each were fully discussed in public assembly in France. In this respect they were most important and suggestive. Particularly is it interesting to know how far an expressed or implied contract could be made by the government with citizen or King, that should remain in any sense inviolable, and with everlasting force and effect. These were all novel questions at that time. The Convention decided them with unerring accuracy and dispatch, and in accordance with the best principles of democratic rule. It declared the omnipotence of the people; that the government was an agent or trustee of the masses; that the nation or people could not be bound by any previously enacted law—fundamental or statute—that was not then regarded as useful and right; that even the deputies had no such right to bind the people; and finally, the tables were turned against royalty by the declaration that "the nation could do no wrong." These principles constitute the essence and spirit of democracy, and to-day they lie at the base of all just governments that profess to be of and for the people. These historic facts should serve to warn those who now exercise temporary power, that they must not violate the principles so ably and so valiantly advocated and established by the French Revolution. The debate on the treason of Louis XVI. foreshadowed the democratic Constitution of 1793. The people of to-day should demand that their temporary power-holders be endowed with full centralized force to act directly and vigorously upon any question that may arise from the condition of things, irrespective of all existing law, and to delegate or deny, in their judgment, what local government may seem needful to the nation. This is the point upon which true democracy rests.

A spirit very much like a religious reformation ran through the French Revolution. "Wherever our generals enter," says Cambon, "let them proclaim the sovereignty of the people, the abolition of feudalism, of titles, of all abuses; let all the old authorities be dissolved; let new local administrations be provisionally formed under the directions of our generals; let these administrations govern the country and devise the means of forming national conventions, which shall decide its lot; let the property of our enemies—that is to say, the property of the nobles, the priests, the communities, lay or religious, of the churches—be immediately sequestrated and placed under the safeguard of the French nation. Peace and fraternity to all friends of liberty, war to the base partisans of despotism; war to the mansion, peace to the cottage."

"The contest henceforth raged not only between nation and nation, but between interest and interest, and the strife of opinion superseded that of glory."

Europe divined the broad field that the Revolution had entered, and England, Austria, Prussia, Holland, Spain, Portugal, the two Sicilies, the Roman States, Sardinia, and Piedmont formed a coalition against France.

The Convention realized the impending danger to the Revolution, and through the Revolution to France. There was no time to be wasted in argument. Action was the watchword of the day. It then solemnly established an "Extraordinary Criminal Revolutionary Tribunal" to take cognizance of any attempt against liberty, equality, the unity or indivisibility of the Republic, the internal and external security of the State, of all conspiracies tending to the re-establishment of royalty, or hostile to the sovereignty of the people. The members of the Tribunal were chosen by the Convention.

A "Committee of Public Safety" was now organized (April 6, 1793), with great power of internal and external defense, to last one month. It could suspend the laws, but had to notify the Convention of its action.

"According to me," said Robespierre (April 10, 1793), "there exists, below the aristocracy dispossessed in 1789, a burgher aristocracy as vain and despotic as that of the nobility. A frank revolution did not exist among this class, and it wanted a King, with a Constitution of 1791, to assure its domination. The Girondists were its leaders. * * * * When the Convention was formed, they made themselves masters of the committees, continued to calumniate Paris, and to represent that city as the focus of all crime, and they perverted public opinion by means of their journals and by the immense sums which Roland devoted to the circulation of his most perfidious writings. Lastly, in January, they opposed the death of the tyrant, not out of attachment to his person, but out of attachment to royalty. * * * * The Girondists desire the war, in order to expose us to the invasion of Austria, which promised a Congress with the burgher Constitution of 1791. They have directed the war with perfidy, and, after employing the traitor Lafayette, they have since employed the traitor Dumouriez to attain the end which they have been so long pursuing."

At this time Danton was disaffected, and advocated the suppression of the "Revolutionary Commission of Twelve." He had no liking for either Marat or Robespierre. Still, he did not wish to meddle with the national representation.

The rapid strides which justice takes in times of revolution often concentrates its action within the compass of a few days that would otherwise extend over centuries.

The Girondists were charged, May 20, 1793, with being the accomplices of Dumouriez, and with desiring to destroy Paris. They were driven from the Convention, and, finally, sent to the scaffold. The Girondins favored what they called a true republic, but they were too moderate to conduct a revolution. Their sympathy with royalty made them reactionary, that is, reactionary to the fierce party at whose head stood Robespierre. The persevering efforts of tyranny without France and the thirst of vengeance within required a different class of torch-bearers to hold aloft the flame of revolution. The fittest survived; the Mountain remained; the Girondins went down. The welfare of the Revolution was the single idea that animated the Mountaineers; no means were too bold, no way too hazardous and costly for these men, whose exaltation of mind led them on in their career of restless activity. "For all the advantages they gained," says Allison, "the Convention were indebted to the energy of their measures, the ability of their councils, and the enthusiasm of their subjects. If history has nothing to show comparable to the crimes they committed, it has few similar instances of undaunted resolution to commemorate. Impartial justice demands that this praise should be bestowed on the Committee of Public Safety. If the cruelty of their internal administration exceeded the worst despotism of the emperors, the dignity of their external conduct rivaled the noblest instances of Roman heroism."

It can be truthfully said that the acts which Allison terms "crimes," were no more crimes than the putting to death of soldiers upon the battle-field who had violated the rules of war; nor were the executions more "cruel." As St. Just said, it was not a matter of law, but of war; and if his proposition be true, the action of the Committee of Public Safety and the killings and slaughter that characterize war are equally criminal and cruel.

Whatever may be the correct historical view of the action of the Convention in ordering the sacrifice of human life upon the guillotine, through its committees of safety and welfare, the development of government was continually going on in the passing of statutes which represented the will and the conscience of the people. The Convention adopted "*citoyen*" and "*citoyenne*" instead of "*monsieur*" and "*madame;*" banished emigrants forever, with death to all who should return; fixed price or maximum on the prime necessities of life; declared war against Holland and Spain; abolished imprisonment for debt; made a forced loan upon the rich; and made levies of 300,000 men, despatched money and stores to the army, and transmitted instructions to the generals in the field. These constitute a few of the acts of the Convention prior to June, 1793.

But to comprehend the position of affairs in this eventful time, it is well to turn from scenes of action to the other evidences of growth of a democracy that were appearing with equal force, namely, the crystallization of these great movements into a fundamental law in the interests of liberty and mankind, although this epoch was characterized by a condition of things which a superficial observer might regard as the mere outbreakings of simple license and massacre, or the manifestation of unbridled passion, uncontrolled by any force or power that might have for its purpose the regeneration of France.

The second Constitution, of which Herault de Séchelles is said to be the author, and under which so much was accomplished in the political evolution of the French people, was drawn up June 24, and adopted August 10, 1793, by its ratification on this date by 44,000 communes.

This Constitution provided that every Frenchman of

the age of twenty-one years, who lives from his labor, or has acquired property, or has married a French woman, or has adopted a child, or supports an aged man, exercised the rights of a French citizen.

The sovereign power rests in the people. One deputy was elected for every 40,000 population.

The French Republic is declared to be one and indivisible. The country is not bounded by village, city, or province. The object was to suppress social rivalries and conflicting legislatures. The people were to form one vast association, whose members were to exist for the whole body-politic. To do any act inimical to the interests of one part would, in effect, attack the whole. These facts gave importance to the expressions of unity and indivisibility. The people are distributed into cantons for the exercise of the rights of sovereignty, that is to say, the representatives are elected by assemblies grouped by cantonal districts. Departments, districts, and municipalities are created for the convenience of administration, of justice, and the establishment of a system under which the different elections may take place. This redivision also had for its object the suppression of all remembrance of the old territorial divisions in the common exercise of direct sovereignty in the election of the deputies. It seemed to be in the thought of the authors of the Constitution to bind together administrative districts which would otherwise remain strangers to each other, to blend the inhabitants of separate localities, and compel them to act in accord in the election of members to the legislative body. Then it was quite necessary to avoid stripping the cantons of that autonomy which may be compatible with the idea of indivisibility.

The legislative body merely proposes law, by printing

and referring the enactment to all the communes of the Republic, under the address of "proposed law." If, forty days after the sending in of the proposed law, of the absolute majority of departments, one-tenth of all the primary meetings, legally assembled by the departments, have not protested, the bill is accepted, and becomes a law.

The executive power shall consist of an Executive Council of twenty-four members. Each electoral assembly nominates a candidate, and the legislative body chooses from this general list the members of the Executive Council, who are renewed each half session of the legislature. Its activity is limited to the execution of the laws and decrees of the legislative body; it shall have its seat near the legislature, which body shall call it into its midst in whole or in part, when it is thought necessary. The Council has no power to dissolve the legislature, nor does the legislature have the right to remove, at any time, the Council according to parliamentary forms.

Although there may be some favorable considerations of this new idea of the impersonal executive, still many serious objections exist as to the manner of selecting the persons who constitute this power, the undue authority conferred upon them, and the fixed period of their office. This Council has the management and supervision of the general administration; it appoints, but not out of its own midst, the highest agents of the general administration of the Republic, and it negotiates treaties. The selection of this executive body through intermediaries, this mixture of constituent and legislative powers, created many sources of conflict. What would have been, however, the practical working of this instrument of the year I, will never be known, for the reason that it was sup-

Marie Antoinette.

pressed two months after its acceptance by the primary assemblies.

The local administrations were under the control of the central government; communal interests were made subordinate to the municipal administration, district interests to an intermediate administration, and departmental interests to a central administration.

The twelve articles devoted to civil justice give to citizens the complete right to have their matters in dispute settled by arbitrators of their own choice, whose decision shall be final, unless the litigants have expressly reserved the right of appeal. Those who do not elect to avail themselves of arbitration may have their differences adjudicated by justices of the peace, who hold court without fees. There shall also be judges of arbitration chosen by the electoral assemblies. They shall render their decisions on oral pleadings and without fees. They shall be chosen annually. There shall be criminal judges chosen annually by the electoral assemblies. There shall be a court of *cassation* for the whole Republic. It shall not take cognizance of the facts. It decides on matters of form and on questions of law.

If, of the absolute majority of departments, the tenth part of their regularly formed primary assemblies demand a revision of the Constitution, the legislative body is obliged to call together all primary assemblies of the Republic, in order to ascertain whether a national convention shall be called.

The Constitution of 1793 guarantees to all Frenchmen equality, liberty, security, property, the public debt, free exercise of religion, general instruction, public assistance, absolute liberty of the press, the right of petition, the right to hold popular assemblies, and the enjoyment of all the rights of man. The French Republic respects loyalty, courage, age, filial love, misfortune. It places the Constitution under the guaranty of all virtues. This instrument is preceded by one of the grandest declarations of the rights of man and of citizens ever framed, and proclaims to the world that France is a place of refuge for all who, on account of liberty, are banished from their native country, and refuses to deliver up refugees to tyrants. "Lastly," says Thiers, "this Constitution, so short, so democratic, which reduced the government to a mere temporary commission, spared, nevertheless, the only relic of the ancient system, the communes, and made no change either in their circumscription or their powers."

"The most popular Constitution that ever was," said Robespierre, "has just emanated from an Assembly, formerly counter-revolutionary, but now purged from the men who obstructed its progress and impeded its operations."

The Constitution of 1793 was now declared to be the battle-flag of the Revolution. Until July 13, 1793, the date of his assassination, Marat was the most prominent man in the work of revolution and in the organization of offensive and defensive operations. He presented himself before the Convention with a list of persons whom he wished to sacrifice. It was he who held the torch aloft; the flame that lighted it was in the hearts and minds of the French people. He was driven on to action by 80,000 foreign bayonets that sharpened his sentences and gave point to his rhetoric. What he did, he was compelled to do; if he had faltered in his daring he would have been hurled from power by those who urged him on. Then the dagger of assassination struck the torch from his hand; it was seized and carried forward by the indomitable Robespierre. These men breathed inspiration from that Revolution upon the success of which depended the fate of the then existing absolutism of Europe. Impelled onward by this force, they did their duty until they fell upon the battle-field of human rights.

"Paris, threatened with destruction," says Hazlitt, "thrilled at Marat's accents. Paris, dressed in her robe of flames, seconded his incendiary zeal. A thousand hearts were beating in his bosom, which writhed like the Sibyl's; a thousand daggers were whetted on his stony words. Had he not been backed by a strong necessity and strong opinion, he would have been treated as a madman; but when the madness arose out of the sacred cause and impending fate of a whole people, he who pointed out a victim was the high-priest of freedom."

In Marat's funeral oration Robespierre urged with great eloquence that he had always been the friend of the people. "Listen to the great spirit of Marat," he said, "which awakes and says to you, 'It was not I whom they meant to assassinate, but the Republic. It is not I whom you must avenge—it is the Republic— the people—yourselves.'"

The Convention possessed all the powers of government; still, it was dissatisfied with the form of its executive. The Committee of Public Safety, which was organized April 6 for one month only, had been continued, and was now placed above the executive council; in fact, it exercised all power. It continued to exhibit extraordinary ability, force, and energy. It reorganized the army of the North and of the Rhine; created the armies of the Pyrénées and of La Vendée; provisioned 126 fortresses, or forts, in the midst of insurrection in the departments.

In the month of August all France was in motion, all resources in activity which served to the advantage of the Revolution, its last and its most terrible crisis.

It was requisite that new financial measures be adopted to place paper money in proportion with the price of articles of consumption; it was necessary to distribute the armies and the generals in a manner suitable to each theatre of war; and, lastly, to appease the revolutionary spirit by great and terrible executions, which urgent want and passion demanded. Inseparable from that force which saves a people in danger is passion.

The autocrats and reactionary parties, perceiving the drift of the Revolution, now expressed a desire for an election under the Constitution of 1793, and united with the moderates; they wanted to establish a Constitutional ministry, fashioned after the English system—with responsibility to the legislature and with power to appeal to the people. The radicals saw that this meant new, unknown, and inexperienced men, and that such a movement would result in ousting the Convention itself and breaking up the supreme power in the presence of hostile armies. "Pitt alone can be the author of that idea!" exclaimed Robespierre.

The men who were in the front of the Revolution were undoubtedly right; for more direct and vigorous machinery is required for revolutionary movements than in a parliamentary government, particularly in France, which had never had a complete legislative system until 1789.

The French now declared the government revolutionary, which signified that the Constitution of 1793 was temporarily suspended, and extraordinary power was conferred on the Convention and the Committee of Public Safety. The Convention, however, acted under and in the spirit of the Constitution, which, of itself, was most simple and direct in its provisions, and, at the same time, the Convention never relinquished its control of the committees, which were required to account to the Convention once a week.

What is known in history as the Reign of Terror was now at its height. Everyone suspected of treason was thrown into prison. The law against visiting a house in the night was repealed. Subsidiary revolutionary committees were appointed for all parts of France. Paris had fifty-eight; every village had one. The prisons were filled. Citizens must go to the field of battle, to the scaffold, or to prison.

Marie Antoinette was condemned and executed October 16, 1793; the arrested Girondist deputies were executed (October 31); some of the leaders of that party, including Roland, perished by suicide. Among the eminent persons sent to the guillotine were the eloquent Vergniaud, Brissot, Bailly, Malesherbes (the advocate who defended Louis XVI.), Madame Roland, and the Duke of Orléans.

This year ended with a condition of affairs in the military situation very favorable to France. The powers of Europe threw the blame of failure on each other.

Danton would have spared the Girondist victims. He halted at this point, where the others advanced. Herbert and the leaders of the commune, with their atheism and licentiousness, were offensive to Robespierre, who was a deist, and had most power with the Jacobins. He opposed the festival of the "Goddess of Reason." He was in position to crush his enemies. The result of the quarrel was that Danton, Camille-Desmoulins, and Herbert were executed (March 5, 1794).

"We have opposed sword with sword," said St. Just, "and the Republic is founded. It has issued from the bosom of storms. It has its origin in common with the world, arising out of chaos, and man weeping at the moment of his birth."

"We must make the body-politic," said Collot d'Herbois, "throw out the foul sweat of aristocracy. The more copiously it perspires, the more healthy it will be."

The Executive Council having been suppressed, it was succeeded by twelve commissions, composed of members of the Convention and made subordinate to the Committee of Public Welfare, of which Robespierre was a member. They were as follows: Committee of civil administration of police and the tribunals; public instruction; agriculture and arts; commerce and articles of consumption; public works; public charity; conveyance, posts, and public vehicles; finances; organization and superintendence of land forces; navy and the colonies; arms, gunpowder, and mines; foreign relations. These committees all drew their powers from the Convention.

The controlling committees of welfare and safety owed their existence to emergency alone, but they had gradually assumed a greater share of power, in proportion as they needed it for the service of the State, and at last attained the dictatorship itself.

Homage had often been paid to moral ideas in the acts of the Convention, by making integrity, justice, and all the virtues, the order of the day. It now turned its attention to religion. It was decreed that the French people acknowledged the existence of a Supreme Being, and the immortality of the soul, and that the worship most worthy of the Supreme Being is the practice of the duties of man.

It was then decreed that festivals be held to the Supreme Being; the human race; the French people; the benefactors of mankind; the martyrs of liberty; liberty and equality; the Republic; the liberty of the world; love of country; hatred to tyrants and traitors; truth and justice; modesty; glory; friendship; frugality and courage; good faith; heroism; disinterestedness; stoicism and love; conjugal fidelity; paternal affection; filial piety; infancy; youth; manhood; old age; misfortune; agriculture; industry; ancestors; posterity; and happiness.

A petition to the " Mountain " declared: " O beneficent Mountain! *   *   *   * From thy boiling bosom darted the salutary thunder-bolt, which crushed atheism, and gave us genuine Republicans the consolatory idea of living free, within the sight of the Supreme Being, and in the expectation of the immortality of the soul." From that day the words *virtue* and *Supreme Being* were on the lips of everyone.

A breach now arose between the Committee of General Safety and the Committee of Public Welfare. Complaints became numerous of the arrests. Robespierre, St. Just, and Couthon were the controlling spirits in the Committee of Public Welfare. Notwithstanding this disagreement, Robespierre was chosen president of the Convention.

The festival of the Supreme Being now took place (June 8, 1794). An amphitheatre was erected in the garden of the Tuileries, upon which the Convention sat. Boys wore wreaths of violets, the youth myrtle, men oak, and the aged ivy and olive. Robespierre appeared dressed with care. There were figures representing Atheism, Discord, and Selfishness, destined to be burned.

" I behold at this moment," said Robespierre, " a whole nation assailed by all the oppressors of mankind, suspending the course of its heroic labors to lift its thoughts and its prayers toward the Supreme Being, who gave it the mission to undertake, and the courage to execute. The statues were burned, and the statue of Wisdom that arose was blackened. There were murmurs of "Tyrant," and Bourdon said: "The Tarpeian rock is close to the capital."

"To-morrow we will combat vice and tyranny," said Robespierre, who was no longer a voluntary agent, but a slave to religious excitement. These pompous ceremonies of the Supreme Being looked like a retrograde movement. Robespierre was told so. He denied it, and upbraided the deputies who suggested this view. Then he had walked in advance of the procession. It was now thought that he wanted to build a despotism on his fantastic religion. This thought had taken lodgment in the minds of the people, and its development brought about the ruin of Robespierre. He demanded the execution of many members of the Convention, whom he called the tail of Danton. This demand was not complied with. Smarting under wounded pride, he withdrew from the Committee of Public Welfare. He now appeared at the Jacobin clubs, and directed their influence to cause the arrest of persons who used the name of the Deity as an oath. The Supreme Being was to become an oppressor, and the inquisition was to be re-established in favor of deism.

On July 28, 1794, Robespierre was executed.

"In my opinion," says Mignet, "Robespierre's destruction was inevitable. He had no organized force; his partisans, although numerous, were not enlisted and incorporated; he possessed only the great power derived from public opinion, and the principle of terror; so that, not being able to surprise his enemies by violence, like Cromwell, he endeavored to frighten them. Fear not succeeding, he tried insurrection. But as the support of the committees gave courage to the Convention, so the sections, relying for support on the strength of the Convention, naturally declared themselves against the insur-

Robespierre.

gents. By attacking the government, Robespierre roused the Assembly; by rousing the Assembly, he let loose the people."

The powers of the Committee of Public Safety were curtailed, and the Revolutionary Tribunal was abolished. The suspected were released, and the Reign of Terror was over.

A decree was passed, closing the Jacobins' clubs. The governmental committees were reorganized, and their powers readjusted by the Convention. The liberty of the press was declared. The Jacobins were attacked by the Gilded Youth. The late members of the Committee of Public Welfare were placed under accusation, and many of them were transported (March 2, 1795), and outlawed deputies were admitted into the Convention. Fouquier-Tinville and fifteen jurors of the Revolutionary Tribunal were executed (May 7), and Charette again took up arms in La Vendée.

A great reactionary crisis was at hand. The majority of the Convention strove to return to moderation. The Jacobins warned them that they were running into counter-revolution. A revolution is like a pendulum. It swings from one extreme to another, but, fortunately for political society and mankind, the pendulum does not go back to the point where it started, and, therefore, while it oscillates, it is seeking the truth. But in its oscillations empire may come. Bloodshed and calamity may occur. Charles I. and his predecessors made a Cromwell possible, and the reaction that followed his death produced a James II., who was driven from England before parliamentary government was established.

A new Constitution was now demanded in France. A commission of eleven was appointed to draft and present a plan. It was reported August 22, 1795, and accepted by the Convention September 23 of the same year.

The preamble of the Constitution of 1795, as well as that of 1793, proclaims that the French people acknowledge the presence of the Highest Being; while the Constitution of the United States provides that all power is derived from the people themselves. The French Constitution of 1795 has a full declaration of rights, as to liberty, equality, security, and property. It was declared that sovereignty abides with the collective mass of all citizens. No one is a good citizen unless he be a good son, a good father, a good brother, a good friend, and a good husband. The French Republic is one, and indivisible, and the collective number of all French citizens is the sovereignty.

France is divided into departments, each department is divided into cantons, and each canton into communes.

Every person born and residing in France, that has attained the age of twenty-one years, and pays direct taxes, is a French citizen. An alien may be naturalized.

Notwithstanding its declaration of rights, which declared that sovereignty resided essentially in the whole body of the people, the republican Constitution of the year III. organized the "powers" upon an artifice, which violated all the principles of '89, and divided the chamber into two parts.

The Legislative Body is composed of a Council of the Ancients and a Council of Five Hundred. The proposing of laws belongs exclusively to the Council of Five Hundred, while the Council of the Ancients adopts or rejects the resolutions of the Council of Five Hundred. The Legislative Body can, neither through itself nor through delegates, exercise either the executive power or the judicial power. This was apparently an attempt to copy the Constitution of the United States, not only in the three great governmental subdivisions, but also the division of the legislature in two parts.

The executive power is given to a Directory of five members, who are nominated by the Legislative Body, which has, in the name of the nation, the character of an electoral assembly. The members of the Directory can only be taken from the citizens who have been members of the Legislative Body, or ministers. The Directory is in part renewed by the election of one new member every year, and during the first four years the casting of lots shall decide on the leaving of those who have been chosen the first time. None of the retiring members can be chosen again before an interval of five years. Relations by blood can not be members of the Directory at one and the same time, nor succeed one another, except after an interval of five years. Each member of the Directory presides, in succession, only for three months. The Directory has the care, according to the laws, of the exterior and internal safety of the Republic. It may issue proclamations, and dispose of the military forces. It appoints the generals-in-chief of the armies, but it can not choose them from among the relations by blood or marriage. The members of the Directory can, when engaged in functions of office, appear neither abroad nor in their dwellings other than in the costumes proper to them.

The Council of the Ancients held its sessions in the Palace of the Tuileries; the Council of the Five Hundred in the Palace Bourbon; the members of the Executive Directory in the Palace Luxembourg.

The Legislative Body established the duties and the number of ministers, who are held responsible for the non-execution of the laws, as for the non-execution of the orders of the Directory.

The ministers are, in point of fact, directorial creatures, and not national functionaries. They have no seat or vote in the chambers. Thus, the bad is mingled with the good.

The Directory may annul directly the acts of the departmental or municipal administrators, and it may also suspend or remove the magistrates both of the departments and cantons, and bring them before the departmental courts.

Each department has a central administration, composed of five members, at least twenty-five years of age. It is renewed every year by one-fifth. The members are elected by the electors, with a prohibition as to relatives by blood or marriage. They are subordinate to the ministers, who can annul their acts when they are in conflict with the laws or regulations of superior orders, and suspend the departmental administrators. No removal or suspension has permanent validity without formal confirmation of the Executive Directory.

Each canton has a municipal administration, formed by the agents of each commune. The president of this administration is chosen by the whole canton.

In the communes, divided into several municipalities, there is a central bureau for matters which the Legislative Body considers indivisible. The bureau consists of three members, nominated by the departmental administrators, and confirmed by the executive power. Communes of less than 5,000 inhabitants nominate only a municipal agent and an assistant. The agents of these small localities assemble in the chief place of the canton to form a cantonal municipality.

The members of each municipal administration are

appointed for two years, and every year one-half of them, or the number nearest to one-half, and thus alternately, now the greater and now the smaller fractional number shall be renewed. They are subordinate to the departmental administration, who can suspend them or annul their acts.

The special mission of the administrators consists, as in 1791, of the distribution of direct taxes, and of the superintendence of the moneys belonging to the public revenues of their district. For these subjects, as well as the other parts of the interior administration, rules, and the mode of their functions are fixed by the Legislative Body. The Executive Directory appoints in each departmental and municipal administration a commissioner, who watches over and sees to the execution of the laws. He is taken from the citizens domiciled for at least one year in the department in which the administration is located. The sanction of this constant surveillance results from the power given to the Executive Directory to annul the acts of all administrators, to suspend or dismiss the administrators, and, when it believes it to be expedient, to send them before the courts and replace them until the following election, but only by former administrators, when the dismissal affects the entire administration. These administrators can not correspond with each other on any subject of general interest to the Republic. They must render an annual and printed account of their acts.

The judicial functions can not be exercised either by the Legislative Body or by the executive power. The judges can be removed only on account of crimes, of which they have been legally found guilty, and can be suspended only by virtue of an accepted accusation.

Voluntary arbitration forms the basis of civil justice.

The decision of the arbitrators chosen by the parties is without appeal, or recourse to the court of *cassation*, unless the parties have expressly reserved this right. Justice is rendered without pay; the sessions of the court are public; judgments express the grounds and apply the law on which they are decided.

In each district specified by law, there are a justice of the peace and his associates. They are chosen for two years, and may be re-elected. The law specifies the subjects on which they may pass with right of appeal.

There are special courts for commerce. Matters which do not belong either before the justices of the peace or before the commercial courts, are brought before the justices of the peace to be settled amicably. If the justice of the peace can not settle them, he sends the parties to the civil court.

There is a civil court in each department. It consists of at least twenty judges, and a commissioner, and a substitute, whom the Executive Directory appoints. This court renders judgment without appeal in the cases specified by law, where appeal has been taken from the justices of the peace, and from arbitrators.

There are courts of criminal and penal jurisdiction, and full provisions guarding against arbitrary arrests. A jury system is provided for, consisting of grand and traverse juries.

There is a court of *cassation* for the whole Republic. This court passes upon questions of procedure, form, and of law, grants new trials, and refers the main subject to courts that have jurisdiction over the matters at issue.

There is a high court of justice to sit in judgment on the complaints preferred by the Legislative Body, both against its own members and against those of the Executive Directory.

If experience should show objections to some articles of the Constitution, the Council of the Ancients shall propose a revision of them. The proposal of the Council of the Ancients is, in this case, subjected to the concurrence of the Council of Five Hundred, and if, in the space of nine years, the proposals of the Council of the Ancients, confirmed by the Council of Five Hundred, have been made at three different periods, each being at an interval of three years at least, an Assembly of Revision shall be called together. In all reactionary constitutions provisions are always adopted which make amendments to the fundamental law next to impossible. The articles bearing on this subject in the Constitution of 1795 had the same practical effect on the French law as the Constitution of the United States has upon revision here.

The French nation intrusts the safe keeping of the present Constitution to the Legislative Body, to the Executive Directory, and to the administrators and judges; to the watchfulness of fathers, and of families; to wives and mothers, to the love of the young citizens, and to the courage of all Frenchmen.

The Constitution of 1795 was adopted after the defeat of all the advanced and radical parties of France. The consequence is that this Constitution is much less democratic than that of 1793. In the first place, the primary assemblies lost all importance. They had no longer legislative power. The deputies were no longer named by them. All citizens of the age of twenty-one met in primary assembly on the 1st of *Prairial*, and nominated electoral assemblies. These electoral assemblies met on the 20th of *Prairial*, and nominated the two Councils, and the two Councils nominated the Directory. This electoral system was fashioned after that of the United

States Constitution, and had for its object the removal of the direct power of choosing the legislature and the executive from the control of the people. The political pendulum at this time swung well back in the direction of monarchy.

The Executive Directory, which was elected by a system of indirect elections, could only be selected from a definite class named in the law, and again followed the Constitution of the United States by nominating its members for fixed periods.

Nothing could be more unscientific than to make an executive body so inflexible and unyielding. Then, as in the case of other countries, where the continuance of the executive is determined by the calendar, great power is conferred on the Directory. Power of appointment, disposition of military forces, issuing proclamations, made this body of men autocrats. Neither the legis'ature nor the executive had any power or control over each other. In their respective spheres each department of government was sovereign, and the framers of the Constitution of 1795 in France followed the misconceptions of Montesquieu, Blackstone, DeLolme, and Paley, in their estimate of the working of the British Constitution, and the acceptance of these misconceptions in the adoption of the Constitution of the United States. The consequence is that a government of conflict was organized, and, in case of conflict, there could be no appeal to the people.

The government as formed provided for a system that was neither responsive nor responsible to the will of the mass. The judiciary was also made sovereign within its limits, and was independent of the executive and legislative departments. Conflicts came at last in France, as conflicts must always come with governments organized

Danton.

under this system, and *coups d'état* were resorted to.
The Directory made two *coups* against the legislative
councils; that of the 18th *Fructidor*, which struck
the Monarchists, and that of the 22d *Froreal*, which
struck the Radicals. On the other hand, the councils made one against the Directory on the 30th *Prairial*.
Then there were conflicts between the five members of
the Directory. Carnot and Barthélemy were exiled. At
last Siéyès and Roger-Ducos conspired against Moulins
and Gohier, and Barras absented himself. Bonaparte
then swept away directors, councils, and Constitution.

The National Convention came to an end October 26,
1795, after having passed 8,370 decrees.

The revolutionary movement in France destroyed
absolutism and established new forms in the structure of
government in Europe, if not throughout the world, and
the great assemblies, particularly the Convention, passed
many beneficial and enduring laws, which still constitute
a monument to the wisdom and statesmanship of the
brave men who sacrificed everything to strike down
tyranny in the interests of humanity.

Among the more important legislation of the Convention, in addition to that already named, may be mentioned
the following: The Convention passed the necessary
acts for the establishment of telegraphs; instituted the
great book of the public debt; adopted the first eight
heads of the Civil Code, which afterward became known
as the Code Napoleon, and remains substantially the law
of France to-day, as well as inspired the enactment of
many laws in other countries; established a new metrical
system; abolished slavery in the colonies, and declared
negroes citizens; passed a decree to remove the remains
of Rousseau to the Panthéon; drew up a moral code of
instructions, tending to encourage a love of industry, and

of the laws, and to enlighten citizens as to the principal events of the Revolution; ordered a plan of a normal school for young persons, with a view to the diffusion of education and knowledge throughout France; directed the committees of finance and commerce to investigate questions of tariff, posts, import trade, and internal taxation; instituted the Conservatory of Arts and Trades; instituted the Central School of Public Works, which afterward became the Polytechnic School; declared foundlings the children of the country; established the uniformity of weights, measures, and coins upon the decimal system; founded the Conservatory of Music; condemned the slave trade; made provision for the aged, and created the Institute of France.

Notwithstanding the great wisdom the Convention displayed in the passage of needful laws for France, there was at times much violence of manner among its members. Deputies carried pistols; and on one occasion the huge knife of a guillotine was brought before the Assembly while in session. The members of this remarkable body of men went forth each day, as the warrior goes to the field of battle, surrounded by danger, but determined to do their duty as their consciences dictated. They cared no more for the guillotine than the soldier for a stroke of a sabre. Citizens often appeared at the sittings to urge more vigorous action. Petitions were at times presented at the end of a pike. The Convention did not falter. It decreed the devastation of La Vendée and the destruction of the city of Lyons. The dangers of the country justified these measures. It was necessary, at the same time, to vanquish European coalition and the internal insurrection. It saved France from foreign invasion. If the emigrants had been allowed to return, there would have been left no vestige of the works of the Constituent Assembly or of the benefits of the Revolution. Instead of those admirable exploits which signalized the Constituent Assembly, the Convention, and the Directory, France would have fallen into a sanguinary anarchy.

"In repelling the invasion of the kings leagued against our republic," says Thiers, "the Convention insured to the Revolution an uninterrupted action of thirty years on the soil of France, and gave its works time to become consolidated, and to acquire that strength which enables them to defy the impotent wrath of the enemies of humanity."

The first matter of controversy that disturbed the political horizon under the new Constitution, familiarly called the Directory, was caused by the decree enacting that two-thirds of the members of the new Assembly should be, for the first time, taken from the Convention. The cry was raised that they were terrorists. Forty thousand men attacked the Convention. Bonaparte, who was sojourning in Paris, having been suspended from his rank, was called to command the 8,000 troops near at hand. Grape-shot mowed down the mob.

At last the one-third that had just been elected by the electoral assemblies joined the two-thirds from the Convention, to divide into the two councils and then to proceed to the nomination of the five directors, who were to constitute the executive power. Both the Moderates and the Radicals showed great animosity against the party that attacked the Convention on the 13th *Vendémiaire;* "they were full of alarm; they solicited one another to unite more closely than ever, in order to resist royalism; they loudly asserted that only such men as were irrevocably bound to serve the cause of the Revolution ought to be called to the Directory and to all public offices; they entertained a great distrust of the deputies of the third, and anxiously investigated their names, their past lives, and their known or presumed opinions."

Victories had diminished at the close of the Convention. There was a relaxation in the discipline of troops. The government was not energetic enough. It was proposed that the credit of the *assignats* should be re-established by the means of 1793: the maximum, requisition and death. The Directory at this time was warmly attached to the Revolution. The sentiment that prevailed was: "Go on; hasten the day when the sacred name of the Republic shall be voluntarily engraven on every heart."

The enemies of the Revolution now declared (early part of 1796) against requisitions, state of the finances, and executive laws against priests and emigrants. The patriots, on the contrary, thought the government was weak, and accused it of indulgences to the counter-revolutionists. The Jacobin clubs reformed at the Panthéon. They were to march forth from their quarters, with banners flying, bearing the inscriptions: "Liberty," "Equality," "Constitution of 1793," and "Common Happiness." Babœuf was arrested and executed.

By the middle of the summer the French armies were masters of Italy, the whole of which they controlled, and half of Germany. Charette was shot, and La Vendée was subdued. The Directory was successful. France had never appeared so great and powerful to the other nations of Europe. But the patriots at home were disgruntled and furious. They could not recover from their chagrin and grief at the execution of Babœuf and their other chiefs. They no longer wished the success of French arms, because it was thought that such successes increased the influence and power of the Directory. The internal condition of affairs could not be compared to the external glory of the nation. Party passion again ran high in the Republic.

But the latter part of 1796 was characterized by a subsidence of open agitation. The murmurs of the contending parties sounded like the last moans of an expiring tempest. "France, at the height of power, was mistress of the whole extent of the country from the Rhine to the Pyrénées, and from the sea to the Alps. Holland and Spain were about to unite their fleets with hers and to attack maritime despotism in concert. She was resplendent with immortal glory. Admirable armies waved her tricolored banners in the faces of kings, who had leagued to annihilate her."

Passions or ideas once engendered in the heart and mind of man seldom die. The Royalists, having become emboldened by temporary success, were about (September, 1797) to collect a band of *Vendémiaires*, under the pretext of organizing the National Guard. Jacobin influence re-asserted itself; the army was republican. It sent many addresses to the Directory. "Of all animals," one of the papers commences, "produced by the caprice of nature, the vilest is a king, the most cowardly is a courtier, the worst is a priest."

The Directory, armed with its immense powers, made a movement against the councils. It suspended electoral functions in forty-eight departments. It banished members of the legislature or sent them to the Temple. Carnot escaped. The Directory assumed revolutionary powers.

A young man of twenty-seven, Bonaparte had given proof of extraordinary military genius. The French victories in Italy followed, and he was able to dictate terms of peace in the treaty of Campo Formio (October 17, 1797).

The Directory now extended a solemn reception to Bonaparte. "The French people," said he, "in order to be free, had kings to combat. To obtain a Constitution founded on reason, it had the prejudices of eighteen centuries to overcome. Religion, feudalism, royalty, have successively, for twenty centuries past, governed Europe; but from the peace, which you have just concluded, dates the era of representative governments. * * * *
When the happiness of the French people shall be seated on better organized laws, all Europe will be free."

Acclamations rent the air. The people thronged the streets. France threw herself into the arms of this extraordinary man.

The Directory was now conscious of its weakness, and looked with alarm and distrust on the young general, who was fast becoming the idol of the people, as well as of the army. He was sent to command the expedition to Egypt (May 19, 1798). He fought the battle of the Pyramids. Here Bonaparte received information that the government at Paris had badly managed the French armies, and that the Austrians and Russians, under Suwarrow, were victorious south of the Alps.

These reverses added to the unpopularity of the Directory. The discontent of the Jacobins with their government had given rise to strong repressive measures. On the other hand, the wealthy class were disgusted with the renewal of war. A rising was threatened in La Vendée. At this juncture Bonaparte appeared in Paris. Siéyès and one other director, with a majority of the Ancients, agreed to another *coup d'état*, which should make Bonaparte the first magistrate. The garrison of Paris lent its aid. The resistance of the Council of Five Hundred, at St. Cloud, was baffled by Lucien Bonaparte and by the use of military force. Thus was accomplished the Revolution of the 18th *Brumaire* (November 19, 1799).

It has been claimed by some writers that this date designates the death of the Revolution. This statement can only be true in a limited sense; for, in point of fact, reform, which is only another word for revolution, was to go on, as it is hoped it ever will. The Revolution had been monarchical, republican, democratic, and, at last, military; it was simply a giant struggle against the old order of things; and that struggle with Europe could only be temporarily suspended. The Revolution proper was the first crisis which prepared Europe for the reception of a higher and broader liberty to come.

By the well-known historical and modern treatment of political, economical, and social questions, it is always essential that the continuity of epochs be shown to exist; how a clear understanding of one dynasty or government is arrived at through a complete examination of the events that precede it. By this process it may be exemplified that there is a gradual growth in most peoples to a betterment of the social, educational, and economical conditions, and what now would appear to be a period of useless despotism, or religious oppression, at first glance, will prove itself to be, on a studious investigation, a regular step toward the formations and mechanisms of more modern times. The old is always the basis of the new. In the examination of governmental development in France, it is just as necessary to be impartial and exact in writing the history of the reigns of Philip le Bel, Louis XI., Henry IV., and Louis XIV., as it is requisite to be patient and dispassionate in describing the great events that took place under the Constituent, the Convention, the Directory, Napoleon, the Monarchies of 1814 and 1830, the

Republic of 1848, the Second Empire, and, at last, the institutions of to-day.

The French kings, for example, successively grouped around their thrones in their struggles against feudal dynasties and rival nations, most of the provinces which constituted ancient Gaul. These provinces in this way lost their sovereignty and became subordinated to a single power. From the chaos of duchies, baronies, municipal republics, and ecclesiastic principalities, there has risen a modern state with its essential organs, its means of attack and defense, an army, a fleet, a diplomacy, and a system of finances. The former exclusive preponderance of the Church has been diminished, the independence of temporal power assured, a free press guaranteed, science gradually emancipated from theology; in a word, the single power of the ancient kings has been developed into a secular State.

From this point of view the Revolution did not come solely to destroy the work of royalty, but, on the contrary, to supplement it; to add to it the needed reforms. The very essence of the Revolution and of democratic government is to enforce a central administration, under the will and guidance of the people. Therefore, the modern government maintains the sovereign power and its preponderance over the individual, thus passing the power from the hands of the king into those of the nation. It strengthens the material unity, by creating a moral one; from provinces reunited by kings it has formed a nation. Louis XIV. and Louis XV., in speaking of the inhabitants of France, were accustomed to say, "Our people;" the Revolution made "the people."

Kings sought to destroy ecclesiastic temporal power, the feudal system, provincial and municipal autonomy, but the Revolution was compelled absolutely and thoroughly

Marat.

to destroy these institutions, equally repugnant to king and democracy; but democratic equality went further, and also required a complete leveling of all classes, and particularly the destruction of all the remnants of absolutism itself.

The Revolution was not an accident in history. Its way was paved by a past of centuries. In the twelfth century commenced the emancipation of the cities; in the thirteenth, abolition of serfdom of the peasantry; in the fifteenth, the renaissance of letters, sciences, and arts; and in the sixteenth, the promulgation of new religious ideas; while the influence of philosophers and economists in the eighteenth was decisive. In 1789, 100,000 Frenchmen talked with d'Argenson, Condorcet, Diderot, Voltaire, Locke, Hume, Rousseau, and Montesquieu. Each day the people took their lesson upon the rights and duties of man to society and to government.

The transformation of ancient France into a new France was accomplished by the people, acting through the three National Assemblies, the constituent, the legislative, and the Convention. The legislative councils of the Directory added little to the work of these great assemblies, which enacted laws and decrees modifying all branches of the national life. The corollaries of the principles of 1789 were formulated in the Constitution of 1791 in its " Declaration of the Rights of Man and of the Citizen." " This page of reason and justice," says Victor Cousin, " is the most sacred, the most beneficent, which has appeared since the Evangels." Even the adversaries of the Revolution invoke these principles as the great charter of their civil rights.

Louis XIV. proclaimed the theory of absolutism, which the Declaration of 1791 opposed. At last, through successive epochs, the principle that sovereignty resides in the people was acknowledged. Nobody, no individual, could exercise any authority except it emanated from the people. There was a negation not only of royal or divine right, but of all authority which pretended to exercise political power, whether through an independent class of men or an aristocratic judicial body.

The Revolution substituted liberty for arbitrary power, equality for privilege, and modern order for the old conflicts.

II.

THE CONSULATE AND THE FIRST EMPIRE.

The Provisional Consulate was instituted by the law of the 18th *Brumaire* (November 19, 1799). The Consuls Bonaparte, Siéyès, and Roger-Ducos, who were then at St. Cloud, repaired to the Palace of the Luxembourg. They fell to work to construct a new government out of the fragments of the old one. The task of forming a new Constitution was assigned to Siéyès, who had long contemplated its mechanism. This instrument, as it was eventually adopted, fell short of its object, because it was not properly based on the facts and experience which preceded it. In fact, any law, either fundamental or statute, which fails to express the will, desire, and conscience of a people is, in point of reason and justice, no law at all.

But the nation was now suffering in the throes of civil war. La Vendée was in a flame. The armies of the Republic were defeated. The soldiers, who had lived on *assignats* and victory, were in a state of destitution. The suppression of the revenue tax upon liquors, salt, articles of consumption, and the right of municipal administrations to make assessments, deprived the government of at least one-third of its revenues.

In lieu of the suppressed paper money the *rentiers* and the pensioners of the State received *bons d'arrérages*, the value of which consisted in their being taken in payment of taxes. The troops were compelled to take subsistence from the country, and to pay for it by means of *bons des réquisitions*, which were also received for taxes, and, lastly, *rescriptions* on the national domains, received in payment for those domains. These bonds were not a forced currency, like the *assignats*, but they stimulated an unhealthy speculation. They were bought up, at the lowest price, from the *rentiers*, the contractors, and the other holders. Thus, at last, all taxes came to be paid in these securities, and the treasury seldom received any specie.

The Directory was charged with the unsettled and troubled condition of the finances, the reverses of the armies, the destitution among the soldiers. The strength of France, however, was still great, and the men who now had clustered around General Bonaparte had the genius to provide for the crisis. Circumstances, or the experiences through which the nation had passed, favored the change for a new Constitution to be framed by the Provisional Consulate.

The law which established the Provisional Consulate also conferred extensive powers upon the three consuls, and it charged them with plenitude of power to restore order, domestic tranquillity, and to obtain for France an honorable and lasting peace. There were, at the same time, associated with the Consuls, two legislative commissions of twenty-five members each, selected from the Councils of the Ancients and that of the Five Hundred, to supply the place of the Legislative Body, and to give legal character to the acts of the Consuls.

The law authorized these two commissions to decree all necessary measures, on the proposition of executive authority, for the preparation of the new Constitution. For this purpose, the time was limited to the following

Ventôse, when the two Councils had full power to assemble again, if in the interim a Constitution had not been promulgated and accepted.

"It was, in fact, a real dictatorship with which they (the Consuls) had been invested, for these commissions, deliberating with closed doors, divided into different sections—on finances, legislation, Constitution—meeting only to legalize what the Consuls had to propose to them, were the surest and most convenient instruments for acting with promptness."

In the natural course of organization, it became necessary to choose a chairman. Roger-Ducos, turning to General Bonaparte, said: "Take the arm-chair, and let us deliberate." Bonaparte complied with the request, and "the chair became a throne."

The General was inexperienced, if not ignorant, of the forms of legislation, but he had quick intuitions. Experience in war gives decision to a man, who there learns to decide, to command, and to govern. Another strong point in Bonaparte's character was that he listened only to specialists. If he was deficient in the knowledge of individuals to be selected for public office, he invariably, at this time in his career, conferred with his colleagues.

It was now decided that Bonaparte was the man of action, and that Siéyès should devote himself specially to preparing the form of the Constitution.

The Consuls had allowed a large number of priests to return to France, and, at the same time, transported some forty members of the revolutionary party. For this reason the Revolutionists regarded Bonaparte as a Cæsar or a Cromwell.

The Royalists, on the other hand, hoped the General would save them from the Revolutionists; assume great powers, which some day he would turn over to them.

Siéyès had long contemplated his plan for a Constitution. His effort was an attempt to reconcile the Republic with monarchy. He borrowed from both, but he distrusted both. He produced what he called a scientific work, so balanced that if it lost one of its counterpoises it would lead to despotism, as it did. He called his proposed government representative; certainly it was one that employed the most indirect means of representation.

However, he went to work and endeavored to combine all the known forms of government in one instrument. Its chief features were the Legislative Body, the Tribunate, the Senate, and the Grand Elector. The last named officer was nothing but royalty confined to the nearly inactive, yet important, part of choosing the chief of government, with infinite precautions against the origin and duration of the office; for it issued from the Senate, and might, upon occasion, be flung back into it again. This proposed Constitution was the product of a man whose mind was disgusted with monarchy by the reign of the last Bourbons, and filled with a dread of a Republic. The paper was called scientific; it was certainly artificial and complicated, if nothing more. The Grand Elector was to have a magnificent income, with little to do. In his stead was eventually, as we shall see, the active chief, General Bonaparte, whom, by a change of a single spring, this Constitution was destined, without any participation of its author, to lead to imperialism.

It was thought that Siéyès had intended the post of Grand Elector for Bonaparte, with a view to tie his hands, and to cause him to be readily and quickly absorbed by the conservative Senate. The friends of liberty were not displeased with the device, but, on the other hand, the partisans of General Bonaparte inveighed against it, and he himself expressed his displeasure with his usual warmth of language, and Siéyès on his part was deeply pained at the disapprobation of his work. Messrs. Boulay de la Meurthe (who had transcribed the Constitution for Siéyès), Roederer, and de Talleyrand exerted themselves to reconcile the General and the legislator. Bonaparte seemed inflexible in his demand that the inaction of the Grand Elector, and the threat of ostracism suspended over his head should be removed.

Whenever it was proposed to Siéyès to let the executive participate in the government, instead of merely naming the executive officers, according to his plan, he would say: "It is a bit of the ancient monarchy, that you want to give me. I won't have it." He threatened to leave Paris, go to the country, and leave Bonaparte alone with his nascent despotism. "He means to go?" said the General: "let him, I will get a Constitution drawn up by Roederer, propose it to the two legislative sections, and satisfy public opinion, which requires the affairs to be settled." Bonaparte's idea was that a people should be fitted to a prepared Constitution, rather than that a Constitution should be prepared to meet the requirements of a nation.

"Your Grand Elector," said he, on another occasion, "is a do-nothing king, and the time of do-nothing kings is gone by. What man of head and heart would submit to such a sluggish life, at the price of 6,000,000, and an abode in the Tuileries? What! nominate persons who act, and not act oneself! it is inadmissible. And then to think, by this device, to prevent the Grand Elector from intermeddling in the government!" The idea of a Grand Elector was laughed to scorn by the young General, and it was agreed to substitute a First Consul in its stead, associated with two others, and thus, in some measure, to disguise the power of the former.

The Constitution of 1799, as it was eventually adopted, is not preceded by a declaration of rights, as were those of the Revolution. This is an ominous fact.

It provided that every man born and living in France, who is twenty-one years old, has his name inscribed on the register of citizens of his communal district, and has resided in the territory of the Republic for one year, is a French citizen.

The citizens of a communal district select by election, from among themselves, those whom they deem most qualified for public administration. Of these a list of citizens is made, who have the public confidence, which list must be equal to one-tenth of the number of all those who have a right to vote. From this first communal list the public officers of the district must be chosen.

The citizens named in the communal list of a department also select one-tenth of their number. In this manner a second list of confidence, the departmental list, is made, from which the public officers of the department must be taken.

The citizens named in the departmental list likewise select one-tenth of their number; hereby a third list of citizens of the department, who are eligible for public national offices, is formed.

These lists of national notability or confidence were well calculated to neutralize the popular action, by rendering it indirect. The revision, instead of being annual, was to be triennial. This system is the groundwork of the whole structure. It is a disfranchisement of the people, and smoothed the way to the despotism which followed.

The legislative power is divided into three assemblies:

Madame Roland.

the Council of State, the Legislative Body, and the Tribunate. No new laws can be promulgated except they have been proposed by the government, that is, the Consuls. The Council of State prepares the laws; then three members of the Council of State and three members of the Tribunate discuss them before the Legislative Body, which takes no part in the discussion. It votes silently. It is an assembly of mutes. It has been said that it is a body "without language, without eyes, and without ears."

The Tribunate only voted for the purpose of deciding what opinion it should support before the Legislative Body. Its vote did not prevent the bill from becoming law, if the Legislative Body adopted it. The Tribunate discussed the laws, but did not vote; the Legislative Body voted, but did not discuss. These provisions constitute a most singular conception in the history of constitutions. The members of the Legislative Body and Tribunate were chosen by the Senate from the list of the persons of note.

A law passed through six processes: initiation, preparation, discussion, vote, confirmation, and promulgation; and, after all, every decree of the Legislative Body was promulgated by the First Consul, provided no appeal had been made to the Senate. The consequence is that no law can be finally operative without the consent of the First Consul. The whole scheme was devised to take the power of legislation away from the will of the people.

The Conservative Senate is another part of this complicated engine of wrong. It consists of eighty members, who are not removable, and are appointed for life. The first Senate was appointed by Siéyès and Roger-Ducos, the Second and Third Consuls—both friends of Bonaparte—and in the future it is to complete itself. All registers of voters in the departments must be sent to the Senate;

the national register is thus formed. The Senate chooses from this register the legislators, the tribunes, the consuls, judges of *cassation*, and commissaries of accounts. The extraordinary power is conferred upon this body of annulling or confirming all laws passed by the Legislative Body which the Tribunate or the government points out as unconstitutional. Its powers were very like those of the Supreme Court of the United States, and may possibly have been fashioned upon that department of government. The government or executive power was intrusted to three consuls, who are chosen for ten years, and may, without exception, be re-eligible. The Constitution appoints citizen Bonaparte, former Provisional Consul, to the office of first consul; to the office of second consul, citizen Cambacérès; and to the office of third consul, citizen Lebrun.

The First Consul had all the powers of a king. He names and removes the ministers, ambassadors, and all officers. He issues orders of arrest and exile against conspirators and the suspected. He is charged with the conduct of the foreign relations, declares war, makes treaties of peace and alliance. This conception of the executive power was diametrically opposed to that of 1791. Bonaparte seized all power, and, in point of fact, made the laws. He made the propositions of law. He could retire a law at any of the halting places, or, by refusing to promulgate it, make it a dead letter. The members of the Senate, of the Legislative Body, of the Consulate, and Council of State are not responsible. The ministers are responsible to the Senate. No responsibility, directly or indirectly, to the people, which characterizes parliamentary government, exists in this monarchical contrivance.

The local administrations, which are established for each commune, and for extensive parts of the territory of

State, are subordinate to the ministers. No one can become or remain a member of these administrations unless his name is inscribed and retained on one of the registers prescribed by law.

Each communal district has one or more justices of the peace, who are directly chosen by the citizens for three years. Their principal duty consists in conciliating the parties, whom they shall advise, and if conciliation can not be effected, to have their matters in dispute decided by arbitrators. Courts of the first resort, and of appeal, are established for all civil suits. Crimes are taken cognizance of by a grand jury, who find a bill of complaint; whereupon a traverse jury passes upon the facts, and a court of criminal jurisdiction decrees the sentences. A court of *cassation* is also established.

"De Tocqueville has given us," says Dicey, "an account of the protection extended over French functionaries in the following passage, which may be considered classical.

"'In the year VIII of the French Republic a Constitution was drawn up in which the following clause was introduced:

Art. 75.—All the agents of the government below the rank of ministers can only be prosecuted for offenses relating to their several functions by virtue of a decree of the *Conseil d'Etat*, in which case the prosecution takes place before the ordinary tribunals.

"'This clause survived the *Constitution de l'an* VIII, and it is maintained in spite of the just complaints of the nation. I have always found the utmost difficulty in explaining its meaning to Englishmen and Americans. They were at once led to conclude that the *Conseil d'Etat* in France was a great tribunal, established in the center of the kingdom, which exercised a preliminary and somewhat tyrannical jurisdiction in all political causes. But when I told them that the *Conseil d'État* was not a judicial body, in the common sense of the term, but an administrative council composed of men dependent on the Crown; so that the King, after having ordered one of his servants, called a prefect, to commit an injustice, has the power of commanding another of his servants, called a councilor of State, to prevent the former from being punished; when I demonstrated to them that the citizen who has been injured by the order of the sovereign is obliged to solicit from the sovereign permission to obtain redress, they refused to credit so flagrant an abuse, and were tempted to accuse me of falsehood or ignorance. It frequently happened before the Revolution that a parliament issued a warrant against a public officer who had committed an offense, and sometimes the proceedings were stopped by the authority of the Crown, which enforced compliance with its absolute and despotic will. It is painful to perceive how much lower we are sunk than our forefathers, since we allow things to pass under the color of justice and the sanction of the law which violence alone could impose upon them.'

"Our author's subsequent investigations," continues Dicey, "make it doubtful whether Article 75 of the Constitution of the year VIII (1799) does more than reproduce in a stringent shape a principle inherited from the *ancien régime;* it at any rate represents the permanent sentiment of French governments with regard to the protection due to officials. This is what gives to a repealed article of a forgotten Constitution a curious speculative importance. If any one wants a proof of the essential difference between French and English ideas as to the relations between individuals and the State, he will find it in the fact that under the monarchy of Louis Philippe, which was supposed to be a copy of the English Constitution, every official in France was entitled to a kind of exemption from ordinary legal process which never has existed in England, and which could not be established here without a revolution in the feelings of the English people. The one thing which to an Englishman is more astonishing than the existence of Article 75 is the date and mode of its abolition. It survived the Consulate, the Napoleonic Empire, the Restoration, the Orléans Monarchy, the Republic of 1848, and the Second Empire. It was abolished on September 19, 1870, by a government which had come into power through an insurrection, and which laid no claim to existence except the absolute necessity of protecting the nation against invasion. It is certainly strange that a provisional government, occupied with the defense of Paris, should have replaced a fundamental principle of French law. It is equally curious that the repeal has been subsequently treated as valid. Of the motives which led men, placed in temporary authority by the accidents of a revolution, to carry through a legal innovation which, in appearance at least, alters the whole position of French officials, no foreign observer can form a certain opinion. It is, however, a plausible conjecture that the repeal of Article 75 was lightly enacted and easily tolerated, because it effected a change more important in appearance than in reality, and did not, after all, gravely touch the position of French functionaries or the course of French administration."

Such were the general provisions of the famous Constitution of the year VIII. Siéyès saw an all-powerful chief substituted for his inactive Grand Elector, which caused this Constitution to lead, a few years later, not to aristocracy, but to despotism.

At this time (December, 1799) it was laid down as a

principle that national rewards should be granted to men who should render eminent services. This was the germ of an institution since known as the Legion of Honor.

The jealousies and rivalries of party, the inefficiency of the Directory, and its final overthrow, had thrown the administration of law in France in great disorder. Bonaparte had had but little experience in the affairs of State, and none as a lawgiver; still, he had great natural qualifications as an organizer, and, assisted as he was by the first specialists of his age, he instituted many reforms which the spirit of the times demanded. Vast labors devolved upon the Legislative Body and the Tribunate. The First Consul caused two bills (*projets de lois*) to be submitted: one established administrative centralization in France; the other, organization of justice. To these two bills were added others relative to emigrants, to the right of making wills, to the prize court, to the appointment of new collectors of taxes, and, lastly, to the receipts and expenditures of the year VIII.

The government now presented a bill designed to close the famous list of emigrants. The list was declared to be closed from December 25, 1799, that is to say, the fact of absence posterior to that date could no longer be construed as emigration, and visited with the existing penalties. People were permitted to absent themselves, and to come from foreign countries.

The reorganization of the finances demanded great attention: the Bank of France was created. The old discounting establishments perished amidst the disorders of the Revolution. This institution has become the most flourishing establishment of the kind in the world.

The Constitution was ratified by the people (February, 1800), and the First Consul had taken up his abode in the

Tuileries. "But he was not to occupy the Tuileries exclusively. His two colleagues were to reside there, too. Lebrun was lodged in the pavilion of the Flora. As for Cambacérès, who ranked before Lebrun, he refused to take up his abode in this palace of kings. This personage, possessing consummate prudence—perhaps the only man of his time who had not given away to any illusion—this personage said to Lebrun, 'It would be wrong for us to go and live in the Tuileries; it is not a fitting place for us, and, for my part, I shall not go. General Bonaparte will soon want to live there alone, and then we should have to move out. 'Tis better not to go there at all.' Neither did he go; but he contrived to get a handsome house in the Place du Carrousel assigned to him, and this he retained as long as Napoleon retained empire."

General Bonaparte, on going over to the palace with M. de Bourrienne, his secretary, said to him: "Well, Bourrienne, here we are, then, in the Tuileries! * * * * And here we must stay now."

It was now claimed by a large party in France (October, 1800) that Bonaparte was as great a statesman as he was a commander; that he belonged to the Moderate party, and deprecated persecution. It was also urged that he was disposed to annul only a few of the laws of the Revolution, and would uphold its principal results; that he honored the arts and sciences, established schools, and opened a temple to art.

"General Bonaparte," says Thiers, "had attained the supreme power November 9, 1799 (18th *Brumaire*, year VIII); it was now the 9th of February, 1801 (20th *Pluviôse*, year X). Consequently, just fifteen months had elapsed, and France, partly reorganized at home, completely victorious abroad, was already at peace with the Continent, and in alliance with the North and the South of Europe against England. Spain was preparing to march against Portugal; the Queen of Naples had thrown herself at our feet; the Court of Rome was negotiating in Paris the arrangement of religious affairs." The Mountaineers, the survivors of the Commune, the Jacobins, the Cordeliers, were irritated at the success of the new government. They called the First Consul a tyrant who wanted to complete a counter-revolution, to abolish liberty, bring back the priests, the Bourbons, and make himself their base servant. He was a Cæsar, who ought to fall under the dagger of a Brutus.

In the early part of 1801 many questions, or *projets de lois*, were brought before the Legislative Body, in respect to the transportation of persons suspected of being concerned in the attempted assassination of Bonaparte, and also in relation to finances and public roads. In the Tribunate there was much opposition at times, and once the cry was raised of *"Vive la République!"*

The government availed itself of the revival of credit to substitute the expedient of *rentes* for that of the alienation of the national domains; paid off certain deficiencies of former years; liquidated the floating debt; and provided for a sinking fund. But other financial propositions met with a violent opposition in the Tribunate.

The First Consul, amid all of these controversies and his military and political occupations, never ceased to give his attention to the subject of roads, canals, bridges, manufactures, and commerce (March, 1801).

At this time he turned his attention to the completion of the Civil Code. This task was confided to several eminent lawyers: MM. Portalis, Tronchet, and Bigot de Preameneu. Their labors were concluded, and the result had been communicated to the Court of Cassation, the

Jean Jacques Rousseau.

Tribunals of Appeal, and the Royal Courts. It was proposed to present it to the Legislative Body.

It was at this time that the Italians contributed to the expense of the opening of the Simplon, and to the endowment of the hospices raised on the summits of the Alps.

It is claimed by some that all these great things were accomplished by the genius of the First Consul. It would seem that it was the faculty he had, at least, of calling around him men of thought and action, and especially those who were eminent in their specialty of work and department of knowledge. The example of the preparation of the Code is one. Then it will be remembered that Cambacérès, one of the first lawyers and statesmen of France, was always near the First Consul. The Civil Code was, however, drawn more from the works of Pothier than the commentaries of any other great lawyer, while Tronchet directed its compilation. At the same time, it must be admitted that Bonaparte always displayed a wonderful energy and great ability in everything he attempted to do. Back of all the work of organization, improvement in the laws, advancement in the art of government, was the spirit of the Revolution, then felt during the epoch of the Consulate and the Empire as it is to this day in France, and throughout the world.

The conqueror of Marengo and Rivoli having concluded peace between France and the rest of Europe, now determined to reconcile France with the Church. This ambitious general knew that the Church must be associated with imperialism, and that by an extension of his great powers as First Consul, the robes of empire could be worn. To keep the clergy from participating in the political affairs of the nation was one of the chief objects of the men of 1793. Under the old monarchy a powerful clergy held possession of a great part of the soil, and failed to contribute to the expenses of government. They formed one of the three orders of the States-general, and claimed the right to express the national will. The Revolution swept the clergy and their fortunes, privileges, and influence away at the time it banished the nobles and destroyed the throne itself. The First Consul had always professed a sympathy with the Revolution, or rather its spirit, but now he undertook an agreement or concordat with Rome, the terms of which were directly in the face of the action and intent of the deists of the Republic.

A law had been passed requiring all priests returning to France to take an oath before entering upon sacerdotal functions. This condition of things made a division among the priests themselves; a part obeying bishops appointed by the civil authorities, the rest refusing to recognize these religious functionaries.

The First Consul wanted to re-establish the old religion for the purpose of satisfying his ambition. The men who surrounded him opposed his course, for they were chiefly the founders of the Revolution, but not, perhaps, from the supporters of Robespierre and St. Just; still they believed in the spirit of 1793. Men of learning, like La Place and Lagrange, told the First Consul that he was about to prostrate himself at the feet of the Vatican; to degrade the dignity of the government and of the age. Even Roederer, a Royalist, and Talleyrand, a Moderate, were not desirous of re-establishing the ancient Catholic Church, with its rules and discipline. The brothers of the First Consul tried to dissuade him from what they termed a premature reaction. Bonaparte was obdurate. He saw the throne awaiting him in the future, and all thrones must have a religion.

"A Pope I must have," said he, "but he must be a Pope who will approximate men's minds to each other. I must have the true Pope, the Catholic, Apostolic, and Roman Pope, whose seat is in the Vatican."

The negotiations were carried on for more than six months; many points of difference occurred between the contracting parties. The Pope yielded the nomination of the bishops to the head of the Republic, provided he was a Catholic. The Church was to pardon the priests who had married during the Revolution; a new body of clergy was formed; and the Church recognized the legality of the sales of its property. The Pope wanted to have the Catholic religion the religion of the State. The First Consul knew that such a provision would meet with great opposition, and would alarm the other religious persuasions. At last, a preamble was agreed on, which provided that the government recognized that the Catholic religion is the religion of the great majority of the French; that the Catholic religion should be exercised in France, and that its forms of worship should be public, in conformity with the police regulations, which are judged to be necessary for the maintenance of tranquillity, and, finally, that there should be a new arrangement of dioceses.

The Concordat was signed July 15, 1801 (26th *Messidor*, year IX). The First Consul did not at first make its provisions public. He gave an analysis of it to the Council of State. The members of this body heard the reasons that led to the signing of this important treaty, which in effect re-established the old religion as the religion of the State. The Council remained sullen and dumb, for the members saw one of the great works of the Revolution perish by the act of a single man, whom the Pope called his "dear son."

The Tribunate, the Legislative Body, and the Senate assembled November 22, 1801 (1st *Frimaire*, in the year X), when active resistance was made against the Concordat, which particularly displeased the Tribunate. The First Consul openly proclaimed that he would crush the bodies that should resist him.

The First Consul virtually destroyed all disgruntled factions, and at the same time proceeded in the pursuit of what he thought was needed reform. He certainly displayed great administrative ability. The forests which belonged to the State, and to the communes, had suffered from the disorder of recent times. He now bestowed particular attention to the preservation of the sylvan wealth of France.

Political reorganization was not neglected. The new institution of prefects and sub-prefects, created by the law of *Pluviôse* (year VIII) had produced immediate and beneficial results. The preparation of assessments and the collection of taxes were regularly and promptly attended to.

In the mean time the tendency of the First Consul to make the consulate pave the way to empire, and to the establishment of a military monarchy, fast developed. He had already (November, 1801) a court around him. He had a military household for himself and the other consuls. He gave Madame Bonaparte a princely establishment. The consular guard was composed of four battalions of infantry, each 1,200 strong, and two regiments of cavalry The ceremonials were fashioned after those that were observed in the monarchical courts of Europe.

There were, at this time, at least, two parties in France. One wanted a moderate democracy, like that of the United States, the other a monarchy, after that of Great

Britain. But there were also those who, when they saw monarchical ideas spreading, a court forming at the Tuileries, the Catholic worship restored, and the emigrants returning in shoals, were ready for open Revolution, and the re-establishment of the Republic of 1793. The Tribunate agitated all manner of social, economical, political, and financial questions. The Concordat, after its full terms were known, excited general opposition and indignation, and it was regarded as the most counter-revolutionary act that could be imagined.

Siéyès was striving, with all the means at his command, to prevent this agitation by constitutional provision. But he soon learned, if he did not appreciate the fact before, that constitutions do not create human passions; neither can any form of law destroy them. A constitution is a mere stage upon which human interests appear, act their part, and then make their exit.

Under the guidance of this statesman, who was indefatigable in his efforts to accomplish his purpose, all activity was centered in the Council of State; declamation took possession of the Tribunate; the Legislative Body answered "yes" or "no;" and the Senate, at long intervals, chose the personnel of the different departments of government, except that of the executive.

While the monarchical governments of Europe were naturally inclined to praise the First Consul for the vigorous manner of conducting his affairs, he was surrounded at home by an active opposition. He called the members of the Senate idealists, the orators of the Tribunate busybodies, and the malcontents of the Legislative Body unfrocked priests.

Events which at first glance appear unimportant, often are, in fact, but the precursors of future movements of great political import. In the scanning of the verbiage of a public paper it was discovered that the First Consul, and his immediate advisers in the Council of State, had acquiesced, in a negotiation with Russia, in the use of the word "subject" in framing a treaty with that power. When this fact was disclosed in the Tribunate, a most violent explosion occurred, and M. Daunou withdrew, saying he would have nothing to do with legislative matters while the tyranny lasted. It was claimed that in a Republic such as the Revolution intended there could be "citizens," but no "subjects." "Five million Frenchmen," said M. Chénier, "have died that they might cease to be subjects, and this word ought to remain buried amid the ruins of the Bastile."

Notwithstanding the vigorous opposition that the Legislative Body made to the adoption of this language in a public document, it, without tumult—for the members of this body were constitutionally silent—ratified the treaty. The consummation of this unpopular act proved that the First Consul could, at his own pleasure, reduce to nothing the provisions of the Constitution of 1799.

Opposition to the rising power of the First Consul continued to grow in the Legislative Body and the Tribunate. The Senate was now the instrument through which he would strike. This body, at the close of January, 1802, proceeded to separate the partisans from the opposers of the government. Sixty members of the Legislative Body who had shown the greatest resistance to the projects of the First Consul, particularly to the re-establishment of Catholicism, and twenty of the most active members of the Tribunate were stricken off the list of membership, by what was called the process of "elimination." This was the end of the importance of the Tribunate, but formally it remained in existence for some time. The open discussion of public affairs which constitutionally took place in this branch of the government always annoyed and displeased Bonaparte. A virtual suppression of this part of the legislature was the course pursued by him to silence it.

The First Consul was fond of drawing attention to the fact that foreigners on arriving in, or passing along the avenues of Paris, were admired by the populace on account of their splendid uniforms and decorations. "See," said he, "these futile vanities which geniuses disdain so much. The populace is not of their opinion. It loves those many-colored cordons as it loves religious pomp. The democratic philosophers call that vanity, idolatry. Idolatry and vanity let it be. But that idolatry, that vanity are weaknesses common to the whole human race, and from both great virtues may be made to spring. With these so much despised baubles heroes are made. There must be a worship for religious sentiment; there must be visible distinctions for the noble sentiment of glory."

If these be correct views of humanity in their practical working; if only through such agencies great men may be produced, great deeds encouraged, what a strange anomaly, what a commentary. It is to be hoped that in the development of society and government such means will not be required, or even used, as an inducement to acts of valor, to self-sacrifice, to energetic action in the affairs of State.

The First Consul resolved to create an order to accomplish his object to inducement to honorable action, and as a new aid for services both civil and military. He called it the Legion of Honor. Each member promised to devote himself to the defense of the Republic, to the integrity of its territory, to the principles of equality, and the inviolability of property called national. What served to complete the institution, and to indicate its spirit, was that civil services in every line, such as the administration of government, distinction in the sciences, letters, and arts were as much an eligibility to admission as military services were. This project of the Legion of Honor was strongly attacked, as the Concordat had been. It was claimed that it was a blow at equality; the recommencement of a once-abolished aristocracy, and an avowed return to the *ancien régime*.

"What is there aristocratic," said he, "in a distinction purely personal, and merely for life, bestowed on the man who has displayed merit, whether civil or military?"

The opposition to the *projet de loi* was formidable, but at last the bill became a law. The will of the First Consul again prevailed against all arguments.

The First Consul now proposed a system of education for the French youth. He desired to rescue education from the enemies of the Revolution to whom it had been abandoned; that the classical studies should take first rank, the sciences to be second. Religious instruction was to be given by chaplains, and military drill by the old officers of the army. All these projects soon became law. This education was to be gratuitous. The youth of the country were to be formed on a common model, regularly and conformably to the principles of the French Revolution.

The fact of the conclusion of peace with Great Britain, May 6, 1802 (16th *Floréal*), was communicated to the Tribunate, which body resolved that General Bonaparte had the strongest claims to the national gratitude for his valor and genius, and that some manifestation of this sentiment should be tendered to him. It was thought that an extension of the term of office of the First Consul to ten years would be acceptable; and the law was passed.

Cambacérès.

He learned this fact with the greatest displeasure. He sent for Cambacérès, who, on consultation with the General, requested him to go to Malmaison. Cambacérès remained in Paris, convoked the Council of State, and induced it to draw up a new proposition.

The First Consul left Paris the next day. Before setting out, however, Bonaparte clearly indicated that he did not accept the extension of his office as was proposed, but would undertake any additional duty the people might impose upon him.

The act was modified to read as follows:

"1. Shall Napoleon Bonaparte be Consul for life? 2. Shall he have the power of appointing his successor?

"Registers shall be opened at all the *mairies*, at the offices of the clerks of the tribunals, the notaries, and the public officers."

The vote was cast in the affirmative on these propositions, in the latter part of July, 1802, and General Napoleon Bonaparte became Consul for life. The proclamation of the plebiscite was made 14th *Thermidor* (August 2, 1802).

Most important amendments of the consular government were now made on the suggestion of the First Consul and his advisers. They were all collected and adopted in the form of a decree of the Senate, called an organic *Senatûs consultum*. In lieu of the list of notables there was substituted a deceptive constituency of electoral colleges appointed for life, which were to assemble only occasionally for the purpose of presenting candidates for the choice of the Senate, which body was already invested with elective functions, and with the duty of watching over the Constitution, of perfecting it, of removing every obstacle in the way of its practical working, the power, in short, of dissolving, if need be, the

Tribunate and the Legislative Body. These decrees not only conferred upon General Bonaparte the consulship for life, with power to appoint his successor, but they bestowed upon him one of the greatest prerogatives of royalty, namely, the power of pardoning offenses. By these alterations, the Tribunate was deprived of its numerical numbers, and almost of publicity in debate, and was thus made merely a second council of State; furthermore, these enactments transferred from the Legislative Body and the Council of State to a Privy Council certain important affairs of administration, as, for instance, the sanction of treaties, and, finally, established a form of government which was little less than an absolute monarchy.

"It was still the aristocratic Constitution of M. Siéyès, apt to turn either to aristocracy or to despotism, according to the hand which guided it; tending, at this moment, to absolute power in the hand of General Bonaparte. But after his death it was capable of being transformed into a downright aristocracy, if, before his death, he did not hurl the whole structure into an abyss." During the life of the First Consul the Senate was his devoted instrument, but at his death or abdication it would in its turn become powerful. The system of electoral colleges created a national aristocracy, from which the Senate was constituted. At the same time, it lay in the power of this aristocracy and the Senate, if they were to combine, to place power in the Legislative Body and the Tribunate that even the First Consul could not defy. Although the Siéyès Constitution with its amendments of 1802 was but a mask for a virtual dictatorship, still, paradoxical as it may seem, there was such a subdivision of political power in its provisions that, under all the circumstances, it tended to serve the interests of liberty. In point of fact, a transitional condition of constitutional and governmental reform was taking place. These powers, as amended in their new form, really did stand ready at this time to oppose and check the dictatorship.

There was a great resemblance between the French Senate and the Senate of ancient Rome. The First Consul had the power of the Roman emperors, with all their hereditary authority. Still, this government in France was called a republic; certainly, it was not a democracy.

The new Constitution was then submitted to the votes of the people, and was approved by an enormous majority. Napoleon Bonaparte assumed the duties of First Consul, and even the Senate was, for the time, silent.

From this epoch the prenomen of Napoleon began to appear in the public acts. He had been called General Bonaparte. How soon would he adopt Napoleon only, like the monarchs of the old world? The First Consul now took possession of the Château of St. Cloud, where he received great personages of all classes, foreigners, and ambassadors.

"This young man," said Tronchet to Cambacérès, one day, "begins like Cæsar. I fear he will end like him."

The First Consul was about to enter into a war with England (May, 1803), and, for the purpose of obtaining money, and, at the same time, of making friends with the Americans, he offered to sell to them the vast territory of Louisiana. This offer was accepted, and the United States was thus indirectly indebted to this war between England and France for the vast additions to its possessions in North America. The price paid was $12,000,000.

One of the strange phases of the character of the First Consul is that, although he was evidently grasping after autocratic power, he continually claimed he was carrying out the spirit of the Revolution. In any event, he seized upon power to be exercised by himself, and not in the interests of the Royalists, against whom, at this time, he always inveighed. Even German territory did not prove a safeguard to the unfortunate Duc d'Enghien.

One day, when the execution of the Duke was brought into consideration, the First Consul said:

"They" (meaning the Royalists) "wish to destroy the Revolution by attacking my person. I will defend it, for I am the Revolution. They will be more cautious in the future, and know of what we are capable."

In April, 1804, the Civil Code was completed. This code was conceived and started by the Convention. Although its completion was earnestly urged by Bonaparte, still it was really the work of the first legal minds of France. The First Consul was about to be made a hereditary sovereign, and it was natural that he would receive even greater credit than he was entitled to for his part in the preparation of the Code, which is certainly a monument of that epoch in the history of the war, and one of the greatest results achieved by the Revolution.

In keeping with the great credit given to the First Consul for this work, there was a growing feeling that the great reforms of the day, the organization and crystallization of many of the projects of the Revolution, were the work of the extraordinary man at the head of the State. The people themselves even seemed to be dissatisfied with the existing government, and demanded a more centralized system.

The idea that the First Consul should be proclaimed Emperor had found favor in the army, and General Soult had written Bonaparte a letter on the subject. The cities of Lyons, Marseilles, Bordeaux, and Paris sent addresses in favor of the re-establishment of monarchy. The popular impulse seemed so general that official steps were sure to follow. The Senate proposed to convert the Consular Republic into an hereditary Empire. It was desirable that the change should be made under the semblance of law, and in accordance with the mechanism then in vogue. The Senate did not publicly discuss questions of State. The Legislative Body heard different orators, and voted in silence. The Tribunate, though narrowed into a section of the Council of State, still preserved the right of speech. The form of a debate with an apparent opposition was then entered into.

The Tribunate passed a resolution, proposing the re-establishment of hereditary succession in favor of the Bonaparte family. It was submitted to the First Consul, who returned it with the words: "Bonaparte family," replaced by the words: " descendants of Napoleon Bonaparte." No explanations were made. The resolution was reported back to the Tribunate. A crowd of orators pressed forward to support it, and vied with each other for the opportunity of distinguishing themselves by an argument upon the advantages of monarchy.

During the discussion it was urged that a monarchy would give, in a higher degree than any other form of government, the utmost liberty, and, besides, the force of action necessary to great military States, and where the habitudes of twelve centuries had rendered this form inèvitable, and thence desirable in a country like France. If that statement were true, would it not be better to admit it, and to organize the government wisely, than to flounder about in a false position which harmonized neither with the ancient customs of France, nor with the want which was then expressed of a stable and permanent government? The thought which seemed to prevail among the old Revolutionists, was that a temporary dictatorship of Napoleon would pave the way, at a future time, to the Republic; according to M. Carnot, to a representative monarchy; to others: Napoleon was to prepare France for a new *régime*, and to deliver her up, aggrandized and regenerated, to those, be they whom they might, who were to govern her after him.

The Senate congratulated the Tribunate upon its labors. Its presiding officer replied to the committee that the Senate did not wish the return of the Bourbons, because it did not want a counter-revolution; that it wished to raise up a new dynasty because it wanted to secure to the French people all the rights they had conquered; that liberty, equality, and enlightenment might be prevented from retrograding; that it was confident Napoleon would not devote his energies to benefit himself, but the nation.

It was evident, from the first steps in this drama, that the Senate did not intend to be second in doing honors to Napoleon. This body determined upon a memorial, which should set forth its views in an organic *Senatûs consultum*.

This document, dated 28th *Floréal*, year XII (May 18, 1804), is most elaborate in its provisions, and sets forth the whole scheme of empire. It consists of fifteen titles on the following subjects: of the government, succession, the imperial family, the regency, the grand dignitaries of the Empire, the grand officers of the Empire, the oaths, the Senate, the Council of State, the Legislative Body, the Tribunate, the electoral colleges, the Imperial High Court, the judicature, and the promulgation of the act.

This decree was adopted through the medium of the farcical plebiscite. The vote took place by inscription upon the registers, and in the absence of all discussion and of all liberty. On the 15th *Brumaire*, year XIII (November 16, 1804), the plebiscite was proclaimed in these terms:

"The Conservative Senate, deliberating upon the message of His Imperial Majesty, of the 1st of this month, declares:

"After having heard the report of the special commission, charged with the verification of the registration of votes cast by the French, by virtue of Article 142, of the Constitutional Act of the Empire, dated 28th *Floréal*, year XII, upon the acceptation of this proposition:

"*The French people desire the succession of the imperial dignity, etc.*

"Considering the minutes of the special commission, which authenticate the fact that 3,580,254 citizens have given their suffrages, and that 3,521,675 citizens have adopted the said proposition, proclaims as follows:

"The imperial dignity is hereditary in the direct, legitimate, and adoptive descendants of Napoleon Bonaparte, and in the direct, natural, and legitimate descendants of Joseph Bonaparte and Louis Bonaparte, as it is decreed by the act of the Constitution of the Empire, dated 28th *Floréal*, year XII."

Liberty, so dearly conquered, no longer existed; and all that remained of the power of the people of France was concentrated in the will and purpose of Napoleon and his band. The executive power swallowed up all right in its arbitrary monstrosity. From 1804 to 1814 this imperial organization was completed.

The hereditary succession was established on the Salic law, from male to male, in the order of primogeniture. The Emperor had the right to determine the imperial decrees, the interior government of the household, and the court etiquette suitable to his imperial dignity. A regency was to be created, in the event of the minority of an heir to the throne, to protect the title and rights of the imperial family. Napoleon, like Augustus, kept up the appearances of republicanism. The coin of the realm had on one side, "*République Française*," on the other, "*Napoléon, Empereur*." None of the different branches of the government refused Napoleon a law—neither the Legislative Body a law nor the Senate a decree. The Tribunate was suppressed, and also the Legislative Body. Napoleon was more powerful, at this time, than Louis XIV. The true name of his *régime* was military despotism, or Cæsarism.

The Consular Constitution of the year VIII, the *Senatûs consultum* of the year X, that of the year XII, and a series of other acts, among which was the Additional Act of 1815, constitute the constitutional compact of the First Empire.

It had been proposed, in order to render the imitation of the Roman Empire complete, to allow the two consuls to remain near the Emperor, at least in a position of quasi-power, as in Rome they were continued in office after the elevation of the Cæsars. It will also be remembered that one of these eccentric Roman consuls attempted to confer the title of "consul" upon his horse, which animal was to be respected as a public officer. By inversion of reasoning it has lately been suggested that General Boulanger's black horse may succeed in making him Emperor.

It was now determined that the Emperor should take an oath to support the Constitution of the Empire in the presence of the grand dignitaries, the officers, the ministers, the Council of State, the Senate, the Legislative Body, the Tribunate, the Court of Cassation, the archbishops, the bishops, the presidents of the electoral colleges, and the mayors of thirty-six principal towns of the Empire. According to the new Constitutional Act an

Empress Josephine.

oath to the French people was to be taken upon the Testament. It read as follows:

"I swear to maintain the integrity of the territory of the Empire, to respect and cause to be respected the laws of the Concordat, and of the liberty of worship; to respect and cause to be respected the equality of rights, political and civil liberty, and the irrevocability of the national property; to raise no impost, and to establish no tax except by virtue of the law; to maintain the institution of the Legion of Honor, and to govern solely with a view to the interest, the happiness, and the glory of the French people."

Thus was completed the third transformation of M. Siéyès' proposed Constitution; the second was that of 1802, and the first that of 1799. The Grand Elector became the First Consul; the First Consul became Consul for life, and the Consul for life became Emperor. These changes were not caused by the single will of one man; they were the result of the spirit of the times, which is always stronger than written constitutions.

No sooner had this republican general, who had supported the Convention, and fought its battles, and the avowed Revolutionist, been proclaimed Emperor of the French by a decree of the Senate— a body very much of his own creation— than he proposed to bring the Pope from Rome, to crown him. This course was without precedence in history; even the great Charlemagne was proclaimed Emperor of the West in the basilica of St. Peter. Cambacérès, who had been made Archchancellor, immediately opened negotiations with the Vatican to accomplish this most extraordinary event.

The French Republic, with its single Chamber and Executive Council of 1793; its two Chambers and Directory of 1795; its Consulate, with its Legislative Body, Council of State, Tribunate, Senate, and the Consuls of 1799; together with the modifications and the Consul for life, of 1802, now disappeared after twelve years' duration, to rise again in 1848; then once more to pass away under the shadow of empire, only to reassume its power and position among the nations in 1871. The French Revolution, thus ever vigorous and indestructible, kept on its course; although, at times, hindered, or apparently destroyed.

The Pope, who had been facetiously called the chaplain of Napoleon, came at last to Paris to conduct the ceremonies of the coronation in the ancient cathedral of Notre Dame. The soldier who sprang from the people was anointed by the Pope, who had quitted the capital of the Christian world to comply with the request of the Emperor. The same words greeted Napoleon that were chanted when Charlemagne was proclaimed Emperor. Napoleon took the sceptre, the sword, and the imperial robe, from the Pope; but, watching his movements for an opportunity, seized the crown and placed it on his own head. The oath, to which reference has already been made, and which embodies many of the principles of the Revolution, was then taken by the Emperor (Dec. 2, 1804).

"It was fourteen years since the Revolution had commenced. A monarchy during two years, a republic during twelve, it had now become a military monarchy, still based upon civil authority and upon the nation's participation in the framing of the laws."

The coronation in Paris was followed by that in the cathedral of Milan (June 4, 1805), where Napoleon was crowned King of Italy, with even more pomp than in Paris, in the presence of the ministers of Europe. Again he placed the crown on his own head, saying: "God hath given it to me; let him beware who shall touch it." Italy was created an empire like that of France.

Napoleon, at this point in his career, brought into action the great energies of his life, and established in the next few years the greatest political, military, and territorial extension of his power. The third coalition had been formed against France. Napoleon found that there was to be no fleet to protect his passage across the Channel. He broke up his camp at Boulogne and led his well-drilled army across the Rhine in order to prevent the Russians and Austrians from uniting. At the battle of Ulm, which followed, 30,000 Austrians were made prisoners.

Two days after this surrender, Nelson achieved a grand victory off Cape Trafalgar, over the French and Spanish fleets.

On the land, however, the career of Napoleon was triumphant. The powerful army of Alexander was defeated on the memorable field of Austerlitz. The peace of Pressburg followed (December 26, 1805).

Prussia now stood by herself. Her army was full of hope, but her methods were old. In the two battles of Jena and Auerstadt, fought on the same day (October 14, 1806), the Prussian forces were routed, and either captured or dispersed. A fortnight later Napoleon was in Berlin.

It now remained for the conqueror to deal with Russia. He had intended to prosecute a winter campaign in Poland, but the severity of the winter and the lack of supplies compelled him to fall back to the Vistula. The Russians now took the initiative. The battle of Eylaw was indecisive, but at Friedland the Russians were routed. Napoleon's method was to move rapidly and to subsist on the country. The consequence was victory. The Emperor Alexander and Napoleon met on the Neimen. At Tilsit, on the North Prussian frontier, peace was concluded (July 7 and 9, 1807).

"No ruler since Charlemagne had held such power as now wielded by Napoleon. Sovereign of France from the Scheldt to the Pyrénées, and of Italy from the Alps to the Tiber, he had given the throne of Holland to his brother Louis, that of Naples to Joseph, and made Jérôme King of Westphalia. Spain was content to do his will, and Germany was under his feet. He was the leader of mighty armies, with no military rival to endanger his supremacy over them. His conquests, it was impossible to deny, carried with them the abolition of numerous time-worn abuses, and the introduction of important material improvements. France was in many respects prosperous under the despotism established over it."

On the morning of July 27, 1807, Napoleon arrived at the palace of St. Cloud. The princesses of his family, the grand dignitaries of State, and the ministers were there to greet him. He had just concluded peace with Russia. "Let us enjoy our greatness," he said, "and now turn to traders and manufacturers. I have had enough of the trade of general. I shall now resume with you that of first minister, and recommence my great reviews of affairs, which it is time to substitute for my great reviews of armies."

He detained Prince Cambacérès for a close conference upon the subjects of legislation, internal administration, finances, and public works.

His mind was not directed to legislation alone, for questions affecting the fundamental law of the State were always of great importance to him. He suppressed the Tribunate (August, 1807). Since it had been reduced to fifty members it was a mere shadow of power. It is true it still conferred with the Council of State; and then one of each body went before the Legislative Body, which voted silently. This body generally did not oppose the *projets de lois* sent to it by the government, but occasionally the old influence of the Revolution would be felt, and certain bills would be deferred. These attempts at independence, at least, show that liberty was not destroyed in France, but only temporarily suppressed.

So far as constitutional forms give expression of the will of the people and perpetuate the purposes of the Revolution, the Tribunate was one of its best expressions, and the suppression of this branch of the government did not please the friends of the Democrats of 1789.

These, among others, constituted members of the government who were distasteful to Napoleon. Cambacérès then proposed a commission which should review the whole magistracy, and designate members who had proved themselves unworthy to administer justice. This *projet de loi* was adopted by Napoleon, and the action taken to carry out its provisions was a complete violation of the spirit of the Revolution.

As to peace and war, Napoleon decided more absolutely than the emperors of ancient Rome, the sultans of Constantinople, or the czars of Russia. He was surrounded by a submissive soldiery, a clergy excluded from public affairs, and an aristocracy he had created himself.

"The Senate, which, since 1805, had, in the absence of the Legislative Body, received the attribution of voting levies of men, paid for those confidences with two or three conscriptions, which the emperor paid for in his turn with magnificent bulletins, with blackened and tattered colors, with treaties of peace, unfortunately too far from durable; and the country, dazzled with all this glory, delighted with its tranquillity, finding internal affairs conducted with superior ability, the external affairs raised to an unparalleled height, wished that this state of things might last for a long time to come; and now and then only, on seeing the French army wintering on the Vistula, and battles fought on the Niemen, began to fear that all this greatness might find an end in its very excess."

Napoleon, by the aid of various financial combinations, in August, 1808, placed it in the power of the French treasury to pay a large part of the enormous debt owing to the United Merchants. A new system of book-keeping was introduced, and the new *caisse de service* was created.

The canal system, which furnished one of the principal means of distribution, at this time, in France, now engaged the attention of Napoleon. To artificial navigation, he justly conceived, ought to be added the full benefits of the natural streams and rivers, and to accomplish this purpose their courses and beds required to be improved. He ordered surveys to be made of eighteen rivers. He passed from canals and rivers to ports. He made basins at Antwerp. He lengthened the piers of Dunkirk and Calais. He continued the work at Cherbourg in the construction of the great pier upon which was to be placed a battery. At this time there was raised at Paris the two triumphal arches of the Carrousel and l'Étoile, the column in the Place Vendome, the *façade* of the Legislative Body, the Church of La Madeleine, and the Panthéon. The Bridge of Austerlitz, thrown over the Seine, was finished, and the Bridge of Jena was in progress.

Napoleon took the most vigorous measures to suppress mendicity by the establishment of houses where mendicants could get food and work.

Cambacérès had had a commercial code, borrowed in many details from the maritime nations, partially prepared. Napoleon ordered it finished. At this time Napoleon ordered the Civil Code to be called the

Napoleon Code. It may be true that this code was partially prepared during his reign; that he favored it, and did all in his power to urge the great lawyers of his day to complete it, but that is the most that can truthfully be said of his connection with the work. The Code was instituted by the great Convention. It was as much the Code of the Revolution as that of Napoleon's reign. The change in title was wrong, except Napoleon may be regarded as the Revolution itself, as he once claimed he was.

It was said of Justinian that he fought by his generals, and thought by his ministers. May not the opposite be true, namely, that Justinian was impelled to action by his generals and ministers?

Could Napoleon have destroyed the Code? Could he have prevented it any more than he could have destroyed the Roman civil law that had been carried by Roman arms and influence over the world, and upon which the French Code was largely founded? Were not the acts of Justinian and Napoleon, in naming those great systems of law for themselves, both unjustifiable and unfair?

While Napoleon encouraged works of genius and literature, he was not always patient, not always willing to wait for results. His intense and active nature led him to interfere and to direct what were, in his judgment, good and bad tendencies in thought, morals, manners, and government. The rival of the regicides at Vincennes, he sought to establish an empire the creator of a military despotism, he proclaimed his intention to lay the foundations of a universal republic; the author of the Concordat, he dethroned and imprisoned the Pope, and suppressed his temporal power.

Napoleon, who was childless, in the hope of founding a dynasty, directed a *Senatûs consultum* dissolving his marriage with the Empress Josephine (December 16, 1809). He then married Maria Louisa, the daughter of Francis I. of Austria, one of the oldest reigning families of Europe. The Archduke Charles personated Napoleon at the marriage (March 11, 1810) in Vienna. The Emperor met her first at Compiègne (March 27), where he had gone to greet her. The religious marriage was repeated in the Tuileries (April 2).

The policy of old Rome was to extinguish the feeling of nationality and patriotism in the provinces she conquered. Napoleon, being a student of that system, followed her example. The consequence was that he did not build up a substantial and continuing power in France. In the meantime he was exhausting her military resources. The time was sure to come when her hunger for glory would be sated, and victories would cease to hide the cost at which they were bought.

His spirit of domination prompted the disastrous Continental System, by which he undertook to cut off trade between the entire Continent and England, by ordering all the merchandise of England and her colonies to be seized and confiscated wherever it might be found. England retaliated by declaring the coast from the Elbe to Brest in a state of blockade; the portion from Ostend to the Seine being declared to be under a rigorous blockade.

These events seemed to stimulate Napoleon's ambition for universal dominion. He invaded and gave the crown of Spain to his brother Joseph; to Murat he gave the throne of Naples. Napoleon now marched an overwhelming force into Spain, and established his brother at Madrid (December 2, 1808). A British army appeared in Portugal, under Wellington, to oppose the French.

Napoleon was at this time called away by the rising of

Marie Louise.

Austria. Within a month from the beginning of the campaign he again entered Vienna as a victor (May 11, 1809). In the desperate battle of Wagram he was triumphant. Austria purchased peace, and joined the Continental System.

The campaign of Wellington produced a strong moral effect in all parts of Europe. France showed signs of weariness with endless war, and a new spirit of patriotism was stirring the hearts of the people of Germany. Societies were formed for the liberation of the Fatherland. Louis Bonaparte abdicated his throne rather than enforce the odious requirements of the Emperor's commercial policy (July, 1810).

The adverse circumstances which now surrounded Napoleon did not prevent him from making the fatal mistake of invading Russia. The Czar would not enforce the commercial restrictions. There were other causes of jealousy and coolness. In June, 1812, Napoleon crossed the Niemen with a force of 450,000 men. The Russians retreated. They declined a battle. When the French arrived at Moscow they found a deserted city already partly wrapped in flames. The only alternative was to retreat. At Smorgoni Napoleon left Murat in command, and hastened in disguise to Paris.

During the first three months of 1813 all North Germany rose in arms. The Prussian contingent furnished, Napoleon went over to Russia. All young men responded with alacrity and joined the volunteer corps. Sweden made a treaty with England, and agreed to help the allies. Napoleon at first was victorious. He had an opportunity to make peace, but he unwisely preferred war. Even Austria was drawn into the alliance against him. The news of the victory of Wellington at Vittoria, in Spain (June 21), turned the scales in Austrian councils. The odds were now against Napoleon. His army was very largely composed of very young men. The battle of Leipsic, in which the French were finally defeated, was the decisive contest in the wars of Europe against Napoleon. He was driven to the Rhine. The Saxon contingent and the members of the Confederacy of the Rhine joined the allies (January, 1814). Holland rose in revolt. Wellington defeated Soult in the Pyrénées, and invaded France from that side. The allies marched on Paris. The city surrendered March 30, 1814.

Napoleon had lost his hold on the ruling bodies in France. The Senate, that had hitherto done his bidding, now came under the influence of Talleyrand, who deserted the fortunes of the Emperor. Alexander was presented to the Senate April 6, 1814, and this body then pronounced the deposition of Napoleon (who had, in the meantime, abdicated), and the abolition of the hereditary sovereignty in the persons of his family. Elba was given to him, with a pension for himself and family, as a sovereign principality. He bade farewell to his veteran guard, which was composed of the soldiers who had followed him from Milan to Rome, from Rome to the Pyramids, from the Pyramids to Vienna, from Vienna to Madrid, from Madrid to Berlin, and from Berlin to Moscow.

The ministers of the different powers, the members of the Provisional Government, which had been established, and Napoleon's representatives, signed the treaty of peace of Paris (May 30). Thus the conqueror, who had signed the treaties of Campo Formio, of Luneville, of Vienna, of Tilsit, of Bayonne, and of Pressburg, was compelled to accept the terms imposed upon him by the allied forces of Europe.

Louis XVIII., the brother of Louis XVI., was placed

on the throne of France. France, by the terms of the treaty, was left with its ancient boundaries, as they were before the Revolution.*

After the whirlwind of change had passed, the Congress of Vienna met (September, 1814) to readjust the map of Europe. The claim of Russia upon Poland and the claims of Prussia on Germany threatened another war. These differences did not prevent the crowned heads assembled in this capital, with their courts and retainers, from indulging in festivities. The participants in these scenes were startled by the news of the reappearance of Napoleon in France. He had apparently engaged in laying out roads and canals in his little kingdom; but, in point of fact, he was observing the state of public opinion in France. With a few hundred men of the Imperial Guard he landed at Cannes (March 1, 1815), and was joined by every regiment that was sent to crush him. Ney was carried away by the popular feeling, and went over to the side of his old commander.

It is not within the province of this essay to recount the brilliant march of Napoleon through France. When he arrived at Lyons he already felt himself in possession of sovereign power. He dissolved the two Chambers of Louis XVIII. He said the Chamber of Peers was composed of old senators of the Empire who had come to terms with a victorious army and with emigrants who had returned in the train of foreigners. As to the Chamber of Deputies, he said that the terms of two-thirds of that body had expired. In all these acts Napoleon assumed

---

* The errors and mistakes of the Bourbons of the Restoration during the eleven months which preceded the "hundred days" will be treated in a subsequent chapter. In the meantime the fortunes of Napoleon will be followed.

that national sovereignty was the source of his power,
and not divine right, as formulated by the Bourbons.
Their rule was unpopular with the French, who
regarded it as the effect and sign of national humiliation.
The returned emigrant nobility made themselves offensive
by attempting the restoration of bygone abuses in government.
The Bourbons had neither learned nor forgotten
anything in twenty-five years. Louis XVIII. had already
fled from Paris.

At four o'clock in the morning of March, 20, 1815,
Napoleon entered the court-yard of the castle of Fontainbleau,
where, eleven months before, he had bidden
farewell to the Imperial Guard. In the afternoon of
that day he was carried up the staircase of the Tuileries
in the arms of the half-pay officers. He was in tears.
On that day France was reconquered, and Napoleon
remounted the throne. He proceeded to make the fullest
preparations for a great armament, and, at the same time,
proclaimed in favor of peace.

Louis XVIII. had promised to give France a Constitution
which would protect the rights of the nation. He
did not fulfill his promise. He entered Paris under the
protection of foreign bayonets. He dated his acts from
the nineteenth year of his reign, and annulled all anterior
acts of the nation. His Constitution was imperfect, and,
in its working, it was worse. He favored the pretentions
of the nobility, deprived the Legion of Honor of its
funds, and put in peril all the Revolution had secured.
His was a government of emigrants.

Napoleon, on his part, returned with the consent of the
nation. That fact made it lawful. He re-established the
nation in its rights. Any class of men claiming to be the
government, that once opposes the will of the people, its
faith, honor, or interests, forfeits its right to govern; for

government should be only an agency of the masses. Beyond this, all is either force or sophistry.

Napoleon promised to change the fundamental law. He favored a constitutional monarchy, in which the monarch would be represented by a responsible ministry, responsible to the Chambers, that should be all powerful. One of his objects was to conquer the foreigner who had humbled France, and, above all, to give her liberty. His supporters were the Revolutionists, the youth of France, and all who wished for liberty. He believed in the necessity of his action. There was, however, a great diversity of opinion; the Revolutionists believed in the Constitutions of '91, '93, and '95; the Liberals in the principles of the British Constitution. He had not time, in the midst of his great preparations for war, to call a constituent assembly, therefore, he determined to frame a Constitution himself, and, after he had made peace, to settle all questions of governmental machinery. The Republicans awakened. A majority of them wanted a constitutional monarchy to be brought about by changing the provisions of the Charter of 1814, granted by Louis XVIII. The Ultra-revolutionists and the Royalists opposed. Siéyès liked the British Constitution. Carnot also favored it. Napoleon consulted, among others, with M. de Bassano, and talked with the independent Lavalette.

Benjamin Constant, the impetuous writer, was at this time concealed in Paris, and waiting for an opportunity to get away. Napoleon heard of this, and, to the surprise of Constant, sent for him. Napoleon, with keen insight, determined to use Constant in his endeavor to frame a Constitution. The talented writer suppressed his prejudices, and accepted the invitation which had been tendered to him. The idea was to frame a temporary Constitution, or, at least, one that should last until the people should take action upon its provisions. The masses wanted Napoleon to take his place at the head of the government. They asked him to rid the nation of priests, nobles, and foreigners. The Emperor told Constant and others that he wanted a government under whose laws the ministers could openly discuss public affairs, with liberty of the press; now the thing to be accomplished was to settle its form. He had numerous plans submitted to him.

"This one is republican," said he, "this, monarchical, of the Mounier school," and a third was pronounced royalistic. "Do what you will with these," said he, addressing Constant; "arrange your ideas, and put them in form."

Napoleon claimed that the country needed a new system of laws, and whatever were his private thoughts, he did not insist upon them, for he now knew that it was impossible to govern a country contrary to its real opinions. He favored a government that would make all ministerial acts to depend on the vote in the lower Chamber. Still, he asked for the power to exercise the right of veto. The Chamber was to revise the laws as it pleased that body; not to beg enactments, as it was expressed in the Charter of Louis XVIII., but to invite the government to propose such laws as might be required by the popular voice. The Chamber was to discuss all questions of taxation, in the first instance; to be elected by the direct vote of the people, and to select military commanders.

Siéyès thought the existing form should be merely modified; that is, the mass should choose about 100,000 electors for life, and these be divided into classes, which bodies should form colleges of departments and of *arron-*

dissements. The formation of a second Chamber presented the greatest difficulty.

"I have always recognized the national sovereignty," said Napoleon, "but that is not conferring a favor, for the nation is sovereign, and no monarch is firmly placed on his throne but he whom the people support. I do not mean to follow the example of Louis XVIII., and grant a Constitution as if emanating from my sole authority. When we shall have finished the work to the best of our ability, I shall present it for national acceptance."

Napoleon did not desire the new Constitution to appear as if granted by a *Senatûs consultum*, at the same time he foolishly wished to continue his former glory in the new law. Therefore, the Constitution was entitled the "Additional Act," added to the Constitution of the Empire. The idea to be conveyed was that he did not intend to destroy the old one, although, in point of fact, he proposed an entire change. The proposed form of the fundamental law was in many respects a well-written and conceived Constitution, so far as an imperial Constitution may be, and in so far as it provided a machinery that would, if properly administered, give expression to the voice of the people. It was finally decided to make the Chamber of Peers hereditary, the members of which were to be appointed by the Emperor, who exercised the executive power; the Chamber of Representatives was to be elected by two series of colleges—those of the departments and of the *arrondissements*. The Chamber of Peers had jurisdiction over the ministers and military commanders. The Chamber of Representatives had the initiative in financial legislation, and in granting supplies and pay to the army and navy. The ministers were responsible to the Chamber of Representatives. The Emperor could dissolve the Chamber, but was bound to summon another within six months. Personal liberty was guaranteed. Misdemeanors of the press were to be tried by jury. This Act was to be presented, for ratification, to the French people. The revision of the votes to be made in an assembly composed of all members of the electoral colleges.

The Additional Act was fashioned closer after the British Constitution than any Constitution that had preceded it. But the title deceived the people. The old Republicans looked upon it as monarchical, the Royalists of 1791 as a monarchy with two Chambers, while the young Liberals considered it an aristocratic monarchy, because of the hereditary peerage, and that it was only a Charter like that of Louis XVIII., which perpetuated a feudal monarchy by the machinery of two Chambers, one of which was hereditary.

Thus the idea was set on foot that Napoleon was not changed, and had no intention of keeping his promises. The old Constitutionalists, however, were flattered because Constant drew the act, and favored it. Madame de Staël approved it. M de Sismondi, a learned publicist, said it had no resemblance to the *octroi* of Louis XVIII. M. de Lafayette disapproved its form, but admired its principles.

Napoleon hesitated to convene the Assembly. He did not want contention in his rear while he was fighting the enemies of France. But as there was so much opposition, he determined to act. A decree was then issued which set forth that Napoleon desired the representatives of the nation to take part in the crisis that was upon the country. It convoked the electoral colleges for the purpose of choosing 629 representatives (April 30, 1815), who were then to meet at Champ de Mai. The communes had power to elect mayors and municipal officers.

Marshal Ney.

The votes were cast; the newly appointed deputies arrived in Paris. The deputies from the electoral colleges assembled on May 29th and 30th.

The number of votes was found to be 1,304,206, of which 1,300,000 were in the affirmative, and 4,206 in the negative. The number of votes cast for the Consulate for life was 3,577,259; for the institution of the Empire 3,521,625. It was seen that the number of voters had been reduced one-fourth. This fact showed that the Counter-revolutionists, and those opposed to war, had abstained from voting. The violent abuse of newspapers and pamphlets against the Additional Act had, however, been silenced by the elections, and the Chambers had been summoned even before the appointed time.

The course pursued by Napoleon, in this eventful epoch in the history of France, disarmed his enemies, and passed power again into the hands of the *bourgeoisie*.

On June 1 Napoleon appeared at the Champ de Mai. He wore silken robes, a plume of feathers, and the imperial mantle. He rode in a coronation-carriage drawn by eight horses. The princes of his family were present. Fifty thousand soldiers cried, " *Vive l'Empereur!* " The blessings of heaven were implored upon a throne restored. Mass was celebrated, and a *Te Deum* sung.

The Act was presented at the foot of the throne. The Emperor signed it. He delivered an address, in which he said: "I have but one thought; that of founding our liberty on a Constitution suited to the wishes and interests of the people."

The representatives were in greater part old magistrates, military officers, holders of national property, and sincere Revolutionists. They were determined to support Napoleon, but at the same time to restrain him.

They thought the Additional Act connected the present government too closely with the First Empire. Napoleon replied: "Revise the laws, while I support the Revolution by cannon-shot."

Waterloo, the second abdication, the overthrow of the Empire, and the annulment of the Additional Act followed. The new representatives had met to deliberate, but the hall where they held their sessions was closed by order of the foreigners who had become the masters of France. The Provisional Government was formed. The barren rocks of St. Helena were ready to receive the conqueror and Emperor.

III.

THE RESTORATION OF MONARCHY.

Let us now turn back the pages of history hastily passed over in the last chapter in following the fortunes of the Empire. Louis XVI. had left a brother, Louis Stanislaus Xavier, now destined to ascend the throne of France under the name of Louis XVIII. It was said he was a savant and a philosopher. There was another brother, the Count of Artois, as well as the nephews, the Dukes of Angoulême and Berry, who, it was claimed, were types of chivalrous honor. In reminding the people of these members of the ancient family of the Bourbons, the audacious antithesis was drawn of these virtuous men, as they were called, in contrast with those of the Revolution, who were referred to as demagogues.

A special commission of seven members of the Senate had been charged, April 5, 1814, to prepare a form of a Constitution. Contrary to the advice of the Abbé Montesquiou, it did not wish to admit the brother of Louis XVI. to take the throne by virtue of a superior right to that of the national will. The members of the commission wished to prove themselves liberal and parliamentary, and, while opposing Napoleonic absolutism, to conserve, under the new reign, the offices and pensions which had been conferred by the usurper. The commissioners determined to conserve the Senate, the Legislative Body, and the system of the plebiscite. This plan, which had been advised by the Emperor of Russia, was voted for by sixty-six senators and promulgated by the Provisional Government.

It provided that the French people should freely call Louis Stanislaus Xavier to the throne of France, and after him, the other members of the House of Bourbon, according to the ancient law. The executive power shall belong to the King; and the King, the Senate, and the Legislative Body shall concur in the making of laws. Laws may be equally proposed in the Senate and in the Legislative Body; those relating to taxation can originate only in the Legislative Body. The King may also invite the two bodies to consider such laws as he may deem desirable. The sanction of the King is necessary to complete a law. Each department shall elect the same number of deputies; they shall be chosen by electoral colleges. The Senate, the Legislative Body, the electoral colleges, the assemblies of the canton shall each elect its own president. The active army, the retired officers, the pensioned widows and officers shall keep their grades, their honors, and their pensions. All acts of government shall be signed by a minister. Ministers are responsible for all laws, for public and individual liberty, and for the rights of the people. Liberty of worship and of conscience is guaranteed. All clergymen are equally treated and protected. Liberty of the press was to be maintained. All Frenchmen are equally admissible to civil and military employment. This Constitution shall be submitted for acceptation by the French people. Louis Stanislaus Xavier shall be proclaimed King of the French as soon as he shall take and sign an oath providing: "I accept the Constitution, I swear to observe and to cause it to be observed."

Ninety-nine deputies of the Legislative Body adopted this Constitution.

This proposed fundamental law attempted to bind Louis and his family as much as possible to the principles of 1789.

The Royalists were not at all satisfied. They were inclined to say to the members of the Senate: "Begone with your master that you knew neither how to restrain nor defend." This proposed Constitution reminded them too much of the principles of 1789; it sacrificed too much to the sovereignty of the people; it recognized rights of which they had a horror. However, they counted upon the unpopularity of the Senate, and upon the concessions in Article 6, which provided for the hereditary feature of the Senate, to reject the whole plan.

The Count of Artois, brother of the future monarch, entered Paris April 12th. The National Guard, with its white cockade, and the army, with its tricolor, united to salute him. He received, without conditions, the title of Lieutenant-general of the Kingdom, which had been conferred upon him by the Senators, but the Provisional Government, sustained by the Czar, exacted that he should declare that he took the office on condition that Louis Stanislaus Xavier of France should accept the Constitutional Charter as already framed. The recognition of this Constitution thus became a formal condition of his election to the throne. It was necessary to subscribe to it; the Emperor Alexander was notified that the promise had been given to the Senate and to the French people. All this time the Count of Artois limited himself to the promise that the King should accept the *groundwork* of the Constitution, and the Senators were contented with this partial adhesion. In order to compensate royalism for this unpleasantness, the tricolor was replaced by the white flag. The Provisional Government added Marshals Oudinot and Moncey to its members, and took the title of the Governmental Council, while around the Count of Artois was forming another council, entirely composed of emigrants.

Talleyrand, who reserved to himself the foreign affairs, hastened to negotiate the evacuation, and caused a treaty to be signed by the Lieutenant-general, which delivered to the allies all places still occupied by the troops outside of the territory of France, as it existed January 1, 1792, about fifty-three fortified places, with 12,600 cannons, and considerable material of war.

Louis XVIII., who, after the death of Louis XVII., the son of Louis XVI., had become, according to the scheme of hereditary monarchy, the King of France, was residing at Hartwell, England, at the time of the overthrow of Napoleon. He thought before entering Paris he would make the acquaintance of as many persons in authority as possible; so he decided to visit the Prince Regent of England. He entered London April 20th. The English gave him a magnificent reception. He was fêted three days in London. A French King receiving homage from the English people under such peculiar circumstances constituted an insult to the people over whom he was to rule by the force of the accidents of war; and he added a double insult to this injury, before leaving London, by investing the Prince Regent with *cordon bleu*, the highest distinction a French monarch could bestow. It almost seems that the Bourbons were destined to commit political errors, if not crimes, from the commencement of their reigns, so little were they *en rapport* with the true spirit of the people. He left London, however, on April 23d, and arrived the same day at Dover, accompanied by the Prince Regent and a number of other English princes. The inhabitants of Dover received him, all wearing the white cockade and waving white handkerchiefs.

The next day he embarked for Calais, escorted by an English fleet of eight ships of the line and several frigates. It was in this way, it may be said, that England gave this gouty personage to the French people to rule over them with sovereign power.

The King went by slow marches to Paris. The marshals of the Empire, Berthier at their head, went to Compiègne to salute the *legitimate King*, and the Legislative Body sent him a deputation.

At St. Ouen he was met and waited on by the Senate, who presented the proposed Constitution, which it had drawn up and published. The King at this place issued his celebrated declaration.

"Having read attentively the plan of the Constitution," said Louis XVIII., "proposed by the Senate at its meeting on the 6th of last April, we find the fundamental principles of the Constitution excellent, but many of the articles bear the impress of the haste with which they were drawn up, and can not, in the present form, become fundamental laws of the State." He then stated that for the purpose of carefully adopting a system of constitutional law, he would appoint June 10, 1814, for the Senate and Legislative Body to meet for the purpose of taking into full consideration the work of the commission.

Thus the King did not accept the senatorial Constitution; he was going to grant *(octroyer)* a Charter. In this way royal sovereignty got the better of the phantom of national sovereignty.

Under the auspices of this declaration, Louis XVIII. prepared to make an entry into Paris May 3. The grand *cortège* entered the city amid the cries of "*Vive le Roi!*" occasionally interrupted by "*Vive la Garde!*" When the party arrived at the Tuileries, they found, to their horror, that it was guarded by the grenadiers of the Imperial Guard.

The commission was chosen by the King and his retinue. He did not put upon it any of the authors of the constitutional plan. Among the old men of the Revolution there was only one who was deemed worthy to figure among the commissioners. This was Boissy d'Anglas, ex-president of the Convention during the days of the "*Prairial*," the reporter of the Constitution of the year III.

Louis XVIII. was an admirer of British parliamentarism, which he held to be the highest kind of liberalism. But he misinterpreted the English Constitution, and adopted a reactionary view of it. He evidently drew his inspiration of the law from a certain class of the people among whom he lived so long, and from the writings of Montesquieu and De Lolme. At any rate, he proceeded to grant a Charter to the French that bore little resemblance to the English Constitution, which had existed as a ministerial government since the Revolution of 1688.

The matter of a fundamental law was now fully discussed.

M. de Bonald expressed a contempt for written Constitutions. When the various Constitutions which had been reduced to writing in previous years are contemplated, it would almost seem that he was right. Except in the periods of revolution, Constitutions should be a growth from customs, habits, and conditions of men. According to this view, ancient France had an unwritten Constitution of absolutism.

In truth, a Constitution should be like any other statute, that is, subject to the varying fortunes and conditions of a people. The Constitution does not make the people, but the people make the Constitution. The Constitution is really only the outward expression of facts that exist

La Fayette.

within the will and the conscience of a nation. An examination of the fundamental law of France will show the progress that liberty and thought have made in that country. There has been great fluctuation in the thought and aspiration of the contending parties. The reform party had been trying to rid itself of a desperate royalty, endowed with great power; first one and then another force would gain the ascendancy. The changes in the law were inevitable. Every law is subject to evolutionary growth and decay, and only expresses the will of to-day, and that is all any law can do—statute or constitutional. Until a people is convinced of its inner and actual wants, its desire, its purpose, it will be necessary for it to have general forms for the guidance of all; but when that condition of society arrives when all questions are understood and agreed to, as if written on the hearts, intelligence, and conscience of the masses, then, perhaps, no written law regulating the mechanism of the government will be required, and the people will simply legislate to interpret and to give expression to the ethical, social, and political sentiments acknowledged by everyone to exist.

With a personal executive claiming that his powers were of divine origin, and granting to the people rights which belong to the people themselves, there could be no progress in the evolution of government that could be regarded as permanent, particularly if everything was not expressed in such a way that the people could understand what the contract was that existed between an individual calling himself a King and those whom he designates as his subjects. The Royalists destroyed the principles of the Revolution, or, rather, as far as they were able to, and then asked why the Constitution of '93 had not been able to settle for all time the questions involved in the construction of that instrument. The

Royalists knew that the written Constitutions had done much for human rights, or at least those who made them had, and, therefore, these nobles were opposed to any of the methods employed by the great men of the revolutionary movement. The Bourbons pretended that they were recalled to the throne in their own right, not by act of the Senate. They proposed to grant a Constitution to the people. The masses foolishly yielded this point to these pretenders.

It was claimed that the new Constitution emanated from royalty itself, acting under the impulse of its own wisdom. Consequently, no mention was made in the new laws and proclamations of the return of the Bourbons to the throne, for, according to the order of primogeniture, they had always reigned, although they had been physically prevented from doing so It was claimed that the rights of the Bourbons needed no enumeration.

In the preamble to the Constitutional Charter, June 4, 1814, Louis XVIII. sets forth as follows:

"Louis, by the grace of God, King of France and Navarre, and to all those to whom these presents shall come, greeting." He states that Divine Providence has called him to his estates after a long absence; that he would like to blot from his memory, and to efface from history all the evils which have affected his country during his absence, and then proceeds to accord, concede, and grant the Charter to his subjects, for himself and his successors, and forever.

The provision on political rights sets forth that "all Frenchmen are equal before the law, whatever their rank or title may be. Individual liberty guaranteed that a person can be prosecuted or arrested only as prescribed by law. Everyone exercises his religion with equal freedom. However, the Roman Catholic religion is the religion of the State."

This act placed all other religions in a condition of dependence.

"Frenchmen have the right to publish and print their opinions, if they conform to the laws, which are to prevent the abuses of this liberty." This was a blow at the liberty of the press, as it was subsequently developed.

"All property was inviolable, not excepting that called national; the law recognizing no difference."

In the discussion that led to this declaration it was plain that the emigrants wanted to get back their property that had been sold by the State to innocent purchasers.

"The person of the King is inviolable and sacred. His ministers are responsible. The King alone has executive power. The King is the supreme head of the State; he commands the forces of the army and navy; declares war; makes treaties of peace, alliance, and commerce; appoints to all offices of public administration, and issues all orders and ordinances necessary for the execution of the laws and for the safety of the State."

The King is thus made the sole responsible executive. It is true that there is an attempt to make the ministry responsible, but as little power is conferred on them, they, in point of fact, become the mere clerks of the King. This part of the Charter displays an effort to combine the features of the English and the American Constitutions. The result is, however, that a personal monarchy was established. At the end of the list of powers is given that "for the safety of the State." This is absolutism itself. This provision gave the King power to overthrow the law at any moment he thought it expedient, although acting within the letter of the law in doing so. A dictatorship was thus concealed.

"The legislative power is exercised in common by the King, and the Chamber of Peers, and the Chamber of Deputies.

"The King proposes laws.

. "The proposition of a law is, at the pleasure of the King, made either in the Chamber of Peers or in the Chamber of Deputies—excepting the law regarding taxes, which must first be brought before the Chamber of Deputies.

"Each law requires free discussion, and the assent of the majority of both Chambers.

"The Chambers have the right to petition the King to propose a law on any subject, and to state what, in their opinion, the laws should contain.

"If the proposition be accepted by both Chambers it will be laid before the King; if rejected, it can not be brought up again in the same session. The King alone sanctions and promulgates the laws."

The King is thus made a legislator as well as an executive, for he not only proposes but sanctions the law. He has an actual and final veto. Although it was claimed that the Charter was fashioned after the British Constitution, it is clear that these provisions were a complete denial of the principles of English law, as well as the Constitutions of '91 and '93. The ministry of a popular government should have had power to initiate laws in the lower house under the direction of the representatives of the people. If the ministry refused to comply, they could then appeal to the people themselves. The personal executive, if one were considered desirable, should have no right to initiate laws, except, possibly, as a recommendation in the way of a communication to the legislature. By this contrivance the actual executive would always be under the control of the will of the masses. The power of veto being vested in the King, left the Chambers no choice between absolute adoption and rejection, and reduced the legislature to extremities and destroyed the spirit of debate. The provision that the Chambers were to petition the King to propose laws on any subject, was, in effect, compelling the sovereign people to beg the King to initiate the laws. This was little less than Asiatic despotism, and it is surprising that the people of France submitted to such a government.

The Chamber of Peers is a privy council of the King.

The best way to prove what a machine of despotism the Charter is, is to state briefly what its provisions are. This branch of the legislature, as well as the Chamber of Deputies, could be called together only by the King. There is no separate power. The action of the legislature depends on the single will of the personal executive. The nomination of the peers belongs to the King. Their number is unlimited, and the King can change the officers at pleasure, he can appoint them during life, or make them hereditary. In this manner the King can control legislation by dismissing one set of peers and appointing another, or by decreasing or increasing them. The members of the royal family and the princes of the blood are peers by right of birth. But the princes can take seats in the Chamber only upon the express command of the King. All deliberations of the Chamber of Peers are secret. The peers decide and adjudicate on treason and high crimes which are alleged to be dangerous to the safety of the State.

"The Chamber of Deputies is chosen by electoral colleges, not directly by the people. No deputy can be admitted unless he has attained the age of forty years, and pays a direct tax of 1,000 francs. The electors who take part in voting must pay a tax of at least 300 francs, and have attained to the age of thirty years. The president of the Chamber of Deputies shall be appointed by the King from a list of five proposed by the Chamber. The sessions are public; the desire of five members, however, is sufficient to oblige the Chamber to form a secret committee of the whole. No alteration can be made in any law, unless it be proposed by the King in a committee and sent to the bureaus, and be there discussed. No taxes can be laid and raised, unless they be assented to by both Chambers, and be sanctioned by the King. The King may call together both Chambers every year; he may prorogue them or dissolve them. All petitions to either of the Chambers must be in writing. The law prohibits presenting them in person at the bar."

In the first place the members of this Chamber were elected indirectly by electors chosen in the departments. The organization of this body of electors is ultra-royal in its contrivance. The property qualification was objected to and the reply came that, "in giving liberty to a country, guarantees should be sought among the holders of property." From what source did Louis XVIII. get his authority to give liberty to the sovereign people of France?

The ministers always have access to the Chambers of Peers and Deputies. The Chambers can impeach for treason or abuse of fidelity. This provision largely increases the executive power of the King, for the ministry really have no separate power, and can not be reached for political misdemeanors.

The whole judicial power proceeds from the King; it is exercised in his name, by judges whom he nominates and appoints, and these judges can not be removed. No extraordinary commissions and tribunals can be established.

The punishment by confiscation of property is abolished.

The King has the pardoning and commuting of punishments.

Two new things were now to be decided upon, namely, the date of the instrument and the title of the King. Louis XVIII. would allow no discussion as to the date. He claimed he commenced to reign the day on which the son of Louis XVI. died, and had reigned even while Napoleon was gaining the victories of Austerlitz, Jena, Friedland, and Wagram, and signing the treaties of Pressburg, Tilsit, and Vienna. "These were only different phases of usurpation, which disappeared before the immutable principle of legitimacy." Consequently, the Charter was dated from the nineteenth year of his reign.

On the question of title Louis said he would follow what Louis le Gros had done, and he denominated the instrument, without any submission of it to the voice of the people, as the "Constitutional Charter."

He then took his seat on the throne (June 4, 1814), surrounded by the bodies of the State, and promulgated the Charter amid the acclamations of "*Vive le Roi!*"

"The Revolutionists and the Imperialists reproached the Bourbons with having returned to France in the train of foreigners, and returned only to communicate the humiliation of the country."

Vestiges of national liberty appeared, as a matter of form, in the articles devoted to political rights; but the rest of the Charter effaced them completely. A State religion is established. The legislative and judicial power resides entirely in the royal person. The right to vote, and eligibility, belong only to the rich. A plutocracy was established. The legislative power oscillated between the two Chambers, which were both equally interested in deceiving the nation for the profit of the Crown. All laws were actually set aside by the right to make ordinances, which power was at the discretion of the King and his ministers. No revision of the Charter was provided for. The projectors of this infamous souvenir of the Middle Ages thought they had enchained France forever.

From its promulgation, the Charter was interpreted in the retrograde sense by the nobility, the clergy, and even by the late constituents, many of whom had returned to their monarchical worship. The men who had fought against France were the objects of all favor, whilst the unfortunate soldiers, returning from the lost provinces, the hulks of England, or the prisons of Germany or Russia, were exposed to attacks of scorn and harshness. To the inward awkwardness of royalty was added the diplomatic silliness of the vain Talleyrand, who wished to intervene in the dissensions of the enemy, not for the purpose of obtaining national advantage, but for the single purpose of sustaining the old aristocracies in other lands, and to put a French army in the service of England and Austria. His pretended skillfulness succeeded in establishing Prussia upon the left bank of the Rhine.

It was in the first days of the Restoration that the law was passed prohibiting work on Sundays. This law was classed among the "customary laws." The situation already existing was aggravated during the winter. Maladroit persecutions, and foolish menaces against everything which recalled the Revolution, alienated many leaders as well as most of the army from this government. Half-pay officers, around the Palais Royal

Fouché.

and on the boulevards, ridiculed the impotent King, and laughed at the household troops.

M. Bouvier-Dumolard proposed a petition to the King requesting a law declaring that the two Chambers were the real parliament of France. He wished to place the two French Chambers in the same position as the English Chambers. He condemned the proclamation of the police concerning holidays and Sundays, the royal ordinance, which placed the press under the same regulations as existed during the Empire. He contended that the police had no right to levy fines under the pretended sanction of ancient edicts. After an acrimonious debate, in which M. Montesquiou supported the King, the ministers amended the bill, and it was passed in this form. This act infused a certain tranquillity in the public mind, which was not destined to endure.

The next question that arose was that of the validity of the sales called national. Questions also of finance arose and were debated.

The Count of Artois, after an absence, returned to Paris. He was dissatisfied with the ministers of the King. He was the object of the hopes and love of the Ultra-royalists. He carried all reports to the King to prove to him that he had badly chosen his officers, and that whilst he was reading his classic authors the monarchy was undermined and threatened with fresh calamities.

Carnot, who, at this time, was living in seclusion in Paris, took little part in affairs; but he was deeply moved at the manner the government treated the ancient patriots, whilst Chouan chiefs were often raised to the rank of nobles.

The princes, the ancient nobility, and the emigrants now demanded the unconditional restoration of the estates which had been seized, but had not yet been alienated. Although much of this land was held for the use of the hospitals, as a sinking fund, the government, in October, 1814, relinquished all that remained unsold, to the emigrants. A plot was now discovered (November 30th) to seize the King on the way to the Odéon, and to throw him into the Seine.

Dissensions and disagreements multiplied. The Bourbons may have reconciled France with the rest of Europe, but in these efforts to re-establish the old *régime* on the ruins of the Revolution and the Empire, were about to set her against herself.

Napoleon surveyed everything from his island home. In the hope of reconquering his throne, he had organized a small troop and a flotilla. He landed in France and appeared before Lyons. The Count of Artois and the Duke of Orléans fled. The same evening Napoleon published a proclamation calling together the extraordinary assembly of the Champ de Mai. Leaving Lyons, he was received everywhere by cries of "*Vive l' Empereur! A bas les prêtres! A bas les nobles!*"

In his rapid course across France Napoleon was given to understand that it was necessary for him to renounce his old way of governing; that, although France wanted to be delivered from the Bourbons, she did not intend to give herself up to the will of a single man. He replied that: "he wished to maintain peace, observe the treaty of peace of Paris, and establish liberty."

Napoleon called Carnot and Davout to the ministry; they accepted the offices, although they were certain that the nation was to be surrounded by great dangers. He gave the department of police to Fouché. He abolished the censorship of the press, prohibited the slave-trade, and the introduction of all slaves into French territory. He even ordered the formation of colored troops at Bordeaux.

Still this incorrigible despot did not believe in peace. He only wished for a respite in order to prepare for his revenge, and to re-establish his own power. But the powerful strangers did not let him have the leisure he needed. The moment the news of his debarkation was received, the coalition reformed and declared that, "it would deliver this enemy and disturber of the peace of the world to public prosecution for crime."

Once again France found herself contending alone against all her enemies.

Louis and his family passed across the frontier.

The "Additional Act to the Constitution of the Empire," was ratified by a plebiscite. The fatal Belgian campaign took place.

France succumbed to this last political mistake of Napoleon, who had been called "an usurper; a man stained with human blood, and more cruel than Attila."

After Waterloo, Napoleon abdicated in favor of his son, on the pretense that he offered himself as a sacrifice to the hatred of the enemies of France.

Napoleon voluntarily terminated his political career, July 13, 1815, by going on board the *Bellerophon*, and surrendering to the British people.

As the ship weighed anchor, one last cry was heard of "*Vive l'Empereur!*" The white flag was hoisted on all the ships in the roads, and the Empire of the hundred days was at an end. As Napoleon paced the deck he was uncertain whether he was in an asylum or a prison.

During the battle of Waterloo Louis XVIII. was at Ghent. The noise of the battle had resounded all day on the 18th day of June. Sinister tidings were spread by the fugitives from the British camp followers. It was to the King and the princes a day of anguish, panic, and despair.

At last Wellington wrote to the Duke of Berry: "As I expect to pass the frontier to-morrow, I beg Your Royal Highness to advance and join us. I wrote to the King to request him to put himself in motion by the same route." On the same night Wellington wrote the old French deserter, General Dumouriez, who was watching the war against his country.

The Duke of Wellington, in his advance on Paris, made the recognition of the rights of Louis XVIII. a condition precedent to all armistice.

Louis, who was really only a vanquished man brought back by a foreign victory, issued a proclamation in the language of a conqueror.

"From the period," he said, at Cateau-Cambrésis, June 15, 1815, "when the most criminal of enterprises, seconded by the most inconceivable defection, constrained us for awhile to quit our kingdom, we have apprised the French people of the dangers which threatened them if they did not hasten to break the yoke of the tyrant usurper." In the same vein he spoke of his subjects, and the blood of his people.

In reascending the throne, Louis was compelled to make friends with Fouché; to take the hand stained with the blood of his brother; to elevate him to the rank of one of his ministers, and to place him at the head of his councils.

Carnot, on hearing that Fouché had been appointed one of the ministers, went before him.

"Where am I to go to, traitor?" said Carnot.

"Where thou wilt, fool," replied Fouché.

Carnot believed that Fouché's ambition sold to the Bourbons the right of re-entry into France, without any conditions of liberty.

A year before his first accession, Louis was nearly

unknown to France. He had presented himself as a
candidate for the throne under foreign patronage. He
represented, in the imagination of France, a *régime* repudiated and superannuated; irreconcilable, perhaps, with
the ideas and interests which had sprung up since his
emigration.

He succeeded a military hero, who had intoxicated
France with the glory and the pride of his conquests, but
who had stumbled from victory and the throne. The
army of this conqueror was even now an empire within
an empire. This element had to be satisfied, or Louis
XVIII. must retire.

Although the second fall of Napoleon and the second
abasement of France had wonderfully smoothed for the
King the difficulties of reigning, still the incompatibility,
which existed since 1789, between renovated France and
the dynasty of the old *régime*, was quite apparent.

" Louis XVIII. returned to the palace of his fathers, but
he returned to it supported on one side by a secularized
bishop: married, a deserter from his church, a negotiator
of the Revolution of 1792, a minister, a favorite, and, may
be, even an accomplice of Napoleon; and supported on
the other side by a regicide, just revolted from the Emperor, and who only opened the doors of his palace to
the King on the condition of chasing from it the friends
of his youth."

These strange circumstances produced the result of a
conspiracy, one against another, in the council of the
royal government. M. de Talleyrand conspired against
Fouché, Fouché against Talleyrand, and the King against
both.

The Chamber of Peers of 1814 was maintained by the
retention of all its members who had not sat in Napoleon's
Chamber of Peers during the hundred days. The peerage,

for the future, was declared hereditary—a vain institution among a people who had, by a revolution, suppressed castes and established the right of popular election based upon personal capacity.

The Chamber of Deputies of 1814 and the Chamber of Representatives of 1815 were dissolved.

The mode of electing the deputies was determined by orders in council. The electors were divided into departmental and district committees. The district committees presented the candidates to the departmental committees, who chose from them one-half of the deputies. Payment of a tax amounting to 300 francs was the qualification for the departmental electors. The ministers, to flatter the army and to introduce a new element presumed to be liberal in the elections, conferred suffrage on those who had been decorated with the Legion of Honor, or who had belonged to the civil service and militia of the Emperor. The Chambers were convoked for September 24, 1815.

The King saw, however, in Napoleon's army a remnant of pretorians. He disbanded it and organized another army upon a new principle. The men must enlist in the department where they were born. This course stifled Napoleonism. But the system was federative and not national.

The era of proscription now commenced. It was declared that the officers and generals who betrayed the King before March 23d were to be brought before courts-martial.

A restoration should have been characterized by amnesty. Pardon should have been its virtue and its law. "Public opinion in France, when irritated, listens neither to middle courses nor to intrigues, nor to prudence; it goes direct from one side to the other, like the ocean in its ebb and flow. This is the whole explanation of the elections of 1815, which sent up to the Crown a Chamber more counter-revolutionary than all Europe, and more Royalist than the King."

M. de Talleyrand was dismissed, and M. de Richelieu accepted the presidency of the Council.

A treaty was arranged and signed by M. de Richelieu in the name of "the most Holy and Invisible Trinity," by the terms of which the allied powers cut up the borders and partitioned them amongst each other. The treaty imposed an indemnity to Europe of 700,000,000 francs for the last war commenced by Napoleon; an armed occupation for five years of 150,000 men, the generalissimo of which was to be nominated by this garrison of security. Each of the States of Europe was to be indemnified for the ravages it had sustained. The entire cost of the last aspiration of Napoleon to the throne amounted to £60,000,000, and 50,000 men.

The Liberal party in France looked upon this treaty as a mutual pledge among kings for the slavery of the people.

"The Chambers voted the restitution of all church property not yet alienated. The Constituent Assembly, when it abolished feudalism, had annihilated the nobility, and created a nation. In reforming the Church, the Revolution of '89 had suppressed the temporal possessions of an established Church, and founded religious liberty. The tendency of the new and religious party in the Chambers in restoring its still unsold possessions to the Church, as a civil body, was an evident return to a State religion."

" Public education, which, since the Revolution, had been principally placed in the hands of an educational body called the University, was reclaimed exclusively for the Church; which also demanded the registry of births and deaths, to the prejudice of the municipal authority, and in order that the people should look upon the priesthood as civil and religious magistrates; a double tie, which should subject the people to the priests, both in soul and body."

Counter-revolutions have their deliriums as well as revolutions. This counter-current, which weak and unreflecting minds took for the real current of human affairs, at first, in the public opinion, carried everything before it.

The ministers, convinced that the reins of government would be wrested from the hands of the King, if they did not prevent the reassembling of the Chamber, formed the bold resolution of dissolving it before it had enacted an electoral law, and to appeal to the country from the violence of its members. The secret of this *coup d'état*, faithfully kept by several men, exploded on the night of September 5, 1816, before the colleagues of the ministers, or even the King's brother himself, could anticipate the blow that was about to strike them. The Chamber was dissolved, and the electors were convoked for October 4, 1816.

The Count of Artois said that this action would be the death-blow of the monarchy. He saw in Louis XVIII. another Louis XVI., and charged M. Decazes with treason.

A new electoral law was submitted to the Chambers, conferring electoral rights upon any individual who paid 300 francs of direct taxes. The act was opposed by the Chamber of Peers.

The law was passed. It constituted an electoral body in France of 100,000 large and moderate proprietors. It excluded the people, and created a political cabal. These

Madame de Staël.

errors produced increasing opposition in the masses and agitation in the assemblies.

In 1818 one-fifth of the Chamber was to be elected. Parties struggled against each other. Journals and pamphlets fanned the opposition to the government, and to the electoral colleges. Never was a government more violently assailed and more bitterly insulted by the jealousy and ambition of its pretended friends.

The president of the Council now formally requested the King to restore harmony between the two deliberative bodies, by creating sixty-three new peers, devoted to the personal policy of the ministers. This was a repetition of the *coup d'état* of September, 1816. The new peers were chosen to influence action at the Luxembourg.

The new electoral law divided the country into two camps. The plebeian nation nominated half the deputies in the chief town of the district, and the aristocratic nation of wealth, composed of proprietors paying taxes, nominated the other half in the capitals of the departments. A foolish law, with all its pretended prudence, which gave to the accident of fortune a title to the right of citizenship—a title of wealth, still more absurd than that of nobility; for family may impart sentiments and virtues, while fortune only bestows means and vulgar power. The law had another danger. It brought face to face, in the same assembly, men issuing from two different elections; an aristocracy of department, and a democracy of district; elements of antipathy, of classification, and civil war, which would rend the country and the government, in contending, as representatives, against each other.

Decazes had made a *coup d'état* against the Royalists on September 5; he was about to make a second against the Liberals. The *coup d'état* he had made only dethroned a party; the one prepared against the Liberals would dethrone public opinion, which had become a popular passion in the masses.

M. de Decazes was now removed and sent to England as minister plenipotentiary.

The government was no longer conducted by authority derived from the Chambers; the government was, in fact, nothing but a succession of *coups d'état;* sometimes for, and at other times against the Charter, victory being generally given by the King's hand.

The laws for the censorship of the press, for the suppression of individual liberty, and the electoral law prepared by M. Decazes, were laid before the Chambers, with some modifications.

M. Pasquier frankly avowed to the Chambers that these proposed laws of the government really demanded a dictatorship. Benjamin Constant, emboldened by the election which absolved his double defection of 1814 and 1815, attacked the ministers with a bitterness of invective as though there was no retaliation to dread.

General Foy was irritated by the insulting apostrophes of the deputies of the right, whom he designated as a handful of wretches who hailed the triumph of foreigners over their country. The Revolution and the counter-revolution personified looked each other in the face during the long debates on the questions involved. M. Benoist exclaimed " that the counter-revolution was accomplished, and that the Charter was nothing but its reign."

The capital, excited every evening by the noise of the combats of the day, took fire at these flashes of the orators. Mobs formed in the public places; the students, the disbanded officers, the conspirators of secret societies, and the men who float with every breeze on the surface of great populations, either gathered at the silent signal or promenaded the thoroughfares. Paris presented every night the aspect and presage of revolution. In the midst of this fermentation the ministry brought forward the electoral law (1820), which was to disarm the nation, and decree a political privilege to the aristocratic classes in the departments.

The basis of civil authority is the doctrine of the rights of man; the theoretic code of the Revolution, elucidated by reason and conscience.

"To support the throne upon an aristocracy in such a country," exclaimed an orator, "is to support it upon an abyss."

"I withdrew myself with grief," he continued, "from the ministers, who were my friends, and I do not hesitate to declare this bill to be the most fatal that has ever issued from the council of kings since those councils of fatal memory which beset and ruined the unfortunate race of Stuarts. It is the divorce between the nation and the family that governs us."

The watchwords of this agitation were renewed at every sitting in the speeches of the opposition members. "For the last eight days," cried an orator, "blood has not ceased to flow in Paris. Thousands of the peaceable inhabitants of the capital were charged upon, sabred, and trodden under the feet of the horses of the cuirassiers."

"Blood is flowing and you refuse to hear us," exclaimed M. de Corcelles.

At these outcries the Chamber rose like two opposing waves which threatened to burst upon each other. The President was compelled to separate the parties by putting on his hat.

The people, being kept down in the public places, retired in anger; and secret conspiracies began to be hatched in the absence of public tumults.

M. de Lafayette declared to his friends that open force was henceforth the only efficacious weapon to overthrow a government which had declared war against the equality of classes. He wished to replace it by a republic, or a constitutional prince responsible to the Revolution and tied up in the trammels of a representative democracy.

At this time a conspiracy was formed for the surprise and capture of the castle of Vincennes. An accidental explosion of powder, on the evening of the day fixed by the conspirators, put the civil and military police on the alert in the principal places where the uprising was to take place.

It has been claimed that Napoleon was an armed missionary of liberty and of revolution in Europe, and that in traversing the Continent to subdue it he had willingly sown the germs of fruitful liberty. This is a sophism. The attempt was now made to create for him a double popularity in the imagination of the people, in order to accumulate around his name all the elements of the opposition which they purposed to offer to the Bourbons, or to the Republic. It is not true that France owes to him her love of liberty.

"That which is true, and is attested by all the revelations of his thoughts, and by all his public acts from the 18th *Brumaire* to the renewed Concordat of Charlemagne, to his feudatories, and his nobility, and to the silence imposed by him upon thought, under the name of ideology, is that he turned back the current of the whole French Revolution; that he pursued the gleams, in order to extinguish them; that he employed force, not to destroy, but to revive the absolute authority of theocracies, of aristocracies, and of thrones; that he was, at all times, the Julian of civil liberty and of liberty of conscience; the great antagonist of the philosophy of the eighteenth century. A hero certainly, but no apostle, or else an untimely apostle of conquest, of glory, and of material force."

When Napoleon died, however, his name was used to attract the discontent of the army, its hatred, and its ambition, round a shadow, in order to make an alliance between the Revolution and the men of the Empire, and thus combine them against the Bourbons.

The Church party, the Royalist majority, the Court aristocracy negotiated by Madame Cayla, the party of the Count of Artois, at last brought about the overthrow of the second ministry of M. de Richelieu. M. de Villèle now became the prime minister of the government.

The new ministry was scarcely formed when the factions, Liberal and Bonapartist, military and revolutionary, felt that the nomination of a ministry avowedly Royalist, was a declaration of war, as it were, on the part of the Crown. Desperate measures were instituted, and conspiracies followed for the next seven years.

The failure of the Carbonari plot, at Belfort, followed. Co'onel Caron's plot arose a short time afterward. It was discovered. The Colonel was condemned to death by court-martial, and shot behind a bastion of the citadel at Strasburg. Similar executions, at Marseilles and Toulon, expiated other abortive conspiracies of the military Carbonari. The air was filled with conspiracies and plotting, but the committee which prompted them remained invisible. Four obscure youths were executed, while thousands of hearts were beating with pity, indignation, and vengeance in their cause. But their blood did not extinguish the flame of revolution that had taken possession of a great part of the people.

Two uprisings occurred February, 1823, under General Berton. Both of the movements were failures. Berton went to the scaffold, exclaiming: "Long live France, and freedom!"

The expulsion of M. de Manuel from the Chamber of Deputies was preceded by one of the most memorable debates of the Restoration. Refusing to retire after the vote of expulsion, he was removed by force.

Manuel opposed the proposition to send French troops into Spain. "Have you then forgotten, gentlemen," he said, "that the Stuarts were dethroned solely because they sought the aid of foreign power? Have I any occasion to add that the dangers of the royal family in France assumed a more threatening aspect when our territory was invaded by foreign troops; and that France, revolutionary France, feeling the necessity of defending herself by new powers, and fresh energy—" Here he was interrupted by cries of "Order!" Such blasphemy must be avenged. "Expel him! Expel him!" arose on every side.
. When the motion of expulsion was carried, Lafayette exclaimed: "What an infamous *coup d'état!*"

"Unhappy men," cried General Foy; "you have destroyed the representative government."

"This Chamber is filled with enemies of the Revolution; myrmidons of the counter-revolution," said General Demarcy.

These cries and protests were communicated, as by electricity, from the hall to the galleries, from the galleries to the lobbies, from the lobbies to the crowds assembled at the doors of the Chamber of Deputies, and along the quays. In vain squadrons of cavalry were sent to restrain and to disperse them. The cry went up "Long live Manuel! Long live the Opposition."

On the expulsion of Manuel, the whole "Left" quitted the Chamber, not to enter it again during the whole session.

In 1824, M. Berthier, in the name of the aristocracy, imperiously promulgated the legal supremacy of the clergy; the endowment of landed estates to the Church, to replace the immense territorial endowments which it had so many times obtained and been so often stripped of by the people; the re-establishment of the national Church.

The press was full of the fire of the opposition. Politicians under the control of the Count of Artois exerted themselves to suppress the organs when they could not corrupt them. Actions were multiplied against the journals. August 15, 1824, a censorship of the press was established.

The Count of Artois, the clerical party, and M. de Villèle concerted measures, which Madame Cayla communicated to the King. Thus the ascendancy of the Church party, the preponderance of the prime minister, and the empire of Madame Cayla were continued. "Louis XVIII. no longer reigned, he simply existed." He yielded to these influences, and avenged himself by sarcasms and prophecies of the punishment that his brother would ultimately call down upon himself. The ambition of Louis was to live and die in the palace of his ancestors, in the midst of a vanquished revolution, and surrounded by an emigration kept within bounds.

The King also tried to mould his minister, M. de Villèle, to the opinions of the Count of Artois, and to the clerical party, in order to soften the transition of his reign to his brother. The prime minister, on his part, serving the reactionary party, urged the King in his last days to sign the ordinances declaring the press under suspicion, and establishing a censorship of all journals in France.

On September 16, 1824, M. Portal, who had been in attendance on the King in his last illness, turned to those who surrounded the bed and said, "Gentlemen, the King is dead;" then, bowing to the Count of Artois, he concluded, "Long live the King!"

It was thought by some that when Charles X. took possession of the Tuileries that he was the King of the two camps which divided France, the hope of one and guarantee of the other, but soon a murmur arose that was caused by the jealous and impolitic measure of his ministers in removing from active service in the army a great number of generals of the Republic and the Empire. When informed of the severity of this measure, he corrected it, and thus effaced, in some degree, the bad impressions that had been made.

On January 3, 1825, his ministers presented to the Chambers the laws characteristic of his reign. The first regulated the endowment of the Crown, during the King's life; the second appropriated to the emigrants, who were ruined by the Revolution, an indemnity of 1,000,000,000 francs, in reparation of their confiscated estates; the third gave the Church satisfaction, by re-establishing the crime of sacrilege in the civil law by punishing it with the penalty of death; the fourth re-established the privileges and immunities of the monks, abolished by the Constituent Assembly, and also the right of monastic orders to inherit inalienable property. Public opinion became greatly excited at these symptoms of a return to the past.

The law of sacrilege particularly excited the indignation of every enlightened mind; while that for the legal re-establishment of monastic orders alarmed the foresight of all. Both of these laws were in defiance of the spirit of the age. They foreshadowed the opinions of the ministers of M. de Villèle. These concessions made to the sacerdotal party comprised measures which

Talleyrand.

placed the public weal and the executioner's axe in the hands of the Church.

Charles X. looked upon his coronation as a sacrament, while the mass of the people regarded it as one of the pomps of the past.

The priesthood, having pretended that they had found the miraculous phial of oil, which the royal superstition of remote ages believed to have been brought from heaven by a dove, to anoint crowned heads, now conducted the coronation with great circumstance. The sword of Charlemagne was presented to Charles, and M. de Talleyrand, the grand chamberlain of the palace, drew on the lily-ornamented boots of the "eldest son of the church."

July, 1830, had arrived, and it was quite evident that a majority for the Crown could not be obtained in the Chamber of Deputies.

M. de Peyronnet now declared himself for "an unavoidable recurrence" to Article 14 of the Charter, and read to his colleagues a plan in conformity with this resolution. This plan, which included a revival of the Assembly of Notables, created, in the place of the Chambers, a Grand Council of France, nominated by the ministers and presided over by the heir to the throne. This Grand Council was to settle all questions that should arise between the King and the people, "for the safety of the State." The scheme was to take, in the name of this article, the momentary dictatorship of the Charter itself.

The King, listening only to reactionary counsels, thought that, in order to subdue the turbulent democracy, which had carried the elections, it was necessary to take measures outside of the legal order. He then signed five ordinances, which were published July 26, 1830, in the *Moniteur*, as "indispensable reforms."

The first suspended the liberty of the press, which had

really been done by the law of August, 1828, and submitted journals and periodicals, without distinction as to matter, to a previous authorization, renewable every three months, and always revocable. All works published without due authorization, were seized, and the presses and type used in their printing were sealed or destroyed. The evidence in law-suits, and productions of the learned societies, fell under the power of the law for fear that there was a political question involved. It was the pure and simple suppression of the pen of the opposition.

The second proclaimed the dissolution of the Chambers, which had not yet reconvened, and consequently annulled the elections.

The third reduced the number of the deputies to 238, and modified dictatorially the law of elections, so that arbitrary power appeared under the mask of a return to the Constitution.

The fourth convoked the departmental colleges for the 6th and 10th of September.

The fifth formed the Council of State from the most detested Royalists and Jesuits.

A *coup d'état* had been expected, but no one expected such a complete one. Journalism, menaced with annihilation, now arose to action. Thiers prepared a protest, inviting legal resistance, and signed it with Armand Carrel, Rémusat, Pierre Leroux, and forty others. Journals appeared without authorization. The police were obliged to close the doors of the printing establishments. The people became agitated; skirmishing took place on the 27th between the masses and the troops. There were wounded and dead. Paris, which had been declared in a state of siege, on the 28th found itself ready for battle. The tricolor floated from the Hôtel de Ville and from the towers of Notre Dame. The students of the Polytechnique School, many old soldiers, and the National Guard had joined the workmen. Marmount, who had been placed in command, had only 14,000 soldiers to resist the people, poorly armed, it is true, but turning everything into arms. His attacking columns were repulsed everywhere and compelled to concentrate in the evening near the Louvre. The following day defections occurred among the regiments; the Tuileries was taken.

At Saint Cloud, the King, who had full confidence in "the protection of the Virgin," did not doubt that the army would put an end to the *émeute*. When he saw himself abandoned by heaven, he withdrew the ordinances and proposed to form a ministry with Mortemart and Casimir Périer. These concessions were no longer admissible. The deputies, who were at first opposed to the insurrection, now decided upon seeing it succeed. Lafayette had accepted the command of the National Guard, and rendered homage to the people of Paris, to the lowest classes of society, which had now become the first.

The people spoke of proclaiming the Republic. The deputy Laffitte saw insurmountable obstacles in this proposition. The crowd of *intrigants* hatched in the guano of the Restoration naturally supported this rich person who was at the head of the finances of the government, when he proposed to marry order and liberty in giving the throne to the Duke of Orléans.

During the night, Thiers, who had kept himself in the background pending the battle, caused anonymous placards to be posted which proclaimed that: "Charles X. can no longer reign. He has shed the people's blood. A republic would expose us to frightful convulsions; it would embroil us with all Europe. The Duke of Orléans is devoted to the Revolution. The Duke of Orléans never fought against us. The Duke of Orléans was at Jemmapes. The Duke of Orléans is a citizen King. The Duke of Orléans has carried the tricolor under fire. The Duke of Orléans can carry it again; we do not wish any other. The Duke of Orléans has declared that he accepts the Charter as we understand it and mean to have it. He will accept the Crown from the French people."

This particular kind of skillfulness, which has always been the bad genius of France, now revealed itself again in the proclamation. The *bourgeoisie* declared themselves satisfied. The people, divided by different opinions, remained undecided. Cries of "*Vive la République!*" mingled with those of "*Vive Napoléon II.!*" But the *bourgeoise* interests could not find a better representative than the crafty prince, who for fifteen years exercised his duplicity in caressing, at the same time, the Court to obtain from it honors and riches, and the Liberals in order to be ready to present himself to them as a candidate for political honors. All danger having disappeared (July 31), the royal family having fled from Saint Cloud, the thirty-five deputies, who had offered the title of Lieutenant general of the Kingdom to the Duke, were now increased to ninety-two.

But Lafayette was at the Hôtel de Ville, the headquarters of the victorious insurgents. The Charter gave neither satisfaction to the students nor to the partisans of the Republic. The deputies saw it would be necessary to promise more. The Duke, escorted by a small number of officers of the National Guard, repaired to the Hôtel de Ville on horseback. Lafayette received him very well. The old Marquis admirer of the American Constitution remained in France a constitutional Royalist. The Feuillant of '91 preserving a weakness for princes, did not believe that the Republic which was effective on this side of the ocean could possibly be suitable on that side. France ought, according to his idea, to content herself "with a popular throne surrounded by republican institutions."

The sly Duke of Orléans, knowing how to flatter the senile *naiveté* of Lafayette, presented himself to him with the tricolored flag in his hand, as "a former National Guardsman of '89 coming to pay a visit to his late general."

An embrace was given and received, and the understanding was sealed.

The game was played; the French nation found itself belonging to new masters without having been consulted. The *bourgeoisie* and the journalists noisily manifested their joy. They made haste to terminate the affair in order not to give the people time to recover themselves—the Republicans the possibility of realizing their position. Some feared, also, the return of Bonapartism. Armand Marrast alone protested against this filching of the popular sovereignty. Charles X. retired to Rambouillet, still preserving his delusions as to the real situation. But as the ambassadors of the powerful strangers did not rejoin him there, he at last accepted the accomplished fact and recognized the nomination of the Duke of Orléans as Lieutenant-general. Then, as the troops were abandoning him little by little, he wrote his abdication and that of his son, in favor of his grandson, the Duke of Bordeaux. He requested his cousin to proclaim this infant under the name of Henri V., and to take the necessary measures to regulate the form of government during the minority of the new King.

The Duke of Orléans had already surrounded himself with a ministry and a private council, among whom figure men who have since **been a heavy** burden to France: Guizot, Casimir Périer, **Dupin**, Laffitte, and de Broglie.

The Duke had convoked the Chambers for August 3, and prepared, with his councilors, an armed demonstration against the provisional residence of his royal kinsman. Charles X. would have defended the rights of Henri V., but the 10,000 men who had remained with him were now rapidly disappearing by continuous desertion. Twenty thousand Parisians were marching upon Rambouillet. He yielded under the advice of d'Odilon Barrot, and, under the escort of his body-guard, set out for Cherbourg, whence he passed to England. England had sent one King to the block and driven another to France; France sent one King to the guillotine and another to England.

France was now delivered from the older branch of the Bourbons; but, unfortunately, the younger ones of the Orléans remained, with all their greedy thirst for intrigue, desire for riches, disdain for the people, and inability to recognize ideas of justice. This class of pseudo-liberals, after having profited by the popular insurrection, was about to shelter its vices under the peculiar form of parliamentarism then existing in France, which was neither the system obtaining in England, nor in accordance with the more advanced theory that had been suggested by certain publicists of that day.

England had reserved for Charles X. the "lonely and recluse hospitality of Holyrood, a palace abandoned by Mary Stuart, and surrounded by memories of dark deeds, and significant of sad lessons of a dynasty dethroned for seeking to inflict upon its subjects, through a pious policy, the yoke of Rome; and for persecuting the freedom of the human mind in its most inviolable place, the conscience of the nation."

"And now I ask," says Louis Blanc, "what have been the fruits of that long series of fluctuations and of postponements of the evil day that made up the reign of Louis XVIII.? On the surface of the political stage discords without end, and beneath it conspiracies, treacherous instigations by paid spies, villainous snares for men's lives, military executions; these were the spectacles that reign presented. The tempest raged everywhere—in the parliament, in the press, at Court, in the towns, in the rural districts. Didier, Tolleron, Berton, Bories—what reminiscences! Ay, methinks that same plastic policy of Louis XVIII. afforded the executioner ample room for the convenient exercise of his craft. *   *   *   *
Whenever there shall be a government of a King and that of an assembly set face to face with each other, there will be disorder, and society will go on its way between dictatorship and anarchy, that is, between two abysses."

IV

THE ORLÉANIST MONARCHY.

The Duke of Orléans, now Lieutenant-general of the Kingdom, opened the session of the two Chambers in the presence of 240 deputies and 60 peers.

He maneuvered skillfully to convert this newly-acquired title into that of King, and to obtain all the rights that might possibly belong to Henri V. under the terms of the abdication. The faction that had grouped itself around him hastened to settle all questions by adopting a moderate and ambiguous Charter, which would be neither a new Constitution nor the re-establishment of the old one. This party wished neither to canvass the electors nor to submit the proposed fundamental law to a constituent assembly, and the question of an hereditary peerage was deferred, for the reason that it was feared that the discussion of this consideration would cause political dissension. The friends of the Duke now entered cautiously upon a course of low hypocrisy. Out of the membership of 430 deputies, 219 against 33 (August 7, 1830), arrogated to themselves, as they possessed no constituent power, the right to publish a declaration that proclaimed, among other things, that the throne of France is vacant, in fact and in law; that in the interest of the French people the preamble of the Constitutional Charter is suppressed, as wounding the national dignity in attempting to grant rights to the people which essentially belong to them; and further, that certain other articles of the same instrument be modified or abolished. All nominations and acts already made by the peers were declared null and void, and Article 27 was to be submitted to a new examination in the session of 1831, and finally, that various considerations, afterward adopted in the Charter of 1830, as Article 69, shall immediately be determined.

The Chamber of Deputies then declared that in the interest of the French people, S. A. R. Louis Philippe d'Orlèans and his descendants, in perpetuity, from male to male, by order of primogeniture, and to the perpetual exclusion of females and their descendants, should be called to the throne; that he be invited to accept these conditions, and, after having taken an oath to support the Constitutional Charter and its modifications, to assume the title of King of the French.

The Chamber of Peers was not called upon to declare itself upon this resolution until it had been presented to the Duke and accepted by him, *as the expression of the national will*. This cunning fellow added that every remembrance of his had tended to create in him a desire that he should never mount the throne, but that the love he bore his country had imposed upon him a duty, and that he would now perform it.

France has not yet liquidated this account thus forced upon her by this generous affection.

The upper Chamber swallowed its humiliation, expressed in an address prepared by Châteaubriand, and indorsed the declaration of the deputies, with the reservation that the matter concerning the acts of the peers during the reign of Charles be submitted to the discretion of the Lieutenant-general.

But what was this monarch to be called? Those partisans who wished to tie the fortunes of the new to the old monarchy wanted him to take the name of Philippe

VII. Lafayette opposed this with all the force which gave him the rank of Commander of the National Guard. Dupin declared, on his part, that the Duke had been chosen *although* Bourbon, and not *because* he was a Bourbon.

The two Chambers reassembled August 9th. They solemnly read the declaration of the deputies, the adhesion of the peers, and the oath of the King. Louis Philippe now sat upon the throne, surrounded with all its paraphernalia, and proclaimed, in the usual official palaver, that he felt the extent of his duties, and that he would conscientiously perform what he had promised; that the modifications added to the Charter guaranteed the security of the future; and finally, that France would be happy at home and abroad.

The Charter of August 9, 1830, is, in the greater number of its articles, only a repetition of that of June 4, 1814. The preamble establishing the pretended right of the Capet family, was the only part that was entirely abolished. The modifications were proposed by a commission whose principal members were Benjamin-Constant, Villemain, Hératry, Bertin de Vaun, Benjamin Delessert, Sébastiani, Bérard, Tracy, Bondy, with Dupin as reporter. It was voted on the 8th, accepted the 9th, and promulgated the 14th of August.

The five first articles of the Orléanist Charter are textually the same as those of the Bourbon Charter, but Article 6, according to the terms of which the Catholic, Apostolic, and Roman religion was the religion of the State, disappeared. This clause is replaced, in the new article, by an addition to the old text, borrowed from the Concordat. "The Catholic religion is professed by the majority of the French people." The word "only," in Article 7, which provided that the non-Christian churches should receive no benefits from the public treasury, was also abolished in the new Charter.

The new Article 7 repeats the old Article 7, less the affirmation that "The law should repress the abuse of the liberty of press." This provision is replaced in the new Charter by a paragraph enacting that "The censorship of the press shall never be re-established." Articles 8, 9, 10, and 11, on the subject of the public rights of the French, repeat, *verbatim*, the Articles 9, 10, 11, and 12, of 1814. The conscription laws, established by the law of the 19th *Fructidor*, year VI, rendered odious by the revolting abuses of the Empire, had been abolished in 1814, and re-enacted in 1818 by the *Recrutement*, in such terms as not materially to change the language of the first statute. The Charter of 1830 preserves this system.

The form of the new government leaves all executive power to the King, whose person is inviolable and sacred. The new Article 13 only deprives him, by reason of the use that Charles X. made of the ordinance, of the faculty of suspending the laws. The provisions as to the safety of the State which terminate the old Article 14 are no longer mentioned in the 13th. It is also provided that henceforth a law shall be indispensable for the introduction of foreign troops into the service of the State. Article 14 of 1830, as in Article 15 of 1814, divides the legislative power between the King and the two Chambers, but the exclusive right to propose and to present, at his pleasure, laws to either of the houses, was taken from the King. Article 16 is the old 18. Articles 19, 20, and 21 of the Restoration, authorizing the Chambers to supplicate the King to propose a law upon any subject which they might indicate, fell by reason of the division of the right of the initiative. The King is continued in his right to sanction and promulgate the laws.

The King is no longer at liberty separately to convoke either branch of the legislature. An exception is reserved in case the upper Chamber assembles as a court of justice. The King may nominate peers for life, or make them hereditary. The princes of the royal family are peers by right of birth. Article 27 makes the sessions of the Chamber of Peers public, for the deliberations of which the old Article 32 had provided secrecy.

The most notable changes take place in the Chamber of Deputies. A renewal of one-fifth of its members every five years is substituted for a renewal of the whole number. The age of eligibility is lowered from forty to thirty years; the age of the electors from thirty to twenty-five years. The provisions of the Charter of 1814, which required the payment of 1,000 francs of direct taxes to make an elector eligible, and 300 francs to give a citizen the right to vote, were re-enacted by the new Charter. The choice of the president of the electoral colleges was taken from the King and given to the electors.

The King preserves the right to convoke and prorogue the two Chambers, as well as to dissolve the Chamber of Deputies.

All other provisions are continued; among others the prohibition personally to present petitions to the Chambers, interdicted by the old Article 53, now become Article 45.

Article 56, which limited the responsibility of the ministers to acts of treason and peculation, is abolished. A law was promised in this regard, and several projects were presented on the subject, and were even discussed from 1832 to 1837, but no law was passed.

All justice emanated from the King, and was administered in his name, by judges appointed by him, who could not be removed from office.

Articles 66 and 67 confide to the patriotism and courage of the National Guard and of the French people, all the rights consecrated by the Charter.

The tricolor was again proclaimed as the national emblem, and this fact of itself, if it did not bring practical reform, through the paltry changes in the fundamental law, made the people feel that they had acquired something for the blood that had been shed.

While the nobility were plotting for the restoration of the ancient *régime*, the *bourgeoisie* were preparing to complete their triumph by the abolition of the hereditary peerage, and by the legal proscription of the elder branch of the Bourbons. The object was to deprive the Chamber of Peers of its very principle of existence by cutting off the right of descent. The *bourgeoisie* wanted to combine a living monarchy with a dead aristocracy.

At last Casimir Périer yielded to an almost universal clamor, and moved the abolition of the hereditary peerage. A committee was appointed by the Chamber of Deputies, it reported, and the debate commenced.

The question arose whether the deputies could pass conclusively upon the proposition, or whether the peers had to ratify the sentence against themselves. It was claimed that for the Chamber of Deputies to act without the consent of the Chamber of Peers was to arrogate to itself the character of a constituent assembly. Because the Chamber of Deputies of 1830 had usurped the sovereignty of the people, is that any reason, it was asked, why the Chamber of 1831 should advance any such theory?

Arguments were advanced in favor of an hereditary monarchy. The King could be an imbecile, it was urged, but there was an intelligent and responsible ministry to answer for him. Attention was drawn to the fact that

England was never more powerful than when Pitt was at the head of affairs, although the sovereign was bereft of his reason.

On the other hand, it was urged that the hereditary house, when strong, gives impulsion to all government, and, when weak, simply follows the lower house.

"Could the House of Lords," it was asked, "check the course of the Commons? It wished to save Strafford, yet pronounced sentence upon him. It wished to preserve the seats of the bishops, yet it voted for their exclusion. It desired peace, yet voted for war. How vain the idea of balancing against each other an hereditary chamber and an elective chamber, in the hope of checking the progressive spirit of society; it is like placing an aristocracy in the bosom of a republic! Rather let us recall the ancient strife between the patricians and the plebeians; between the decrees of the Senate, which legalized usurpation, and the edicts of the people, which legalized violence; a strife which so long consumed the Roman Empire. The notion of averting such a contest through the agency of a monarchy, which shall mediate between the two, is preposterous. In the face of an elective assembly, the interest of an hereditary monarchy and an hereditary peerage is identical. On the contrary, granting that the hereditary peerage has a will of its own, how may this will be subdued if it shall obstinately stand in the way of desirable innovations? By swamping it with a batch of new peers? Adieu, then, to all respect for it, and to all its independence; it merges the moderator into the slave. But now look at the peerage as a representative body;—with what interests, in a state of society born of revolutions, can the principle of political inheritance assimilate? Are the fiefs abolished; is not feudalism extinct; is not nobility, which no longer transmits its functions, but only its titles, forever discredited; have we in France, as in England, a higher class who have joined with the people against monarchical oppression, and who have so acquired a title to the respect of future generations; have we anything in France which approximates to the relations of patron and client? An hereditary peerage, then, is in a false position, since it represents no national interest, and keeps alive the recollections of that odious mass of privileges against which the people, in 1789, rose as one man. Do you count the universal dislike of the hereditary peerage, which now exists, of no moment? What more would you have then, to prove its manifest disagreement with the tendencies, progress, and the manners of the age? Would the hereditary peerage have so often exhibited the spectacle of its meanness had it struck root in the nation? What did it do for Napoleon, conquered at Waterloo? What for Louis XVIII., when threatened by the exile of Elba? What did it do, on the 29th of July, for Charles X.? What has it been able to do for liberty?"

The advocates of the hereditary principle claimed that the devolving of the largest functions of government on a certain number of great families created a practical school for statesmen. "Besides, it does not follow that a chamber of peers should consist wholly of eminent men, in which case the advantage would be far exceeded by the dangers, since all would aspire to the first place."

M. Thiers thought that the bicameral feature of the government was essential; that, logically speaking, a republic and a single chamber would be the result of the abolition of the peerage.

Louis Blanc, in discussing this momentous question, said that "the simultaneous existence in the bosom of nations of two interests, ever at variance with each other, is a fact; but it is also an evil. Watch it; not to regulate, but to destroy it. As regards the advantages peculiar to each form of government, such is their nature that, to bring them together, without altering their character, is to neutralize one by the other, and to pass through disorder to arrive at powerlessness. To establish a compound power is to organize anarchy."

The contest over this question involved the entire government. The Chamber of Deputies called on the peerage to decide its own fate. It refused to commit suicide, and voted for the maintenance of its hereditary succession. Political passions were ready to burst forth. A collision was imminent. A revolution was impending. The ministry then created, by royal ordinance, thirty-six new peers. This was regarded by the opposition as a *coup d'état*. The hereditary peerage was then abolished, and the elder branch of the Bourbon line was banished from France.

Under Louis Philippe the French nation, instead of lifting itself out of the condition of prostration into which the Empire and the Bourbon Restoration had plunged it, descended another degree into degradation. If the Catholic clergy lost a little of their power, the science of obtaining and holding office (*fonctionnarisme*) visibly increased. The mass of the people (*les administrés*) were openly treated as an inferior class. The military caste was reinforced under the homage given, under color of patriotism and liberalism, to the memory of Napoleon and the "glorious" recollections of the Empire. The *bourgeoisie*, which found its own image in the person of the King and the reflection of its egotistic inclination in the *régime* of 1830, placed its sons in the employ of the government and in the service of the military schools,

Guizot.

It followed that, to amount to anything in the State, it was necessary either to dangle a sword at one's side or to wear an official livery.

Above the mass of the proletariats, working for their masters and furnishing the soldiers who were destined to maintain the "respect for the institutions," were the "superior classes," who strongly organized themselves for concert of action, while they drew their numbers from that inexhaustible seed-plot of prefects, magistrates, *curés*, and officers. Under the powerful influence of the bishops, the deputies, and the peers, France was locked in the thousand arms of the bureaucratic administration, which rested upon the mitre and pompoon. It was a tortuous despotism, produced by an official blending of the interests of the bureau, the sacristy, the barracks, and the shops, constituting an unhealthy medley of Empire, Restoration, and constitutionalism. This system extended over the nation, effacing all sentiment other than that of gain, and forming minds for cabal and hearts for cowardice.

Eighteen years of this *régime* finished the emasculating work commenced by Napoleon, and continued by Louis XVIII. and Charles X. Imposture and baseness became, under this sad reign, the indispensable condition of existence; money was the supreme power before which all were compelled to bow or be destroyed. Orléanism, which had commenced by a swindle, had passed its meanness and venality to the "middle class," and that class did its best to transmit these characteristics to the "lower classes."

Although for a half century this great people had been under the demoralizing influence of their rulers, there still remained in their breasts a love of country, which was soon to manifest itself. In 1847 the words *liberty* and *citizen* were again found on the lips of intimate friends.

The revolutionary idea, which had been many times suppressed by military and police rigor, was nevertheless constantly in the minds of the workmen and "ideologists." The founders of the various schools were busy agitating social, economical, and political problems. The autocratic Orléanist laughed at these "reveries," because at this time there had been no serious disturbances of the peace. Guizot was at the head of the conservative and reactionary party, while Thiers formulated the maxim, after an English authority, that: "The King reigns, but he does not govern." The good sense of the people replied that if the King did not govern, he was useless, and should be excused from acting at all.

Should not all citizens have the right to vote? Is not a republic more loyal and simple than any form suggested by political sophistry? Are not the affairs of a country identical with the interests and rights of its inhabitants? Should not the direction of public affairs cease to be the exclusive right of any certain class?

These thoughts were born in the minds of the artisans and of the *petits bourgeois*. A vast work develops slowly in the general intelligence. Aspirations arise, the will commences to form. It manifests itself when the government, disturbed by what it is pleased to call blind impulse and unfriendly passion, interdicts the reform banquet about to take place in Paris. As in 1830, the legal opposition soon transferred itself into an open insurrection, and when Louis Philippe felt his throne shaken beneath him, he was disposed to grant the reforms that had been demanded; but he was too late, as Charles X. had been, eighteen years before.

The police having forbidden the banquet, Odilon

Barrot, Thiers, and their colleagues, were not slow to recognize the mistaken policy, and hastened to revoke the order. In spite of the counter-order that they caused to be circulated, the uprisings took place in every direction, to the cry of: "*Vive la réforme!*" The "Marseillaise" resounded from the Latin quarter to the Madeleine.

The government had made military preparations. They had 30,000 men in Paris. Louis Philippe, who was as blind as his predecessor, counted upon his soldiers to put down the Revolution. Guizot ridiculed the timidity of the Left, who were trying to mask their retreat under a demand for a vote of want of confidence in the ministry. But a more advanced element had taken the place abandoned by the panic-stricken members. The activity of a small group of Republicans supplied the numerical weakness of their party. The skirmishes of the first day were succeeded, on February 23d, by more serious disturbances. Laughter ceased at the Tuileries. Guizot was replaced by Molé, who was charged with the task of bringing about a compromise.

The Moderates, on learning of the fall of Guizot, thought that a settlement had been effected. The boulevards were illuminated, and the saunterers were happy. In the meantime, however, the men who knew something about Orléanist cunning continued to erect barricades in the most populous parts of Paris.

At last a battalion of the line suddenly fired on a crowd This act now justified the defiance of the people and changed the whole face of things. Dead bodies were carried along the streets; the cry of vengeance went up; the people armed themselves. Molé refused to form a ministry. The King even asked Thiers to attempt the task. Then the Court hastened on to its ruin by giving the command of the troops to General Bugeaud, one of the most unpopular of the superior officers.

Louis Philippe heard the fusillade before the gates of his palace. He abdicated February 24, 1848, in favor of his grandson, the Count of Paris. The King now indulged himself in a final misrepresentation of the facts by stating that he voluntarily gave up the Crown which the "national voice had called upon him to wear."

The Duke of Nemours, who had been designated by the law of 1842, and the widow of the Duke of Orléans, preferred by the latest advisers of the King by reason of the liberal opinions she had avowed, repaired to the Chamber of Deputies in order to proclaim the regency.

Louis Philippe had left for Saint Cloud, thinking he had arranged all the details of his abdication. But the republican idea had gained during the last days of the struggle. The Chamber of Deputies was invaded by combatants, who demanded its fall. Ledru-Rollin and Lamartine proposed the nomination of a provisional government charged to submit all questions to the entire country in order to have a decision upon all that concerns the rights of man and of the citizen. The cry of "*Vive la République!*" threw the Royalists in a state of consternation. Lists of names for the provisional government circulated in the midst of disorder. Dupont de l'Eure, Arago, Lamartine, Ledru-Rollin, Garnier-Pagès, Crémieux, and Marie, who were successively proclaimed by the people, now repaired to the Hôtel de Ville, where Garnier-Pagès had just been selected as the mayor of Paris. Louis Blanc; Flocon, representing *La Réforme;* Marrast, *Le National;* and Albert, an intelligent workman and friend of Louis Blanc, were added to the first-named as secretaries.

This provisional government was recognized without

contest. Bugeaud and Changarnier gave their assent. Caussidière, late insurgent at Lyons, was installed in the prefecture of police, and Etienne Arago was given the direction of the post office department.

The overthrow of the monarchy of July has been attributed to many causes, among which were the electoral reforms of that day, but, possibly, looking at history in its continuity, the whole reign of Louis Philippe was in conflict with the principles of the revolutions which preceded him, particularly the more immediate one of 1830, one of the most important in the annals of history.

The movement that drove Charles X. out of France frustrated the repressive policy of the great powers. This was a new era in the liberties of Europe. It gave great impulse to the revolutions in Belgium, to the insurrection in Poland, to the democratic Constitution of Switzerland, to political freedom in the several States of Germany, and to parliamentary reform in England. Its influence was felt in Italy, Spain, Portugal, and Hungary, and in the Sclavonic part of Austria, and reached from Egypt and Syria in the East, to South America in the West, in fact throughout the world, it aided in the progressive development of liberty and freedom.

Louis Philippe, assisted by the commercial *bourgeoisie* that surrounded him, gave serious offense to the spirit of the age in which he lived, and he was allowed quietly to embark for England.

V.

THE SECOND REPUBLIC.

Was it necessary immediately to invite the citizens of France to choose an assembly with power to decide what the form of government should be? Or, better, ought the Republic to be instantly proclaimed, either in a definite manner, or by reserving the rights of the nation? The fear of committing an usurpation arrested the action of some of the members of the Provisional Government. After a long discussion, the Republic was proclaimed, subject to the ratification of the people. The Chamber of Deputies was dissolved, and that of the peers was forbidden to reassemble, and a convocation of a national assembly was proclaimed as soon as the necessary delay in organizing the details of the suffrage of all citizens should allow this action to be taken.

The situation was surrounded by difficulties. The most difficult questions arose for the consideration of the moderate Republicans, the journalists, and the theorists who composed the government. By the side of the question of suffrage, so suddenly brought before the public intelligence of the country, that had been for a long time silenced or misled, appeared another of absolute urgency that affected the existence of a large population without work.

Uneasiness for the welfare of the future blended itself with the hope for the creation of republican forms, and with that fever of reorganization that held the people in alarm, the labor problem was plainly set forth in a petition by masses of workmen. In the presence of an express demand they had not foreseen, the members of the Government promised to guarantee "the existence of the workingmen by labor, and to give employment to all citizens," without taking good account of the bearing of such a promise and the cruel deceptions they were preparing.

To perform this self-imposed obligation, the Government could find nothing better than to create on the one side "*la garde mobile*," and, on the other, national workmen. Both of these creations were badly conceived.

A decree, February 26th, announced in the following terms the proclamation of the Republic:

"Citizens:—Monarchy, under whatever form, is abolished. No legitimism, no Bonapartism, no regency.

"The provisional government has taken every necessary measure to render impossible the return of the ancient dynasty, or the event of a new one.

"The Republic is proclaimed.

"The people are united.

"All the forts which surround the capital belong to us.

"The brave garrison of Vincennes is a garrison of brothers.

"Let us preserve with respect the old republican flag, whose three colors our fathers carried around the world.

"Let us show that this symbol of equality, of liberty, of fraternity, is, at the same time, the symbol of the most lasting order, since it is founded on justice and the entire people.

"Let Paris resume its accustomed appearance, its commerce, its activity, and its confidence; let the people maintain their rights, and continue to assure, as they have done to the present time, the public tranquillity and security."

Divided between their sentiments of honesty and their terrors of anarchy, between the desire to conserve the popular sympathies and the wish not to alienate any class, not to repel any adhesion, the Government of February had to make the greatest effort to arrange a date for the re-assembling of the Constituent Assembly. The clergy exercised their conciliating functions; the Catholic priests lavished their consecrated water upon the trees of liberty; pastors and rabbis mingled together under the protection of universal fraternity. Falloux and Veuillot passed from the most ultramontane monarchism to a recognition of the "social principles which had just triumphed." Legitimists and Orléanists cried out loudly that the Republic had been irrevocably established. The financial power united itself with the judicial, administrative, military, and commercial departments, in order to simulate an attachment for the "gentle Republic," which so complacently closed its eyes upon all former misdeeds.

. The Bonaparte family hastened to profit by the exhibition, of so much good will. Louis Napoleon left England to place himself under the Republican flag, "without other ambition," said he, "than that of serving his country." The Government did not dare to apply to him the law of expulsion of 1832, and, after trying to learn the sentiments of this "Destroyer of Poverty," who was posing as the vindicator of his uncle's rights, and could only be dangerous to the public weal, asked him to remove himself, which he did, protesting, at the same time, the purity of his intentions, and of his patriotism.

The popular weaknesses, the blunders of the representatives, and the intrigues of the "*amis de l'ordre*," soon facilitated the accession to power of the corsair, who carefully hid his rascally designs under a display of humanitarian sentiments.

From the month of March, serious divergencies as to

Grévy.

the policy of the government occurred, and enormous differences grew up in the consideration of the form of the Republic. Many laborers thought that the State should include a system of socialism, extolled by Louis Blanc, for the organization of labor, as well as the amelioration of the condition and complete emancipation of the proletariats. These persons were persuaded that it was only necessary to pass an enactment to put into operation an immediate and radical reform. The rapid expansion of ideas so long repressed, the warmth with which they were discussed in the clubs, the most pronounced follies controlling the best balanced thought, marvelously served the designs of those who had only accepted the Republic, while they contemplated its overthrow. They inspired the shopkeepers, the stockholders, the property owners, and agriculturists, with a fear of communism. From this time, there were two Republics: the "red" and the "blue;" the former represented the destruction of society; the latter, the safety of the world. Under the first denomination they classed all the adversaries of monarchical *régimes;* they depicted them as wishing to overthrow and destroy everything by fire and blood, to strip everyone naked who possessed anything; these were the "*partageux*," "*buveurs du sang*," etc. The second division applied to those who called themselves peaceable, honest, moderate, and enlightened friends of progress, not wishing to destroy, and always placing faith in Providence. The credulous and faint-hearted multitude naturally ranged themselves with the skillful manipulators of political affairs under the conservative flag.

Throughout the agitations in the streets; at the meetings, and in the press; in the midst of manifestations and counter-manifestations; in the chaos where everything moved without compass or guide, the Provisional

Government declared the abolition of the political oath, of titles of nobility, of slavery, of the tax upon the voice of the press, of the regulations of 1832 of the periodicals, of corporal punishment in the marine; annulled political condemnations; called all citizens from twenty-one to fifty-five years to join the National Guard and to elect their officers; suppressed the companies called the "*élite;*" declared the unremovability of the magistracy as incompatible with the Republic; proclaimed the right of meeting; organized, in aid of commerce, banks of discount, and sought to re-establish the great traditions of the Convention in all branches of public instruction.

But by the side of these laudable efforts, gross faults were committed. The "moderate system," to which the greatest portion of the members of the Provisional Government belonged, was enraged against the revolutionary acts, and allowed reaction to organize itself in the name of liberty. In all religious congregations "free associations" were found, having the right to develop, to teach, and to transform liberty into an instrument of servitude, and of moral and material ruin.

Louis Philippe had left the finances of the country in a deplorable condition. Garnier-Pagès, who took the place of Goudchaux, now entered upon a policy of inflation of the currency in order to escape bankruptcy.

The elections were first set down for April 9th, by a decree of March 5th, the terms of which were universal suffrage, with a direct ballot, the vote taking place by departments. This manifestation of the national will was not without danger. Beyond the material difficulties, the mental condition of the rural masses was of such a nature as to convey the most serious apprehensions to the friends of the Republic. The elections were also postponed to April 23d, in order to give the commissioners of the Government ample time to explain to the people all the questions that were at issue. In spite of this precaution the result was that a majority of those elected had very little attachment for the Republic. Legitimists, Clericals, members of the old "Left Center" and Orléanist "Left," two cousins of Louis Napoleon, and a large number of Republicans "*du lendemain*" were now ready to join their fortunes with the lukewarm Democrats who had been elected in Paris.

The National Assembly inaugurated its labors, May 4th, by the cry of "*Vive la République!*" It would have been better to acclaim itself less vigorously and to constitute itself more seriously. This Assembly seemed to make use of words which it either did not understand or wish to translate. It rested its initial proclamation upon the following act, which was unanimously carried on the proposition of the representatives of the Department of the Seine:

"The National Assembly, being the faithful interpreter of the sentiments of the people, who have just called it together, before commencing its labors, declares:

"In the name of the French people, and before the world, that the Republic, proclaimed February 24, 1848, *is and shall remain* the form of the government of France.

"The Republic wishes that France should have for her device: Liberty, Equality, and Fraternity. In the name of the whole country the Assembly conjures all Frenchmen, of all shades of opinion, to forget old dissensions, and in the future to constitute only one family. The day which unites the representatives of the people is a *fête* for concord and fraternity to all citizens."

The Provisional Government now rendered the account of its acts and transmitted its powers to the Assembly, which body decreed that it deserved the thanks of "*La Patrie.*"

A Commission of five members was appointed to prepare a report upon the subject of executive power. It should also choose the ministers outside of its own members. It should not have a fixed duration. It was thus revocable and had no more authority than the ministers appointed by it.

The Commission was chosen May 10th, and was composed of Arago, Garnier-Pagès, Marie, Lamartine, and Ledru-Rollin. The term " Constituent " was then added to that of the " National Assembly."

The Assembly decided on the 12th to nominate a Commission of eighteen members to prepare a Constitution. The commissioners elected during the sessions of May 17th and 18th were: Cornemin, Marrast, Lamennais, Vivien, de Tocqueville, Dufaure, Martin (of Strasbourg), Voirhaye, Coquerel, Corbon, Tourret, Dupin, Gustave de Beaumont, de Vaulabelle, Odilon Barrot, Pagès, (de l'Ariège), Doinès, and Victor Considérant. These persons formed a medley of the most dissimilar opinions. A decree of June 2d enacted that the first report should be discussed in the committees, and that each committee should nominate a delegate in order to transmit its observations to the commissioners; after which the Commission should present its report to the Assembly.

Another decree of August 11th enacted that the Assembly should deliberate upon all the articles of the report, and that then the Commission should make a new report embodying the modifications that may have been made, and, after a second deliberation, the vote should be taken on the whole instrument.

After preliminary reports, minority reports, modifications, and deliberations, the whole Constitution was adopted by a vote of 739 against 30, November 4th, after three days of discussion. The composition of the Chamber being known, the figures indicated how little democratic the new Constitutional Act would be. The cruel spirit of division which had been bequeathed to the people by the preceding monarchies soon showed the peculiar influence that it exerted over this Constitution and over the march of subsequent events.

In imitation of the constitutions of the first Republic, that of 1848 commences by a preamble which sets forth the object, the principles, and the reciprocal duties of citizen and State. Higher rights than the specific law are affirmed, but they are carefully enumerated.

The reciprocity of duty between the State and the citizen is an advance upon the Constitution of the year III, which only imposes upon the State the duty of contributing to primary instruction. Paragraph VIII, Article 13, enlarges the circle of the obligations of society toward the citizen. To protect the person, property, religion, and labor; to put necessary instruction within the reach of all men, by means of primary and gratuitous instruction; to favor the development of labor by education in the skilled trades, in the agricultural and voluntary institutions; to provide for public labor in order to alleviate the condition of those forced to a respite from labor; to extend fraternal assistance to the weak and incapacitated, and succor in default of family aid: the men of '48 declared that society should perform all these charitable acts. But this is only a program composed of beautiful words which could be applied to the most varied combinations and to all *régimes*, and nothing is said in the Constitution which follows about the accomplishment of these social duties.

This instrument reduced all the traditions of the past relative to sovereignty to twenty or thirty words; restated that the person and the domicile of citizens shall be as inviolable as the laws to be passed may permit; re-abolished slavery, and the death penalty in political cases; strengthened the chain that binds Church and State together; permitted meetings, association, the manifestations of the liberty to think and write within the absolutely uncertain limit of what is called public security; proclaimed *free* instruction which it may please the law and the surveillance of the State to impose; suppressed confiscation of property, however illegally acquired, to the minimum; guaranteed the payment of the public debt; thus approving the disorders of predecessors, and sanctioning *sacred* and monarchical plunder, and established the most iniquitous taxation—and this *ensemble* was presented under the nomenclature of guaranteed constitutional rights.

All the rest treats of " powers " and of " force." Rights of man, and duty of society to him, remain a pure delusion. The recognition inserted in paragraph III is only a deception, and the assurance contained in paragraph V, never to employ military force against the liberties of another country, was about to become, as against the Romans, an audacious lie.

A bill, proposing the settlement of the rights of labor, was discussed for four days, and, finally, lost by a vote of 596 against 187. Thiers and Dufaure maintained that this right supposed an organization of labor by the State, a thing deemed impracticable. In repeating the question and pushing its difficulties to the utmost, they succeeded in making their advice dominate in an Assembly already frightened by the idea of according any formal protection to the laborer. The right to live by working was only recognized " within the limits of the resources of society," that is to say, the whole subject was submitted to the arbitration of those who are in position to exercise the governing power.

Members of the Liberal party infuse the same light and good faith into their political as into their social conceptions. It appears to them that the Republic should be administered according to imperial ways, in so far as it may exercise the absolute power of the sovereignty of the people. Article 19 declares that the separation of powers is the first condition of a free government. Without bestowing attention upon the weakness which invades this principle, the framers of this constitution give the nomination of judiciary functions to the executive power as well as the right of this same power to impose his ministers and his commissioners upon the legislative body.

A mixture, in badly defined proportions of former charters and constitutions, more particularly illustrated by the American system, this Constitution is governed by two culminating points: universal suffrage and the presidency of the Republic. The direct vote, without any property qualification of any kind whatsoever, was acquired by the law of February 24th. The members of the Assembly did not dare to take away this right from the people, but they proceeded to restrict it, not by submitting it to certain conditions of elementary education requiring citizens to know what they voted for, but by depriving the moving population of the great cities of the right to vote because of the want of a fixed domicile. As to the presidency, the people were too much impregnated with a monarchical education to admit that they could wisely rid themselves of a magistrate at the head of affairs who, representing the country by election to office, combined the faculty of double dealing with the authority of execution. All the difficulty then depended upon the manner in which this personage, who was playing a comedy that everything foretold would end tragically, should be nominated.

The Commission decided from the beginning in favor of the election of a President by the people. It had given to this supreme magistrate all the attributes of a constitutional monarch, save the right to dissolve the Chamber. No one had proposed to nominate him by the Assembly.

It was desired to have a strong power face to face with the nation, and it was not apparently understood that, in nominating the chief of this power by the entire people, an enormous force was placed in juxtaposition to the Assembly. It was believed that all peril could be avoided by limiting the executive functions to four years and by prohibiting the re-election of the President during the lapse of equal time. In this way a provocation to organize *coups d'état* was added to the certainty of conflicts between an Assembly and a man claiming authority from the same ballot-box.

Considérant perceived the danger and demanded that the President should be elected by the Assembly, lest the executor of the law should rise above the legislator. He was supported by Odilon Barrot, who predicted that any other expedient would lead to civil war. But the majority of the Commission, veiling its love of authority under a pretended respect for the national will, did not wish to hear anything more on this subject. It also rejected a proposition of Pagès to exclude members of families who had reigned over the country from the presidency.

Thiers, Lamartine, Cavaignac, and their followers held that the President should be elected by the people. Grévy opposed this proposition and offered the following resolution:

Thiers.

"The National Assembly delegates the executive power to a citizen who shall receive the title of President of the Council of Ministers. The President of the Council is nominated by ballot, by a majority of the National Assembly. He is elected for a limited time and is always removable."

Supported by the Extreme Left, Grévy showed that an election by universal suffrage would render the President more powerful than a king. He described the perils which would follow "the elevation to the throne of the presidency" of an ambitious man, offspring of a royal family, masking under seductive promises his real intentions against the Republic. This danger was known to all, but whimsical statesmen, like Lamartine, persuaded the Chamber that God and the people should choose whom they liked.

Infatuation and indifference could go no further. Everything was unfortunate. Rashness of some and foolishness of others, personal vanity and ambition favored the cabals of the Monarchists, who were working for the overthrow of the Republic. But the majority of the representatives, trusting to appearances, were of the opinion that he who bore the dreaded name, after all, would prove himself so ridiculous that it was quite impossible that such a pretender was seriously to be feared.

Other amendments, proposing the election of the President by the Assembly, or by a choice from a list of candidates designated by universal suffrage; a system of double election; the exclusion of general officers, etc., were rejected, as well as that of M. Grévy. By 587 votes against 232 the Assembly decided that the people should elect the President of the Republic.

As the pretensions of Louis Bonaparte were again

mentioned, he mounted the tribune, October 26th, and clearly stated that "he accepted as a popular sentiment, the candidature he had not personally sought." But the country was infested with Bonapartist agents, who presented the "melancholy sire of Boulogne" under the triple face of Socialist, of moderate Republican, or seeker for the throne, according to the districts in which they operated. Thanks to these maneuvers, Napoleonic fetishism had taken possession of the rural and urban masses.

The Commission had decided, by thirteen votes against three, that a single Assembly was preferable to two Chambers. Duvergier de Hauranne proposed to divide the legislative power into two Assemblies. His amendment, supported by Rouher, Thiers, Odilon Barrot, and by the Monarchists, was combated by Lamartine, who saw in a single Chamber "a dictatorship, necessarily temporary," without perceiving that this argument of the dictatorship of a single Chamber would reject the independent presidency which he sustained. Five hundred and thirty votes against 289 wished to strengthen the legislative power by the unity of action. The force of power was the supreme argument, the single purpose of these legislators calling themselves Republicans.

The executive power, being confided, by a fiction entirely monarchical, to a single functionary, the ministers become only his agents, as under the royal charters. Consequently, the Constitution does not define their attributes.

As under the Empire, the Restoration, and the Orléanist monarchy, the judiciary power is subjected to the executive power. Unremovability gives the department a false appearance of independence. The High Court is established to judge, in theory, the President and his ministers, but, in practice, to punish more surely those who may be guilty of conspiracies, real or supposed, against the safety of the State, that is to say, against the executive power.

The judges incurred no responsibility; either for their mistakes or for their faults. The President, his ministers, and their employés of every kind are constitutionally responsible, but no legislative measure furnishes the means to render this responsibility effective with respect to the nation.

The public forces, always held in a passive submission, are entirely at the disposition of the executive, although Article 32 leaves to the Assembly the right to arrange the military forces for his safety, and to dispose of them.

Among other acts, the President negotiates and ratifies treaties; he promulgates the laws; all envoys, and ambassadors of foreign powers are accredited to him; he nominates as well as revokes the commissions of all diplomatic agents, commanders of the armies and naval forces, on land and on sea, the prefects, the commandant of the National Guard of the Seine, the governor of Algeria, and all superior officers of the State.

The constituent power is confounded with the legislative power. Everything foretells the violation of the Constitution by the very powers it creates. It is imagined that sufficient precautions have been taken by confiding "the rights which it consecrates" to the patriotism of all Frenchmen, imposing an oath upon the chief of power, and by inviting all citizens to refuse obedience to him if he act against the National Assembly. Still, these two last dispositions, aimed personally at Louis Bonaparte, whose election to the presidency already ap.eared certain, were only added in the course of the final discussions.

"Presidency is an institution," says Louis Blanc, in an article in the *Nouveau Monde*, 1849, entitled "*De la Présidence dans une République*," "which can become more baleful than royalty itself. Monarchy baffles ambitions; presidency prevails by setting them in motion and exasperating them. He whom birth calls to a throne does not have to open a road for himself across an agitated people. His need of tools costs neither factious attempt nor bloody effort. The lot which releases him from the need to merit power by virtues, also releases him from the need of acquiring it by intrigues. Without having to disquiet himself, without need of devices, he sees approaching a crowd eager to obey. Why seize by ruse or violence what he possesses without even extending his hand? Fortune has undertaken to supply him partisans in advance; he finds them pressing around his cradle; he has begun to reign in his mother's womb. Fantastic conventionalism, certainly! A conventionalism humiliating to the human species, but which at least can not trouble the society it debases. In the canvass for presidency there is nothing of that kind. Here success can be the prize only of prodigious efforts. In the midst of a society where interests are very diverse, and relations complex, distinguished merit, unquestionable services, a well-founded popularity, will not always constitute sufficient chances. It is then necessary to eke them out by force of skill and audacity; it will be necessary to calumniate rivals, to make ignominious advances to former enemies, to sacrifice friends to partisans, the sacred rights of justice to the violence of majorities; it will be necessary to add to the echo of his name the noise of a thousand venal clamors, to accept fraudulent engagements; to open for all parties, fawned on in turn, deceitful prospects; to create a train of subordinate ambitions, an environment of false leaders; to lose self-respect for the suffrage of others, and stoop to become the master; *omnia serviliter pro dominatione*. When the heir of a monarch reaches the crown, no one finds himself humiliated. The event was foreseen; this is not the victory of one man over another; it is the triumph of an insolent abstraction at which the philosopher is indignant, which the publicist condemns, but which does not wound the ambitious. It may, perhaps, be a misfortune for all; for no one is it an offense. Even the mediocrity of a prince, if it is recognized, pleases the statesmen; they are consoled for having a chief; involuntarily placed under one elected by accident, their high-spirited minds indemnify with disdain the necessity of submission. When it comes to be one elected by a people, what a difference! Superiority of rank, able to establish that of merit, in this case establishes between the most distinguished men a strife in which self-love is naturally called to play an implacable part. The passions of the chiefs traverse society. I am not among those who excuse, or even comprehend, monarchical superstitions. But it is only just to recognize that what, under the constitutional *régime*, Royalists honor in their king, is an idea rather than an individual. Well! human dignity has less to lose by worship of a principle than by worship of a man, however false the principle and however grand the man."

"I have a letter," says Moncure D. Conway, who translated the above paragraph, "received fifteen years ago from Louis Blanc, in which he says: 'At the time when Louis Napoleon Bonaparte was coming forward as a candidate for the presidential office, I thought it my duty to point out the direful consequences likely to flow from the election of a President. The solemn warning I then gave to my countrymen was expressed as follows: "Whenever a man and an Assembly stand face to face, that Assembly brings with it a 10th *Août*, and that man has behind him an 18th *Brumaire*." But as you have rightly observed, there are political as well as religious superstitions, nor are the former more easily uprooted than the latter. At the time alluded to it seemed next to impossible that there should be a Republic without a President. A strange aberration this—more especially on the part of the French, as they had been taught by experience how readily a President or Consul is turned into an Emperor. However, the warning was disregarded, and, on the 2d of December, we had to undergo the unspeakable humiliation of another 18th *Brumaire*. My prediction was thus fulfilled even sooner than I expected.' "

The question of progressive taxation was agitated, but it was defeated by 694 votes against 96. The freedom of education gave place to a lively discussion. Its consideration was vigorously urged by M. de Montalembert. The Clerical interests, however, were supported, under a pretext of equality, by a number of Liberals always unconsciously ready to play into the hands of the enemies of liberty. The question was left to the vague terms of Article 9, which provides that free education is under the surveillance of the State, and its conditions shall be determined by law. There did not seem sufficient determination clearly to define these conditions, and the passage of the law was indefinitely postponed.

The right of ratification by the people was cleverly juggled. The discussion on the subject was at last suppressed, and the sovereignty of the people was buried by 733 votes against 42. Article 1 was thus violated by the constituents themselves, and the Republican principle, so loudly proclaimed, was trampled under foot. A fatal war was thus initiated between the legislature and the executive, with power on the side of the latter.

The following is the provision of the Constitution on the subject of revision, and Article III provides: Whenever, in the last year of a legislature, the National Assembly shall have expressed the wish that the Constitution should be modified, in whole or in part, this revision shall be entered upon in the following manner: The wish expressed by the Assembly shall not be converted into a definitive resolution until after three successive deliberations held upon the subject, at the interval of one month between each deliberation, and the measure shall only be carried by a vote of three-fourths of the Assembly. The number of votes must be 500 at least. The Assembly for revision shall only be appointed for three months. It *shall only engage* in the special revision for which it has been assembled; nevertheless, in cases of emergency, it *may provide* for legislative necessities.

This is a piece of legislation intended to defeat the objects for which it was ostensibly passed. This provision was maladroitly borrowed from the monarchical Constitution of 1791.

The work of the men of '48, from the beginning to the end, was commonplace and barren of results. The gravest questions were left in doubt, and relegated to the organic law in order to finish by piece-meal that which should have been done by a single act. The liberties and the rights of the people were not at all guaranteed, and the manner in which the " powers " were organized, rendered illusory the principles that had been affirmed. The Republic found itself condemned even by its godfathers, for there had been no change made in the national organization; the pyramid of tyrannies constructed by Napoleon remained intact; the officials continued to dominate the nation, the army, the police, and the clergy divided everything, as the magistracies and the bureaus did under the Empire and the Monarchy; and the contradiction between the facts and the word *Republic* persisted in asserting itself.

The Constitution in its entirety was adopted November 4, 1848, and the *fête* of its promulgation was celebrated on a sad and sombre day, on the Place de la Concorde. Armand Marrast presided on this occasion, and was assisted by Cavaignac and Marie, Minister of Justice, partisan for the amelioration of workingmen in 1847, and who became, in 1848, the instigator of the *émeutes* of June by the severity of his treatment of laborers.

A mass, followed by a *Te Deum*, was solemnized upon a high altar by Archbishop Sibour, the prelate who pretended to teach the people "the redemption of the proletariat by work," and who, January 3, 1852, celebrated Bonaparte's *coup d'état* by the same chant, under the vaulting of Notre Dame.

The mental condition of the people, as well as the state of the atmosphere, lent to this *fête* of the Constitution every appearance of a funeral solemnity.

The presidential election was fixed for December 10th. The names of Bonaparte, Cavaignac, Ledru-Rollin, and Raspail were most discussed. Lamartine's star, which had shed a faint light over the events of February, was nearly eclipsed. Raspail, the learned editor-in-chief of the *Réformateur*, the adversary of scientific and political poisoners, was only supported by 36,000 socialistic Republicans. Ledru-Rollin found his supporters among the "*petite bourgeoisie*," calling themselves Republicans, but he was reproached in the advanced camp for having

Marshal MacMahon.

supported the sham "*amis de l'ordre*," though, since the sinister days of June, he had sought to regain his popularity by speaking against "infamous capital" and the "selfishness of the rich."

For General Cavaignac was a large army of *bourgeoisie*, who defended the blunders of the Orléanists and had no confidence in the pretender of Cæsarian socialism. But the laboring masses were allured, either by their resentments against the *bourgeoisie*, or by the unwearied Bonapartist propaganda, which took every form to advance the fortunes of "the nephew of the Emperor," in favor of whom leaned the leaders of the "*Comité de la rue de Poitiers*," Thiers at the head, guided by his grudge against Cavaignac, and by his hope to direct, by his abilities and intrigues, the inanity of the "Prince."

The most opposite tendencies, ranging from misunderstood socialism to the most reactionary clericalism, were favorable to the man who, in his manifesto of November 29th, affirmed that his name was a symbol of order and security; that he would, upon his *honor*, at the end of four years, leave power affirmed and liberty intact to the custody of his successor. The inexperience of the great majority of electors found satisfaction suited to all tastes in this skillfully drawn and widely distributed document. To the people he promised diminution of taxation, the amelioration of the burdens of conscription, the establishment of savings banks, and the granting of pardons; to Catholics, the liberty of education and the protection of religion; to soldiers, an assured existence; to financiers, a resumption of credit, and to property-owners, the security of their estates. Cavaignac, having shown unfitness for his position, by commencing the culpable affair of Rome by sending troops to protect Pius IX., Louis Napoleon criticised this expedition in a letter to the newspapers, and, at the same time, in another letter addressed to the ambassador of the Pope, he declared himself in favor of temporal power.

A report of the presidential election showed that Bonaparte received 5,434,226 votes, Cavaignac 1,448,107, Ledru-Rollin 370,119, and Lamartine fell to 7,910. Marrast proclaimed Louis Napoleon Bonaparte President of the Republic.

"In the presence of God and before the French people," Bonaparte swore "fidelity to the democratic Republic and to the Constitution." "My duty is set forth," said he. "I shall fulfill it as a man of honor. Those who shall attempt to destroy, by illegal ways, that which all France has established, I shall regard as enemies of the country. We have a great mission to fulfill; it is to found a Republic in the interest of all, and a just and firm government, which may be animated by a sincere love of progress, without being reactionary or utopian. God aiding us, we shall do our best, even if we can not accomplish great things."

Subsequent events disclosed the meaning of this hypocritical language. The unhappy people, by trusting themselves to the guidance of this dishonest man, destroyed the Republic. "They stabbed themselves to death" by placing their destinies in the hands of a man, who, by theft upon theft, untruth upon untruth, was about to cast the whole country into the depths of shame.

The efforts of the government were directed against the Assembly, which showed some pretension to respect the Constitution, and to complete it by enacting organic laws. The Monarchists and Bonapartists joined together to demand its dissolution. The commencement of the *coup d'état* took place during the night of January 28 and 29, 1849. The Palais Législatif was surrounded by troops, and arrests were made among the Democrats. Rateau moved that the election of a legislature be set down for March 19th. The Assembly exerted itself only to procure a vote on the budget and the electoral law. Things drifted on until May 27th. Its last infamous action was upon a favorable report of Jules Favre to vote a credit of 1,200,000 francs for the Mediterranean expeditionary corps, that is to say, the overthrow of the Roman Republic.

The election of May 13th and 14th disclosed a majority of two-thirds for the "party of order," which consisted of a union of Bonapartists, Legitimists, and Orléanists against the Republicans. The "moderate" faction almost disappeared. The struggle was now to take place between the Conservatives, numbering about 450, who hid their project of overthrowing the Republic under this false appellation, and the Democrats, represented by 180 members, who assumed the old title of Mountaineers.

The French army laid siege to Rome, in violation of all the governmental promises, and of the Constitution, and insurrections were provoked in Lyons and in Paris. Both of these cities were placed under martial law. The right of meeting was suspended by the law of June 19, 1849. Democratic journals were discontinued; thirty representatives were prosecuted before the High Court at Versailles. In the place of the organic law for the press, promised by the Constitution, the law of July 27th was passed. It was proposed by Odillon Barrot, and seconded by Thiers, Dufaure, and Montalembert. This law recalled and exaggerated the old provisions of 1835, punished attacks upon the President, and the publication of false news, and submitted the sale and distribution of all printed and written matter to the authorization of the prefecture. Other restrictive measures followed. Victor

Hugo, upon this occasion, who had voted until this time with the " Right," separated from the Conservatives.

The election of July 8th, held in the interests of this *régime*, caused the already compact ranks of the reactionary coalition to grow. The most detestable influences of the First Empire manifested themselves. The Bonapartist committees wanted an appeal to the people, in order to give the presidency for life to Louis Napoleon. The use of physical force was already so probable that the " Left " alleged the peril of another 18th *Brumaire* in order to oppose the prorogation of the Chamber. The Prince had the audacity to protest "his respect for the laws of his country," to reassure the representatives. Upon this assurance a recess of six weeks was agreed upon, after having decided that there was no need to reform the judiciary organization, and that the magistrates suspended by the Provisional Government should be reseated.

An organic law upon the subject of state of siege, announced December 11, 1848, was voted August 10, 1849. M. Grévy maintained, against M. Dufaure, that Article 8 of this law violated Article 4 of the Constitution prohibiting extraordinary tribunals. But a majority of 419 against 153 sanctioned this violation. Then a law of August 11th, placed upon the active list the notoriously Royalist generals whom the Provisional Government had retired. Thus the military element was avenged as the magistracy had been.

Napoleon commenced from this time to modify his tactics, and aimed to govern without the Assembly, and to make himself more popular at the expense of the national representatives. In his message of October 31, 1849, he declared that parties were awakening; that France was restless, because she could not see the proper course to take, and sought the will of him who was elected December 10th; that the name of Napoleon was to him only a programme, signifying: at home, order, authority, religion, and the well-being of the people; abroad, national dignity.

Rouher became Minister of Justice; Fould took the finances; Parieu, education; Bineau, public works; Ferdinand Barrot, the interior; d'Hautpoul, war. This change surprised the majority, but it made no objection, pursued its reactionary march, and did not disapprove of the police organization which the executive power extended over all France, alleging that these precautions were directed against socialism.

Thiers associated himself with Falloux, in order to prepare a law upon the "Liberty of Education." In his terror of socialism, which threatened, according to him, to destroy society, the former minister of Louis Philippe pushed clericalism further than the most fiery Ultramontane. He wished to deliver over to the clergy all primary instruction and to suppress the lay institutions. Dupanloup did not ask so much. All that the clergy desired was that they should control primary and secondary instruction, by directing the teachers and professors, and making them their docile instruments.

The "Left," through Edgar Quinet, asserted that all instruction should be given by the State, outside of any religious dogma, and the organ of Victor Hugo formulated the doctrine that "*l'Église restât chez elle et l'État chez nous*"; and pleaded in favor of gratuitous and compulsory education.

The contempt of the Republic attracted public attention in all the acts of the majority and of the government. Trees of liberty planted in 1848 were cut down with ostentatious insolence. The anniversary of February 24th was disregarded by the Assembly; an act of February 12, 1850, ordered the formation of five grand commands—a military precaution openly taken against the Republicans. Public opinion protested against this audacious defiance in the elections of March 10th. Carnot, the Minister of Public Instruction of 1848, had 132,000 votes; de Flotte, insurgent of June, obtained more votes in the army than General de la Hitte, Minister of Foreign Affairs; the socialist Vidal, editor of the *Travail Affranchi*, was elected in Paris and in the Provinces; Eugene Sue also obtained a large majority. These results were largely brought about by the fact that the Parisian "*petite bourgeoisie*" returned to vote with the workingmen. These elections had a considerable moral effect, and they frightened the Chamber, which determined instantly to attack universal suffrage.

Urgency on this subject was declared May 18, 1850, by 451 votes against 239, and May 31st the electoral law of March 15, 1849, was modified by a vote of 433 against 239. Montalembert said, facetiously, that the law was only a point of departure, for it was "necessary to have a Roman expedition at home." Thiers supported it by his garrulity. The danger that was to be avoided was not, in his eyes, the communism that claimed private ownership in landed property, but industrial communism, the expropriation of manufactories, and the instruments of labor, to the use of the working community. He affirmed that the law would only exclude " vagabonds, the dangerous classes, and the vile multitude " from the electorate, and that the true people would not be affected. An examination of the text of the law will show the falsity of these allegations. To require three years' domicile instead of six months, was to deprive three millions of citizens of the right to vote; it was the suppression of universal suffrage and the overthrow of the Constitution. While the Chamber was losing its hold on the people, Louis Napoleon was actively carrying out the Bonapartist propaganda and organization. The "Left" contented itself by protesting in flowers of rhetoric against the violation of the Constitutional law. The members of this party did not believe in the possibilities of a *coup d'état;* they depended on the want of intelligence of the President, upon the energy of Changarnier, on the boldness of Dupin, President of the Assembly, and upon the vigilance of the commission appointed to supervise public affairs during the recess from August 9th to November 12th.

This recess was utilized by Napoleon by taking trips through France, and fawning upon the civil and military authorities. He caused the General Councils to issue a demand for the revision of Article 45 of the Constitution, which prohibited the re-election of the President of the Republic. At the reviews and the soldiers' banquets the cry was heard of "*Vive l'Empereur!*" The solution of the political problem was thus settling itself under the eyes of the permanent commission, composed of Legitimists and Orléanists. These two parties worked actively, but were unable to arrive at an agreement; some of them dreamed of a fusion of the elder and younger branches of the Bourbons; others, with Chambord, refused to lend themselves to such an arrangement; while there were those who wished to address themselves to the people, through the mutilated suffrage, for the return of the King.

The danger did not exist in the Royalist intrigues, but in the Bonapartist plots. The paid bands of "December 10" acclaimed the President everywhere, and maltreated those who did not approve of their enthusiasm. Changarnier wished to prohibit the cries and demonstrations of the soldiers under arms. A conflict appeared imminent.

The Prince seemed to recede; at the opening of the session of November 12, 1850, he caused a message to be read, in which he presented himself simply as a man occupying a position of public trust; above all things, not preoccupied in finding out who should govern France in 1852, but in employing his time in such a way that the transition, whatever it might be, should be made without agitation and without trouble. He was not yet quite sure of succeeding.

Changarnier was relieved of all command January 10, 1851. The ministry was partially renewed. The "Right" now saw that it was deprived of the sword, upon which it depended for the restoration of monarchy. Rémusat demanded the formation of a commission charged to take such measures as the circumstances should require. The Commission, having been named, had the courage to ask a vote of censure, on account of the recall of the General. Thiers, comprehending too late that the danger did not come from the people, tried to arrest the reaction to which he had so actively contributed, and to persuade his accomplices that, after all, the Republic was the government of all, and it was necessary to give it a complete and loyal trial. "If the Assembly yield," said he, "the Empire will be established."

The Chamber limited itself to a vote of want of confidence in the ministry. Napoleon then appointed a "*Cabinet de transition*," composed of MM. Germiny, Magne, Randon, Royer, Schneider, Vaillant, and Vaïsse. He demanded money of the Assembly. This was the second time; for he had already received 3,000,000 francs for election expenses. This time the credit was refused, and the "Elysian" press lamented upon the poverty to which the chief of State had been reduced.

The majority rendered itself odious by abrogating the

Victor Hugo: 1884.
(From the Bronze by Rodin, Institute, 1884.)

law which exiled the Bourbons, and also showed itself disposed to favor a restoration.

During these agitations between the ministry and the Chamber, the country was stirred by the prefects, who urged a constitutional revision. The Republicans, on their part, and before any revision, claimed the repeal of the law of May 31st; the Bonapartists defended this law before the Assembly, and attacked it everywhere else. At Dijon Napoleon delivered a speech, in which he claimed that the representatives were opposed to all measures which he wished to advocate in the interests of the people.

Petitioners to the number of 1,360,000 asked for a total revision of the Constitution. Some saw in the revision a means of stopping the use of force, and of fixing the powers of the President; others wished to make it a stepping-stone for the re-establishment of monarchy. The "Left" feared that, in revising the fundamental law, the Republic would be overturned.

The necessary three-fourths to reform the Constitution was not obtained. The proposition of the government —sustained by Falloux, Berryer, Odillon Barrot, and Baroche; opposed by Cavaignac, Michel de Bourges, Victor Hugo, and Dufaure—obtained only 446 votes (July 19, 1851). The Assembly was then prorogued to November 4th.

Napoleon no longer hesitated in his scheme of violence. He sought a soldier of fortune, without either honor or scruples, to command the troops. Fleury, his aid-de-camp, procured Saint Arnaud, but he hesitated to accept. Baraguay d'Hilliers, who commanded the garrison of Paris since the dismissal of Changarnier, and who was judged too honest, was replaced by Magnan. Granier (de Cassagnac) and Louis Napoleon prepared a project for revision which they kept secret, while Morny, Rouher, Persigny, and Carlier, Prefect of Police, arranged the details of a *coup d'état*, at Saint Cloud. But Randon, the Minister of War, was not in the plot, and the necessary dispositions of the police could not be made, therefore, the contemplated action against the Assembly was postponed.

The Constitution of 1848 had organized in advance a conflict between the legislature and the executive. Napoleon saw if he could control the majority of the Assembly by a combination of parties, that his path to empire would be smoothed. If the people could be made to believe in him as a leader and statesman, he could then seize upon power without serious opposition. To hoodwink the masses and to enlist them on his side in the overthrow of the "Right," he proposed to become the vindicator of universal suffrage, and to demand the abrogation of the law of May 31, 1850. Léon Faucher, vexed at having served as a mask to the presidential tactics, resigned. The ministry was replaced by lackeys and accomplices. Saint Arnaud accepted the portfolio of war, and Carlier yielded the police to Maupas, who had distinguished himself by arbitrary acts against the Republicans in the prefecture of Haute Garonne.

The troops were advised that they ought to know only one law—the will of the commander; only one duty—passive obedience.

The "Left" sustained the government; the "Right" opposed and offered to re-enact a law of 1848, giving the President of the Chamber the power to make requisition of armed forces. Upon the decision of this question the whole matter was at last to turn. Nearly all the "Left," not believing that the Bonapartist peril was as formidable as the Legitimist danger, voted with the Napoleonic party. The Assembly was thus disarmed in the interest of the executive power. Charras, Quinet, Bixio, Dufaure, Grévy, Chauffour, and Kestner, more clear-sighted, voted against the Bonapartists. The proposition of the "Right," to take away the control of the army from Napoleon, was defeated by 408 votes against 300, while his attitude in relation to the abrogation of the electoral law already guaranteed the neutrality of the masses.

The unskillfulness of the Republican representatives was striking. In their opinion they had vanquished the Empire, when, on the contrary, they had assured its success. In the meantime the babbling and idling Chamber was passing the time in the fabrication of municipal laws.

Napoleon celebrated the anniversary of the coronation of his uncle, and that of the battle of Austerlitz. On December 2, 1851, the man who had posed as the champion of duty and law, finished by destroying the Republic, and slaughtering an unarmed population by a drunken soldiery.

Henceforth, everything that was done in the name of constitutional law was an infamous and ridiculous parody.

In the night of December 1 and 2, 1851, the following decree was posted upon the walls of Paris:

"The President of the Republic decrees:

"The National Assembly is dissolved. Universal suffrage is established. The law of May 31 is abrogated. The French people are convoked to meet in their polling places, beginning December 14 and ending December 21. The state of siege is decreed in the first military district. The Council of State is dissolved. The Minister of the Interior is charged with the execution of this decree."

A second decree enacted that the plebiscitory vote should take place, as in the time of the Uncle, upon open registers. But the Nephew wished to perfect the system, and a decree on the 4th ordered that all citizens who had a six months' domicile in the district should cast a closed ballot. Each was to put in the ballot-box, if approving, a ballot having on it the word *yes;* if disapproving, the word *no.*

Since the cold-blooded massacres committed in the capital terror reigned everywhere. Republicans were tracked throughout the territory of France, and treated with a barbarity only exceeded by that of M. Thiers. The authorities prosecuted, as an act of insurrection, the distribution of negative ballots. In thirty-two departments, where martial law was proclaimed, the military commissioners made their arrests without interrogating the prisoners. Every citizen who was not in prison, concealed, or in flight, was compelled to vote "yes," if he wished to protect his liberty.

The canvass of the votes was made by a consulting commission, appointed to take the place of the Council of State, and the result of the December election was proclaimed in a decree setting forth the result of the vote on the adoption or rejection of the following plebiscite:

"The French people wish the maintenance of the authority of Louis Napoleon Bonaparte, and delegate to him the necessary power to establish a Constitution upon the basis proposed by him in his proclamation of December 2, 1851."

The total number of votes was 8,016,773; affirmative, 7,439,216; negative, 640,737; annulled as irregular, 36,820.

"Prince," said Baroche, in congratulating Louis Napoleon upon the result, "establish in France the principle of authority so often disturbed in the last fifty years * * * * that France may at last be delivered from the men who are always ready for murder and pillage, and who horrify civilization." And the chief of conspirators then replied: "France has responded to the loyal appeal that I have made to her. She has comprehended that I only passed beyond the limits of legality in order to re-enter the precincts of the law."

The Napoleonic *régime* is entirely embraced within this official conversation. The antithesis of "legality," and "law" was suggested by Menjaud, Bishop of Nancy, who was named Grand Chaplain of the Court, with a salary of 120,000 francs. The clergy, constant to their principles, sanctified the crime to the weight of gold. "We pray God," said Archbishop Sibour, "for the success of the high mission confided to you." A *Te Deum* was chanted at Notre Dame, January 1, 1852. The imperial eagle was placed on the flags, and the hero of December 2d was installed in the Tuileries, "the only residence worthy of him," according to the noble Ségur d'Aguesseau.

On January 9th sixty-five representatives of the people were expelled from French territory, with a threat of transportation if they returned to it, eighteen others were sent away for the general safety, five were destined for Guyane, and the prisons commenced to overflow into Cayenne and Lambessa.

Mixed commissions were directed to purify the departments. In each of them tribunals, more ignoble than the magisterial courts of the Restoration, were invested with power to inflict the following punishments solely on account of political antecedents: Sending before the Council of War, which meant shooting; transportation to Cayenne, or to Algeria; expulsion from the country; seclusion in some fixed locality, and surveillance of the police.

Their decisions were made without procedure and without witnesses.

We now arrive at the Constitution which was imposed upon deceived and terrorized France. Napoleon had already indicated its groundwork in his proclamation of December 2d. He repeated it in the five paragraphs of the preamble. In order to fulfill his *great* mission, and being persuaded that "the preponderancy of a single Assembly and the instability of power are the permanent causes of trouble and discord," he demanded a "return to the system initiated by the First Consul, in the commencement of the century—a system which had given *prosperity* and *repose* to France, and can only guarantee them to her in the future." Such was the "profound conviction" of this man without convictions. "If you share it with me," he impudently continued, "declare it by your suffrages. If, to the contrary, you prefer a government without force, monarchical or republican, borrowed from some past I know not of, or some chimerical future, then reply negatively. If I do not obtain the majority of your suffrages, I shall convene a new Assembly, and commit to it the charge which I have received from you. But if you believe in the cause of which my name is the symbol, that is to say, *France regenerated by the Revolution of* 1789, *and organized by the Emperor*, then proclaim it by consecrating the power which I have asked of you.

By the vote of December 20th the French people acknowledged they accepted this tissue of lies as the truth, renounced that liberty which the Republic only could secure, and replaced themselves under the yoke, thus showing into what condition of political incapacity and obtuseness they had fallen in the last sixty years.

The fundamental groundwork of the plebiscite recommitted all power, for ten years, *to a responsible chief*. It was the repetition of the commencement of the First Empire. Nothing could disguise the final result. The ministers depended alone upon this chief, who was invested with the most effective power. Not only was the parliamentary *régime* destroyed, but the representative system lost all semblance of truth; those elected by the people could do nothing, either against the ministry or against the supreme chief, whose pretended responsibility covered, under all circumstances, the acts of his "clerks." A personal dictatorship, without any restriction, was thus instituted. The Council of State, re-established according to the Constitution of year VIII, and the "equipoising" Senate, open to all "distinguished men" of servility, were to assist the master in his work of moral destruction and spoliation, by surrounding him with an appearance of greatness.

The Constitution of 1852 embodied all the essential points decided by the monosyllabic plebiscite. The President held absolute power in his hands. The organic law was elaborated conformably to the proposition of the Prince, by a commission composed of Rouher, Troplong, Persigny, Flahault, and Mesnard. By a cruel irony they pretended to guarantee the grand principles of '89, although the instrument they produced was a most formal violation of them. The principles were replaced by a fact: the most sweeping autocracy—there was not a word on rights or liberty.

The President, chief of State, governs by his ministers, his Council of State, his Senate, his Legislative Body. He is reputed to divide the legislative power with the senators and deputies; but this is false, since he alone can initiate laws; after the vote he can refuse his sanction, and consequently render the laws ineffective, even after having proposed them, if they cease to please him. Better still, he can dismiss the deputies and do without them for six months. His *responsibility* before the people is a lie, since it would take a revolution to render it effective. His action is free, without any limit whatever. He commands all, designates all employments, even the functions of the mayors, outside of the municipal councils, if it is his pleasure to do so. After having caused the laws to be made in accordance with his will, he regulates their execution. Justice is rendered in his name, and all functionaries swear obedience to him. He commands the army in person, declares war, and makes treaties. The ministers, chosen as it suits him, are not bound as a whole. He can accept or dismiss them in whole or in part. Functionaries and magistrates are only servants of the master, in whom resides all sovereignty. The entire nation is incarnated in him. If he die, his successor, whom he designates, shall be recommended, that is to say, imposed *upon the confidence of the electors*, by the senators and ministers who form the council of government.

The Council of State is presided over, nominated, and revoked by Napoleon. Reconstituted upon the models of year VIII and year XII by an organic law of February 25, 1852, the Council deliberates with closed doors, draws up the bills according to superior authority, and supports them by discussion before the Legislative Body, and gives its advice upon questions which are endorsed by the master or his ministerial lackeys. It is composed of forty to fifty members, not including the substitute of the President, councilors in extraordinary service, auditors, and secretaries, making in all 167 valets, with salaries ranging from 80,000 to 2,000 francs, according to rank and class, and not counting gratuities.

Napoléon III.

The Senate, as a moderate, conservative, and equipoising body, is declared the guardian of *public liberties*, which, in fact, have no existence. It appears to be reclothed with considerable authority, for it can oppose the promulgation of laws which may be an attack on the Constitution, on religion, on morals, on freedom of worship, on individual liberty, on the equality of citizens in the eye of the law, and on the integrity of the territory. But the Cerebus is muzzled, his teeth are drawn, for the only citizens that the President of the Imperial Republic judges worthy to constitute members of the Senate are cardinals, marshals, and admirals. These members are unremovable, and the importance of their services is such that they are gratuitous, at least in theory, for His Highness may allow or refuse, at his pleasure, a donation of 30,000 francs a year. This *grand body* interprets the Constitution, regulates all that it does not provide for, and can propose modifications of it; in the event of the dissolution of the Legislative Body, it governs under the orders of the grand chief, who convokes or prorogues it as he pleases. It is composed of eighty members for the first year, and this number may be raised to 150. In this manner, all inclination to insubordination may be paralyzed by the master, if it were possible for such a thing to exist among his creatures. The First Consul did not arrogate to himself such an extensive power by the *Senatûs consultum* of the 16th *Thermidor* of year X.

A Legislative Body exists as a matter of show. Direct universal suffrage shows itself obliging enough to permit itself to act, but only in such a contracted way that it is completely swallowed up. This other "grand body" is composed of 262 members, one for every 35,000 electors (Article 35), although Article 34 says that this election shall be based on population. Soldiers are only electors to nominate the President. The "*scrutin de liste*" is inhibited. The Constitution does not mention official candidature, but, in *the interest* of the electors, the government believed itself *compelled* to present the candidates in each district, considering that it was quite impossible for citizens to know the *good* candidates.

The deputies are elected for six years. Their services are gratuitous, which forcibly eliminates all men without fortunes. The president and vice-presidents of the Legislative Body are nominated by the executive. The Chamber can approve only what has been proposed to it; it possesses neither the parliamentary initiative, nor the right of interpellation, nor even the right to amend the bills that have been presented to it; for all amendments must, to be submitted to the Assembly, have been previously approved by the commission charged to examine the bill, and then accepted by the Council of State. If the bill does not come out victorious from these two trials, it is buried, without any possible recourse. The president of the Chamber, whose emoluments are fixed by a decree, has alone the right to draw up the minutes of the sitting, in order that nothing of a disagreeable character shall go before the public. All petitions being addressed to the Senate, the Legislative Body can receive none. Publicity of the sittings is tolerated, but the public shall be expelled on the demand of only five members. Finally, the convocation, the adjournment, the prorogation, and the dissolution are left to the caprice of the President of this strange Republic. The legislative power is thus only a lower court of the executive power, doing only what it is ordered to do, and has no need of legislators, save for parade.

The High Court of Justice, instituted to try, without appeal, or without recourse to *cassation*, upon the order of the President, all persons charged with crime, *attentats*, or conspiracies against his august person, or the safety of his State, is the only judicial power which obtains under the Constitution of '52.

Article 1 sets forth clearly enough that justice is the will of him, in whose name it is dispensed, and therefore, its *rôle* is reserved to magistracy.

All legislation contrary to this Constitution is abrogated; the municipal organization is relegated to a former law, making the decree of the *coup d'état* the supreme law.

The Constitution of 1852 is largely inspired by the despotic work of the year VIII; it even notably amplifies it. In hypocrisy and villainy the scholar goes beyond the professor. This instrument, signed January 14, 1852, was not put in force until March 29th, following. Until this date, Napoleon governed by decrees. When his satellites judged that the purification was nearly complete, that there was no opposition to be feared, the raising of the state of siege was proclaimed, and a pretended constitutional *régime* succeeded, in appearance, at least, to dictatorial power.

Soon after the *coup d'état*, Napoleon, being desirous of conciliating the clergy, dedicated the Panthéon to Catholic worship, in conformity to a decree of 1806, and prescribed the suspension of labor on Sundays and *fête* days.

A decree, dated January 31st, and simply authorized by the executive power, established congregations of women devoted to the "education of youth and amelioration of the condition of the poor." March 22d a community of priests was instituted "to perform service at Sainte Geneviève, and to prepare men as religious teachers." Another decree, March 25th, re-established the salary of the canonry of Saint Denis.

On February 2, 1852, an organic decree upon the mode of choosing deputies appeared. Its preamble provided that " Louis Napoleon, President of the Republic, upon a report of the Secretary of the Interior, decrees."

It must be borne in mind that all the decrees issued after the *coup d'état* were considered as likewise ratified, under the provisions of Article 58 of the Constitution of 1852. The acts were denominated as belonging to the work of centralization. This included the transportation of members of secret political societies, without trial, and by which authority many persons deemed dangerous were transported to Cayenne. The same may be said of the stringent laws of the press, according to which every paper existed at the will of the President. Titles of nobility, abolished February, 1848, were re-established January 24, 1852. The municipality of Lyons was suppressed March 24th; that of Paris had already disappeared July 3, 1848. The edifice was completed; it only remained to withdraw the false republican standard, and under its true colors to launch the ship of Empire.

VI.

THE SECOND EMPIRE.

The presidential voyage was at an end. The last formality that preceded the loud acclaim of "*Vive l'Empereur!*" was skillfully arranged by the "*Décembristes.*" The famous words, "*L'Empire c'est la paix,*" resounded.

"The civilizer, apostle, and future sire" promised to make himself master of all, by the conciliation of disgruntled parties, by the aid of religion and morality, and by the co-operation of the masses of the people.

On arriving in Paris, this illustrious traveler was besought by the Prefect of the Seine, in the name of the so-called Municipal Commission, "to deign to reassume the crown of the founder of his dynasty." The refrain of the Marseillaise was mingled with the Imperialist chorus; the clergy burnt their incense; the boulevards presented a continuous scene of ovation. Triumphal arches proclaimed Napoleon III. "the savior of modern civilization." The people looked on, but did not understand.

The *Moniteur* declared the following day, October 17, 1852, that a transcendent manifestation imposed upon the President the "duty" of consulting the Senate upon the subject of the re-establishment of the Empire. A message proposed the question to the Senators, who were convoked November 4th. A commission immediately nominated affirmed that its members were men *providentially* chosen to repair the evils of revolutions; to declare that France, being, at the same time, monarchical and democratic, the Empire would unite in itself both the monarchy and the republic.

The Senate deliberated in conformity with Articles 31 and 32 of the Constitution, and, by a vote 86 against 1, enacted a *Senatûs consultum*, November 7, 1852, providing that:

The imperial dignity is re-established. Louis Napoleon Bonaparte is Emperor, under the name of Napoleon III.; that the imperial dignity is hereditary in the direct and legitimate issue of Louis Napoleon Bonaparte, from male to male, in the order of primogeniture, and with perpetual exclusion of females and their descendants. Then follow most minute provisions, providing for the default of heirs, the forms of adoption of male children by the Emperor, the fixing of titles, and the condition of other members of his family.

This decree then sets forth that: The Constitution of January 14, 1852, is maintained in all those dispositions which are not contrary to the present *Senatûs consultum;* it can not be modified, except in the forms and by the means there prescribed.

The following is then presented for the acceptation of the people, in the forms determined by the decree of December 2 and 4, 1851: "The people wills the re-establishment of the imperial dignity in the person of Louis Napoleon Bonaparte, with inheritance in direct legitimate or adoptive descendants, and gives him the right to regulate the order of succession to the throne in the Bonaparte family, in the manner described in the *Senatûs consultum* of November 7, 1852."

The senators repaired to Saint Cloud, to present this *Senatûs consultum* to Louis Napoleon. Forty-eight years before, another Senate, as vile as this one, had offered, in the same palace, the imperial crown to the head of this inauspicious family. The descendant did not fail to remember the touching souvenir. "He flattered himself that he felt the spirit of the Emperor."

As the re-establishment of the hereditary monarchy modified Article 1 of the plebiscite of December 20, 1851, it was necessary to consult the nation, in order to make the buffoonery complete. A decree, therefore, was issued the same day, calling upon all Frenchmen twenty-one years of age to declare themselves, on November 20th and 21st, upon the proposition, by voting "yes" or "no," in accordance with the *régime* of the Constitution and the additional decrees; that is to say, outside of all guarantees of liberty. Marines and soldiers voted "militarily," and the electors absent from their domiciles were invited to deposit their votes in any locality where they found themselves. It was thus intended to facilitate the floating vote.

The Legislative Body, December 1, 1852, declared the result of the vote on plebiscite, which established the imperial dignity. According to the figures, as to the honesty and accuracy of which many were incredulous, over 8,000,000 voted "yes." The French people seemed thus to absolve all the crimes which were subsequently committed against them. The abdication was complete.

The Legislative Body joined the Senate and the Council of State; these three "grand bodies" together made the pilgrimage to Saint Cloud, in order to present this authentification to the new Emperor, who affirmed that his reign had not originated in violence and deceit; that his government would have for its groundwork religion, justice, probity, and love for the suffering classes. The following day, the anniversary of the great crime, Napoleon, flanked by Persigny and by Saint Arnaud, promoted Marshal of France for "services rendered," proceeded to take possession of the Tuileries. The plebiscite was read from the balconies of the palace and the Hôtel de Ville, to the army, to the National Guard, to the people, and the *Moniteur* made known the names of the illustrious scamps composing the "*Maison de l'Empereur.*"

The succession to the throne was provisionally regulated by a decree, December 18, 1852. It commences with these words: "Napoleon, by the grace of God, and the national will, Emperor of the French, to whom these presents shall come, greeting." It provides, among other things, that in case he leaves no direct, legitimate, or adopted heir, that his uncle, Jerome Napoleon Bonaparte, and his direct descendants, according to the rule of primogeniture, shall succeed him.

December 25th the attributes of the executive power were largely augmented by a *Senatûs consultum* enacting many changes to the Constitution of January 14, 1852, and abrogating many other articles.

A law of May 3, 1855, abrogating that of March 21, 1831, as well as the provisions of the decree of July 3, 1848, and July 7, 1852, regulated the composition of and the nominations to the municipal councils; the conditions of eligibility; of the meetings and deliberations, and the right of suspension and dissolution. This law maintained a special *régime* (the nomination of its officers by the Emperor for five years), for Paris and Lyons. The fifty-one articles of this law augmented the power of the government.

A *Senatûs consultum* of July 17, 1856, regulated the question of the regency, by giving the Emperor the right to dispose of it, and conferring the same power upon the Empress in case he did not make the designation.

The number of deputies, fixed at 261 by the decree of

Henri Rochefort.

February 2, 1852, was raised to 267 for the legislative election which took place five years afterward, by virtue of a *Senatûs consultum* of May 27, 1857. Six candidates were elected as Republicans June 21st of the same year: Cavaignac, Carnot, Goudchaux, Émile Ollivier, and Darimon, for the Seine; Hénon for the Rhône. Cavaignac died before the opening of the session; Carnot and Goudchaux refused to swear obedience to the Constitution and fidelity to the Emperor. Hénon had refused the oath in 1852; this time he looked at the matter differently in accepting the formula of it, although he had not changed his sentiments, because the electors had nominated him no longer to remain upon the threshold of the Assembly, but to pass beyond it. In order to prevent the recurrence of such a vexation a *Senatûs consultum* of February 17, 1858, required that all candidates should take the oath at least eight days before the opening of the polls.

The Orsini bombs (January, 1858), which wished to avenge Italian independence lost by the fault of the French, gave Napoleon III. a pretext to reduce all factious opposition to silence. On February 27, 1858, he caused a monstrous law to issue, in the name of general safety, by which innocent citizens were fined, imprisoned, and transported. Morny, President of the Legislative Body, was the initiator of this law. He praised the moderation of the government, and protested against the qualification of the law in relation to "suspects." It was adopted by 227 votes. Only twenty-four deputies dared to enter their protest. In the Senate MacMahon was alone in pointing out the fact that these measures did not conform to the Constitution.

The execution was more cruel than the law. Napoleon charged General Espinasse with it, one of the men of the *coup d'état* and the mixed commissioners, whom he named as Minister of the Interior. Although the Republicans were strangers to Orsini's act, Espinasse asserted in a circular to his prefects that "the execrable *attentat* had just revealed the savage resentments of this party, whose odious attempt aroused the apprehensions of the country."

Even before the law was passed, the proscriptions commenced. The individuals who were to be arrested were named in each department; the prefects looked after those who remained.

Victims were selected apparently by chance from the liberal *bourgeoisie*, from honest workmen, from old men, and persons suffering from disease; and even women were torn from their families. The list of delinquent persons made by the Chambers was not followed. But this terror did not always attain its object, for Jules Favre, the defender of Orsini, was elected in Paris with Ernest Picard to replace Carnot and Goudchaux. They formed, with Ollivier, Hénon, and Darimon, the group of "Five," who for several years represented the only opposition to the odious *régime* of the Empire.

When Espinasse ceased to preside over the matter of arrests and transportations, he was replaced by Delangle, as minister of the "general safety."

The year 1859 was signalized by a full and complete amnesty to all persons condemned for political crimes and misdemeanors, and in cases where they had been victims of measures taken for the "general safety." A decree also annulled the admonitions to the press.

Napoleon did not take this action because he had any intention of showing any respect for political rights. He simply wished, by a measure of clemency, to calm the discontent caused by his peace of Villafranca, which left the Italian war unfinished, and to prove that his government was strong enough not to fear the hostility of parties.

In order to be in high favor with the government of Great Britain, he signed a commercial treaty with England, January 23, 1860, without having done anything to protect French industry against the crisis which this sudden change in the international commerce was certain to produce.

The year 1860 saw the annexation of Savoy and Nice to France, by the treaty of March 24th with Victor Emmanuel, and ratified by a plebiscitory consultation with the interested departments.

The imperial arms now had occasion to distinguish themselves by pillage and conflagrations in China. In order to make the "glorious" expedition remembered, General Cousin-Montauban was decorated with the title of Count Ta-li-Kao. The proposition to vote him a large sum of money was rejected.

The conquest of Cochin China, accomplished by sacrifices upon sacrifices, follies upon absurdities a long time afterward, involved the nation in the Tonkin, Chinese, and Annamite complications.

This same year there appeared, under the title of "liberal concessions" certain fragments of parliamentarism, in an imperial decree of November 24th, concerning the Senate and the Legislative Body enacting the creation of ministers "without portfolio."

Billault, Magne, and Baroche were named ministers "without portfolios," and Walewski, who was appointed Minister of State, became a kind of central minister, who had precedence over his colleagues.

This paroxysm of "liberalism" very much disturbed the enraged Bonapartists. They were, however, reassured by a circular from Persigny, showing that this decree made no changes in the *régime*, and, further, that the lists of "suspects" were regularly kept in force in all the departments.

The discussion of the Address brought about debates, which had been unknown for a long time. The opposition came chiefly from the clergy, who were furious against the government for failing to maintain the temporal sovereignty of the Pope, although at this time there were French troops in garrison in Rome. There was a strong minority opposition of 131 votes against the Address. The clerical demonstrations were carried to such an extent that the Central Committee of the Society of Saint Vincent de Paul was suppressed.

The year 1861 brought two other modifications of the Constitution of 1852; one relative to the publicity of the sittings of the Legislative Body and of the Senate; the other, upon the report of M. Fould, member of the Private Council, who replaced Magne in charge of the finances, pretending to remedy the excess of the supplemental credits.

At the close of 1861 the unhappy expedition to Mexico commenced—a movement brought on by the intrigues of usurers with the servile dependents of the Court.

The year 1863 marked a curious halt in the march of the Empire. In the general elections of May 31st the various opposing parties—Orléanists, Legitimists, and Republicans—combined together against the common enemy. Independent candidates presented themselves, in spite of the order everywhere displayed by the prefects, who were goaded on by Persigny, by a circular in which he denounced to the people the coalition of the men of 1815, of 1830, and of 1848. Haussmann went so far as to threaten Paris with *émeutes*, which would destroy all business, if the citizens voted *badly*. The official candidates were most vigorously imposed upon the people as men already chosen by the masses, and *who, by their providential election, would realize for the people all the hopes of France*. This administration, from the ministers to the rural guard, pursued the electoral masses and tried to bind them hand and foot. Judges, gendarmes, mayors, commissioners of police, attorneys, functionaries of all kinds—all who wore a uniform or robe—struggled with zeal to accomplish this object, with the aid of the secret police. The clergy supported the governmental candidates with all their avowed and latent power and means of intimidation.

On the other hand, those who abstained from voting in 1857 were upon their reserve. They regarded the candidates as a means to fight the Empire. Thiers was accepted on the list of the Democratic committee, which took for its device: "Inaction is suicide; action is liberty."

In nine districts of the Seine the Opposition came out of the struggle victorious. It also succeeded at Marseilles. Hénon and Jules Favre were elected in Lyons; a dozen anti-Bonapartist deputies, if not Republicans, came to increase the little group of Five; fifteen others, nominated against the official candidates, formed, at the same time, a dynastic and liberal clan.

This awaking of public opinion, occurring with the events taking place in Denmark, Poland, and Mexico, presented a strong reason for the hallucinated person of the Tuileries seriously to contemplate the situation. He avenged himself upon Persigny, whom he replaced by Boudet; upon Walewski, who had to submit to the influence of Thiers, and whose office was given to Billault, although he remained, as the supporter of the government, in the Chamber, notwithstanding the provision of the Constitution, which inhibited a minister with port-

folio from accepting membership of the Legislative Body.
But the most remarkable fact in this revulsion was the
nomination of M. Duruy, considered as a reformer, as
Minister of Public Instruction. The death of Billault
soon occurring, brought Rouher to the first rank.

Thiers, renewing his tortuous cunning and servile skillfulness, sought to profit by all the imperial mistakes, in
order to bring back that system which had been known
in France as "parliamentarism," and which had generally promoted cabals and conflicts, reassumed his *rôle* as
leader of the Opposition, in order to promote the practical fulfillment of certain liberties accorded by the
decree of 1860. The financial situation powerfully aided
him in this design; the deficit was always growing, and
borrowing was going on without cessation. In 1864
Thiers acquired a dominant position between the little
group known as Republican and the Liberal party, by
setting forth the principles of what he called the "necessary liberties," and by maintaining that it was also essential to treat with Juarez. On his side, Morny pretended
to reconcile liberty with the Empire, and won Émile
Ollivier over by this chimera, or rather by the promises
which were made to him.

The International Association of Workmen organized
itself. The Pope launched the "Encyclical Quanta Cura,"
followed by the "Syllabus" enumerating the "guilty
errors" of modern societies, and attacking all the principles of the Revolution. Agitation was everywhere,
when the soul of December 2d went out forever, with
Morny (1865).

After this death, the false prestige which success had
given to the Empire soon faded away. There were no
longer around the husband of Eugénie but "unknown
incapables," who, according to the *mot* of Bismarck,

came to Paris to study the ground, laugh at Napoleon, and prepare, against Austria and France, the elevation of Prussia. Napoleon and his ministers allowed the enemy to grow in Europe, while in America they were obliged, at last, under the menace of intervention of the United States, to withdraw the French troops from Mexico, and to abandon Maximilian to his merited destiny.

The Opposition, profiting by the accumulation of mistakes, attributed to the Imperial Constitution the origin of the humiliations suffered by France on two continents. The Empire tried to defend itself by interdicting all constitutional discussion, by a decree issued July 18, 1866, modifying Article 40 of the Constitution, and also by augmenting the salaries of the deputies.

But the Opposition did not limit itself to the slight shades of the "Reds" and the "Blues," for there was an opposition of the "Whites," over-excited by the foundation of Italian unity, and the reduction of the temporal sovereignty of the Pope to the territory of Rome, and of Civita Vecchia. Whilst Thiers declaimed in the name of the Revolution, the clergy accused the Empire of making an alliance with Revolutionists against the Church. In the midst of this confusion, Emile Ollivier placed himself at the head of a clique claiming the extension of parliamentary prerogatives without ceasing to support the throne. During the discussion of the Address of 1866 an amendment was presented by Buffet and forty-one other deputies, *praying* the Emperor to associate the nation more intimately in the conduct of his affairs. This petition rallied sixty-three votes.

Napoleon, who was urged on by the different opinions held by Ollivier, Rouher, the Prince Napoleon, the Empress, and her following, at last allowed himself to be persuaded to take a course that would bring about an important constitutional change without compromising his cherished "institutions," and thus pacify discontent and facilitate the transmission of the Crown to his heir. Rouher solemnly announced in a letter that great reforms were under consideration, and that the time had come when it was fitting to give imperial institutions their full development, and a new extension to public liberties. This decree appeared January 19, 1867.

The relations between the government and the Chambers were again modified. The "right of address" gave way to a limited right of interpellation. By virtue of a special delegation of the question under consideration, each minister had the right to debate the subject before the two Chambers.

The power of the Legislative Body was increased in such a manner that in place of the Address being discussed for several days at the opening of each session, all public affairs could be debated during the entire session.

Rouher's letter also announced the presentation of two bills; one abolishing the discretionary power of the government over the press, in order to give the right to pass judgment in the case of misdemeanor committed by it to the correctional tribunals; the other regulating the right of meeting, particularly during the electoral period. These two bills were presented March 13, 1867, but they dragged their slow length along until May 11th and June 6th, when they became laws. A *Senatûs consultum* of March 14, 1867, gave the Senate the right to examine into the expediency of a law, as well as its constitutionality, and to submit it during the following session to a second examination before the Chamber of Deputies.

These illusory changes, accompanied by a rearrange-

Empress Eugenie.

ment of the rules of the Legislative Body and Senate, by a modification of the personnel of the ministry, by a slight increase of the attributes of the municipal councils, and the re-establishment of the Legislative Tribunal (suppressed since December 2d), formed what was pompously called: "The crowning of the edifice raised by the national will."

The negative value of these measures resulted in making Rouher their public defender.

The law affecting the press, made remarkable by the amendment of Guilloutet, creating "*le mur de la vie privée*" carried upon its face the stamp of equivocation and corruption, which were the characteristic features of the Empire. Heavy fines replaced the prison; condemned authors were made felons; the correctional tribunals continued to be the judges of opinion, and reports of trials by the press remained interdicted. The right of suffrage was curtailed. The maintenance of the "caution" left periodicals to be controlled by intriguers and capitalists.

The law of June 6, 1868, upon public meetings, no longer required the previous authorization, *except political and religious matters were to be discussed*, and permitted the holding of electoral meetings between the date of the convocation of the college and the fifth day preceding the opening of the polls. The five days of silence before the vote were reserved for the last maneuvers of the official candidates. This was called "the period of reflection." This law was a mass of snares and formalities.

The tide of loans rose without filling the gulf caused by the deficits. Four thousand millions of francs had been borrowed; the budget constantly increased. Money destined for the materials of war served for the orgies of libertines, while the "peaceful and pious" German was seeking a pretext to throw his 1,000,000 soldiers upon French soil. The supporters of the government audaciously proclaimed that the deficit did not exist, that it was a calumny to assert it, only meriting disdain; that no fault had been committed; that peace was certain, and the public full of worthy confidence. However, a majority of the nation seemed to give faith to these statements of the government which then redoubled its efforts to intimidate the people. It was at this time that an ambitious advocate had occasion to conjure up the spectres of the victims of the crime of December, and to enlarge upon the criminal origin of a despicable power.

The servile Chamber elected in 1863 was renewable by the general elections of May 24, 1869. The number of deputies had been fixed at 292. The electors sent a stronger numerical opposition, incapable, however, of arresting France in its fatal decline.

The "Dynastico-Liberal party" which maintained itself between a minority more or less Republican or Royalist, and the docile majority furnished by the official candidature, was now controlled by the bold intriguers, who pushed the hesitating Emperor into the troubled waters of French parliamentarism, by persuading him to facilitate the accession of Napoleon IV., to lighten the government of part of its authority, and to make apparent concessions to new ideas.

Rouher feigned to accept these views. He thought that a little liberty would bring about disorders which he could encourage and provoke, if necessary, and thus frighten the *bourgeois* class, who, being terrorized by the cries of "*blouses blanches!*" by the police, would be thrown back upon Cæsarism.

On July 12th, with the intent of anticipating popular

aspirations, there was read a message announcing
very important constitutional modifications. The Senate was convened August 2d to pass upon the proposition. Jerome's son loudly praised his noble cousin for
wishing to favor the progress of democracy, and to
transform the authoritative Empire into a "liberal Empire." While the changes displeased the senators, the
habit of obedience alone induced them to vote for the
modifications of the Constitution.

The Emperor stripped himself of part of his autocracy
in favor of the Legislative Body and the Senate; the
special ministerial body disappeared; ministers could
now be members of either one or the other Chamber.
The hypocrisy and the ambiguity of the system only grew
the faster. This false parliamentarism badly adapted
itself to the constitutional arrangements which had been
allowed to remain. The political edifice which had been
thus hurriedly erected then broke into pieces in every
part.

Napoleon's faculties, which were already much impaired, could not now resist the assaults of the illness
that was wasting him away, and the intrigues of the
boudoir, of the clergy, and the ministry with which he
was surrounded. Fatigued by Rouher's fierce activity,
which disturbed his peace, and hoping to find some tranquillity in a change of *régime*, he placed implicit confidence
in Ollivier's ambiguous combinations. France learned,
with astonishment, January 2, 1870, that she had a *Liberal*
Ministry, composed of Émile Ollivier, Daru, Chevandier
de Valdrôme, Louvet, Maurice Richard, Rigault de
Genouilly, and Lebœuf. Haussmann, the great "demolisher," was sacrificed, and replaced by Chevreau. The
assassination of Victor Noir by Pierre Bonaparte, Rochefort's prosecution, his condemnation, and Flourens' gen-

crous illusions, provoked a state of over-excitement in Paris which the zeal of the police, and cavalry charges rapidly increased.

By the side of this popular fever, Ollivier's "*Constitutional* Empire" developed itself. Extensive liberal reforms were to strengthen the edifice that had been shaken by the immoderate desire for change, and to assure a graceful transmission of the crown to the illustrious offspring, as well as to place insuperable limits to instability in the new Constitution. The ministry were then invited to prepare this model Constitution. A commission, among whom shone Baroche, Drouyn de Lhuys, Boudet, Magne, Maupas, Chasseloup-Loubat, Rouher, and Devienne, combined Ollivier's newly-elaborated arrangements with those provisions of 1852 not abrogated, and from this condition of things sprang the *Senatûs consultum* of April 20, 1870, which claimed to produce an entirely new Constitution.

The Senate was too well domesticated not to vote unanimously for this measure. The nation was then called upon to pronounce its verdict by virtue of a decree of April 23d. The Society of the Prince Imperial had inundated France with its agents and printed matter, and for the eighth time the farce of the Napoleonic plebiscite repeated itself.

The Legislative Body, without waiting to hear from the most distant localities, which would not have materially changed the result, published, on May 18, 1870, its declaration that the French people, convoked in their polling places, May 8th, had accepted the following plebiscite:

"The French people approve of the liberal reforms made by the Emperor and introduced into the Constitution since 1860, and with the concurrence of the great departments of State, ratify the *Senatûs consultum* of April 20, 1870."

This declaration was received with cries of "*Vive l'Empereur!*"

Napoleon, at last, on May 21, 1870, sanctioned and promulgated the whole instrument, which had been countersigned by Émile Ollivier, as the law of the State.

There is no need of analyzing this fundamental law. However, Persigny has recapitulated its provisions as follows: "The Emperor preserves all his power. In creating the Liberal Empire, he continues the authoritative Empire's powers."

This Constitution can not be classed under the great subdivisions of organic law of other countries and epochs. In the latter days of the Empire it was claimed that it was inclined to be parliamentary. In no true sense, certainly not in the English sense, is this statement correct, for how could a ministry operate under parliamentary rules when there existed above it a potentate endowed with nearly absolute authority? One of the chief features of such a government is that the cabinet or ministry is an executive power itself, and that the figure-head, who nominally rules, has little or no control over the affairs of State. The Constitution of 1852, adopted during the so-called Republic, was substantially continued under the modifications of the Empire. The Constitution of 1870 (as well as that of 1852) was decreed. It is difficult to find an appropriate name for a thing which is the result of a confused mixture of absolutism, popular sovereignty, violence, of breaking of oaths, and the prescribing of others, of *coups d'état*, and of the idea of the incarnation of popular absolute power in one person. "Louis Napoleon has been called," says Lieber, "the incarnation of a great principle. I do not pretend to find a philosophical name for this product. Probably the whole Constitution belongs to the ' Napoleonic ideas,' of which we read so much; or we may call it in future an imperatorial or Cæsarean Constitution."

Napoleon and his following were now advised that "they could look the future in the face without fear." The Empire needed only a fortunate war to perpetuate Bonapartist liberalism, and, seating the dynasty solidly upon thousands of corpses, to impose a salutary terror upon enemies at home and abroad.

The pretext for a conflict, which Prussia was really waiting for, sprang from the arcana of diplomacy. The rulers of France foolishly gave the provocation before any preparation had been made for serious war. The spies simulated patriotic manifestations by provoking the cry "to Berlin!" and maltreating intelligent citizens who begged for peace.

An old man who wished to carry on "*his war*," the rascality of ministers, the unskillfulness and treason of generals, the shame of Sedan and Metz, the tortures of the siege of Paris, and the disgraceful capitulation which followed the infamies of Bordeaux and Versailles, made up the closing scenes of the Second Empire.

VII.

THE THIRD REPUBLIC.

When the disaster of Sedan was known in Paris, September 3d, Jules Favre presented a proposition to the Legislative Body, signed by twenty-seven members, proclaiming Napoleon's forfeiture of his throne and the rights of his dynasty, and confiding the supreme power to a council to be named by the Chamber. The following day Thiers, who had been offered the premiership by the terrified Empress, set forth another proposition supported by forty-eight signatures. This skillful personage, without reciting the forfeiture, demanded that power should be referred to a council, charged to convoke a " Constituent" as soon as circumstances would permit. Palikao had also prepared a project instituting a governmental council of five members, to be nominated by the Legislative Body; he reserved the lieutenant-generalship to himself. The three schemes were referred to a committee, by a vote of urgency.

While the deputies were conspiring together, the Palais Bourbon was invaded by the crowd; the police gave way before the recently formed National Guard; the Regent and her partisans, having lost their presence of mind, did not dare to give orders to the few thousand soldiers who remained in Paris. It was no longer a forfeiture of the throne, but the Republic that the people demanded. The Bonapartists either shared the fright of their mistress or proclaimed themselves Republicans.

The deputies of the Seine now instituted a government. Thiers, holding himself in reserve to participate in the intrigues, which he saw a vast field for, did not wish to compromise himself in the provisional installation. The garrulous and devout General Trochu, whose liberal proclamations had seduced the Parisians, assumed the presidency of the Decemvirate, as military commander. Rochefort, whom Jules Favre would rather have with him than against him, was admitted among the incumbents, to serve as a screen to cover themselves from the view of the people.

Whilst the members of the government were installing themselves at the Hôtel de Ville, where they were soon surrounded by a number of nobodies, forming a hot-bed of future rulers, certain deputies, who had collected around the president of the Chamber, had voted for the Thiers proposition. They delegated Grévy and a few others, with instructions to learn the intentions of the improvised rulers. But these veritable usurpers, who were acting without any right, without having been delegated by any authority, and feeling only the popular pressure, replied that having thus taken possession, they could not resign. The Republic, which had been proclaimed amidst the general enthusiasm, caused the irregularity of the proceeding to be forgotten, and cast a veil over the insufficiency of the legal authority of those who had thus seized upon the direction of affairs.

On September 4, 1870, the following proclamation was issued:

Citizens of Paris!

The Republic is proclaimed.

A Government has been named by acclamation. It is composed of citizens: Emmanuel Arago, Crémieux, Jules Favre, Jules Ferry, Gambetta, Garnier-Pagès, Glais-

Jules Ferry.

Bizoin, Pelletan, Picard, Jules Simon, representatives of Paris.

General Trochu is charged with full military power for the national defense. He is called to the presidency of the Government.

The Government invites all citizens to be calm; the people will not forget that they are in the face of the enemy.

The Government is, above all, a government of national defense.

It is believed by many that if France had properly and legally been directed under the Republic, which had been everywhere proclaimed, she would have come out of the struggle victorious, and ready to redeem her faults, and her many weaknesses, which a harsh experience had made her exhibit. But the ambitious incapables, who had seized upon her in this terrible moment, only continued the mistakes and disorders of the Empire. As soon as the new masters had divided the places and the monarchical offices between themselves and their friends, it was easy to see that there was no change in governmental practices, and that the French people were marching on to disaster.

By virtue of the decrees of September 8th and 15th, this Government, which so badly responded to the title with which it had adorned itself, convoked the electoral colleges for October 16th, in order to nominate a National Constituent Assembly. The elections were to take place according to the departmental system (*scrutin de liste*), in conformity with the law of March 15, 1849; the number of representatives was fixed at 750. Another decree (September 16th) advanced the elections to October 2d; then a fourth decree of the 23d adjourned them indefinitely. Paris was invested by the Germans, or, rather, it was so regarded; for nothing had been done to prevent

the investment that had been declared impossible by the
Prussians themselves. The grand preoccupation of the
" chiefs of power " was not how to save the country, but
the appearances of defeat. Their purpose seemed to be
to suppress everything that seemed " revolutionary." The
foolish hope had been conceived that they must enlist the
good will of Prussia, and to obtain an European intervention that Thiers was about to implore in all the courts of
the great " powers."

After six months of shameful maneuvers and culpable
failure to arm France, the final disaster followed in the
surrender of Paris, which had falsely been called an
armistice. Every kind of fear and baseness then prompted
the sending of an obnoxious mixture of Legitimists, Orléanists, and intriguers to an anti-National Assembly, convoked at Bordeaux, which hastened to nominate Thiers
as " Chief of Executive Power," depending on him to
overthrow the Republic.

In the act of February 17, 1871, making this nomination, the Assembly declared itself the " Depositary of
sovereign authority." It conspired to establish another
form of government, after having charged upon the Republic the responsibility of the ignoble bargain which it
had just concluded with the enemy.

The preliminaries of peace, which ceded Alsace and
Lorraine to Germany, were signed at Versailles, February 23d.

March 1st the Assembly confirmed the fall of Napoleon
and his dynasty, and declared that he was responsible for
the ruin, the invasion, and the dismemberment of France.
After this platonic execution of Bonapartism, it turned
all its furies against the Republic and against the Republican deputies, who, computing all the different shades of
opinion, had risen to 150. It now insolently declared its

intention of re-establishing monarchy, and did not hide its desire to chastise Paris for her excess of patriotism, which had prolonged resistance to the enemy almost beyond hope. At last, more distinctly to mark its hostility to the capital, the Bordeaux Assembly decided to transfer itself to Versailles on March 20th. Many other measures accentuated this declaration of war of the provincial Royalists against the Republicans of Paris.

The Parisians were disarmed, under the pretext that their munitions of war belonged to the Prussians under the treaty; and the position they had assumed was declared to be an insurrection against the will of France. The cry went up to punish the bandits of the war *à outrance*. The armies, which had surrendered like a flock of sheep, were now let loose, by the Germans, upon the city they had not, in point of fact, conquered by war. The *bourgeoisie*, always controlled by their cowardly terrors, thought only of saving their own persons and goods. After two months of horrors, the mournful history of which will never be known, order reigned over the bodies of 50,000 Frenchmen slaughtered in the presence and to the great joy of the enemy. The sword of the officers of the Empire became a law to M. Thiers, and now judged the miserable people who had not been mowed down by the *mitrailleuses*.

The Bonapartist, Royalist, and Clerical vengeance surpassed in infamous ferocity anything that history records. For a month, the soldiers of France enraged themselves against all who were guilty, or even suspected of having wished to defend surrendered France and a betrayed Republic. Blood flowed in the prisons, in the barracks, where, without defense, men exhausted by misery and famine were massacred. Old men, women, children, the wounded and invalids, all furnished the material for the destruction of life. The squares were converted into charnel-houses, the casemates and the ditches of the fortifications received more dead and dying than quick-lime could consume. Assassination had become such a habit with the soldiery that the imperial officers became afraid of the brutes they commanded.

After this butchery came the twenty-six Councils of War, composed of sanguinary idiots, who ordered executions and transportations in mass, by the semblance of judgments rendered "between two absinthes." Never did a nation exhibit less pity toward itself; never was a savage tribe more horribly cruel toward a vanquished horde, than were this rural soldiery, in their treatment of the defenders of the great city.

Arrests and condemnations continued for a long time. For eight years the menace of prosecution was held suspended over the heads of those who escaped indictment during the first months of the occupation of the Versailles Government. It was during these days of carnage that M. Thiers repeated Cavaignac's barbarous words: "Let justice take its course."

On the conclusion of peace with Germany, the ambitions of parties, which had temporarily been mingled in the common hate of the Republic, were more bitterly revived. On June 8, 1871, the Chamber abrogated the laws of 1832 and 1848, which had banished the Bourbons and the Orléanists. The bill which M. Batbie reported blended the older and the younger branch of this family under the name of the "princes of the House of Bourbon." This Assembly wished to weld the two monarchies into one. It was necessary to prepare this event before imposing it upon France.

August 12, 1871, a Conservative by the name of **Rivet** proposed to confer the title of President of the Republic upon Thiers, and to prolong his powers for the duration of the Assembly, or, at least, for three years. This was for the purpose of continuing the Republic until everything was in readiness for a change. The majority accepted the proposition, reserving to itself certain powers. This provisional solution, which is comprised in a preamble and three short articles, and decorated with the name of the Rivet Constitution, was passed by 491 votes against 94, though Louis Blanc, Gambetta, and Pascal Duprat demonstrated in the course of the discussion that the Assembly had no constituent power.

These concessions on the part of the Royalist majority were the result of the impotency caused by the differences that had arisen in their own party. Each branch of it wished to reconstruct an edifice of its own liking upon the ruins of the nation. The Clericals and the Legitimists aspired to elevate the Bourbon throne again. The rich and cunning Orléanists relied upon the old compeer of Louis Philippe. At one time it was believed that monarchy would be restored by a co-operation of the two branches of the House of Bourbon.

But the Monarchists were soon incensed by seeing their efforts remain sterile in the presence of the inertness of their "little executive." They found that he imposed himself too much on the Chamber, by talking like a deputy in the important deliberations. Things were made worse, when, November 13, 1872, a presidential message was received telling them that the Republic was the legal government, *the only one possible*, and inviting the members to organize it promptly. A majority of 407 to 225 votes replied to him, upon a report of the Duke of Broglie, by an act which limited the President's right of speech. But it was not yet possible to do without him, and he was compensated for this loss

of influence by a grant of a certain suspensive vote.
The majority then promised to occupy itself, in the future,
with the organization of which the government had submitted the outline. The act upon the attributes of public power and upon ministerial responsibility bears
date March 13, 1873, and provides that the Chamber
shall not separate until it has passed laws upon the
organization and the mode of transmission of legislative
and executive power; upon the creation and specification
of the attributes of a second Chamber, and upon the
electoral law.

Thiers soon presented his proposition on these questions. He was then accused, by the majority, of
insensibly conducting it into the hands of the Radical
party. M. de Rémusat's defeat in the partial election
of the Seine (April 27, 1873), appeared to be a striking
proof of the growth of radicalism. After the return
from the Easter vacation, there was an interpellation
from the "Right," and a vote of a want of confidence
against the presidential policy, was carried by 360 to
344.

His egotism being attacked by the ungrateful vote of
May 24, 1873, Thiers offered his resignation, calculating
that it would not be accepted, and that the repentant
Monarchists would return to his support. But all precaution had been taken. The same evening MacMahon
was nominated in his stead.

The monarchical restoration was then very near being
fulfilled, by reason of certain measures taken by the
Count of Paris at Frohsdorf, August 5th. But the stubbornness of the Count of Chambord, who wished to preserve his white flag, baffled these projects and destroyed
the compact which had been tacitly entered into at Bordeaux. The necessity of preparing a Constitution, or

rather something which would pass for one, seemed impending. The Provisional Government could not always last.

On November 9th Changarnier, who had presided over the Royalist conspiracies in the hope of obtaining the marshal's baton, the object of his dreams, demanded the nomination of a commission of thirty members to examine the two constitutional laws prepared under Thiers. Although M. Grévy maintained that the Assembly had no constituent power, it persisted in investing itself with all authority and fixing the term of the MacMahon presidency at seven years. The Monarchists relied upon their "loyal soldier" to favor their designs, and to find, in the lapse of time, an occasion to cede his office to some monarch. The law confiding the executive power for seven years to Marshal MacMahon, Duke of Magenta, was passed November 20, 1873.

The Commission of thirty occupied itself at first with two propositions upon the public powers, and the elections, presented by Thiers before his fall, then with the new project upon powers brought forth May 15, 1874, in the name of the Government, by the Duke of Broglie. Casimir Périer's motion, demanding the proclamation of the Republic, as a settled and definite government, was rejected, July 23d, by 374 against 333 votes, and the session terminated without seriously entering into the discussion of the subject.

January 21, 1875, the debates opened upon the Ventavon bill, called the organization and transmission of executive power. This project established two Chambers, and gave to the Marshal, without conditions, the right to dissolve the Chamber of Deputies, and ascribed exclusively to him, during the entire term of seven years, the authority to institute revision. On the expiration of his powers, or in the event of premature adjournment, the two Assemblies were to meet in a congress to enact measures necessary to be taken. The personal Septenate was a special government, which did not provide so much for the future as it left to everyone the indulgence of his own aspirations. It acted as an institutional barrier, erected in the interests of the Royalists, and its wrongs were soon to be seen. M. Laboulaye begged his colleagues in vain; he conjured them to have pity on France, and to content themselves with a constitutional monarchy under the name of a Republic; as there was not a suitable king to offer, the amendment of the "Left Center," which he supported, declaring the Republican form, was defeated on the 29th, by 359 to 336 votes.

But on the following day, January 30th, by a sudden change which presents a just estimate of this ridiculous Assembly, it adopted, by 353 to 352 votes, M. Wallon's (Right Center) amendment, which added to the proposition of a commission a paragraph enacting: "The President of the Republic is elected for seven years, by a plurality of votes, by the Senate and the Chamber of Deputies, meeting in a National Assembly."

This act incidentally recognized the Republic, without proclaiming it, as M. Wallon said, simply to take what existed, "as nothing better could be found as a substitute for it. Make," said he, "a government which has the power to transform itself not at a particular date (1880 had been proposed), but when the exigencies of the country shall demand the change."

The Republic, with a single vote in reserve, was pitifully admitted, by an absolutely strict majority. This lucky vote, which the Royalists had previously declared sufficient to establish royalty, turned itself against them. Cast in the midst of dissensions and interminable

Count de Paris.

negations, they appeared so astonished that the situation was accepted as a revelation. After several attempts at resistance on the part of the Commissioners, the rest inclined to the Republican side. The "Right Center," placing in the scales its fear of the Empire and its hostility to "*le linge blanc*," passed over in a body to the "Wallonnat."

The two laws organizing the public powers were passed February 24 and 25, 1875, one by 425 to 254 votes, and the other by 435 to 234 votes. The Republic found itself accepted as a dilatory measure; a kind of interlude in which everyone had tried to profit by the ruin of his adversary. These two constitutional laws, which were completed by a third, regulating the relations of the powers that had been instituted by the two first, were to the Royalists only a net so arranged that the Republic would sooner or later be entangled in its meshes. As to the Republicans, satisfied as to the acknowledgment of its name, they now sought to establish the thing. Mental restrictions and impotency pervaded this last-shift compact in all its parts.

This Chamber, usurper of the constitutional power, which the majority had created for the purpose of restoring monarchy, died in giving birth to this fœtus of a Republic. After this work, well worthy of its origin, it had only to disappear. Its false Constitution, condemned from its birth, has since crept along through ambiguities, uncertainties, pullings and haulings, the intrigues of cliques, the apathetic indifference of the masses, and the illusions of certain honest minds, habituated by a superficial education to skim ideas, and to attach themselves to names, to pretense, and to momentary satisfaction.

The first of the constitutional laws, dated February 24, 1875, refers to the organization of the Senate. It provides that this body shall be composed of 300 members, 225 of whom shall be elected by the departments and the colonies, and seventy-five by the National Assembly. Each senator shall be a Frenchman, of at least forty years of age, and enjoying all his civil and political rights. The senators of the departments and colonies are elected by a majority vote, on a general ticket (*scrutin de liste*), by an electoral college composed of: 1st, the deputies of the department in which the election is held; 2d, the councilors-general (*des conseillers généreaux*); 3d, district councilors (*des conseillers d'arrondissement*); 4th, delegates, one for each commune, elected by the municipal councils, by the communal electors.

The senators elected by the Assembly are unremovable. The Senate has concurrent right with the Chamber of Deputies to initiate and pass laws.

The second of the constitutional laws, dated February 25, 1875, refers to the organization of the public powers, and the third, dated July 16, 1875, defines the relations of the public powers.

The legislative power is exercised by the two Assemblies. The deputies are elected by universal suffrage, in manner to be prescribed by law.

The President is elected by a majority vote of the Senate and the Chamber of Deputies, sitting as a National Assembly. He is elected for seven years, and is re-eligible. He has concurrent power with the Chambers to initiate laws; he promulgates and executes the laws that are passed. He has the right to pardon, but amnesty is accorded only by law. He disposes of the armed forces. He nominates all the civil and military employees and officers. Envoys and ambassadors are accredited to him. Each act of the President shall be countersigned by a minister. The President may, with the consent of the Senate, dissolve the Chamber of Deputies before the expiration of its legal term; in which case an election shall take place within three months. The President pronounces the closing of the session; he has the right to convene extraordinary sessions of the Chambers, and he must convoke both Houses on the request of a majority of each Chamber. The President can adjourn the Chambers for a term not longer than one month; he negotiates and ratifies treaties, and informs the Chambers of them, as soon as in his judgment the interest and the safety of the State will permit. But treaties of peace, of commerce, and those which involve the finances of the State, and rights of public and private property shall, to be operative, be voted by the two Chambers. The President of the Republic can not declare war except by the previous consent of the Chambers. He can only be impeached by the Chamber of Deputies, and only judged by the Senate. The ministers can be impeached for crimes committed in the exercise of their duties, and in this case they are judged by the Senate. The President can, by a decree made in the Council of Ministers, constitute the Senate as a court of justice to try any person charged with an act committed against the safety of the State.

The authors of these constitutional laws, which make up what is known as the Constitution of 1875, and organize a lame system of parliamentarism, claimed that they had set on foot a representative *régime*.

The improprieties and contradictions with which the instrument is filled have been described by the press and by orators of every shade of political belief. It is notorious that this irregular organization was instituted for the destruction of democracy. A restricted suffrage is made the ruler of the Republic, by submitting universal suffrage to the caprices of privileged intermediaries, who exercise their powers through various processes. More extended attributes and duration are given to the Chamber which only represents an arbitrarily chosen minority than to the Chamber which is the result of the direct vote of the nation. In the first place an upper Chamber is instituted, and whose decisions the lower Chamber is bound to follow, under penalty of being dissolved, or creating a conflict by putting the country in danger. Difficulties are multiplied in every way to prevent the people from exercising a surveillance over the representatives they have elected. It is impossible to hold the intermediary electors to any responsibility. Every agreement made by them with the electors is absolutely void in law.

In addition, these laws, which took great care to order public prayers, and to establish the capital of France in the city where the German Empire had just been formed, have omitted to touch upon a great number of essentially constitutional points. The result is that all dispositions of previous constitutions can be made to pass through these intended gaps, provided they are not manifestly in conflict with the clauses enacted by the legislators of 1875.

Only to cite a single example, the President of the quasi-Republic has the right to dispose of the armed forces. It does not say that he can, or not, command them in person.

The present instrument does not in any terms interdict him, and as—by virtue of the anterior Constitution, that of 1852, modified in 1870—the chief of State commanded the land and sea forces, the President could now make use of this right by arguing, by force of legal construction, that the precedent provisions are continued when not formally abrogated by the new text. A President *Im-*

perator is thus provided for, that is to say, an empire, in fact, is created.

This Assembly also re-enacted the system of district in the place of department voting. By this "*uninominal* vote" the political power was thus very largely placed in the hands of the "illustrious men" of the canton and the village "notables," who were generally rich enough to spend 20,000 or 30,000 francs, and sometimes more, for their election, with a hope of reimbursing themselves from the tax-payers. Those who had done everything they could to strip the nation of its constituent power, now wished to bequeath the fruit of their robbery to their progeny.

Article 8 of the law of February 25th clothed the two Chambers with this power, exactly as if the people had no existence whatever. It provides as follows: The Chambers shall have the right, by separate deliberations taken in each body by a majority vote, either on its own motion or that of the President of the Republic, to declare that a constitutional revision shall take place. After each of the two Chambers shall have passed this resolution, they shall unite in a National Assembly and proceed to the revision. The revision of the constitutional laws shall be passed by a majority vote of the members of the National Assembly. During the continuance of the power conferred by the law of November 20, 1873, upon Marshal MacMahon, this revision can only take place on the proposition of the President of the Republic.

In this way, on any day, by a well-conducted conspiracy, the Republic could be converted into a monarchy, by the simple substitution in a few articles of the word "Emperor," or the word "King," for the title of "President." And this was the dream of very many of those then in power.

The constitutional laws did not provide for the details of the election of senators and deputies. These were provided for by laws passed August 2 and November 30, 1875. These "organic" laws, as they were called, completed the structure called the Constitution of 1875. There never was any pretense made to submit it to the people, but it was claimed that there had been a tacit ratification of it by the elections that had taken place since its formation.

At last many deputies and ministers became disgusted with their enforced sojourn at Versailles, and, tired of the incessant journeys from the real to the fictitious capital, determined to modify Article 9 of the law of February 25, 1875. The proposition met with the violent opposition of the "Center" and the terrors of the Senate (March, 1879). The resistance lasted three months. However, on June 18th the two Chambers voted that the seat of the executive power should henceforth be located in Paris, and that the Senate and Chamber of Deputies repair to that city on November 3, 1879. But it was provided that in the event of action being taken in conformity with Articles 7 and 8 of the law of February 25, 1875, relative to the organization and amendment of the public powers, that the joint session forming the National Assembly should be held at Versailles in the hall then occupied by the Chamber of Deputies.

This removal did not remedy any of the original defects of the pretended Constitution of 1875. Royalists, Bonapartists, and Republicans conspired against each other in the pursuit of their cunning and low combinations. In the meantime, the public was agitated by a revival of socialism; labor recommenced its enraged struggle against capital; and anti-religious sentiments, advocated by the free-thought clubs, signaled the approaching reawakening of all shades of political opinion.

M. Lenglé now proposed in the Chamber to revise the Constitution, and demanded:

1st. The responsibility of the President of the Republic, and an obligation upon him to choose his ministers outside of the two Chambers.

2d. The election of the Senate by universal suffrage, and the erection of this body into an assembly no longer having legislative power, but charged with the nomination of magistrates.

3d. The right of the Chambers freely to fix the time and duration of their sessions, and to name their committees as they shall desire.

4th. The ratification of the constitutional laws by the people, by a vote that shall signify "yes" or "no."

These apparent concessions to the republican idea simply tended toward an indirect restoration of Bonapartism, in the interest of the Prince Napoleon. Several journals commenced, at this time, a revision campaign, in the sense of a ratification of a reformed Constitution, by representatives elected by universal suffrage, and specially instructed to this effect.

M. Barodet, and sixty-four of his colleagues, formulated a revision, having for its object the suppression of the right of dissolution; equality of legislative rights between the two Chambers; modification of the electoral law of the Senate, and the election of a Constituent Assembly. A special provision demanded that the electoral law of the deputies should be made a part of the Constitution; the object was to put a stop to the debate that was about to open upon the re-establishment of department voting. This proposition was defeated in the month of May, on the motion of M. Cazot, Keeper of the Seals, and M. Ferry, President of the Council of Ministers. In the meantime, Bardoux's project caused discussion for and against the return to department voting (*scrutin de liste par département*) in the legislative elections. Parliamentary groups, and the ministry itself, were largely divided on this question. Most of the Monarchists saw in the system of district voting (*scrutin d'arrondissement*) a guarantee for the success of conservative ideas and maneuvers, while others among them hoped that the *scrutin de liste* would lead to the destruction of the Republic. Certain Republicans, misconceiving the democratic traditions, rested themselves upon the following specious argument: That the close connection that should always exist between the electors and the elected could only be made possible by "*le petit scrutin*," and they maintained that the vote by districts had strengthened the Republic, by sending 363 members to the Chamber.

These diverse opinions, into which entered more of calculation than conviction, led to the production of a curious compromise, demanding the maintenance of *uninominal* voting in 236 districts having only one deputy, and the establishment of the *scrutin de listes* by departments in the others. This obstructing combination gave satisfaction to no one, and was defeated by the Commission.

After an eloquent address by Gambetta, in the month of May, 1881, in which he spoke against the system of official candidature, the Chamber adopted the re-establishment of the *scrutin de liste* by department, at the rate of one deputy for every 70,000 inhabitants. But the assent of the Senate was necessary. By 148 to 114 votes the senators refused, May 9, 1881, to pass the law which had been adopted by the deputies.

The elections of August 21st were a triumph of Gambetta's mild program, but were, at the same time, a per-

Leon Gambetta

sonal check to him in the second circumscription of Belleville. The new Chamber was largely Opportunist (Union Republicans, "Left Centers," and "Left" Republicans, making in all 411 deputies out of a membership of 557).

The fall of the Ferry ministry, November 10, 1881, caused by the Tunis affair, brought the Gambetta cabinet, which was, in the opinion of the Republicans, a complete dissolution. The declaration of November 15th, by which the new ministry indicated its policy, was so vague, that it was an easy matter to predict its overthrow in the near future.

Gambetta was defeated January 26, 1882, upon the question of the *scrutin de liste*, by a majority which feared that they would be sent home before the expiration of their terms. The Chamber had three other ministries in a year.

The revision was again advocated on the reformation of the Ferry ministry, February, 1883; but the Chamber refused to take into consideration the propositions formulated by Barodet and Andrieux. The adjournment of this question caused the formation of the Revision League, by means of which the deputies of the extreme "Left" sought to organize a vast agitation in the country against the Constitution of 1875. Conducted without energy, with an object governmental and ministerial, rather than democratic, this attempt, which should have produced the best results, was nearly deprived of its just fruits. The men who were at the head of the Central Committee soon found that the departmental committee of the Seine wished to take a too advanced position in social and political affairs. A disavowal of the objects of the extreme "Left" followed, and the *statu quo* was recommended as the surest means of making a healthy advance.

A project of *partial* revision, presented May, 1883, by the government, as against an *integral* revision, was not brought forward again until a year afterward, June 9, 1884, by M. Ferdinand Dreyfus. The initiator of this measure opposed all radical amendment, and concluded to revise only: paragraph 2 of Article 5, of the law of February 25, 1875; Article 8 of the same law; Articles 1 to 7 of the law of February 24th; Article 8; and paragraph 3, Article 1, of the law of July 10, 1875.

The Senate decided that this was too great a revision for a single time; it reduced the proposition. Deputies and ministers accepted with resignation the reduction of the proposition they had voted.

The two Chambers, united in National Assembly at Versailles, August 4, 1884, showed, by the violent disorder of their debates, the wrong that this pretended Constitution had done to the country. Opposition was made to all liberal propositions; each favorable amendment for a convocation of a constituent assembly was rejected, and finally a bill was presented by an entirely official commission (named in committee by *scrutin de liste*, without previous discussion, upon lists furnished in advance by members of the majority); such was the "Congress," which brought forward the following paltry law, enacting a revision of the constitutional laws, August 14, 1884.

ARTICLE 1. Paragraph 2 of Article 5 of the constitutional law of February 25th, relative to the organization of the public powers, is modified as follows:

In this case [anticipated dissolution of the Chamber] the electoral colleges shall be called together for the new election after a delay of two months, and the Chamber shall meet ten days after the vote is declared [in place of a delay of three months for the convocation of the electors].

Art. 2. Paragraph 3 of Article 8, of the same law, is completed as follows:
The republican form of the government can now be made a subject of revision.
The members of the families who have reigned over France are ineligible to the presidency of the Republic. [The only amendment which escaped the previous question, because it was not opposed by the ministry].

Art. 3. The Articles 1 to 7 of the constitutional law of February 24, 1875, relative to the organization of the Senate, shall not have a constitutional character.

This law was modified on December 9, 1884. The amendment provides that as the vacancies occur among the senators elected by the National Assembly they shall be filled by senators elected for the term of nine years. These seats have thus been distributed among the different departments—proportionately to population. The senators consist of three classes; one retiring every three years. They are elected indirectly, as has already been described.

Art. 4. Paragraph 3 of Article 1 of the constitutional law of July 16, 1875, upon the relations of the public powers is abrogated [Suppression of public prayers on the opening of the Chambers].

This pitiful miscarriage only surprised the senators and deputies who had entertained the vain hope of obtaining a more important result. If the politicians who prided themselves on their advocacy of advanced principles had had the true political sense, they would forthwith have comprehended that it was first necessary to defeat before the people the many servants of monarchy who were serving in the deliberative assemblies before a democracy could be founded.

The Departmental League for the Seine, for the revision of the Constitution, issued the following manifesto on September 6, 1884, addressed to the French democracy.

Citizens:

We submit to a pretended Constitution, which is essentially monarchical, but under republican forms.

From this pitiable comedy, which has just been played at Versailles, has come the pretended revision made by an Orléanist majority.

The Constitution and revision have been voted by men who did not have the right either to create the instrument nor to revise it.

Both acts are flagrant usurpations of the national sovereignty.

Republican France will only have a Constitution when the rights of the people shall be placed above such injuries, when the depositaries of power shall be relegated to their *rôle* of simple trustees, when neither ministers nor representatives shall believe themselves to be the masters of the nation; in a word, when single, undoubted, and incontestable sovereignty shall be recognized. The people should freely express its will by means of universal suffrage. Beyond that, the Republic becomes a mere shadow, the Constitution a fiction, and revision a parody.

We wish a true and complete revision. We demand a democratic Constitution, prepared by a constituent assembly, specially elected by universal suffrage, with formal power to introduce radical, as well as social and political reforms into our institutions, which can alone found a republic, assure its existence, and guaranty its progress.

The Constitution shall be submitted to the sanction of the people.

Behold, citizens, the revision we demand, and which we invite you to demand with us, until we shall obtain by legal ways, if that may be possible, otherwise by all legitimate means which a people that wishes to be free can command.

It need scarcely be remarked that this radical programme met with no extended response, in fact, the members of the central committee of the League still had hopes of bringing such an influence to bear upon the "Congress" that other important reforms might be accomplished— such as the election of the Senate by universal suffrage, and the creation of a republican Constitution by a constitutent assembly. The Assembly at Versailles continued, to the end of the session, its defiance of the spirit of the Revolution, and the traditions of the Republican party.

On June 8, 1885, the law re-establishing the *scrutin de liste* was enacted. The Chamber of Deputies had given this measure a large majority, and the Senate was compelled to give its assent, after attacking an amendment which reduced the representation in several large cities by deducting the foreign population from the basis of representation, and, in effect, cutting down the number of deputies in these localities.

But the rapid rise of Boulangism has demonstrated that the Republicans misjudged the effect of department elections, and in February of this year (1889) the ministry introduced a bill for the restoration of the system of district voting adopted in 1875, which measure shortly afterward became the law of the land.

The constitutional laws upon which the present government rests, are, upon their face, largely monarchical, but, in their practical working, there are many considerations that are suggestive of the future destiny of France.

VIII.

CONCLUSION.

France has, at all times, in greater or less degree, acknowledged that just government rests on communal institutions. Particularly is this true since she has had constitutional forms. The principle established is that the citizen first owes his duty to the State, which manifests itself in the crystallization of the thought of the indivisibility of sovereignty; and secondly, that he owes his duty to his neighbors, to succor and provide for the poor and helpless, to educate children, to establish lunatic asylums and hospitals; and negatively considered, to do nothing that shall be an injury or nuisance to others. The practical idea of the Revolution is that the national spirit being once so aroused as to form a central constitutional government with unlimited power, that such a government naturally proceeds, in the interests of freedom, to give back to the people, from whom its power proceeds, a system of local administration. The process of evolution may have been that the local governments being first formed, and they, at last, perceiving that there could be no protection to them, no real liberty with freedom, except by the formation of an absolute central government above all other political forms, proceeded to formulate the nation; and that the nation, becoming absolute in unity and power, and inspired with magnanimity and with a spirit of justice, extends a protection to and requires a support from the entities which go to make up the whole body-politic, and reconveys to them so much of autonomy as seems expedient.

France, for the purposes of local government is divided into eighty-seven departments, and subdivided into 362 arrondissements, 2,865 cantons, and about 36,000 communes.

The government of the department is conducted by a prefect and a general council, the former having the executive power, while the latter exercises deliberative functions. The prefect is appointed by the President of the Republic; he has power to issue local decrees; he appoints and dismisses a large number of agents who are directly responsible to him; he controls the police in the maintenance of public order, and for this purpose can call on the military forces for assistance; he superintends the collection of taxes; he transmits the instructions of the ministers to all subordinate functionaries; in fine, he is the general representative of the central government in all affairs of local administration. The general council, which is elected by universal suffrage—the councilors being elected for six years, one-half retiring every three—and the council of prefecture, which is nominated by the executive power, and assists the prefect in the performance of his duty. The council of prefecture gives its opinion on all legal questions, and advises the prefect when requested to do so. The general council assesses the taxes, authorizes the purchase, sale, or exchange of departmental property, superintends the management of the same, controls the construction of departmental roads, railways and canals, bridges and ferries, and is responsible for their repair; votes the budget for sanitary and charitable institutions belonging to the department. Lunatic asylums, the maintenance of poor children and the poor-houses, are all within its jurisdiction. The departmental budget is published annually; it includes the ordinary and extraordinary receipts, such as special taxes and loans. Although political questions of general interest are strictly excluded, still a recent law invested these councils with great political importance in the event the national legislature is violently dissolved by a *coup d'état*, by conferring upon them the duty immediately to assemble and elect new delegates.

The arrondissement is presided over by a sub-prefect, who is appointed by the executive power, and the elective council, to which each canton sends one member, which body examines the assessment made on the arrondissement by the general council, and contests it if it thinks fit. It further fixes what proportion of the assessment is to be paid by each commune.

The commune is the administrative unit in France. It is a corporate body. It is presided over by a mayor and his deputies, who are chosen by the municipal councils. The mayor has a double part to perform, as he represents both the government and the commune. His duties are, therefore, difficult and complicated. The mayor is an unpaid officer and the prefect has the power to suspend him. He is registrar of births, deaths, and marriages. He appoints the communal officials and is empowered to make by-laws on such subjects as the abatement of nuisances and other matters relating to public health, the sale of provisions, the regulation of street traffic, the preservation of order in public places, and the control of theatres. The communal budget is presented by the mayor and voted by the municipal council. The members of the municipal council are elected for three years. The duties of that body consist in assisting and to some extent controlling the mayor, and in the management of communal affairs and property. Among the functions allotted to the commune are the making and repair of communal roads, the inclosure and maintenance of burial-grounds, and the provision of moneys for the local police, elementary education, and the care of foundling children. The communes vary in size, but the only difference in constitution between a small and a large commune consists in the number of members in the municipal council. This number varies from ten to thirty-six, according to population.

The cantons serve chiefly as mere political divisions, but each one has a commissary of police, who exercises complex duties, being at the same time a governmental, judicial, and municipal officer. Paris and Lyons have exceptional administrations.

Judicial proceedings are classed under civil, commercial, and criminal jurisdictions; there are also special departments, such as military and maritime tribunals, councils of discipline, *cours des comptes,* and the court of justice of the Senate.

In civil matters every canton has a *juge de paix,* whose decision is final when the amount in dispute does not exceed 100 francs; up to 200 francs he can only give judgment subject to appeal. His principal business is, however, one of conciliation, and no suit can be brought before the tribunal of the first instance until he has endeavored, without success, to bring the parties to an amicable settlement.

A tribunal of first instance, or primary court, is established in every arrondissement. Its decision may be appealed against for a sum above 1,500 francs. The *cours d'appel* hear the appeals. Tribunals of commerce are organized to decide questions arising out of business transactions. They are instituted in all the more important

commercial towns, and consist of judges chosen from
among the leading merchants, and elected by their
fellows.

The criminal courts are of three kinds: The justice of
the peace courts in each canton, which have cognizance
of small offenses. When they are of a more serious character, which the French laws call *délits*, they are judged
by a special section of the tribunals of first instance, bearing the name of correctional tribunal. This tribunal can
be appealed to from judgments pronounced by tribunals
of police, but its judgments are also subject to the revision
of the *cours d'appel*. Offenses which rank as crimes are
heard by the *cour d'assises*, consisting of three magistrates
and twelve jurors. The jury decides the facts, leaving
the application of the law to the judges. Above the
various courts, the court of *cassation* is supreme It is
held in Paris, and is composed of three chambers—the
chambre des requêtes, the *chambre civile*, and the *chambre
criminelle*. Its province is to decide all appeals from the
other courts, to investigate, not the facts, but the law, in
order to grant a new trial, if need be.

There are also special jurisdictions, such as the military
tribunals, councils of war, the maritime tribunals, and the
councils of discipline for lawyers and professional corporations. There are also the *cours des comptes*, which control the accounts of the government officials.

The Senate can be formed into a court of justice by
a decree of the President of the Republic, decided upon
in a council of ministers, to judge any person charged
with an attempt (*attentat*) committed against the safety
of the State.

One of the most difficult subjects for an American or
an Englishman to comprehend is that system of rules,
regulations, and laws which obtains in France and is

known as the *droit administratif*. The words "administrative laws," which are well understood in one form or another in most Continental States as well in France, are unknown to American and English judges.

Even a publicist of the ability of De Tocqueville, during his visit to the United States in 1831, was surprised at the absence of anything answering to the administrative laws in the United States, and, strange as it may appear, while he was investigating this question, serious doubts occurred in his mind as to the general ideas (*notions générals*) which govern this system in his own country. In any event, he, at that time, wrote to M. de Blosseville, a French judge, asking an authoritative explanation of this law.

The *droit administratif* is defined by the French authorities as consisting of "the body of rules which regulate the relations of the administration, or of the administrative authority, toward private citizens." "Administrative law determines," says Aucoc, in his work on *droit administratif*, "the constitution and the relations of those organs of society which are charged with the care of those social interests which are the object of public administration, by which term are meant the different representatives of society, among which the State is the most important, and the relation of the administrative authorities toward the citizens of the State.

"So far, however, as an Englishman may venture," says Dicey, "to deduce the meaning of *droit administratif* from foreign treatises and reports, it may (at any rate, for our present purpose) be best described as that portion of French law which determines: (i) The position and liabilities of all State officials, and (ii) the civil rights and liabilities of private individuals in their dealings with officials as representatives of the State, and (iii) the

procedure by which these rights and liabilities are
enforced. The effect of this description is most easily
made intelligible to English students by giving examples
of the sort of matters to which the rules of administrative
law apply. If a minister, a prefect, a policeman, or any
other official commits acts in excess of his legal authority
(*excès de pouvoirs*), as, for example, if a police officer in
pursuance of orders, say from the Minister of the
Interior, wrongfully arrest a private person, the rights of
the individual aggrieved and the mode in which these
rights are to be determined are questions of administrative law. If, again, a contractor enter into a contract
with any branch of the administration, e. g., for the supply
of goods to the government, or for the purchase of
stores sold off by a public officer, and a dispute arises as
to whether the contract has been duly performed, or as
to the damages due to the contractor for a breach of it
by the government, the rights of the contracting parties
are to be determined in accordance with the rules of
administrative law, and to be enforced (if at all) by the
methods of procedure which that law provides. All
dealings, in short, in which the rights of an individual in
reference to the State or officials representing the State
come in question, fall within the scope of administrative
law."

In his work on "The Law of the Constitution," Mr.
Dicey makes a careful examination of this subject.
In the following statement his language is substantially employed. Every servant of the government possesses, as representative of the nation, a whole body
of special rights, privileges, or prerogatives as against
private citizens, and the extent of these rights, privileges,
or prerogatives is to be determined on principles different
from the considerations which fix the legal rights and

duties of one citizen toward another. An individual in his dealings with the State does not, according to French ideas, stand on anything like the same footing on which he stands in dealing with his neighbors.

A, for example, enters into a contract with N, an official acting on behalf of some department of the government. N, or in fact the department, breaks the contract. A has a right to claim from the government, not, as in the case of an action against a private citizen, damages equivalent to the gain which he would have made if the contract had been kept, but only damages equivalent to the loss (if any) which A may have actually suffered by the breach of the contract. In other words, the State, when it breaks a contract, ought, according to French ideas, to suffer less than a private person. In the example here given, which is one among many, the essential character of the *droit administratif* becomes apparent—it is a body of law intended to preserve the privileges of the State.

The second general idea of this peculiar system is that of the so-called separation of powers (*separation des pouvoirs*), in other words, of preventing the government, the legislature, and the courts from encroaching upon one another's province. This expression is entirely different from what is known in the United States and England as "the independence of the judges," or similar expressions. It means, as interpreted by French history, legislation, and decisions, that the ordinary judges ought to be irremovable, and independent of the executive of the government; and its officials ought, while acting officially, to be independent of, and to a great extent free from the jurisdiction of the ordinary courts.

This theory of the separation of powers seems to rest upon the misconceptions of Montesquieu as set forth in his work on the "Esprit des Lois." Whatever may be the evolution of these laws and decisions, the teachings of these writings underlie the institutions of the French Republic. It must be borne in mind that the maxims of administrative law are not reduced to a code, but rest largely on what is known in the United States and England as "case" law, and, therefore, possess the element of expansiveness, which, whether it be counted as a merit or a defect, is inherent in this kind of law.

Questions of right between private citizens and all accusations of crime fall within the jurisdictions of the civil tribunals, or of the common law courts. But ordinary courts are unable to pronounce judgment on any administrative act; that is, any act done by any official, high or low, in his official character. The judges can not pass upon the validity of the decrees issued by the President of the Republic, as for example, the decrees with reference to "unauthorized congregations;" the judges can not determine the meaning or legal effect of official documents, as for example, of a letter addressed by a minister of State to a subordinate, or by a general to a person under his command; the judges have no jurisdiction as to questions arising on a contract made between a private person and a department of the government; they have no right to entertain an action brought by a private individual against an official for a wrong done in the discharge of his official duty.

A person who is wronged by an official can not claim redress from the ordinary judges, but he has a remedy from the proper official authorities called the "*tribunaux administratifs.*"

"For the third salient feature of French *droit administratif*," continues Dicey, "is that it is administered by administrative courts, at the head of which stands the

Council of State. These so-called 'courts' have, of comparatively recent times, acquired, to a certain extent, a quasi-judicial character, and have adopted a quasi-judicial procedure. We must take care, however, not to be deceived by names. The administrative authorities which decide all disputes in regard to matters of administrative law (*contentieux administratif*) may be called 'tribunals,' and may adopt forms moulded on the procedure of a court, but they all of them, from the council of the prefect (*conseil de préfecture*) up to the Council of State, bear the more or less definite impress of an official or governmental character; they are composed of official persons, and as is implied by the very pleas advanced in defense of withdrawing questions of administrative law from the civil courts, look upon the disputes brought before them from a governmental point of view, and decide them in a spirit different from the feeling which influences the ordinary judges. * * * * The separation of judicial and administrative powers, combined with the co-existence of 'ordinary' courts and 'administrative' courts, results, of necessity, in conflicts of jurisdiction. * * * * There exists in France a *Tribunal des Conflits*, or court for deciding conflicts of jurisdiction. The special function of this body is to determine finally whether a given case, say an action against a policeman for an assault, comes within the jurisdiction of the civil courts, or of the administrative courts. On this matter of jurisdiction, judges and officials are certain to form different opinions; a glance, moreover, at the head 'Compétence Administratif,' in the 'Recueil Periodique de Jurisprudence,' by Dalloz, shows at once the constant occurrence of cases which make it necessary to fix the limits which divide the spheres of the judicial and the administrative authorities. The true nature, therefore, of administrative law, depends, in France, upon the constitution of the *Tribunal des Conflits.*"

The Constitution of 1875 has been commented on. It remains to notice its practical working, and to inquire how far important modifications of it have been accomplished by the demand for a more democratic interpretation of the organic forms; how far its monarchical provisions are held in abeyance, or actually perverted from the original intent.

The ministry, whom the law provides shall be named by the President, are, in point of fact, elected by the majority of the Chamber of Deputies; on the face of the Constitution the ministry are responsible to both Chambers; practically, a hostile vote of the upper Chamber does not overthrow the government, while a vote of a want of confidence of the lower Chamber compels the ministry to resign. A new one is then named by the Chamber of Deputies, through the President, who has not, since the administration of MacMahon, dissolved the Chamber, with the consent of the Senate, as he had a right to do. Thus the President has become, in one sense, a premier at the head of a removable executive council. The appeal to the people has, practically, been lost, and the chief feature of the English parliamentary procedure suppressed. Want of power in the ministry to conduct governmental affairs, and to dissolve the Chamber of Deputies, has subjected them to numerous changes, and made them dependent on the will of the existing deputies. If greater power resided in the ministry, the members of the lower Chamber would hesitate to bring about so many ministerial crises, and thus jeopard their chances of re-election before the people; and naturally greater stability would prevail. If parliamentary forms are to be continued, why should they not be

Sadi Carnot.

enforced according to the well-known principles which
obtain in England?—for it is in that country that this system exists in its perfection. So far as the Chamber of
Deputies assumes power over a Senate and a President
selected by a restricted electoral vote, it is a step in the
direction of the authority of the people and of democracy,
but why should this branch of the legislature exercise all
power and suppress the right of the ministry (if parliamentary forms prevail) to dissolve the popular branch,
with a view to procure a new interpretation of the will of
the masses?

A strange anomaly occurred in the latter part of President MacMahon's administration. Although the Chamber of Deputies had been hedged around by an aristocratic
Senate and a President endowed with extraordinary authority, it had gradually been gaining power. Under the
leadership of Gambetta this Chamber had become assertive
and aggressive. In 1877 the soldier President had, with the
co-operation of a complacent Senate, dissolved the Chamber of Deputies. A new election was held, and when the
electors assembled it was found that they constituted a still
more active opposition to the two privileged departments
of the government. The conflict between these discordant
elements reasserted itself. The President was charged
with interfering with the recent elections. The deputies
condemned him, and although his term of office was still
unexpired, Gambetta, speaking for the popular branch of
the government, told him he must submit or resign.
MacMahon then (1879) voluntarily gave up power.

The Republican *régime* in France has thus developed
the power of the Chamber, and, also, as has been shown,
encroached upon the rules that generally govern the
proper working of a ministry. The facility, however, with
which presidential elections are conducted in France

seems almost incredible to Americans. President Grévy, long considered an almost necessary man in the Élysée, resigned one day and was replaced the next, and in this way, after an hour's session of the National Assembly, the chief executive office was filled. No extraordinary stress of popular excitement, nor menace of revolution, accompanied the act. It must be remembered, too, that Grévy was forced to resign by the Chamber of Deputies. The members of his family, if not himself, were under the suspicion of wrongful practices. This resignation was almost a confession. Still, he yielded to the demand that was made upon him.

Americans who criticise France on account of her unstable government may well reflect when they recall the turmoil, expense, and vexation of the year's campaigning that precedes a presidential election in the United States. In France, ministers, premiers, and presidents go down before an omnipotent National Assembly, really before the popular branch of that body; while, in America, an attempt to interfere with the executive power by the legislature would create civil war. It is very true that this complete simplicity of constitutional mechanism is not provided for in the letter of the law of France, which embraces checks, balances, and monarchical contrivances. The Constitution is actually in conflict with this central idea of the supremacy of the deputies. Undoubtedly, if the advanced Republicans had been allowed to form a Constitution in 1875, there would have been but one Chamber, and, possibly, after the experiences of 1852, no personal executive; at any rate, if one had been provided for, he would not have been endowed with the monarchical attributes with which the present chief of State is armed. But the fact remains that, theoretically, the Chamber is restricted; practically, it is the center of political power, and, by means of the establishment of bureau committees, controls the administration of the government.

Whatever may be the opinion of the French people of the working of the presidential system in the United States, it has certainly been conducted with disastrous results in France.

M. Grévy established a *régime* of presidential inertia; M. Carnot has followed the example set him. Neither of these Presidents has availed himself of his right to address the Assembly.

Each of the political parties of France has a plan for the "revision" of the fundamental law, which, on account of its unsettled condition, lends uneasiness to the general situation of public affairs. It is difficult, at times, to distinguish what constitutes the real ambition and object of these contending factions. The discussion of Boulangism involves some of the principal features of this contention. The issue which is forced upon the consideration of France by the National Republican Party is set forth in two articles in *The New Review*, June, 1889.

"Everyone is aware," says Alfred Naquet, who states General Boulanger's case, with his authority, "that, in order to work properly, parliamentary government requires two great parties, and only two parties, which succeed each other in power alternately, and which, disciplined like an army, obey their leaders implicitly, and without ever breaking their ranks. With universal suffrage, however, it is totally impossible to realize this ideal (if, indeed, it be an ideal). The country is divided by countless shades of opinion—it may almost be said that each individual forms a party by himself. The Chamber, which reflects the country accurately, also shows an infinite variety of colors and shades. It no longer contains blues and whites, or blues and reds, but gradations of every tint, from pure white to scarlet, like the box of a painter in colored chalks. How can any government command a majority in an assembly of this nature? It is simply impossible. No doubt, there must be a majority about each question, as it arises; but this majority, ever shifting, ever new, composed on each occasion of fresh elements, can never have that fixity without which a responsible ministry can have no duration, nor, while it exists, that security which alone permits administrators to work to good purpose. Moreover, personal interest, with which we must always reckon, since we must deal with men, contributes to this instability and confusion. * * * *

"There remains the possibility of Cæsarism, but aristocracy and monarchy are quite dead. It may be matter for regret. * * * *

"Therefore, we are confronted, on the one hand, with the responsibility of reconstructing all forms except the *simulacrum* of a monarchy more frail than the worst republic—partly because a monarchy would bring in its train the parliamentary system, and especially because monarchy is a species of religion, and you can not call to life a religion which is no more; on the other hand, with the necessity of escaping from the condition of anarchy under which we are suffering, and which, if it endure, must destroy the country. Such was the problem before us when General Boulanger appeared on the political scene. * * * *

"It is enough to recognize that these two terms, authority and liberty, which have been considered as two formulas mutually exclusive, may be united under a single republican formula. America and Switzerland have found this formula in the separation of the executive and legislative powers, and we have only to borrow it from them and apply it to France, introducing, at the same time, certain modifications of detail, in order to adapt it to our national genius.   *   *   *   *

"The possibility of saving the situation by constituting a republic, unequivocal, national, non-parliamentary, under which all Frenchmen can be reconciled—has been opened to us by the popularity of General Boulanger. This is why the whole people flock to his standard, the masses, instinctively; the politicians who follow him, deliberately.

"Thanks to him we shall have a revision of the Constitution by a constitutional assembly, which, elected to carry out a very simple and very distinct programme, far from being an incoherent assembly, will be disciplined and under the direction of the General, will do for France that which, under the direction of Washington, another assembly did just a century ago for free America. To attain this result; to conquer the resistance of the representatives of the present system of the Chamber, of the President of the Republic, of the Senate, a strong current of opinion was required, one of those currents which sweep away everything in their torrent; and such currents are not determined by abstraction. Some personality is needed to give them unity and direction.

"From 1871 to 1877 there was a man in whom the republican principle or current was incarnate—Gambetta, and to him are due the triumphs of the Republic. Since his death the Republic has steadily declined. In the same way that Gambetta represented the republican idea, considered generally, General Boulanger represents to-day the idea of revision, and of the foundation of the only government which can flourish among us: a representative Republic based on the *referendum*.   *   *   *

"We are certain that when the Constitution is revised and sanctioned by the *plébiscite*, and the General is elected chief of the executive power, all opposition will rapidly subside. * * * *

"France will at length have found what England has had for two centuries, and what we have been seeking since 1789—a form of government which all French citizens can accept and live under."

In the same magazine, Camille Pelletan follows with an impeachment of General Boulanger.

"An hereditary title in old monarchical countries, even in many republics," says Pelletan, "has often explained the extraordinary popularity or extraordinary success of second-rate men; the addition of a handsome face made the effect irresistible. Under the old *régime*, the part played by the second Duc de Guise at the time of the Ligue, and by the Duc de Beaufort at the time of the Fronde, may be readily accounted for in this manner, and in more recent days who can wonder that after the Napoleonic epic, whose effect was heightened by legend, the great movement of 1848 should have taken place in the name of Bonaparte, to which we owe the 2d of December and Sedan. But M. Boulanger is neither a Guise nor a Bonaparte, nor does the blood of Henri IV. flow in his veins.

"Still more frequently it is a victorious general who profits by those outbursts of popular enthusiasm which are so dangerous to liberty. Able conduct in war is often enough, even when displayed without success, to raise a man to formidable popularity. But M. Boulanger can boast neither feats of arms nor victory. * * * He took no part in the expedition to Tunis, nor in that to Tonquin. He has risen in rank for the last eighteen years in public offices and ante-rooms, and had his latest military exploit been earlier known, it might have strangled his popularity at the birth; for he was certainly implicated in the horrible massacre which stains the suppression of the Commune in 1871. * * *

"Neither do his political ideas afford any explanation of his success. Not only has he borrowed from others those out of which he makes capital to-day—revision—dissolution—but he thought of producing them only after two years of a popularity he had won without their aid.

"Such a condition of affairs is very dangerous in a land where the people have, so to speak, an intellectual attachment to the freedom of the representative system, but whose temperament and character yet retain something of the manners of an age of personal power. To the early habit of feeling the grasp of a firm hand on the reins of power we must add the military sentiment excited in the masses by long space; and we shall easily understand how, after ten years of enthusiasm for parliamentary strife, of horror of a dictatorship, of attachment to the civil government, successive mistakes may arouse the most dangerous instincts of the past—instincts which lie deep, and are quite unconscious, which can not be expressed in words, and which, reduced to a political formula, would be denied by the vast majority, but which exercise their influence even on those who believe themselves freest from them. * * * *

"M. Goblet had been thrown out on a question of finance; M. Grévy took advantage of this to dismiss M. Boulanger from office by means of a very unpopular junction of the Moderate Republicans and the Royalists. Naturally, M. Boulanger's popularity was only heightened. The Wilson scandal and M. Grévy's fall followed. Shameful abuses in the President's palace necessarily lowered the executive power in public opinion, which pronounced itself against the parliament, and held the Chamber responsible. M. Boulanger had no need either to speak or act—everything was in his favor. The rest was thrown in. I mean by the rest, everything that belongs to fashion. The trivial songs, sung in music halls, amid the clinking of glasses and the fumes of tobacco, and the little plaster images sold at the street-corners, followed the general vogue. * * * *

"When the agitation had reached these proportions, and money was thus scattered broadcast, it was naturally joined by every form of discontent. From this point of view, the total absence of political programme with which it commenced, far from being a weakness, was a source of strength. If M. Boulanger had been a personality, if Boulangism had represented an idea, opposite parties could not have allied themselves to the movement. But the successful protest against the actual government was full of ambiguity. Each party hoped to profit by the attack on those in power. Ardent Catholics, Socialists of the most violent type, Republicans, Royalists, Bonapartists, all hoped to utilize it. From this point of view there would be a certain advantage in replacing the party leader by a figure-head; though he says very little, even in the few words he utters there is a risk of compromising the alliance of these contradictory hopes.

"For it must be noted that Boulangism represents nothing but the hatred of that which exists. Its formula — revision, dissolution — expresses but two ideas: a change in the Constitution and an expulsion of the members of the present Chamber. But in what direction is the change to be made? Who is to profit by this expulsion? Were these questions answered there would be an immediate division in the camp. The little that is added—a

General Boulanger.

strong executive, the *plébiscite*—are but the formulas of every despotic government.

"After the man, and the organization, we pass on to consider the composition of the party. Behind the staff, which is of small importance, is the army; and in the van the Roman Church, whose riches and power are alike threatened by the Republic, whose doctrine of authority and whose interests attach her to despotic governments, and who recognized her champion from the first, even while he yet wore the Radical colors. The whole clergy, burning with a suppressed and for years an impotent hatred of the democracy, felt a thrill of hope at the sight of the General's plume and sabre. * * * *

"We can only watch events, as they occur, with the deepest anxiety. It is a fatal mistake, and one whose punishment is sure, for a country to abandon herself to despotic power, even though the ruler be a man of genius. The danger is greater when the country yields to an average man."

Such is the gist of the statement of the issue created by Boulangism, an issue which includes the salient points of the political questions the French people must soon meet—shall there be a dissolution, and who shall replace the present representatives? Shall there be a revision, and what shall the form of the government be?

In his charge that instability is inseparable from parliamentarism the writer states his conclusion, and not the causes which led to this alleged truth. In the first place, he fails to disclose the fact that a strong monarchical minority exists in the Chamber, and that the members of this faction are the firm friends of the General; that it is they who largely bring about the ministerial changes by voting with any clique when there is an opportunity of producing an overthrow of the government. As soon as a cabinet falls, they will say: "Ah! you see how impossible it is for ministers to gain experience under a republic. How much more wisely things are managed in Prussia! There, when the sovereign has got an able minister, he keeps him. In Prussia a minister may learn by a long experience, and he has time to carry out great projects."

The unfairness of these persons is apparent, for they first create a change and then affect to lament it. They could easily form an alliance with Moderate Republicans, and formulate a stable government, but they prefer to join their fortunes, for the moment, with the Reds, the Socialists, or any disgruntled faction, in hopes to create a political chaos out of which to construct, if possible, monarchical forms. "Royalists we are," said the Duke of la Rochefoucauld, in stating the case of the Royalists, on the return of the Duke of Aumale, "and Royalists we shall remain."

The statement that two parties only are necessary to the success of parliamentary government is not correct, for in England there is an Irish minority always standing ready to make a coalition with either of the two great parties in order to overthrow the ministry. And this theory has often taken objective form.

In fact, there is another consideration that is almost startling. Since the fall of Marshal MacMahon, it is true, there have been many cabinets, but, paradoxical as it may appear, not much change of policy. There has been far more governmental change in England than in France. Liberals have been a power since Grévy's accession to the presidency. Moderate Republicans are still in possession. The rule in France for the last eighteen years has been: Changes of men, with monotony of government. In England the inverse is true.

Nor is it true that universal suffrage is radically antagonistic to parliamentarism. The House of Commons, that embraces all power, springs from a suffrage that is substantially universal. Only those without a permanent home are disfranchised there. Who doubts the stability of the government of Great Britain; its immense power and greatness, and its ability to extend its dominion?

The writer, who claims to state the opinion of the General, says that the formula of the separation of the executive and legislative powers obtains in America and Switzerland, and that this principle should be applied to France. In the opinion of many this separation of powers is a great weakness in the Constitution of the United States. Great Britain has a strong government, and the sovereignty in that system rests in the people as represented by their trustees in the Commons. To divide the sovereignty in France as proposed would violate the spirit of the Revolution, which provided, in the Constitutions of '91 and '93, and even in the reactionary forms of '95 and '99, that the "sovereignty is one, indivisible, inalienable, and imprescriptible; it belongs to the nation; no section of the people, nor any individual, can claim the right to exercise it," and the Constitution of '48 states that the "sovereignty resides in the whole body of the French people." The idea of a democracy is that the people shall always be the power, and that the representatives shall constitute the temporary power-holders, who are always subject to recall. To delegate this power to great departments is to subdivide the sovereignty and to weaken the political authority of the masses.

The "modifications" which it is proposed to adopt from the Constitution of the United States, are, possibly, in point of fact, only certain forms that may be found in the French Constitution of '52. The General knows how easy it would then be to change a few words of such an organic form, and "*à lancer sous son véritable nom la galère impériale.*"

The cry that has been raised in Europe of late years, "to Americanize," is pregnant with great interest to Americans. With the exception of Mr. Gladstone and his followers, who make use of this proposition chiefly in connection with the Irish question, in order to apply certain principles of the United States Constitution which bear on the subject of confederation, the admirers of our fundamental law have largely been Royalists. Sir Henry S. Maine, who did not believe in the present working of parliamentary government in England, placed great value on our system, at least that part of it which puts checks and balances upon the direct action of the people—as a whole. Mr. Froude and many others have expressed themselves as favorable to the views held by Maine. The resemblance of our President to a European king has often attracted the attention of publicists.

The great weakness of the present Constitution of France is its attempt to blend the features of the English parliamentary government with the American presidential system.

Gambetta was a popular hero, with great ambition. He thought that the *scrutin de liste* was the most favorable form of voting to facilitate the procurement of what is known as a "mandate" from the people. But the Chamber, ever alive to prevent personal government, refused. After his death it was established, and was the law when Boulangism developed itself. Its chief idea is to make each department vote for its representatives together. If there are twelve in number, each elector has twelve votes. He gives them to any of the twelve candidates he pleases, but, in practice, opposite lists, which have been made up by the politicians, are presented to him. The supposed utility was to deliver the votes from local influence, and the deputies, after election, from local pressure. The objection is that the local elector can not know all the men in the list, and therefore votes blindly, and generally in the interests of "the machine." The *scrutin de liste* becomes a sort of a *plébiscite*. Another objection is that in case a deputy resigns or dies, all the electors of a department have to vote on the election of a successor, as in the case of the recent election of Boulanger in the Department of the Seine. This system was fast giving Boulanger a great advantage of position. The Chamber then repealed the law and established the *scrutin d'arrondissement*, which is district voting. Under this form the candidates are generally known to the voters. The system is simple and direct. Upon the people of France, who are now divided into four great parties, rests the responsibility of settling the great issues of to-day. While it is claimed that monarchy and aristocracy are dead in France, the Legitimists are confessedly aristocratic, clerical, and reactionary. They would establish a despotism sterner than that of Louis XI. or Louis XIV. In their belief there is no remedy except in a restoration. They charge upon the Revolution that it tended to a despotic centralization, forgetting that they themselves were ruined by centralization and despotism, and that the kings wasted their treasures on favorites, while they upheld a system of robbery of one tax-payer at the expense of another.

The Orléanist party is quasi-liberal and *bourgeois*, and the Bonapartist is aristocratic, democratic, and reactionary, at once.

On account of the many subdivisions, the Republican

party is the most difficult to define. It is "moderate, with a tendency to conservatism, radical, if not revolutionary, and democratic, if not socialistic." It is divided into Independents, Opportunists, Radicals, and Extreme Left, with a decided preponderance with the Radical group.

Under the Republican *régime* France has repaired her losses, recreated the army, given new impulse to education, and increased her colonial power. She has enjoyed liberty of speech and of the press, and developed charitable and hygienic institutions for the benefit of children. The intellectual, artistic, and scientific progress made in France will bear favorable comparison with that of any other country.

The Radicals, however, demand that the country shall be completely democratized, the Church disestablished, and the whole system of taxation readjusted, religious fraternities suppressed, education secularized, and the *laïcisation* of hospitals established.

The Radicals charge that the Republicans have injured themselves by the invasions and massacres in the East, and have drawn too heavily upon the resources of the country in support of militarism. They attack the obstinacy of the Royalists in clinging to a defunct ideal, instead of supporting the Republic by co-operating with some branch of the party in power, and, above all, they criticise the monarchical features of the present Constitution.

Political mechanism may not, of itself, form the character of a people, for that is the result of evolutionary action as manifested through the influence of the inexpressible force which produces the growth of ethics, economics, and self-government. These principles must be stamped upon the heart, mind, and genius of man. But organic form, when it approximates to a truthful expression of the higher thought and true aspiration of a nation, may assist in the endeavor to give outward voice to the subjective intent and purpose of sovereignty.

Government is not an abstraction, but to the contrary, it is, or ought to be, an agency of the people for performing acts, obeying directions and requests, for the benefit of the masses. It is, therefore, within the scope of the science of politics to show what would naturally be the evolution, development, or fate of a government, viewed in the light of reason and of history. Constitutions can not be ready-made; government is, after all, a fact. If a people believe they are living under a system of laws that obstructs liberty, or extends an invitation to some "political idol," then the honest way is to suggest and adopt new processes to meet the requirements of the age, and thus to establish the needed reform. When this change is determined upon, its crystallization ought to be simple and swift.

The French people are fitted for a spontaneous initiative and free control in the conduct of their own affairs. To accomplish all that this statement implies, their government must be simplified upon the line of democracy. This is the burning question of the day. The best hope of this people is that no fabric will stand before them, after it has been demonstrated, by the logic of events, and by the historic facts, that its forms are unavailing, mischievous, and wrong.

The Radicals believe, that as France is a country of solidarity, and has no confederative features in her composition, no series of statelets to be represented in an upper Chamber, that, therefore, there is no need for one.

They desire a revision of the Constitution which shall establish one central Chamber composed of temporary power-holders, who shall always be subject to recall by their constituencies. Their representatives shall not be in any sense rulers or governors, but trustees, with power to pass upon routine legislation, submitting all matters of important governmental policy to the people for ratification. This body to have full authority within these conditions A wise people, feeling that they control their own destiny, would then provide for the administration of justice by the existing courts, or create new ones, if need be; ratify existing local government, so far as expedient, within well-defined limitations, and take all necessary measures for the execution of the law through a responsible executive council.

This plan would rid France of the political superstition of a personal ruler, and at the same time do away with that system of parliamentarism, which, at least, in the English sense, has never been fully and properly introduced into that country. In Great Britain this system embodies the true essence of democracy, but as it exists in France it destroys stability and creates unrest.

The hope is, that the people of France, inspired by the spirit of the Revolution, filled with its love of liberty, equality, and fraternity, are about to enter upon an era of constitutional and legislative reforms, which will effect a true application of political power.

APPENDIX I.

THE CONSTITUTION OF 1791.

TITLE I.
Fundamental Provisions Guaranteed by the Constitution.

The Constitution guarantees as natural and civil rights:

1. That all citizens are admissible to public office and employment without any other distinction than that of virtue and talent.
2. That taxation shall be equally divided between all citizens in proportion to their means.
3. That the same crime shall be punished by the same penalty, without distinction of persons.

The Constitution guarantees, in like manner, as natural and civil rights:

The liberty of all men to move about, to remain, or to depart, only being subject to detention or arrest under the forms determined by the Constitution.

The liberty of all men to speak, to write, to print, and to publish their thoughts, without first submitting their writings to any censorship or inspection before their publication, and to exercise the religious worship to which they may be attached.

The liberty of citizens peaceably and without arms to assemble, under the police regulations.

The liberty to address individually signed petitions to the constituted authorities.

The legislative power shall not pass any law which shall prejudice, or place any obstacle in the way of the full exercise of the natural and civil rights set forth in this title, and guaranteed by the Constitution. But as liberty consists only in doing that which shall injure neither the rights of others, nor the public security, the law may establish penalties against acts which attack either the public security, the rights of others, or would be injurious to society

The Constitution guarantees the inviolability of property, or a just and previous indemnity of that which public necessity, legally constituted, shall demand the appropriation of.

Goods intended to meet the expenses of worship and of all public uses, belong to the nation, and are at all times at its disposal.

The Constitution guarantees the alienations that have been, or shall be made under the forms established by law.

Citizens have the right to elect or choose the clergymen of their own religious beliefs.

A general establishment of public aid shall be created and organized to bring up abandoned children, to alleviate the condition of the infirm poor, and to furnish work to the sturdy poor who have not been able to procure it.

Public instruction, common to all citizens, and gratuitous with respect to the amount of education indispensable to all men, shall be created and organized, and whose establishments shall gradually be distributed, according to a full report of the divisions of the kingdom.

National *fêtes* shall be established to conserve the remembrance of the French Revolution, to preserve fraternity among citizens, and to attach them to the Constitution, to the country, and to the laws.

TITLE II.

Of the Division of the Kingdom and of the Condition of Citizens.

ARTICLE 1 The kingdom is one and indivisible. Its territory is divided into eighty-three departments, each department into districts, each district into cantons.

ART. 2. French citizens are: Those who are born in France of a French father; those who, born in France of an alien father, have fixed their residence in the kingdom; those who, born in a foreign country of a French father, have come to settle in France, and have taken the civic oath; finally, those who, born in a foreign country, and a descendant, in whatever degree of consanguinity, of a French man or of a French woman, expatriated on account of religious belief, come to live in France and take the civic oath.

ART. 3. Such residents of France who were born out of the kingdom, of foreign parents, become French citizens after five years of continuous domicile in the kingdom, provided they have acquired real estate, or married a French woman, or founded an agricultural or commercial establishment, and if they have taken the civic oath.

Art. 4. The legislative power may, for important considerations, naturalize a foreigner without other conditions than a domicile in France, and the taking of the civic oath.

Art. 5. The civic oath is: *I swear to be faithful to the nation, to the law, and to the King, and to maintain with all my power the Constitution of the Kingdom, decreed by the National Constituent Assembly in the years* 1789, 1790, *and* 1791.

Art. 6. The right of exercising French citizenship is lost: 1, by naturalization in a foreign country; 2, by condemnation to penalties which carry civic degradation, so long as the condemned is not restored to his rights; 3, by a judgment of contumacy, so long as the judgment is not annulled; 4, by affiliation with any order of foreign chivalry, or with any foreign corporation, which would require either proofs of nobility, or distinctions of birth, or exact religious vows.

Art. 7. The law only considers marriage as a civil contract. The legislative power shall establish for all inhabitants, without distinction, the manner in which births, marriages, and deaths shall be authenticated, and it shall designate the public officers who shall receive and preserve the records.

Art. 8. French citizens, considered with reference to local relations which arise from their reunion in cities and in certain districts of the country, form communes.

The legislative power shall fix the boundaries of the district of each commune.

Art. 9. Citizens who compose each commune have the right to elect, at stated times, and following the forms determined by the law, those among them, who, under the title of municipal officers, are charged with the administration of the local affairs of the commune.

The law shall delegate to municipal officers certain functions relative to the interest of the State.

Art. 10. The rules which the municipal officers shall be required to follow in the exercise, both of municipal functions and those which have been delegated to them in the general interest, shall be determined by the law.

TITLE III.

Of the Public Powers.

ARTICLE 1. The sovereignty is one, indivisible, inalienable, and imprescriptible; it belongs to the nation; no individual, no fraction of the people can claim the right to exercise it.

ART. 2. The nation, from which emanate all powers, can only exercise them by delegation.

The French Constitution is representative; the representatives are the Legislative Body and the King.

ART. 3. The legislative power is delegated to one National Assembly, composed of temporary representatives, freely elected by the people, in order to be exercised by it, with the sanction of the King, in the manner which shall be determined hereafter.

ART. 4. The government is monarchical; the executive power is delegated to the King, in order to be exercised, under his authority, by ministers and other responsible agents, in the manner which shall be determined by law.

ART. 5. The judiciary power is delegated to judges elected at stated times by the people.

CHAPTER I.

OF THE NATIONAL LEGISLATIVE ASSEMBLY.

ARTICLE 1. The National Assembly, forming the Legislative Body, is permanent, and is only composed of one chamber

ART. 2. It shall be formed every two years by new elections. Each period of two years shall constitute a legislature.

ART. 3. The provisions of the preceding article shall not be operative in respect to the next Legislative Body, whose powers shall cease the last day of April, 1793.

ART. 4. The Legislative Body, on its renewal, shall assume full authority.

ART. 5. The Legislative Body can not be dissolved by the King.

SECTION I.

Number of Representatives.—Basis of Representation.

ARTICLE 1. The Legislative Body shall consist of 745 representatives, to be apportioned among the eighty-three departments of which the kingdom is composed, and independent of those who may be accorded to the colonies.

ART. 2. The representations shall be distributed among the eighty three departments, in the proportions of territory, population, and direct taxation.

ART. 3. Of the 745 representatives, 247 are assigned to territory. Each department names three of them, except the department of Paris, which names only one.

ART. 4. Two hundred and forty-nine representatives are credited to population. The total amount of the active population of the kingdom is divided into 249 parts, and each department names as many deputies as it has parts of the population.

ART. 5. Two hundred and forty-nine representatives are credited to direct taxation. The total sum of the direct taxation of the kingdom is also divided into 249 parts, and each department names as many deputies as it pays parts of the whole taxation.

SECTION II.

Primary Assemblies. Nomination of Electors.

ARTICLE 1. In order to form the National Legislative Assembly, all *active* citizens shall meet every two years, in primary assemblies, in the towns and cantons.

The primary assemblies shall meet, with full authority to act, on the second Sunday in March, if they have not been convoked sooner by the public functionaries appointed by law.

ART. 2. To be an *active* citizen, it is necessary to be born, or to become a Frenchman; to be full twenty-five years of age; to be domiciled in the town or the canton for the period determined by law; to pay in some part of the kingdom a direct tax, at least of the value of three days' work, and to present a receipt for it; not to be in a state of servitude, that is to say, in service for wages; to be registered in the municipality of his domicile, on the roll of the National Guard—to have taken the civic oath.

ART. 3. Every six years the Legislative Body shall fix the minimum and the maximum of a day's labor, and the administrators of department shall give it local application in each district.

ART. 4. No person shall exercise the rights of an active citizen in more than one place, nor shall he be represented by another.

ART. 5. The exercise of the rights of active citizenship shall be denied to.

Those who are under indictment; those who, having been adjudged in a state of bankruptcy or insolvency, proved by authenticated records, do not produce a general discharge from their creditors.

ART. 6. The primary assemblies shall nominate electors in proportion to the number of active citizens domiciled in the town or the canton. One elector shall be nominated for 100 active citizens, present or not, at the assembly. Two electors from 151 to 250, and thus one after the other.

ART. 7. No one can be chosen elector unless he unites all the necessary conditions to be an active citizen, that is to say:

In towns above 6,000 inhabitants, that he is the proprietor or beneficiary of an estate valued, upon the tax rolls, at a revenue equal in local value to 200 days' labor, or an occupant of a tenement valued, upon the same rolls, at a revenue equal in value to 100 days' labor.

And in the country, that he is the owner or beneficiary of an estate valued, upon the tax rolls, the income of which is equal in local value to 150 days' labor, or that he is the tenant or farmer of estates valued, on the same rolls, at the value of 400 days' labor.

In regard to those who are in part proprietors or beneficiaries, and in part occupants, tenants, or farmers, their estates are estimated together, in their different characters, to the amount of tax requisite for their eligibility.

SECTION III.

Electoral Assemblies. Nomination of Representatives.

ARTICLE 1 The electors chosen in each department shall meet in order to elect the number of representatives who have been credited to their department, and a number of alternates equal to one-third of the representatives. The electoral assemblies shall meet with full power, on the last Sunday in March, if they have not been sooner called together by the public officers appointed by law.

ART. 2. The representatives and the alternates shall be elected by an absolute plurality of votes, and can only be chosen from the active citizens of the department.

ART. 3. All active citizens, whatever may be their condition, profession, or amount of taxes paid by them, may be elected representatives of the nation.

ART. 4. If any one of the following officers be chosen a representative, he shall be required to make election between such office and the one he may then hold: the ministers and other agents of the executive power, revocable at will; the commissioners of the national treasury; the

CONSTITUTION OF MDCCXCI.

collectors and receivers of direct taxes; the overseers of collections; the excisemen of indirect taxation, and of the national domains; and those who, under whatever denomination, are attached by their employment to the military and civil household of the King; and also the administrators, sub-administrators, municipal officers, and commandants of the National Guard.

ART. 5. The exercise of judicial functions shall be incompatible with the duty of the representatives of the nation during the session of the legislature. The judges shall be replaced by their substitutes, and the King shall, by commission, fill the vacancies from his commissioners at the tribunals.

ART. 6. The members of the Legislative Body can be re elected to a subsequent legislature, but only after the interval of one legislature.

ART. 7. The representatives named in the departments shall not be representatives of any particular department, but of the entire nation, and no mandate to execute any fixed commission shall be imposed upon them.

SECTION IV.

The Sessions and the Government of the Primary and Electoral Assemblies.

ARTICLE 1. The functions of the primary and electoral assemblies are limited to election; they separate as soon as the elections are made, and can only meet again when they are convoked, except in the cases above provided for in Article 1 of Section II, and of Article 1 of Section III.

ART. 2. No citizen, if he is armed, can enter, or exercise the right of suffrage in an assembly.

ART. 3. An armed force can not be introduced into an assembly, without its express vote, unless violence is committed, in which case the order of the President will suffice to call the public force into requisition.

ART. 4. Every two years lists shall be prepared in each district, by cantons, of the active citizens, and lists of each canton shall be published and posted therein two months before the time of meeting of the primary assembly.

All claims which may be made, either to contest the qualifications of citizens entered upon the lists, or on the part of those who allege an unjust exclusion therefrom, shall be carried to the tribunals to be there summarily judged. The lists shall regulate the admission of citizens into the next primary assembly, except in such cases as may have been decided, by judgments rendered before the session of the assembly.

ART. 5. The electoral assemblies have the right to verify the qualifications and the powers of those who shall present themselves to them, and their decisions shall be provisionally executed, subject to the judgment of the Legislative Body at the time of the verification of the powers of the deputies.

ART. 6. In no case, and under no pretext, may the King, or any of the agents named by him, take cognizance of questions relating to the regularity of the meetings, to the sitting of the assemblies, to the form of elections, or to the political rights of citizens, without prejudice to the King's commissioners in cases determined by the law, where the questions relating to political rights of citizens ought to be carried before the tribunals.

SECTION V.

Meeting of Representatives in National Legislative Assembly.

ARTICLE 1. The representatives shall assemble on the first Monday of the month of May, in the place in which the sittings of the last legislature was held.

ART. 2. They shall provisionally form themselves in assembly, under the presidency of the oldest member, in order to verify the credentials of the representatives present.

ART. 3. As soon as there shall be 373 members verified, they shall formally constitute themselves under the title of the National Legislative Assembly. It shall nominate a president, a vice-president, and secretaries, and commence the exercise of its functions.

ART. 4. During the month of May, if the number of representatives present shall fall below 373, the Assembly shall not pass any legislative act. It may pass a resolution requiring absent members to return within fifteen days, under penalty of a fine of 3,000 livres, unless they present an excuse which shall be judged legitimate by the Assembly.

ART. 5. On the last day of May, whatever may be the number of members present, they shall form themselves into a National Legislative Assembly.

ART. 6. The representatives shall pronounce in unison, and in the name of the French people, an oath to live as freemen or to die. They shall then take individually an oath, to maintain with all their power the Constitution of the kingdom, decreed by the National Constituent Assembly, in the years 1789, '90, and '91; and neither to propose nor to consent to anything, in the course of the legislature, that may assail it, and to be in all respects faithful to the nation, to the law, and to the King.

ART. 7. The representatives of the nation are inviolable; they can neither be apprehended, indicted, nor judged at any time, on account of what they may say, write, or do in the exercise of their functions as representatives.

ART. 8. They may, on account of criminal actions, be arrested, when taken in the act, or by virtue of an order of arrest; but immediate information must be given thereof to the Legislative Body, and the prosecution can not be proceeded with until the Legislative Body shall decide that there are grounds for the prosecution.

CHAPTER II.

OF ROYALTY, OF THE REGENCY, AND OF MINISTERS.

SECTION I.

Of Royalty and of the King.

ARTICLE 1. Royalty is indivisible, and is transmitted by inheritance to the reigning family, from male to male, in the order of primogeniture, to the perpetual exclusion of females and their descendants.

ART. 2. The person of the King is inviolable and sacred, his only title is that of King of the French.

ART. 3. In France there is no authority superior to the law; the King only reigns by virtue of it, and it is only in the name of the law that he can require obedience.

The King, on his accession to the throne, or as soon as he shall attain his majority, shall take, before the nation and in the presence of the Legislative Body, an oath to be faithful to the nation, and to the law and to employ all the power that is delegated to him to maintain the Constitution decreed by the National Constituent Assembly, and te execute the laws.

ART. 4. If the Legislative Body is not assembled, the King shall publish a proclamation in which he shall express the oath, with a promise to repeat it as soon as the Legislative Body shall meet.

ART. 5. After one month from the call of the Legislative Body, if the King shall not have taken the oath, or if, after having taken it, he retract it, he shall be accounted as having abdicated the throne.

ART. 6. If the King shall place himself at the head of an army, or direct its forces against the nation, or if he does not oppose, by a formal act, such an attempt made in his name, he shall be accounted as having abdicated the throne.

ART. 7. If the King, having passed beyond the territory of the kingdom, does not re-enter it upon the call of the Legislative Body, within a time which shall be fixed by proclamation, which shall not be less than two months, he shall be judged to have abdicated the throne. The delay shall commence to run from the day the proclamation of the Legislative Body shall have been published at its place of sitting, and the ministers shall be required, under their responsibility, to do all executive acts, the exercise of which have been suspended by the absence of the King.

ART. 8. After an actual or legal abdication, the King shall be classed as a citizen, and may be accused and judged in the same manner for acts done subsequent to his abdication.

ART. 9. The private property which the King possessed on his accession to the throne is irrevocably transferred to the estates of the nation; he has the disposition of that to which he acquires personal title, still, if he has not disposed of it, it is appropriated, in like manner, at the end of his reign.

ART. 10. The nation provides a sum of money for his household, which amount the Legislative Body shall determine at each change of reign, and for the duration of the reign.

ART. 11. The King shall nominate an administrator of the civil list, who shall carry on all judicial suits of the King, and against whom all actions, on account of the King, shall be commenced and judgment entered. The judgments obtained by the creditors of the civil list shall be executed against the administrator personally, and satisfied out of his personal property.

ART. 12. The King shall have, independent of the guard of honor which shall be furnished by the citizen National Guard at the place of his residence, a guard paid from the funds of the civil list; it shall not exceed 1,200 infantry and 600 cavalry. The rank and the rules of promotion shall be the same as that of the troops of the line, but those who compose the guard of the King shall be advanced for all grades exclusively among themselves, and shall not be promoted in the troops of the line. The King shall only choose the men of his guard from those in active service in the line, or from citizens who have seen one year's service in the National Guard, provided they are resident citizens in the kingdom, and have previously taken the civic oath.

The guard of the King shall not be ordered nor required for any other public service.

Section II.
Of the Regency.

ARTICLE 1. The King shall be a minor until he arrives at the full age of eighteen years old, and during his minority a regent of the kingdom shall be appointed.

ART. 2. The regency belongs to the relative of the King who is nearest in degree according to the order of inheritance to the throne, if he is fully twenty-five years of age; provided he is a Frenchman and native born; that he is not presumptive heir to another crown; and that he has previously taken the civic oath. Females are excluded from the regency.

ART. 3. If the King, in his minority, has no relative who unites the above expressed qualifications, the regent of the kingdom shall be elected according to the following articles.

ART. 4. The Legislative Body shall not elect the regent.

ART. 5. The electors of each district shall meet in the chief place of the district, after a proclamation shall have been issued in the first week of the new reign, by the Legislative Body, if it be sitting, or, if separated, the Minister of Justice shall be required to make the proclamation during the same week.

ART. 6. The electors shall nominate in each district, by individual vote, and by absolute plurality, an eligible citizen who is domiciled in the district, to whom they shall give, by the minutes of the election, a special mandate, limited to the single function to elect a citizen whom he shall, on his soul and conscience, judge to be most worthy of being chosen the regent of the kingdom.

ART. 7. These special electors named in the districts must assemble in the city where the Legislative Body is sitting, to begin, at the latest, from the fortieth day after the accession of the King, during his minority, to the throne, and they shall form an Electoral Assembly which shall proceed to the nomination of the regent.

ART. 8. The election shall take place by individual vote, and be decided by an absolute plurality of votes.

ART. 9. The Electoral Assembly can only provide for the election and then terminate its session; all other acts which it may attempt are declared unconstitutional and of no force.

ART. 10. The Electoral Assembly, by its president, shall cause the minutes of the election to be presented to the Legislative Body, which after having verified the regularity of the election, shall cause it to be published, by proclamation, throughout the kingdom.

ART. 11. The regent exercises, until the majority of the King, all the functions of royalty, and is not personally responsible for the acts of his administration.

ART. 12. The regent can only enter upon the exercise of his functions after he has taken, before the nation and in the presence of the Legislative Body, the oath to be faithful to the nation, to the law, and to the King; to employ all the power delegated to the King, the exercise of which has been confided to him during the minority of the King; to maintain the Constitution decreed by the National Constituent Assembly in the years 1789, '90, and '91; and to cause the law to be executed. If the Legislative Body is not sitting, the regent must publish a proclamation, in which he shall express the oath, with the promise to repeat it as soon as the Legislative Body shall meet.

ART. 13. As long as the regent is not exercising his functions, the sanction of the laws shall remain suspended; the ministers, under their responsibility, continue to do all acts of executive power.

ART. 14. As soon as the regent shall take the oath, the Legislative Body shall determine what income shall be paid to him, which, being established, can not be changed during the regency.

ART. 15. If, by reason of the minority of the relative entitled to the regency, it has devolved on a relative farther removed, or has been decreed by election, the regent who shall enter upon the exercise of the office shall continue his functions until the majority of the King.

ART. 16 The regency of the kingdom confers no right upon the person of the King during minority.

ART. 17. The guardianship of the King, during his minority, shall be confided to his mother; and if he has no mother, or, if she has married again at the time of the accession of her son to the throne, or, if she marries again during his minority, the guardianship shall be decreed by the Legislative Body. Neither the regent nor his offspring, nor a female, can be elected to the guardianship of the King during minority.

ART. 18. In the event of the notoriously recognized insanity of the King, legally authenticated and declared by the Legislative Body after three successive deliberations taken from month to month, the regency shall continue as long as the insanity lasts.

Section III.
Of the Family of the King.

ARTICLE 1. The heir presumptive shall bear the name of the Prince Royal. He can not go beyond the borders of France without a decree of the Legislative Body and the consent of the King. If he is absent, and if, having arrived at the age of eighteen years, he does not return to France after having been required to do so by a proclamation of the Legislative Body, he is adjudged to have abdicated his right of succession to the throne.

ART. 2. If the heir presumptive is a minor, the relative being of full age, and having the first right to be called to the regency, shall reside in the kingdom. In the event of his being absent, and he should not return upon the requisition of the Legislative Body, he shall be adjudged to have abdicated his right to the regency.

ART. 3. The mother of the King who is a minor, and being his guardian, or the elected guardian, and if she leaves the kingdom, she forfeits the guardianship. If the mother of the heir presumptive who is a minor, goes beyond the kingdom, she can, even after her return, have the guardianship of her minor son, who has become King, only by a decree of the Legislative Body.

ART. 4. It shall pass a law regulating the education of the King and the heir presumptive, who are minors.

ART. 5. The members of the family of the King called by contingent succession to the throne enjoy the rights of active citizens; but they are not eligible to any office, function, or employment in the gift of the people. With the exception of the ministerial departments, they are eligible to office and employment on the nomination of the King; nevertheless, they can not command in chief any land or sea force, nor fill the position of ambassador, without the consent of the Legislative Body, accorded on the proposition of the King.

ART. 6. The members of the family of the King called by contingent succession to the throne shall have added the denomination of French Prince to the name that shall have been given to them by the civil act authenticating their birth, and this name shall be neither patronymic nor based upon any of the qualifications abolished by the present Constitution. The denomination of Prince can not be given to any other individual, and shall carry neither privilege nor any exception to the common rights of all Frenchmen.

ART. 7. The acts which shall legally authenticate the births, marriages, and deaths of the French Princes shall be presented to the Legislative Body, who shall order them deposited in its archives.

ART. 8. It shall not accord any support to the members of the family of the King. On arriving at the full age of twenty-five years, or upon their marriage, the younger sons of the King shall receive an income, which shall be fixed by the Legislative Body and terminate on the extinction of their male offspring.

SECTION IV.
Of the Ministers.

ARTICLE 1. The King alone shall have power to appoint and revoke the appointment of the ministers.

ART. 2. The members of the present National Assembly and following legislatures, the members of the Tribunal of *Cassation*, and those who shall serve on the grand jury, shall not be promoted to the office of minister, nor receive any office, gift, pension, honor, or commission from the executive, or from its agents, during the duration of their functions, and for two years after they shall cease in the exercise of them. It shall be the same with those who are entered on the list of the grand jury during the time of their inscription.

ART. 3. No one can enter upon the exercise of any employment, either in the offices of the ministers or those of the excisemen, or of the administration of public revenues, or generally in any employment by the executive power, without the civic oath, or proving that he had taken it.

ART. 4. No order of the King can be executed unless it is signed by him and countersigned by the minister or the auditor of the department.

ART. 5. The ministers are responsible for all misdemeanors committed by him against the national safety or against the Constitution; for all acts against property and individual liberty; for all expenditure of all revenues intended for the expenses of their departments.

ART. 6. In no case can the written or verbal order of the King relieve a minister from responsibility.

ART. 7. The ministers are required to present each year to the Legislative Body, at the opening of its session, a statement of the expenses to be incurred in their departments and to render an account of the sums already appropriated, and to indicate the abuses which may have been introduced in the different parts of the administration.

ART. 8. No minister, in office or out of office, can be prosecuted criminally for an act of his administration without a decree of the Legislative Body.

CHAPTER III.
OF THE EXERCISE OF LEGISLATIVE POWER.

SECTION I.

Powers and Functions of the National Legislative Assembly.

ARTICLE 1. The Constitution delegates exclusively to the Legislative Body the following powers and functions:

1. To propose and decree the laws; the King can only invite the Legislative Body to take a subject into consideration. 2. To determine the public expenses. 3. To establish public taxes; to determine their nature, the quota, the duration, and the mode of collection. 4. To cause a distribution of direct taxes between the departments of the kingdom, to guard the employment of all public revenues, and to cause an account to be rendered of them. 5. To decree the creation or suppression of public offices. 6. To determine the title, the weight, the impress, and the denomination of moneys. 7. To permit or forbid the introduction of foreign troops upon French territory, and of foreign naval forces in the ports of the kingdom. 8. To legislate, annually, upon the proposition of the King, upon the number of men and vessels of which the land and sea forces shall be composed; upon the pay and number of persons in each service; upon the rules of admission and promotion, the forms of enrollment and of discharge; the organization of ships' crews; upon the admission of troops or of foreign naval forces into the service of France, and upon the pay of troops in case of disbandment. 9. To legislate upon the administration of law and to order alienation of national domains. 10. To prosecute before the national High Court the responsibilities of ministers and the principal agents of the executive power; to accuse and to prosecute before the same court those who shall be charged with an attempt or conspiracy against the general security of the State, or against the Constitution. 11. To legislate in what manner purely personal marks of honor or decoration shall be accorded to those who have rendered service to the State. 12. The Legislative Body, only, has the right to order public honors to the memory of great men.

ART. 2. War shall only be declared by a decree of the Legislative Body, rendered by the formal and necessary proposition of the King, and sanctioned by him. In the event of imminent or commenced hostilities, of an ally to be sustained or a right calling for protection by the force of arms, the King shall, without any delay, give notice of it to the Legislative Body; and make known the questions involved. If the legislative corps decides that the war ought not to be made, the King shall immediately take measures to put an end to it, or prevent hostilities, the ministers remaining responsible for delays.

If the Legislative Body finds that the existing hostilities were the result of culpable aggression on the part of the ministers, or of any other agent of the executive power, the author of the aggression shall be prosecuted criminally.

At any time during the war, the Legislative Body can require the King to negotiate peace, and the King is compelled to yield to this requisition. Immediately after the war, the Legislative Body shall determine when the troops raised above the peace footing may be disbanded, and the army reduced to its ordinary condition.

ART. 3. It belongs to the Legislative Body to ratify the treaties of peace, of alliance, and of commerce, and no treaty shall have effect without this ratification.

ART. 4. The Legislative Body shall have the right to determine the place of its sittings, to continue them as long as it may judge them necessary, and to adjourn. At the commencement of each reign, if it is not in session, it must assemble without delay.

It has the police control at the place of its sittings, and within a circumference it shall determine. It has the right to discipline its members, but it can not pronounce punishment greater than censure, arrests of eight days, or prison for three days. It has the right, for its safety, and to maintain the respect due to it, to dispose of the forces, which, by its consent, shall be established in the city where its sessions are held.

ART 5. The executive power can not march nor bivouac any troops of the line within thirty miles of the Legislative Body without its requisition or authority.

SECTION II.

Of the Holding of Sessions and the Form of Deliberation.

ARTICLE 1. The deliberations of the Legislative Body shall be public, and the minutes of its sessions shall be printed.

ART. 2. The Legislative Body may, however, on any occasion, form itself in general committee. Fifty members shall have the right to demand it. During the session of the general committee the assistants shall retire; the chair of the President shall be vacant; order shall be maintained by the Vice-President.

ART. 3. A legislative act can only be deliberated upon and decreed in the following manner:

ART. 4. There shall be three readings of a bill, at three intervals, each of which shall be eight days.

ART. 5. The discussion shall be open after each reading, but the Legislative Body may declare, after the first or second reading that it shall be adjourned, or that no discussion shall take place; but in this last case, the bill may be presented again during the same session. All bills must be printed and distributed before the second reading.

ART. 6. After the third reading, the President must bring the bill forward for discussion, and the Legislative Body must decide whether it is ready to decide, or the decision shall be postponed in order to procure the clearest light upon the subject.

ART. 7. The Legislative Body can not deliberate unless the session is composed of at least 200 members, and a decree shall only be passed by an absolute plurality of votes.

ART. 8. Every bill which has been acted on and rejected after the third reading can not be brought up again during the same session.

ART. 9. The preamble of each decree shall definitely express:

1. The days of the session on which the three readings of the bill took place. 2. The act by which it was, after the third reading, declared to decide definitely.

ART. 10. The King shall refuse his sanction to a decree of which the preamble does not attest the compliance with the above forms. But if such a decree is sanctioned, the ministers must not seal and promulgate it, and their responsibility in this regard shall last six years.

ART. 11. Decrees recognized and declared urgent by a previous declaration of the Legislative Body are excepted from the above provisions, but they may be modified and revoked in the course of the same session. The decree by which the matter shall have been declared urgent shall express the reasons for it, and it shall make mention of the previous decree in the preamble of the final decree.

SECTION III.

Of the Royal Sanction.

ARTICLE 1. The decrees of the Legislative Body are presented to the King, who may refuse to give his consent to them.

ART. 2. In cases where the King refuses his consent, this refusal shall only be suspensive. When the two legislatures which follow the one which shall have presented the decree shall successively present again the same decree in the same terms, the King shall be deemed to have given his consent.

ART. 3. The consent of the King is expressed upon each decree by this formula, signed by him: *The King consents, and it shall be executed.* The suspensive refusal is expressed in these words: *The King will advise upon it.*

ART. 4. The King must express his consent or his refusal upon each decree within two months of its presentation.

ART. 5. All decrees to which the King has refused his consent can not be presented to him again by the same legislature.

ART. 6. The decrees sanctioned by the King, and those which shall have been presented to him by three consecutive legislatures, have the force of law, and bear the name and title of law.

ART. 7. The acts of the Legislative Body concerning its rules as a deliberative assembly, its interior police, and that which it controls within the exterior environs which it shall have determined, the verification of its present members, its injunctions to absent members, the convocation of primary assemblies that have not voted, the exercise of the constitutional police over the administrators, and over the municipal officers, whether the question is that of eligibility or of the validity of elections, shall, nevertheless, be executed as laws, without being subject to the royal sanction. Neither the acts relative to the responsibility of ministers, nor the decrees bearing upon grounds of indictment, are required to secure the royal sanction.

ART. 8. The decrees of the Legislative Body concerning the establishment, the putting off, and the collection of public taxes shall bear the name and title of law. They shall be promulgated and executed without the sanction, unless they are provisions which shall establish penalties other than fines and pecuniary coercion. These decrees can only be passed after the observance of the formalities prescribed in Articles 4, 5, 6, 7, 8, and 9 of Section II of this chapter, and the Legislative Body shall not insert in these laws any provision foreign to their object.

SECTION IV.

Of the Relations of the Legislative Body with the King.

ARTICLE 1. When the Legislative Body is definitively organized it sends a deputation to the King to inform him of the fact. The King can, each year, open the session, and propose that which he believes should be taken into consideration during the session, but, nevertheless, this formality shall not be considered as necessary to the activity of the Legislative Body.

ART. 2. When the Legislative Body wishes to adjourn beyond fifteen days, it shall give notice to the King by a deputation, at least eight days in advance.

ART. 3. Eight days before the end of each session the Legislative Body sends a deputation to the King to inform him of the day upon which it proposes to terminate its sitting. The King may close the session.

ART. 4. If the King finds it important for the welfare of the State that the session should be continued, or that the adjournment should not take place, or that it should be for a shorter period, he may send a message to this effect upon which the Legislative Body is compelled to deliberate.

ART. 5. The King shall convoke the Legislative Body during the interval of its sessions, at all times when the interests of the State shall appear to him to require it, as in cases which shall have been foreseen and determined by the Legislative Body before adjourning.

ART. 6. The King may repair at all times to the place of the sitting of the Legislative Body; he shall be received and reconducted by a deputation; he shall only be accompanied in the presence of the legislature by the Prince Royal, and by his ministers.

ART. 7. The President can in no case constitute a member of the deputation.

ART. 8. The Legislative Body shall cease to be a deliberative body as long as the King shall remain present.

ART. 9. The correspondence of the King with the Legislative Body shall always be countersigned by a minister.

ART. 10. The ministers of the King shall have the right to appear before the National Legislative Assembly; a place shall be reserved for them. They shall be heard at all times they shall demand, upon questions relating to their administration, or when they shall be required to give information. They shall also be heard upon considerations foreign to their administration, when the National Assembly shall give them liberty to speak.

CHAPTER IV.
OF THE EXERCISE OF THE EXECUTIVE POWER.

ARTICLE 1. The supreme executive power resides in the King. The King is the supreme head of the general administration of the kingdom; the care of guarding public order and tranquillity is confided to him. The King is the supreme head of the land and marine forces. To the King is delegated the care of guarding the exterior safety of the kingdom, and to maintain its rights and possessions.

ART. 2. The King appoints ambassadors and all other public agents. He names the commander of the army and navy, marshals of France, and admirals. He names two-thirds of the rear-admirals, one-half of the lieutenant-generals, adjutant-generals, post-captains, and colonels of the national *gendarmerie*. He names one-third of the colonels and lieutenant-colonels, and one-sixteenth of the lieutenants of men-of-war. All of these shall conform to the laws of promotion.

He appoints in the civil administration of the marine, the orderers, the comptrollers, the treasurers of arsenals, the chiefs of works, under-chiefs of civil buildings, one-half of chiefs of administration and under-chiefs of construction. He appoints the commissioners of tribunals. He appoints the overseer-in-chief of the excisemen of indirect taxes, and of the administration of national domains.

He oversees the coining of money, and names the officers charged to exercise the superintendence in the general commission and in the mints. The image of the King is impressed on all money of the kingdom.

ART. 3. The King causes letters patent, warrants, and commissions to be delivered to the public functionaries, or to others who ought to receive them.

ART. 4. The King causes the lists of pensions and bounties to be drawn up and presented to the Legislative Body at each of its sessions, and decreed if it so order.

SECTION I.
Of the Promulgation of Laws.

ARTICLE 1. The executive power is charged to seal the laws with the seal of State, and to cause them to be promulgated. It must also promulgate and execute the acts of the Legislative Body which do not need the sanction of the King.

ART. 2. It shall make two original copies of each law, both signed by the King, countersigned by the Minister of Justice, and sealed with the seal of the State. One shall be deposited in the archives of the seals, and the other remitted to the archives of the Legislative Body.

Art. 3. The promulgation shall be thus expressed: "N (the name of the King) by the grace of God and by virtue of the Constitutional law of the State, King of the French, to all to whom these presents shall come, greeting. The National Assembly has decreed, and we wish and order that which follows (a literal copy of the decree shall be here inserted without any change):

"We direct and order all administrative bodies and tribunals that these presents shall be recorded in their registers, read, published, and posted in their departments and respective jurisdictions, and executed as laws of the kingdom. In witness whereof we have signed these presents, to which we caused the seal of State to be affixed."

'Art. 4. If the King is a minor, the laws, proclamations, and other acts emanating from the royal authority, during the regency, shall be expressed as follows:

"N (the name of the regent) regent of the kingdom, in the name of N (the name of the King) by the grace of God and by virtue of the constitutional law of the State, King of the French, etc., etc."

Art. 5. The executive power shall send the laws to the tribunals, and cause the transmittal to be certified, and to authenticate the fact to the Legislative Body.

Art. 6. The executive power can make no law, even provisional, but only proclamations for the purpose of ordering or recalling their execution conformable to the laws.

Section II.

Of the Interior Administration.

Article 1. There is in each department a superior administration, and in each district a subordinate administration.

Art. 2. The administrators have no representative character. They are agents elected at stated times by the people, to exercise administrative functions, under the superintendence and the authority of the King.

Art. 3. They can neither interfere in the exercise of legislative power, nor suspend the execution of laws, nor undertake anything of a judicial order, nor of military provision or operation.

Art. 4. The administrators are essentially charged with the distribution of the direct taxes, and with the superintendence of the moneys accruing from all public taxes and revenues in their territory.

The legislative power determines the rules and mode of their functions, both in regard to these subjects and all other parts of the interior administration.

ART. 5. The King has the right to annul the acts of the department administrators which are contrary to law or to the orders that he has given them. He may, in case of continued disobedience, and where they compromise, by th ir 'acts, the public safety and tranquillity, suspend them from their functions.

ART. 6. The department administrators have the same right to annul the acts of the district sub-administrators which are contrary to law, or the resolutions of the department administrators, or to the orders which these last named shall have given or transmitted to them. They can also, in cases of continued disobedience, or if they compromise, by their acts, the public safety and tranquillity, suspend them from their functions, on condition that notice is given to the King, who can disapprove or confirm the suspension.

ART. 7. The King may, when the department administrators shall not have used the power delegated in the above article, annul directly the acts of the sub administrators, and suspend them in the same cases.

ART. 8. At all times, when the King shall have pronounced or confirmed the suspension of the administrators, or sub administrators, he shall notify the Legislative Body of the fact. It shall disapprove or confirm the suspension, or even dissolve the guilty administration, and, in such case, send all the administrators, or a portion of them, to the criminal tribunals, or procure against them a direct indictment.

SECTION III.

Of the Exterior Relations.

ARTICLE 1. The King only may maintain public relations with foreign nations, conduct negotiations, make preparations for war proportionate to those of neighboring States, distribute the land and marine forces as he shall deem expedient, and regulate their conduct in the event of war.

ART. 2. All declarations of war shall be made in these terms: On the part of the King of the French and in the name of the nation.

ART. 3. The King shall enter into and sign, with all foreign powers, all treaties of peace, of alliance, and of commerce, and other agreements which he shall judge necessary for the welfare of the State, subject to the ratification of the Legislative Body.

CHAPTER V.

OF THE JUDICIAL POWER.

ARTICLE 1. The judicial power can neither be exercised by the Legislative Body nor by the King.

ART. 2. Justice shall be rendered, without pay, by the judges elected at stated times, by the people, instituted by letters patent of the King, who can not refuse them.

They can be removed only on account of crimes of which they have legally been found guilty, and can be suspended only by virtue of an accepted accusation.

The public prosecutor shall be named by the people.

ART. 3. The judges can not interfere with the exercise of the legislative power, nor suspend the execution of the law, nor interfere with administrative functions, nor summon before them the administrators, in regard to the functions of their office.

ART. 4. No citizens can be separated from the judges who have been assigned to them by law, by any commission, in any other way which is not pointed out by law.

ART. 5. The right of citizens definitively to terminate their controversies by arbitrations can not be taken away by any act of the legislative power.

ART. 6. The ordinary tribunals can not determine any civil action, except it is authenticated to them that the parties have appeared, or that the plaintiff has cited the adverse party before the arbitrators in order to arrive at a settlement.

ART. 7 There shall be one or several justices of the peace in the cantons and in the cities; their number shall be determined by the legislative power.

ART. 8. It belongs to the legislative power to regulate their number and the jurisdiction of the tribunals, and the number of judges of which each tribunal shall be composed.

ART. 9. In regard to crimes, no citizen can be prosecuted, except by virtue of an accusation preferred by a jury, or passed by the legislative body in cases where the latter has the right to pass the same.

After an accepted accusation, the fact shall be recognized and declared by a jury.

The accused has the right, without assigning reasons, to reject at least twenty of the jurors.

The jury, which shall declare the fact, shall not be less than twelve in number.

The application of the law shall be made by the judges.

The proceedings shall be public, and the accused shall not be denied the aid of counsel.

He who has been acquitted by a legal verdict of the jury can not be again put on trial or accused for the same cause.

ART. 10. No person can be legally arrested, except for the purpose of being brought before a police officer, and no one can be arrested or detained, except by virtue of a warrant of a magistrate of police, on a warrant of arrest issued by a court, or a decree of accusation of the Legislative Body, in those cases in which it is allowed to issue the same, or on a sentence of imprisonment or correctional detention.

ART. 11. Every person who has been arrested and brought before a magistrate of police, shall forthwith, or at least within twenty-four hours, be examined. If it appear upon the examination that there is no ground of accusation against the accused, he shall be set at liberty forthwith, or, if there is reason to send him to prison, he shall be taken there within as short a time as possible, which, in no case, shall exceed three days.

ART. 12. No person arrested can be detained, if he give sufficient bail, in all cases where bail is allowed by law.

ART. 13. No person, in case his detention is authorized by law, can be taken or detained anywhere except in places legally and publicly assigned as places of arrest, of justice, or of imprisonment.

ART. 14. No keeper or jailor can receive or detain any person, unless by virtue of a warrant of arrest, of indictment, or judgment mentioned in Article 10, as above, and without a transcript has been made of it upon his register.

ART. 15. Every keeper and jailor is compelled, and no order can exempt him from it, to bring the arrested person before the civil officer who has the police of the jail under his control, at all times when this officer shall demand it.

Access to the arrested person can not be denied to his relations and friends, if they present an order of the civil officer, who is always compelled to give it, unless the keeper or jailor produce an order of the judge, transcribed on his record, providing that the accused be held in secret confinement.

ART. 16. Any person, whatever may be his place or employment, other than those to whom the law gives the right of arrest, who shall issue, sign, execute, or cause to be executed, an order of arrest of a citizen, or if any person, even in cases of authorized arrests by law, shall bring, receive, or detain a citizen in a place of detention not publicly and legally assigned as such, and all keepers and jailors who shall violate the provisions of Articles 14 and 15, as above, shall be guilty of the crime of arbitrary arrest.

ART. 17. No person can be arrested or prosecuted by reason of writings he shall have caused to be printed or published upon any subject whatever, unless with the design to provoke the disobedience of the law, the disgrace of the constituted authorities, the resistance to their acts, or certain acts declared crimes and misdemeanors by law.

Censure upon the acts of the constituted powers is permitted, but voluntary calumnies against the probity of public functionaries and the integrity of their intentions in the exercise of their functions, may be prosecuted by those who are the object of the attacks.

ART. 18. No one may be judged, either in a civil or criminal way, for written, printed, or published facts, unless a jury has recognized and declared that there is a crime in the writing complained of, and that the person prosecuted is guilty.

ART. 19. There shall be a Court of *Cassation*, established near the Legislative Body, for the whole kingdom. It shall have the following jurisdiction:

Upon appeals from judgments rendered in other courts; on application for removal of cases from one court to another, by reason of lawful prejudice; on orders of judges, or on complaint against a whole court.

ART. 20. In matters of appeal, the Tribunal of *Cassation* shall not examine the main subject of the lawsuit; but, after having annulled the judgment which shall have been rendered in a proceeding in which forms shall have been violated, or which shall contain an express contravention of the law, it shall send the main subject of the action to a court which has jurisdiction over it.

ART. 21. If, after two appeals, the judgment of the third tribunal shall be attacked by the same legal means as in the first two actions, the question can no more be acted on by the Court of *Cassation*, without having been submitted to the Legislative Body, which shall pass a decree declaring a law by which the Court of *Cassation* shall be governed.

ART. 22. The Tribunal of *Cassation* shall send, every year, to the bar of the Legislative Body a deputation of eight of its members, which shall present to it the state of the judgments rendered; opposite each shall be an abridged statement of the action, and the text of the law on which the decision shall have been made.

ART. 23. A National High Court, formed of members of the Tribunal of *Cassation*, and of the grand juries, shall have jurisdiction of the misdemeanors of ministers, and principal agents of the executive power, and crimes which attack the general safety of the State, in cases where the Legislative Body shall have passed a decree of indictment.

The High Court shall assemble on the proclamation of the Legislative Body, and at a distance of at least thirty miles from the place where the legislature has its seat.

ART. 24. The writ of execution of the courts shall be expressed as follows:

"N (the name of the King), by the grace of God and by constitutional law of the State, King of the French, to all these presents shall come, greeting. The Tribunal of * * * has rendered the following judgment:"

(Here shall be a copy of the judgment, in which the name of the judges shall appear.)

"We decree and order all sheriffs, upon this requisition, to place the said judgment in execution; to our commissioners at the tribunals to keep it in force, and to all commanders and officers of the public forces to lend assistance when they shall legally be required to do so. In witness whereof the present judgment has been signed by the president and the clerk of the tribunal."

ART. 25. The functions of the commissioners of the King at the tribunals shall be to require the observance of the law in the pending cases, and to cause the final judgments to be executed.

They shall not be public accusers, but they shall be heard upon all accusations, and shall require the observance of forms in the preparation for the hearing of a cause, and, before judgment, in the application of the law.

ART. 26. The commissioners of the King at the tribunals shall inform the foreman of the jury, either as a duty, or in accordance with orders which shall have been given to them by the King:

All attempts against the individual liberty of citizens, against the free circulation of subsistence and other objects of commerce, and against the collection of taxes; crimes by which the execution of the orders given by the King, in the exercise of the functions which are delegated to him, would be disturbed or hindered; attempts against the rights of the people; revolts against the executions of judgments and against all executory acts emanating from the constituted powers.

ART. 27. The Minister of Justice shall inform the Tribunal of *Cassation*, through the commissioner of the King, and without prejudice to the rights of the interested parties, the acts by which the judges shall have exceeded the limits of their power.

The Tribunal shall annul these acts, and if they call for forfeiture, the fact shall be laid before the Legislative Body, which shall pass a decree of indictment, if there be cause, and shall send the accused before the National High Court.

TITLE IV.
Of the Public Forces.

ARTICLE 1. The public force is established to protect the State against foreign enemies, and to secure in the interior the maintenance of order and the execution of the laws.

ART. 2. It is composed of the land and marine forces, of the troops specially designated for home service, drawn from the active citizens and their sons who are able to bear arms, and registered on the roll of the National Guard.

ART. 3. The National Guards neither form a military body nor an establishment of the State; they are the citizens themselves, called into the service of the public force.

ART. 4. Citizens can neither form themselves nor act as National Guards, except by virtue of a requisition, or of a legal authorization.

ART. 5. They submit in this regard to an organization determined by the law; there can be but one discipline and uniform throughout the kingdom. Order of rank and subordination take place only in regard to the service, and during the same.

ART. 6. The officers are elected at stated times, and can only be re-elected after an interval of service as soldiers. No one can command the National Guard for a greater territory than a district.

ART. 7. Every part of the public forces employed for the safety of the State against foreign enemies shall act under orders of the King.

ART. 8. No corps or detachment of the troops of the line shall operate in the interior of the kingdom without a legal requisition.

ART. 9. No agent of the public forces can enter the house of a citizen, unless it is for the execution of a police or judicial mandate, or in cases formally provided for by law.

Art. 10. The requisition of the public force in the interior of the kingdom belongs to the civic officers, following the rules determined by the legislative power.

Art. 11. If troubles agitate the whole of a department, the King shall give, under the responsibility of his ministers, the necessary orders for the execution of the laws, and for the re-establishment of order, but on condition that he inform the Legislative Body of his action, and to convoke it if it has adjourned.

Art 12. The public forces shall always obey orders. No armed body can deliberate.

Art. 13. The land and marine forces and the troops intended for the safety of the interior are subject to special laws, either for the maintenance of discipline or the form of sentences and nature of punishments in all military crimes.

Title V.
Of Public Taxation.

Article 1. The public taxes shall, every year, be considered and established by the Legislative Body, and can not exist longer than the last day of the following session, unless they are expressly renewed by the same.

Art. 2. Under no pretext may the necessary funds for the discharge of the national debt or the payment of the civil list either be refused or suspended. The stipend of the ministers of the Catholic worship pensioned, maintained, elected, or nominated by virtue of the decrees of the National Constituent Assembly forms part of the national debt.

The Legislative Body can, in no case, charge the nation with the debts of any individual.

Art. 3. The detailed accounts of the expenses of the ministerial departments, signed and certified by the ministers or the general orderers, shall be made public in a printed statement at the commencement of the sessions of each legislature. The same rule applies to the accounts of the income of the different taxes, and of all public revenues. The accounts of these expenditures and receipts shall be stated separately, according to their nature, and shall express the sums received and expended, year by year, in each district. The special expenses of each department relating to the tribunals, to the administrative body, and other establishments, shall equally be made public.

Art. 4. The departmental administrators and sub-administrators shall not create any public tax, nor make any assessment beyond the time and the sums fixed by the Legislative Body, nor consider nor permit, without being authorized by it, any local loan to be a charge upon the citizens of the department.

ART. 5. The executive power directs and superintends the collection and the disbursement of taxes and gives all necessary orders to that effect.

TITLE VI.

Of the Relations of the French Nation with Foreign Nations.

The French nation disclaims all wars conducted for conquest, and will never employ its forces against the liberty of any people.

The Constitution does not admit the right of escheat.

Foreigners, settled or not, in France, inherit from their kin, whether they be foreigners or native born.

They may enter into contracts, buy and take estates situate in France, and dispose of them like French citizens, in any manner allowed by law.

Foreigners in France shall submit, in the same manner, to the criminal and police laws, as French citizens, subject, however, to the treaties with foreign powers; their persons, their estates, their industries, their worship, are equally protected by the law.

TITLE VII.

Of the Revision of the Constitutional Acts.

ARTICLE 1. The National Constituent Assembly declares that the nation has the inalienable right to amend its Constitution, and considering that the national interest is better served by making use of the means provided for in the Constitution itself, of the right to reform such articles which experience shall show the expediency of, decrees the formation of an Assembly of Revision, in the following manner:

ART. 2. When three consecutive legislatures shall have issued a request for an amendment of a constitutional article, the revision demanded shall then take place.

ART. 3. The next legislature, or the one following it, can not propose any reform to a constitutional article.

ART. 4. Of the three legislatures, which shall be able, one after another, to propose certain amendments, the two first shall only occupy themselves with this object during the last two months of their last session, and the third at the end of its first annual session, or at the commencement of the second. Their deliberations upon this matter shall be submitted to the same forms as the legislative acts, but the decrees by which they shall emit their request shall not be subject to the sanction of the King.

ART. 5. The fourth legislature, augmented by 249 members elected in each department, by doubling the ordinary members which are furnished according to population, shall form the Assembly of Revision.

These 249 members shall be elected after the nomination of the representatives to the Legislative Body shall have been terminated, and separate minutes of the same shall be made.

The Assembly of Revision shall only be composed of one chamber.

ART. 6. The members of the third legislature who shall have requested amendments shall not be elected to the Assembly of Revision.

ART. 7. The members of the Assembly of Revision, after having pronounced the oath together to live as freemen or to die, shall then take an oath, individually, to limit themselves to the objects which shall have been submitted to them by the uniform request of three preceding legislatures, to maintain, moreover, with all their power, the Constitution of the kingdom decreed by the National Constituent Assembly in the years 1789, 1790, and 1791, and to be in all respects faithful to the nation, to the law, and to the King.

ART. 8. The members of the Assembly of Revision shall then, without delay, be compelled to occupy themselves with the objects which shall have been submitted to them; as soon as their labors shall have terminated, the additional 249 members shall retire, without taking any part in the regular legislation.

TITLE VIII.

Various Provisions.

ARTICLE 1. The French colonies and possessions in Asia, Africa, and America, although they formed part of the French empire, are not comprised within the present Constitution.

ART. 2. No power instituted by the Constitution has the right to amend it in whole or in part, except the reforms to be made by way of revision, and conformably to the provisions of the above title.

ART. 3. The National Constituent Assembly intrusts itself to the safe-keeping and to the fidelity of the Legislative Body, to the King, and to the judges, to the watchfulness of fathers of families, to the wives and mothers, to the love of young citizens, and to the courage of all Frenchmen.

ART. 4. The decrees rendered by the National Constituent Assembly which are not comprised within the Constitutional Act, shall be executed as laws, and the anterior laws, which have not been abrogated, shall equally be observed, so long as they have not been repealed or amended by the legislative power.

ART. 5. The National Assembly having heard the Constitutional Act read, and after having approved it, declares that no further changes can be made, and that the Constitution is completed.

APPENDIX II.

CONSTITUTION OF 1793 (YEAR I).

OF THE REPUBLIC.

1. The French Republic is one and indivisible.

OF THE DIVISION OF THE PEOPLE.

2. The French people is, for the purpose of exercising its sovereignty, divided into primary assemblies by cantons.

3. For the purpose of administration and justice, it is divided into departments, districts, and municipalities.

OF THE RIGHT OF CITIZENSHIP.

4. Every man born and living in France, of twenty-one years of age, and every alien who has attained the age of twenty-one, and has been domiciled in France one year, and lives from his labor, or has acquired property, or has adopted a child, or supports an aged man; and, finally, every alien whom the Legislative Body has declared as one well deserving of the human race, are admitted to exercise the rights of a French citizen.

5. The right of exercising the rights of a citizen is lost: by naturalization in a foreign State; by acceptance of functions or favors which do not proceed from a democratic government; by condemnation to dishonorable or corporal punishments, until reinstated in civil rights.

6. The exercise of the rights of citizens is suspended: by indictment; by a sentence *in contumaciam*, so long as this sentence has not been annulled.

OF THE SOVEREIGNTY OF THE PEOPLE.

7. The sovereign people embraces all French citizens.

8. It chooses its deputies directly.

9. It delegates to electors the choice of administrators, of public arbitrators, criminal judges, and judges of *cassation*.

10. It deliberates on laws.

OF THE PRIMARY ASSEMBLIES.

11. The primary assemblies are formed of the citizens who have resided six months in a canton.

12. They consist of at least 200 and no more than 600 citizens, called together for the purpose of voting.

13. They are organized after a president, secretaries, and collectors of votes have been appointed.

14. They have their own police.

15. No one is allowed to appear there with arms.

16. The elections are conducted either by secret or open voting, at the pleasure of each voter.

17. A primary meeting can not prescribe a uniform mode of voting.

18. The collectors of votes note down the votes of those citizens who can not write and yet prefer to vote by ballot.

19. The votes on laws are given by "Yes" and "No."

20. The vote of the primary assemblies is published in the following manner:

The united citizens in the Primary Assembly at ———, numbering ——— votes, vote for, or vote against, by a majority of ———.

OF THE NATIONAL REPRESENTATION.

21. Population is the only basis of national representation.

22. For every 40,000 individuals one deputy is chosen.

23. Every primary assembly, which is formed of from 39,000 to 41,000 individuals, chooses directly a deputy.

24. The choice is effected by an absolute majority of votes.

25. Every assembly makes an abstract of the votes, and sends a commissioner to the appointed central place of general record.

26. If, at the first voting, no absolute majority be effected, a second meeting shall be held, and those two citizens who had the most votes shall be voted for again.

27. In case of an equal division of votes, the oldest person has the preference, either in selecting the person to be voted for, or to decide if he be elected. In case of an equality of age, the casting of lots shall decide.

28. Every Frenchman who enjoys the rights of a citizen is eligible throughout the whole Republic.

29. Every deputy belongs to the whole nation.

30. In case of non-acceptance, of resignation, or forfeiture of office,

or of the death of a deputy, the primary assembly which had chosen him shall choose a person to fill the vacancy.

31. A deputy who tenders his resignation can not leave his post until his successor shall have been appointed.

32. The French people assembles every year on the 1st of May to take part in the elections.

33. It proceeds thereto, whatever the number of citizens present may be who have a right to vote.

34. Extraordinary primary meetings are held at the demand of one-fifth of the eligible citizens.

35. The meeting is, in this case, called by the municipal authority at the usual place of assembly.

36. These extraordinary meetings can transact business only when at least more than one-half of the qualified voters are present.

OF THE ELECTORAL ASSEMBLIES.

37. The citizens united in primary assemblies nominate one elector in proportion to 200 citizens (present or not); two for from 301 to 600.

38. The holding of electoral assemblies and the mode of elections are the same as in the primary assemblies.

OF THE LEGISLATIVE BODY.

39. The Legislative Body is one, indivisible and continual.

40. Its session lasts one year.

41. It assembles on the 1st of July.

42. The National Assembly can not be organized unless at least one more than one-half of the deputies are present.

43. The deputies can at no time be held answerable, accused, or condemned on account of opinions uttered within the Legislative Body.

44. In criminal cases, they may be arrested if taken in the act; but the warrant of arrest and the warrant of committal can be issued only by the authority of the Legislative Body.

MODE OF PROCEDURE OF THE LEGISLATIVE BODY.

45. The sessions of the National Assembly are public.

46. The minutes of their sessions shall be printed.

47. It can not deliberate unless it consist of at least 200 members.

48. It can not refuse the floor to members in the order in which they demand the same.

49. It decides by a majority of those present.

50. Fifty members have the right to demand a call by names.

51. It has the right of censorship on the conduct of its members.

52. It exercises the power of police at the place of its sessions, and within a certain jurisdiction it has determined.

OF THE FUNCTIONS OF THE LEGISLATIVE BODY.

53. The Legislative Body proposes laws and issues decrees.

54. By the general name of law are understood the provisions of the Legislative Body which concern the civil and penal legislation; the general administration of the revenues of the Republic; the national domains; the inscription, alloy, stamp, and names of coins; the nature, the raising, and the collection of taxes; declaration of war; every new general division of the French territory; public instruction; public demonstrations of honor to the memory of great men.

55. By the particular name of decrees are understood those enactments of the Legislative Body which concern: the annual establishment of the land and marine forces; the permission for or refusal of the marching of foreign troops through French territory; the admission of foreign vessels of war into the ports of the Republic; the measures for the general peace and safety; the distribution of annual and momentary relief, and of public works; the orders for the coining of moneys of every description; the unforeseen and extraordinary expenses; the local and particular measures for an administration, a commune, or any kind of public works; the defense of the territory; the ratification of treaties; the nomination and dismissal of the commanders-in-chief of the armies; the carrying into effect the responsibility of members of the Council, and of public officers; the accusation of discovered conspiracies against the common safety of the Republic; every alteration in the division of the French territory, and the national rewards.

OF THE MAKING OF LAWS.

56. A report must precede the introduction of a bill.

57. Not until after a fortnight from the report can the debate begin and the law be provisionally enacted.

58. The proposed law is printed and sent to all the communes of the Republic, entitled *Proposed Law*.

59. If, forty days after the sending in of the proposed law, an

absolute majority of the departments, and one tenth of all the primary assemblies of each department, legally assembled, have not protested, the bill is accepted and becomes a law.

60. If protest be made, the Legislative Body calls together the primary assemblies.

ON THE SUPERSCRIPTION OF LAWS AND DECREES.

61. The laws, decrees, sentences, and all public acts are superscribed:—

In the name of the French people, in the — year of the French Republic.

OF THE EXECUTIVE COUNCIL.

62. There shall be an Executive Council, consisting of twenty-four members.

63. The electoral assembly of each department nominates a candidate. The Legislative Body chooses the members of the Executive Council from this general list.

64. It shall be renewed each half session of every legislature, in the last months of its session.

65. The Executive Council is charged with the management and supervision of the general administration. Its activity is limited to the execution of laws and decrees of the Legislative Body.

66. It appoints, outside of its own body, the highest agents of the general administration of the Republic.

67. The Legislative Body establishes the number and the business of these agents.

68. These agents do not form a council. They are separated one from the other, and have no relation with each other. They exercise no personal power.

69. The Executive Council chooses, outside of its own body, the foreign agents of the Republic.

70. It negotiates treaties.

71. The members of the Executive Council are, in case of violation of duties, accused by the Legislative Body.

72. The Executive Council is responsible for the non-execution of the laws and decrees, and the abuses of which it does not give notice.

73. It recalls and substitutes the agents at pleasure.

74. It is obliged, if there is cause, to inform the judicial authorities regarding them.

OF THE MUTUAL RELATIONS BETWEEN THE EXECUTIVE COUNCIL AND THE LEGISLATIVE BODY.

75. The Executive Council shall have its seat near the Legislative Body. It shall have admittance to, and a special seat at the place of session.

76. It shall be heard at all times when it shall have a statement to make.

77. The Legislative Body shall call the Council before it, in whole or in part, when it is thought necessary.

OF THE ADMINISTRATIVE AND MUNICIPAL BODIES.

78. There shall be a municipal administration in each commune of the Republic, and in each district an intermediate administration, and in each department a central administration.

79. The municipal officers are chosen by the assemblies of the commune.

80. The administrators are chosen by the electoral assemblies of the departments and of the districts.

81. The municipalities and the administrations are annually renewed one-half.

82. The administrators, authorities, and municipal officers have not a representative character. They can, in no case, modify the acts of the Legislative Body, nor suspend the execution of them.

83. The Legislative Body assigns the business of the municipal officers and of the administrators, the rules regarding their subordination, and the punishments to which they may become liable.

84. The sessions of the municipalities and of the administrations are public.

OF CIVIL JUSTICE.

85. The civil and penal code is the same for the whole Republic.

86. No encroachment can be made upon the right of citizens to have their matters in dispute decided on by arbitrators of their own choice.

87. The decision of these arbitrators is final, unless the citizens have reserved the right of protesting.

88. There shall be justices of the peace, chosen by the citizens of the districts, according to law.

89. They shall arbitrate and hold court without fees.

90. Their number and jurisdiction shall be established by the Legislative Body.

91. There shall be public judges of arbitration, who are chosen by electoral assemblies.

92. Their number and districts are fixed by the Legislative Body.

93. They shall decide on matters in controversy, which have not been brought to a final decision by private arbitrators or by the justices of the peace.

94. They shall deliberate publicly. They shall vote orally. They decide in the last resort on oral pleadings, or on a simple petition, without legal forms and without costs. They shall assign the reasons of their decisions.

95. The justices of the peace and the public arbitrators are chosen annually.

OF CRIMINAL JUSTICE.

96. In criminal cases, no citizen can be put on trial, except a true bill of complaint be found by a jury, or by the Legislative Body.

The accused shall have advocates, either chosen by themselves or appointed officially.

The proceedings are in public.

The facts and the intention are passed upon by a jury.

The punishment is executed by a criminal tribunal.

97. The criminal judges are chosen annually by the electoral assemblies.

OF THE COURT OF CASSATION.

98. There is a Court of *Cassation* for the whole Republic.

99. This court takes no cognizance of the facts. It decides on the violation of matters of form, and on questions of law.

100. The members of this court are appointed annually by the electoral assemblies.

OF THE GENERAL TAXES.

101. No citizen is excluded from the honorable obligation to contribute toward the public expenses.

OF THE NATIONAL TREASURY.

102. The national treasury is the central point of the revenues and expenses of the Republic.

103. It is managed by responsible agents, whom the Executive Council shall elect.

104. These agents are supervised by commissioners, whom the Legislative Body shall appoint, but who can not be taken from their

own body; they are responsible for abuses of which they do not give legal notice.

OF THE RENDITION OF ACCOUNTS.

105. The accounts of the agents of the national treasury, and those of the administrators of public moneys are rendered annually to responsible commissioners appointed by the Executive Council.

106. Those persons appointed to revise the accounts are supervised by the commissioners, who are elected by the Legislative Body, not out of their own number; and they are responsible for the frauds and mistakes of accounts of which they do not give notice.

The Legislative Body passes upon the accounts.

OF THE MILITARY FORCES OF THE REPUBLIC.

107. The general military force of the Republic consists of the whole people.

108. The Republic supports, also, in time of peace, a paid land and marine force.

109. All Frenchmen are soldiers; all shall be exercised in the use of arms.

110. There is no generalissimo.

111. The distinction of grade, the military marks of distinction and subordination, exist only in service and for the time of its duration.

112. The public force employed to maintain order and peace in the interior acts only on a written requisition of the constituted authorities.

113. The public force employed against foreign enemies is under the command of the Executive Council.

114. No armed body can deliberate.

OF THE NATIONAL CONVENTION.

115. If the absolute majority of departments and the tenth part of their regularly formed primary assemblies demand a revision of the Constitution, or an alteration of some of its articles, the Legislative Body is compelled to call together all primary assemblies of the Republic, in order to ascertain whether a National Convention shall be called.

116. The National Convention is formed in like manner as the legislatures, and unites in itself the highest power.

117. It is occupied, as regards the Constitution, only with those subjects which caused it to be called together.

OF THE RELATIONS OF THE FRENCH REPUBLIC TOWARD FOREIGN NATIONS.

118. The French nation is the natural friend and ally of free nations.

119. It does not interfere with the affairs of government of other nations. It suffers no interference of other nations with its own.

120. It offers an asylum for all who, on account of liberty, are banished from their native country. These it refuses to deliver up to tyrants.

121. It concludes no peace with an enemy that holds possession of its territory.

OF THE GUARANTY OF RIGHTS.

122. The Constitution guarantees to all Frenchmen equality, liberty, security, property, the public debt, free exercise of religion, general instruction, public assistance, absolute liberty of the press, the right of petition, the right to hold popular assemblies, and the enjoyment of all the rights of man.

123. The French Republic respects loyalty, courage, old age, filial affection, misfortune. It places the Constitution under the guarantee of all virtues.

124. The declaration of the rights of man and the Constitutional Act shall be engraven on tables, to be placed in the midst of the Legislative Body and in public places.

APPENDIX III.

CONSTITUTION OF 1795 (YEAR III).

ARTICLE 1. The French Republic is one and indivisible.
ART. 2. Sovereignty consists of the collective number of all French citizens.

TITLE I.
DIVISION OF TERRITORY.

ART. 3. France is divided into departments.
ART. 4. The boundaries of the departments may be altered or rectified by the Legislative Body, but in that event, the area of a department can not exceed 100 square myriameters (about 400 square miles).
ART. 5. Each department is divided into cantons, and each canton into communes. The cantons preserve their present circumscription.
ART. 6. The French colonies are parts of the Republic, and are subject to the same constitutional law.
ART. 7. They are divided into departments (the names are then given).

TITLE II.
POLITICAL CONDITION OF CITIZENS.

ART. 8. Every person born and residing in France, who has attained the age of twenty-one years, and whose name is inscribed in the civic register of his canton, and who has lived in the territory of the Republic for one year, and who pays a direct tax, real or personal, is a French citizen.
ART. 9. All Frenchmen who shall have made one or more campaigns for the establishment of the Republic, are citizens, without condition as to taxes.
ART. 10. An alien becomes a French citizen if, after having attained the age of twenty-one years, he has declared his intention to settle in

France, and has resided there for seven consecutive years, provided he pays a direct tax, and is possessed of real estate, or carries on an agricultural establishment, or has married a French woman.

ART. 11. French citizens can only vote in the primary assemblies and be appointed to the offices created by the Constitution.

ART. 12. The right of the exercise of the rights of citizenship is lost: 1. By naturalization in a foreign country. 2. By admission into any foreign corporation which requires distinction of birth, or religious vows. 3. By accepting offices or pensions tendered by a foreign government. 4. By condemnation to corporal or dishonorable punishment, until restoration to former rights.

ART. 13. The exercise of the rights of citizenship is suspended: 1. By a judicial decree on account of insanity, idiocy, or imbecility. 2. When a person is bankrupt, or takes of his own free will, as immediate heir, the whole or a part of an insolvent estate of a deceased bankrupt. 3. By being a servant for wages in the employment of a person or a household. 4. By indictment. 5. By judgment of contempt of court, so long as the judgment is not annulled.

ART. 14. The exercise of the rights of citizenship is neither lost nor suspended, except in the cases enumerated in the two preceding articles.

ART. 15. Every citizen who shall have resided seven years out of the territory of the Republic, without a mission or authorization given in the name of the nation, is regarded as an alien; he can only become again a French citizen after having complied with the conditions prescribed by Article 10.

ART. 16. Young men can not be inscribed on the civic register if they can not prove that they can read and write and practice a mechanical trade. The manual work of agriculture belongs to the mechanical trades. This article shall only be enforced from the twelfth year of the Republic.

TITLE III.

PRIMARY ASSEMBLIES.

ART. 17. The primary assemblies consist of the citizens residing in the same canton. The qualification for voting in these assemblies is acquired by one year's residence, and is lost by one year's absence.

ART. 18. No one can be represented by another in the primary assemblies or vote on the same subject in more than one of the assemblies.

CONSTITUTION OF MDCCXCV.

ART. 19. There is at least one primary assembly in each canton. If there are several, each one shall consist of at least 450, and no more than 900 citizens. This number includes both absent and present citizens entitled to vote there.

ART. 20. The primary assemblies are formed provisionally under the presidency of the oldest person; the youngest performs provisionally the duties of secretary.

ART. 21. They are permanently organized when a president, a secretary, and a collector of votes are chosen by vote.

ART. 22. If doubts arise in regard to the qualifications for voting, the assembly shall decide, conditionally subject to an appeal to the civil tribunal of the department.

ART. 23. In all other cases, the legislative body alone pronounces upon the validity of the acts of the primary assemblies.

ART. 24. No one shall appear armed in the primary assemblies.

ART. 25. They have their own police.

ART. 26. The primary assemblies convene: 1. To accept or reject amendments to the constitutional act proposed in the assemblies of revision. 2. To hold those elections which belong to them according to the constitutional act.

ART. 27. They convene with full power on the 1st of *Germinal* (21st March to 19th April) of each year, and proceed to the election according to the order of legality: 1. Of the members of the electoral assemblies. 2. Of the justice of the peace and his associates. 3. Of the president of the municipal administration of the canton, or of the municipal officers in communes of over 5,000 inhabitants.

ART. 28. Immediately after the elections, in communes under 5,000 inhabitants, the communal assemblies meet to elect the agents of each commune and their assistants.

ART. 29. All that is done in the primary or communal assemblies beyond the objects for which they were convened, and against the forms of the Constitution, is void.

ART. 30. The assemblies, primary or communal, shall hold no other elections than those specified by the constitutional act.

ART. 31. At all elections the voting is by ballot.

ART. 32. Every citizen who has been legally convicted of having sold or bought a vote, is excluded from the primary assemblies and from all public office, for twenty years, and in case of a second transgression, forever.

Title IV.

ELECTORAL ASSEMBLIES.

ART. 33. Each primary assembly nominates one elector for every 200 present or absent citizens who have the right to vote in said assembly. Up to 300 citizens (inclusively), one elector is chosen, for 301 to 500, two electors are chosen; three for 501 to 700; four for 701 to 900.

ART. 34. The members of the electoral assemblies are chosen annually and they can not be re-elected until after an interval of two years.

ART. 35. No one can be chosen elector unless he has attained the age of twenty-five, and unless he unites with the qualifications requisite for the exercise of the rights of a French citizen one of the following conditions:

In communes of over 6,000 inhabitants, that he is the proprietor or beneficiary of an estate valued at a revenue equal to the local value of 200 days' work, or that he is the occupant, either of a habitation valued at a revenue equal to the value of 500 days' work, or of a rural estate valued at 200 days' work; in communes under 6,000 inhabitants, that he is the proprietor or beneficiary of an estate valued at a revenue equal to the local value of 150 days' labor, or that he is the occupant either of a tenement valued at a revenue equal to the value of 100 days' labor, or of a rural estate valued at 100 days' labor; and in the country, that he is the proprietor or beneficiary of an estate valued at a revenue equal to the local value of 150 days' labor, or that he is a farmer or tenant of a farm valued at the value of 200 days' labor.

In regard to those who are, in part, proprietors or beneficiaries, and, in part, tenants or farmers, their estates are estimated together, in their different characters, to the amount requisite for their eligibility.

ART. 36. The electoral assembly of each department meets annually on the 20th of *Germinal* (from March 21st to April 19th), and terminates, at the longest, in one session of ten days, without the power to adjourn, all the elections which are to be made, whereupon it shall be dissolved.

ART. 37. The electoral assemblies can not be occupied with any subject foreign to the elections with which they are charged; they can neither send nor receive any address, petition, or deputation.

ART. 38. The electoral assemblies can not hold correspondence with each other.

ART. 39. No citizen, having been a member of an electoral assembly, can bear the title of elector, nor, in this relation, combine with those who have been members with him in the same assembly.

The violation of this article is an attempt against the general safety.

ART. 40. The Articles 18, 20, 21, 23, 24, 25, 29, 30, 31, and 32 of the preceding title, on primary assemblies, are applicable to electoral assemblies.

ART. 41. The electoral assemblies elect, as the case may be: 1. The members of the Legislative Body; namely, the members of the Council of the Ancients, then the members of the Council of the Five Hundred. 2. The members of the Tribunal of *Cassation*. 3. The grand jurymen. 4. The departmental administrators. 5. The presidents, public attorneys, and clerks of the criminal courts. 6. The judges of the civil courts.

ART. 42. When a citizen is elected by the electoral assemblies in the place of an officer who is either deceased or has resigned, or is removed, this citizen is only chosen for the time left of the term of the past officer.

ART. 43. The commissary of the Executive Directory at the departmental administration is compelled, under penalty of dismissal, to inform the Directory of the opening and closing of the electoral assemblies. This commissary can neither arrest nor suspend the operations, nor be present at the place of their sessions; but he has the right to demand the minutes of each sitting within the following twenty-four hours, and he must inform the Directory of the violations of the constitutional act.

In all cases the Legislative Body alone decides on the validity of the transactions of the electoral assemblies.

TITLE V.

THE LEGISLATIVE POWER.—GENERAL PROVISIONS.

ART. 44. The Legislative Body is composed of a Council of the Ancients and of a Council of the Five Hundred.

ART. 45. The Legislative Body can in no case delegate to one or several of its members, nor to anybody else, any of the functions which are assigned to it by the present Constitution.

ART. 46. It can neither through itself nor through the delegates exercise either the executive power or the judicial power.

ART. 47. The qualifications of a member of the Legislative Body are incompatible with the holding of another public office, except that of the keeper of the records of the Republic.

ART. 48. The law determines the permanent and temporary substitution of public officers who have just been elected members of the Legislative Body.

ART. 49. Each department concurs, only in proportion to its population, in the nomination of the members of the Council of the Ancients, and of the members of the Council of the Five Hundred.

ART. 50. Every ten years the Legislative Body, by the lists of population forwarded to it, decides on the number of members of both Councils which each department must furnish.

ART. 51. During this interval, no change can take place in the apportionment.

ART. 52. The members of the Legislative Body are not representatives of the departments which have elected them, but of the nation as a whole, and no instruction can be given them.

ART. 53. Both councils are renewed every year by one-third.

ART. 54. Members whose term of three years has expired may immediately be re-elected for the following three years, after which an interval of two years must take place before they can be chosen again.

ART. 55. No one can, in any case, be a member of the Legislative Body for more than six consecutive years.

ART. 56. If, by extraordinary circumstances, the number of members of one of the two councils should be reduced to less than two-thirds of its members, it shall immediately give notice thereof to the Executive Directory, which shall, without delay, convoke the primary assemblies of those departments which have places of members to fill in the Legislative Body. The primary assemblies shall forthwith choose electors, who shall fill the vacancies.

ART. 57. The newly elected members to both councils assemble on the 1st *Prairial* of every year, in the commune which has been fixed by the foregoing Legislative Body, or in the same commune where it held its last session, if no other has been designated.

ART. 58. Both councils have their sessions in the same commune.

ART. 59. The Legislative Body is continual; it may, nevertheless, adjourn for periods of time it shall designate.

ART. 60. Both councils can in no case assemble in the same room.

ART. 61. The duty of president and of secretary, neither in the Council of the Ancients nor in the Council of the Five Hundred, can exceed the term of one month.

ART. 62. Both councils have, each for itself, the right of police in the place of its sittings, and the environs determined by them.

ART. 63. They have each police authority over their members, but they can award no greater punishment than reproof, arrest for eight days, or imprisonment for three days.

ART. 64. The sessions of both councils are public; the audience can not exceed in number one-half of the respective members of each council. The records of the sessions are printed.

ART. 65. All voting is done by keeping seat and rising; in doubtful cases the names are called, but then the voting is secret.

ART. 66. At the request of 100 of its members each council can resolve itself into a general or a secret committee, but only for discussion, and not for the transaction of business.

ART. 67. Neither of the councils can, from its own body, create a permanent committee. But each council has the right, when a subject seems to require a preliminary examination, to name a special committee, which confines itself to the matter referred to it. This committee is dissolved as soon as the council has legislated on the subject.

ART. 68. The members of the Legislative Body receive a yearly salary; it is determined for either of the councils at the value of 3,000 myriagrammes of wheat (613 hundred-weight and thirty-two pounds).

ART. 69. The Executive Directory can not cause any body of troops to march through or to bivouac at a distance of six myriameters (twelve miles of middle length) from the commune where the Legislative Body holds its sessions, unless it be at the request or with its authorization.

ART. 70. A guard of citizens shall be stationed near the Legislative Body, which is taken from the inactive National Guard of all the departments, and chosen by their comrades in arms. This guard can not consist of less than 1,500 men in active service.

ART. 71. The Legislative Body determines the character and duration of its service.

ART. 72. The Legislative Body shall not attend a public ceremony, nor send a deputation to it.

THE COUNCIL OF FIVE HUNDRED.

ART. 73. The Council of the Five Hundred is unalterably fixed at this number.

ART. 74. In order to be eligible to the Council of the Five Hundred, a person must be thirty years old, and have been domiciled in the territory of the Republic for ten years immediately preceding his election. This condition of age is not required before the seventh year of the Republic; until this time the age of twenty-five years will be sufficient.

Art. 75. The Council of Five Hundred can pass no act unless there are at least 200 members present.

Art. 76. The initiation of laws belongs exclusively to the Council of Five Hundred.

Art. 77. No bill can be discussed nor passed in the Council of Five Hundred unless the following forms are observed: There must be three readings of the bill; the interval can not be less than ten days between two of these readings; after each reading the discussion may take place, but after the first or second reading the Council of Five Hundred may declare that it shall be adjourned, or that no discussion shall take place. Every bill must be printed and distributed two days before the second reading, and after the third reading the Council of Five Hundred decides whether an adjournment shall take place or not.

Art. 78. Every bill which has been rejected after the third reading can not be brought forward again before the lapse of a year.

Art. 79. The propositions adopted by the Council of the Five Hundred are called resolutions.

Art. 80. The preamble of each resolution sets forth: 1. The days of the session on which the three readings of proposition took place. 2. The act by which it was, after the third reading, declared that no adjournment should take place.

Art. 81. The propositions recognized as urgent by a previous declaration of the Council of Five Hundred are excepted from the forms prescribed by Article 77. This declaration states the reasons for the vote of urgency, and mentions them in the preamble of the resolution.

THE COUNCIL OF THE ANCIENTS.

Art. 82. The Council of the Ancients is composed of 250 members.

Art. 83. No one can be chosen a member of the Council of the Ancients until he has attained the age of forty years, and unless he is, moreover, married or a widower, and unless he has resided in the territory of the Republic for fifteen years immediately preceding his election.

Art. 84. The condition of residence required by the preceding article, and that prescribed by Article 74, do not apply to citizens who have left the territory of the Republic on a mission of the government.

Art. 85. The Council of Ancients can not transact business unless at least 126 members are present.

Art. 86. It belongs exclusively to the Council of the Ancients to approve or reject the resolutions of the Council of the Five Hundred.

Art. 87. Whenever a resolution of the Council of the Five Hundred has arrived at the Council of the Ancients, the president orders the preamble to be read.

Art. 88. The Council of the Ancients refuses to approve of the resolutions of the Council of the Five Hundred which do not follow the forms of the Constitution.

Art. 89. If a proposition of urgency has been declared by the Council of the Five Hundred, the Council of the Ancients passes on the acceptance or rejection of the act.

Art. 90. If the Council rejects the act of urgency, it does thereby pass upon the subject of the resolution.

Art. 91. If the resolution is not preceded by an act of urgency, three readings must be had of the same. The interval between two of these readings can not be less than five days. The discussion is opened after each reading. Every resolution is printed and distributed at least two days before the second reading.

Art. 92. The resolutions of the Council of the Five Hundred, adopted by the Council of the Ancients, called laws.

Art. 93. The preamble to the laws states the dates of the sessions of the Council of the Ancients, in which the three readings were had.

Art. 94. The decree by which the Council of the Ancients recognizes the urgency of a law is with its reasons set forth in the preamble of the law.

Art. 95. The proposition of a law made by the Council of the Five Hundred embraces all the articles of the same bill; the Council of the Ancients must either accept or reject them all in their entirety.

Art. 96. The acceptance of the Council of the Ancients is expressed upon each proposition of law with this formula, signed by the president and the secretaries: The Council of the Ancients approves.

Art. 97. The refusal to approve by reason of non-conformance with the forms prescribed in Article 77 is expressed by this formula, signed by the president and the secretaries: The Constitution declares it null and void.

ART. 98. The refusal to approve of the subject-matter of the law is expressed by this formula, signed by the president and the secretaries: The Council of the Ancients can not accept it.

ART. 99. In the case of the preceding article, the rejected bill can not again be presented by the Council of the Five Hundred before the lapse of a year.

ART. 100. The Council of the Five Hundred may, nevertheless, at any time, propose a bill containing articles which constitute a part of the rejected bill.

ART. 101. The Council of the Ancients sends the laws which it has accepted on the same day to the Council of the Five Hundred and the Executive Directory.

ART. 102. The Council of the Ancients may change the place of meeting of the Legislative Body; in this case it appoints a new place, and the time when the two councils have to repair to the same. The decree of the Council of the Ancients on this subject is irrevocable.

ART. 103. On the same day of this decree neither of the councils can longer transact business in the place where they heretofore held their sessions. The members who should continue these acts there make themselves guilty of an attempt against the safety of the Republic.

ART. 104. The members of the Executive Directory who retard, or refuse to seal, promulgate, and forward the decree of removal of the Legislative Body, are guilty of the same crime.

ART. 105. If, after the lapse of twenty days from the day which the Council of the Ancients has appointed, the majority of both councils shall not have made known to the Republic their arrival at the newly-designated place, or their meeting at some other place, the departmental administrators, or, in their default, the civil courts of the departments, shall convoke the primary assemblies for the purpose of choosing electors, who proceed to the formation of a new Legislative Body, by the election of 250 deputies for the Council of the Ancients, and 500 for the other council.

ART. 106. The departmental administrators, who, in case of the preceding article, shall delay to convoke the primary assemblies, are guilty of high treason and of an attempt against the safety of the Republic.

ART. 107. Of the like crime are guilty all citizens who, in case of the 106th Article, shall hinder the calling together of the primary and electoral assemblies.

ART. 108. The members of the new Legislative Body assemble at the place to which the Council of the Ancients had transferred the sessions.

ART. 109. Except in the case of Article 102, no bill can originate in the Council of the Ancients.

OF THE GUARANTY OF THE MEMBERS OF THE LEGISLATIVE BODY.

ART. 110. Citizens who are, or have been members of the Legislative Body, can at no time be prosecuted, accused, or judged on account of what they have said or written in the exercise of their duty.

ART. 111. Members of the Legislative Body can, from the moment of their nomination until the thirtieth day after the expiration of their official duties, in no other way be brought before court than in the manner prescribed in the following articles:

ART. 112. They may, for criminal acts, be arrested when taken in the act; but immediate information must be given thereof to the Legislative Body; and the prosecution can not be proceeded with until the Council of the Five Hundred shall have proposed the trial and the Council of the Ancients shall have decreed the same.

ART. 113. Excepting the case of being caught in the act, the members of the Legislative Body can not be brought before a magistrate of police, nor be arrested, before the Council of the Five Hundred shall have proposed the trial, and the Council of the Ancients shall have decreed the same.

ART. 114. In the cases of the two preceding articles, a member of the Legislative Body can be brought before no other court than that of the High Court of Justice.

ART. 115. They are brought before this same court on the charge of treason, squandering of public moneys, plans for the overthrow of the Constitution, and infringements of the internal safety of the Republic.

ART. 116. No information against a member of the Legislative Body can furnish grounds for prosecution unless it be in writing, signed and addressed to the Council of the Five Hundred.

ART. 117. If the Council of the Five Hundred, after having acted on the information in accordance with the forms prescribed by Article 77, shall accept it, it declares this in the following words:

The information against ——— , on account of ——— , dated ——— signed by ———, is accepted.

ART. 118. The accused is then summoned; he has full three days to make his appearance; and when he appears he is heard in the hall where the Council of the Five Hundred meets.

ART. 119. Whether the accused has appeared or not, the Council of the Five Hundred declares, on the expiration of the time, whether or not there is cause for an examination into his conduct.

ART. 120. If the Council of the Five Hundred declare that an examination shall be had, the accused is summoned by the Council of the Ancients. He has full two days to appear, and when he appears he is heard in the hall where the Council of the Ancients meets.

ART. 121. Whether the accused is present or not, the Council of the Ancients, after the time has expired, and after having deliberated according to the forms prescribed in Article 91, pronounces the accusation, if there is cause, and sends the accused before the High Court of Justice, which must prepare the trial without any delay.

ART. 122. All discussion, in both councils, relative to the complaint or accusation against a member of the Legislative Body, is had in the general committee. All deliberative action on these subjects is taken by calling the names and by secret voting.

ART. 123. An accusation against a member of the Legislative Body involves his suspension. If he is acquitted by the judgment of the High Court of Justice, he resumes his duties.

RELATIONS OF THE TWO COUNCILS BETWEEN ONE ANOTHER.

ART. 124. When the two councils are definitively organized they give each other due notice of the fact by a messenger of State.

ART. 125. Each council appoints four messengers of State for its service.

ART. 126. They carry the laws and the acts of the Legislative Body to each of the councils and to the Executive Directory; for this purpose they have admission to the place of session of the Executive Directory. Two ushers precede them.

ART. 127. Neither of the two councils can adjourn for more than five days without the consent of the other.

PROMULGATION OF THE LAWS.

ART. 128. The Executive Directory causes the laws and the other acts of the Legislative Body to be sealed and published within two days after they have been received.

ART. 129. The laws and acts of the Legislative Body which are preceded by an act of urgency must be sealed and published on the same day.

ART. 130. The publication of the laws and the acts of the Legislative Body are ordered in the following form:

"*In the name of the French Republic (the law) or (the act of the Legislative Body)*——— *The Directory orders that the above law or act be published, and executed, and that the seal of the Republic be affixed to the same.*"

ART. 131. The laws, the preambles of which do not attest the observance of the forms prescribed by Articles 77 and 91, can not be promulgated by the Council of the Ancients.

TITLE VI.
EXECUTIVE POWER.

ART. 132. The executive power is delegated to a Directory of five members, nominated by the Legislative Body, which has, in the name of the nation, the character of an electoral assembly.

ART. 133. The Council of the Five Hundred makes out, by ballot, a list of ten times the number of individuals to be appointed, and presents it to the Council of the Ancients, who chooses, also by ballot, from this list.

ART. 134. The members of the Directory must be at least forty years old.

ART. 135. They can only be taken from citizens who have been members of the Legislative Body or ministers. The provisions of this article will not be observed until the 9th year of the Republic.

ART. 136. From the first day of the fifth year of the Republic members of the Legislative Body can not be appointed members of the Directory or ministers, either during the term of their legislative duties or during the first year after the expiration of the same.

ART. 137. The Directory is partially renewed every year, by the election of a new member. During the first four years, on the going out of office of those who have been named the first time, the casting of lots shall decide.

ART. 138. None of the members going out of office can be chosen again until after an interval of five years.

ART. 139. Relations by blood in direct ascending or descending line—brothers, uncle, and nephew, cousins in the first degree, and relations by marriage in their different degrees—can not be members of the Directory at the same time, nor succeed one another, except after an interval of five years.

ART. 140. In case of vacancy by death, resignation, or other retirement of a member of the Directory, his successor is chosen by the Legislative Body within ten days at latest. The Council of the Five Hundred must propose candidates within the first five days, and the Council of the Ancients must consummate the election within the last five days. The new member is only chosen for the unexpired term of him whom he succeeds. If, however, this time does not exceed six months, he who is elected shall remain in office to the end of the following fifth year.

ART. 141. Each member of the Directory presides, in succession, only for three months. The president has to sign and keep the seal. The laws and acts of the Legislative Body are directed to the Directory, in the person of its president.

ART. 142. The Executive Directory can not act unless at least three members are present.

ART. 143. It chooses out of its own number a secretary, who countersigns the documents and records the deliberations upon a register, where each member has the right to have his opinions inscribed. The Directory may, if it chooses, deliberate without the presence of its secretary; in this case, the transactions are recorded by one of its members in a special book of record.

ART. 144. The Directory provides, according to law, for the external and internal safety of the Republic. It may issue proclamations, according to law, and for the execution of the same. It disposes of the military forces; however, neither the whole Directory nor any of its members can command them, either during the term of office, or within the next following two years.

ART. 145. If the Directory is informed that a conspiracy exists against the internal or exterior safety of the State, it may issue warrants of arrests and summons against those who are suspected as the authors of or participators in the same; it may examine them, but it is compelled under the penalties for these punishments awarded against arbitrary arrest, to send them, within two days, before the police magistrates, to be proceeded against according to law.

ART. 146. The Directory appoints the generals-in-chief; but it can not choose them from among the relations by blood or marriage of its members within the degrees expressed by Article 139.

ART. 147. It supervises and secures the execution of the laws in the administrations and courts through commissioners of its own selection.

ART. 148. It appoints, but not from its own members, the ministers, and revokes their appointment at its pleasure. It can not choose them under the age of thirty years, nor from among relations by blood or marriage within the degrees specified in Article 139.

ART. 149. Ministers correspond directly with their subordinate authorities.

ART. 150. The Legislative Body establishes the duties and the number of ministers. This number will be at least six, and no more than eight.

ART. 151. The ministers form no council.

ART. 152. The ministers are responsible, each for himself, as well for the non-execution of the laws as for the non-execution of the orders of the Directory.

ART. 153. The Directory appoints the receiver of direct taxes in each department.

ART. 154. It appoints the superior officers in the administration of indirect taxes, and in the administration of national domains.

ART. 155. All public officers in the French colonies, excepting the Isle of France and de la Réunion, shall, until peace, be appointed by the Directory.

ART. 156. The Legislative Body may authorize the Directory to send into all French colonies, according to the exigencies, one or more special agents, named by it for a specified time. The special agents shall exercise the same functions as the Directory, and shall be subordinate to it.

ART. 157. No member of the Directory is permitted to go out of the territory of the Republic until two years after the expiration of his office.

ART. 158. He is compelled, during this interval, to give the Legislative Body proofs of his residence. Article 112, and the following, to Article 123 inclusively, relative to the security of the Legislative Body, apply to the members of the Directory.

ART. 159. In case there are more than two members of the Directory under indictment, the Legislative Body shall, according to the ordinary forms, provisionally supply their places during the prosecution.

ART. 160. Except in cases provided for in Articles 119 and 120, the Directory, or one of its members can not be summoned either by the Council of the Five Hundred nor by the Council of the Ancients.

ART. 161. The accounts and the explanations, demanded by either council of the Directory, are furnished in writing.

ART. 162. The Directory is compelled, each year, to present in writing to both councils, a statement of the expenses, the state of the finances, the condition of existing pensions, as well as a proposition of those which it is thought advisable to raise. It must indicate the abuses which have come to its knowledge.

ART. 163. The Directory may, at all times, in writing, invite the Council of the Five Hundred to take a subject into consideration; it may propose measures, but can not lay the propositions before the council in the form of laws.

ART. 164. No member of the Directory can be absent more than five days, nor go beyond four myriameters (eight middle miles) from the place of sitting of the Directory, without the authority of the Legislative Body.

ART. 165. The members of the Directory can, when engaged in the functions of office, appear, neither abroad nor in their dwellings, other than in the costumes appropriate to them.

ART. 166. The Directory has a guard, paid by the Republic, composed of 120 infantry and 120 cavalry.

ART. 167. The Directory is accompanied by its guard in public ceremonies and processions, where it has always first rank.

ART. 168. Each member of the Directory, when separated from his associates in office, is accompanied by two guardsmen.

ART. 169. Each military body must show to the Directory, and to each of its members, the highest military honors.

ART. 170. The Directory has four messengers of State, whom it may appoint and dismiss. They carry the writings and memorials of the Directory to the two legislative councils; they have for this purpose admittance to the places of session of the legislative councils. Two *huissiers* go before them.

ART. 171. The Directory has its seat in the same commune with that of the Legislative Body.

ART. 172. The members of the Directory have their dwelling at the expense of the Republic, and all occupy the same edifice.

ART. 173. The salary of each of them for one year is fixed at the value of 50,000 myriagrams of wheat (10,222 hundred-weight).

TITLE VII.

ADMINISTRATIVE AND MUNICIPAL BODIES.

ART. 174. There is in each department a central administration, and in each canton at least one municipal administration.

ART. 175. Every member of a department or municipal administration must be at least twenty-five years of age.

ART. 176. Relations by blood in direct ascending and descending line, brothers, uncle, and nephew, and connections by marriage in the same degree, can not be members of the same administration at the same time, nor succeed one another, except after an interval of two years.

ART. 177. Each departmental administration consists of five members; it is renewed every year one-fifth.

ART. 178. Every commune, the population of which is from 5.000 to 100,000 inhabitants, has a municipal administration of its own.

ART. 179. In every commune, the population of which is less than 5,000 inhabitants, there is a municipal agent and an assistant.

ART. 180. The meeting of the municipal agents of each commune forms the municipality of the canton.

ART. 181. There is, moreover, a president of the municipal administration, who is chosen by the whole canton.

ART. 182. In the communes, the populations of which amount to from 5,000 to 10,000 inhabitants, there are five municipal officers; seven, from 10,000 to 50,000; nine, from 50,000 to 100,000.

ART. 183. In communes, the populations of which amounts to over 100,000 inhabitants, there are at least three municipal administrations. In these communes, the distribution of the municipalities is made so that the population in the district of each is not above 50,000 individuals, and not less than 30,000. The municipality of each district is composed of seven members.

ART. 184. In the communes, divided into several municipalities, there is a central bureau for matters which the Legislative Body considers indivisible. This bureau is composed of three members named by the department administration, and confirmed by the executive power.

ART. 185. The members of each municipal administration are appointed for two years, and every year one-half of them, or the number nearest one-half, and thus alternately now the greater, and now the smaller fractional number, shall be renewed.

ART. 186. The departmental administrators and the members of the municipal administrations, may once be re-elected without any interval.

ART. 187. Every citizen who has been chosen twice in succession a departmental administrator or member of a municipal administration, and who has performed the duties imposed on him by virtue of both elections, can not be chosen again, except after an interval of two years.

ART. 188. In case a departmental or municipal administration should lose one or more of its members by death, resignation, or otherwise, the remaining magistrates may, to complete their number, elect temporary magistrates, who shall remain in office until the next election.

ART. 189. The departmental and municipal administrations can neither modify the acts of the Legislative Body, nor those of the Executive Directory, nor suspend the execution of them. They can not interfere with judicial matters.

ART. 190. The administrators are essentially charged with the distribution of direct taxes and the superintendence of moneys accruing from public revenues in their territory. The Legislative Body establishes the rules and the mode of their functions, both in regard to these subjects, and the other parts of the interior administration.

ART. 191. The Executive Directory appoints at each departmental and municipal administration a commissioner, whom it may recall at pleasure. This commissioner watches over and requires the execution of the laws.

ART. 192. The commissioner in each local administration must be taken from the citizens domiciled for one year in the department where this administration is established. He must be at least twenty-five years old.

ART. 193. The municipal administrations are subordinate to the departmental administrations, and these to the ministers. Consequently, the ministers, each in his department, may annul the acts of the departmental administrations, and these the acts of the municipal administrations, if they be contrary to the laws or orders of the superior authorities.

ART. 194. The ministers can also suspend the departmental administrations who have contravened the laws or orders of the superior authority; and the departmental administrations have the same right in regard to the members of the municipal administrations.

ART. 195. No suspension or annulment becomes final without the formal confirmation of the Executive Directory.

ART. 196. The Directory may annul directly the acts of the departmental and municipal administrations. It can, if it deem it necessary, immediately suspend or dismiss the magistrates both of the departments and cantons, and send them, if there be cause, before the departmental courts.

ART. 197. Every decree which orders the cancellation of acts, suspension, or removal of magistrates, must assign the reasons thereof.

ART. 198. If five members of a departmental administration are removed, the Executive Directory provides the filling of the offices, until the next election; but it can only choose the temporary representatives from among former magistrates of the same department.

ART. 199. The administrations, either department or canton, can only correspond with each other on business which the law refers to them, and not on the general interests of the Republic.

ART. 200. All administrations should render an annual account of their management. The accounts rendered by the departmental administrations are printed.

ART. 201. All acts of the administrative bodies are made public by depositing the record in which they are written, and which is open to all citizens. This register is closed every six months, and is deposited from the day when it is closed. The Legislative Body may, according to circumstances, extend the period for the depositing of the record.

TITLE VIII.

JUDICIAL POWER. GENERAL PROVISIONS.

ART. 202. The judicial functions can neither be exercised by the Legislative Body, nor by the executive power.

ART. 203. The judges can not interfere with the exercise of the legislative power, or make enactments. They can neither delay nor suspend the execution of any law, nor summon the administrators before them, in regard to the functions of their office.

ART. 204. No one can be withdrawn from the judges whom the law assigns to him, by any commission, nor by any other way not set forth in the existing law.

ART. 205. Justice is rendered gratuitously.

ART. 206. Judges can only be removed on account of misdemeanors of which they have been found guilty, and only suspended by virtue of an accepted accusation.

ART. 207. Relations by blood in direct ascending and descending lines, brothers, uncle, and nephew, first cousins, and relatives by marriage in all these degrees, can not be members of the same court at one and the same time.

ART. 208. The sittings of the courts are public; the judges deliberate in secret; the judgments, with the grounds upon which they are based, are pronounced orally, together with reference to the language of the law which applies.

ART. 209. No citizen who is not thirty years old can be elected departmental judge, nor justice of the peace, nor associate to a justice of the peace, nor judge of a commercial court, nor member of the Court of *Cassation*, nor juryman, nor commissioner of the Executive Directory in the courts.

OF CIVIL JUDICATURE.

ART. 210. The right to have matters of controversy passed upon by arbitrators, chosen by the parties, can not be taken away.

ART. 211. The judgment of arbitrators is without appeal, and without recourse to *cassation*, unless the parties have expressly reserved the right.

ART. 212. There is a justice of the peace, and his associates, in each district determined by law; they are all elected for two years, and may be re-elected immediately and indefinitely.

ART. 213. The law determines the subjects which the justices of the peace and their associates decide without appeal. It assigns other subjects on which they may render judgment with right of appeal.

ART. 214. There are special commercial and marine courts. The law appoints the places where they shall be held. Their power to give judgment without appeal can not extend beyond the value of 500 myriagrams of wheat (about 102 hundred-weight).

ART. 215. Matters in controversy, which neither belong to the justices of the peace, nor to commercial tribunals, either of last resort, or of appeal, are brought immediately before the justices of the peace and their associates to be arbitrated upon. If the justice of the peace can not settle them, he sends the parties to the civil courts.

ART. 216. There is a civil court in each department. Each civil court consists of at least twenty judges, of a commissioner, and of a substitute. The Executive Directory names and recalls the clerk of the court. The members of the court are elected every five years. The judges may be re-elected.

ART. 217. At the election of the judges, there is also named five substitutes, three of whom are taken from the citizens residing in the commune where the court is held.

ART. 218. The civil court renders judgment without appeal, in the cases determined by law, upon appeals from judgments, either of the justices of the peace, or arbitrators, or from the commercial courts.

ART. 219. Appeals from judgments of the civil court are taken to the civil court of one of the nearest three departments, as regulated by law.

ART. 220. The civil court is divided into sections. A section can not give judgment if less than five judges be present.

ART. 221. The aggregate judges in each court name between themselves, by ballot, the president of each section.

OF CORRECTIONAL AND CRIMINAL JUDICATURE.

ART. 222. No one can be legally arrested except for the purpose of being brought before a police magistrate; and no person can be arrested or detained, except by virtue of a warrant of arrest of a police magistrate, or of the Executive Directory, provided for in Article 145, or by virtue of an order of arrest, either by a court, or by the foreman of a grand jury, or by an indictment of the Legislative Body, in those cases in which it is allowed them to issue the same, or by virtue of a sentence of imprisonment, or correctional detention.

ART. 223. That the warrant which orders the arrest may be executed, it is necessary: 1. That the same state the ground of the arrest, and the law by virtue of which it is issued. 2. That a copy thereof be left with the person arrested.

ART. 224. Every person who has been arrested and brought before the police magistrate shall, forthwith, or at least the same day, be examined.

ART. 225. If it appears from the examination that there is no ground for the arrest, he shall immediately be at liberty; or, if there is cause to send him to prison, he must be conducted there in the shortest possible time, which in no case may exceed three days.

ART. 226. No person can be detained, if he give sufficient bail, in all cases where bail is allowed by law.

ART. 227. In cases where his detention is authorized by law, a person can only be brought to and detained in places legally and publicly assigned to serve as prisons, court-houses, or places of detention.

ART. 228. No jailor can receive or detain any person unless by virtue of an order of arrest, according to the forms prescribed in Articles 222 and 223; of a warrant of arrest, decree of indictment, or a sentence of imprisonment, or correctional detention, of which a copy must be transcribed upon his register.

ART. 229. Every jailor is compelled, and no order can release him from the duty, to bring the arrested person before the civil officer having the police of the jail under his control, whenever the officer shall demand it.

ART. 230. Access to the arrested person can not be denied to his relations and friends, if they produce an order of the civil officer, who is at all times bound to accord the same, unless the jailor produce an order of the judge, entered on his register, to keep the person in close confinement.

ART. 231. If any person, of whatever place or office, in whom the law does not assign the right to arrest, shall issue, sign, execute, or cause to be executed, a warrant of arrest; or, if any person, even in case of legal arrest, shall bring, receive, or detain any person at a place of detention which is not publicly and legally assigned as such, and all jailors who shall contravene the provisions of the three preceding articles, shall be guilty of the crime of arbitrary arrest.

ART. 232. All severities exercised in making arrests, custodies, or executions, other than those prescribed by law, are crimes.

ART. 233. In each department there are at least three and no more than six correctional courts to take cognizance of offenses for which there is neither a corporal nor an infamous punishment. These courts can award no greater punishment than two years' imprisonment. The jurisdiction of offenses, the punishment of which does not exceed either the value of three days' labor or imprisonment for three days, is delegated to the justices of the peace, who pass on them without appeal.

ART. 234. Every correctional court is composed of a president, two justices of the peace, or associates of the justices of the peace, of the commune where it is established, a commissioner of the executive power, and a clerk.

ART. 235. The president of each correctional court is taken every six months, in succession, from among the members of the sections of the civil court of the department, excepting the presidents.

ART. 236. An appeal lies from the judgments of the correctional courts to the criminal court of the department.

ART. 237. In respect to crimes which draw after them corporal or dishonorable punishments, no person can be prosecuted, except by an indictment preferred by a jury, or decreed by the Legislative Body, in cases where it has a right to pass the same.

ART. 238. A first jury decides whether an indictment ought to be accepted or rejected, a second jury passes on all matters of fact, and the punishment, fixed by law, is awarded by the criminal courts.

ART. 239. The jurymen vote by secret ballot.

ART. 240. In each department there are as many grand juries as there are correctional courts. The presidents of the correctional courts, each in his district, are their directors. In communes of over 50,000 persons there may, by law, be appointed, beside the president of the correctional court, as many directors of the grand juries as the expedition of business may require.

ART. 241. The functions of the commissioner of the executive power, and the clerk to the director of the grand jury, are performed by the commissioner and the clerk of the correctional court.

ART. 242. Each director of the grand jury has the immediate supervision over all the police officers of his district.

ART. 243. The director of the grand jury immediately prosecutes, as police magistrate, according to the indictments presented to him by the public prosecutor, either ex-officio or on the orders of the Executive Directory: 1. Infringements of liberty, or security of citizens. 2. Those committed against the laws of nations. 3. Revolt against the execution either of judgments or any executory act emanating from the constituted authorities. 4. Disturbances and violences committed in order to hinder the collection of taxes, the free circulation of provisions, and other subjects of trade.

ART. 244. In each department there is a criminal court.

ART. 245. The criminal court consists of a president, a public prosecutor, four judges taken from the civil court, the commissioner of the executive power of the same court, or his substitute and his clerk. In the criminal court of the Department of the Seine there is a vice-president and a substitute of the public prosecutor. This court is divided into two sections; eight members of the civil court act as judges.

ART. 246. The presidents of the sections of the civil court can not fill the offices of judges in the criminal court.

ART. 247. The other judges fulfil the duties of their office, each in their turn during six months, in the order of their nomination, and during this time they can exercise no functions in the civil court.

ART. 248. The duty of the public prosecutor shall be: 1. To prosecute crimes according to the indictments found as true by the first juries. 2. To deliver to the police magistrates the information directly made to him. 3. To watch over the police officers of the department, and in case of negligence or greater crimes, to proceed against them according to law.

ART. 249. The duty of the commissioner of the executive power shall be: 1. During the course of the prosecution to require the due observance of forms, and, before the sentence, the due application of the law. 2. To see to the execution of the sentences passed by the court.

ART. 250. The judges can not submit to the juries any complicated question.

ART. 251. The traverse jury consists of twelve jurymen; the accused has the right, without assigning reasons therefor, to reject such a number of them as the law shall determine.

ART. 252. The proceedings before the traverse jury are public, and the accused can not be denied the aid of counsel, whom they themselves may choose, or who is appointed for them by the court.

ART. 253. All persons acquitted by a legal jury can not again be put on trial nor accused for the same cause.

OF THE COURT OF CASSATION.

ART. 254. There is a Court of *Cassation* for the whole Republic. It has jurisdiction over: 1. Applications for *cassation* of judgments rendered by courts of last resort. 2. Applications for the removal of cases from one court to another by reason of legal prejudice, or of the public safety. 3. Orders of judges, or of complaints against a whole court.

ART. 255. The Court of *Cassation* does not take cognizance of the facts on which the action is based, but it annuls judgments rendered in proceedings in which the forms of procedure have been violated, or which express a violation of the law, and it refers the main question to a court which has jurisdiction over it.

ART. 256. When, after one *cassation*, the second judgment is attached on the facts, by the same means as the first, the question involved can no longer be acted on by the Court of *Cassation* without having been submitted to the Legislative Body, which shall pass a law by which the Court of *Cassation* is to be governed.

ART. 257. The Court of *Cassation* is compelled annually to send to each division of the Legislative Body a deputation which shall lay before the latter a list of judgments rendered, with marginal notes, and the text of the law on which the judgment is based.

ART. 258. The number of the judges of the Court of *Cassation* can not exceed three-fourths of the number of the departments.

ART. 259. This court is renewed every year by one-fifth. The electoral assemblies of the departments nominate alternately the judges who are to replace those who leave the Court of *Cassation*. The judges of this court can always be re elected.

ART. 260. Each judge of the Court of *Cassation* has a substitute elected whom the same electoral assembly nominates.

ART. 261. In every Court of *Cassation* there is a commissioner and a substitute whom the Executive Directory names and recalls.

ART. 262. The Executive Directory gives notice, through its commissioner, and without prejudice to the parties interested, to the Court of *Cassation* of the acts by which the judges have exceeded their power.

ART. 263. The court annuls these acts if it finds that a misdemeanor of office has been committed. The fact is communicated to the Legislative Body, which passes a decree of impeachment, after having called and heard the accused.

ART. 264. The Legislative Body can not annul the judgments of the Court of *Cassation*, but it may prosecute the judges in person who have been guilty of a misdemeanor or a crime.

OF THE HIGH COURT OF JUSTICE.

ART. 265. There is a High Court of Justice to sit in judgment on the complaints preferred by the Legislative Body, either against its own members or against those of the Executive Directory.

ART. 266. The High Court of Justice is composed of five judges and two national prosecutors taken from the Court of *Cassation*, and from the grand juries named by the electoral assemblies of the departments.

ART. 267. The High Court of Justice is only organized by a proclamation of the Legislative Body, which the Council of the Five Hundred draws up and publishes.

ART. 268. It is formed and holds its sessions in the place designated by the proclamation of the Council of the Five Hundred. This place must be at least twelve myriameters (twenty-four middle miles) distant from the place where the Legislative Body sits.

ART. 269. When the Legislative Body has proclaimed the organization of a High Court of Justice, the Court of *Cassation* chooses, by lot, fifteen of its members in public session; it nominates, hereupon, in the same session, by ballot, five of these fifteen; the five judges thus named are the judges of the High Court of Justice; they choose their president from their own number.

ART. 270. The Court of *Cassation* nominates, in the same session, by ballot and absolute majority, two of its members to perform the duties of national prosecutors to the High Court of Justice.

ART. 271. The acts of impeachment are prepared and drawn up by the Council of the Five Hundred.

ART. 272. The electoral assemblies of each department nominate, annually, a juryman for the High Court of Justice.

ART. 273. The Executive Directory causes, one month after the date of the elections, a list of the jurymen chosen for the High Court of Justice to be printed and published.

Title IX.

OF THE ARMED FORCES.

ART. 274. The armed force is organized to defend the State against foreign enemies, and, in the interior, to maintain order and to execute the laws.

ART. 275. The armed force is essentially obedient; no armed force can deliberate.

ART. 276. It is divided into the inactive National Guard and the active National Guard.

ART. 277. The inactive National Guard is composed of all citizens and sons of citizens able to bear arms.

ART. 278. Its organization and its discipline are the same throughout the Republic; they are determined by law.

ART. 279. No Frenchman can exercise the rights of citizenship unless he is inscribed on the list of the inactive National Guard.

ART. 280. Order of rank and subordination take place only in regard to the service, and during the same.

ART. 281. The officers of the inactive National Guard are elected, at stated times, by the citizens who compose it, and can only be re-elected after a certain interval.

ART. 282. The command of the National Guard of a whole department can not be assigned permanently to a single citizen.

ART. 283. When it is necessary to assemble the whole National Guard of a department, the Executive Directory may appoint a temporary commander.

ART. 284. The command of the inactive National Guard in a city of 100,000 inhabitants and over, can not be permanently assigned to one man.

ART. 285. The Republic maintains, even in times of peace, a paid land and marine force, under the name of the National Guard in active service.

ART. 286. The army is made up by volunteer enrollment, and, if required, in the manner prescribed by law.

ART. 287. No alien who has not acquired the rights of a French citizen can, hereafter, be received into the French armies unless he has made one or several campaigns for the establishment of the Republic.

ART. 288. The commanders, or chiefs on land and sea, are only appointed in time of war; they receive their commissions, revocable at will, from the Executive Directory. The duration of these commissions is limited to one campaign, but they may be continued.

ART. 289. The command of the armies of the Republic can not be confided to one man.

ART. 290. The discipline, the form of sentences, and the nature of punishments of the land and sea forces are subject to special laws.

ART. 291. No part of the inactive National Guard nor of the active National Guard can operate in the interior service of the Republic, except on the written requisition of the civil authorities, and according to the forms of law.

ART. 292. The public force can only be called upon by the civil authorities within their territory; it can not be passed from one canton into another, without the movement is authorized by the departmental administration, nor from one department into another without the orders of the Executive Directory.

ART. 293. The Legislative Body determines, nevertheless, the means to secure, through the public force, the execution of sentences, and the prosecution of the accused throughout the French territory.

ART. 294. In time of imminent danger the municipal administration of a canton can call upon the National Guard of the neighboring cantons. In this event, both the administration which has made the requisition and the commandants of the National Guards who have been called into service, are compelled to give immediate notice thereof to the departmental administration.

ART. 295. No troops can be introduced into French territory without the previous consent of the Legislative Body.

TITLE X.

PUBLIC INSTRUCTION.

ART. 296. There shall be established in the Republic primary schools, where the pupils may learn to read and write, and the elements of arithmetic and morals. The Republic provides dwelling-houses for the teachers who preside over these schools.

ART. 297. There shall also be, in different parts of the Republic, high schools, distributed in such a manner that there shall be at least one for two departments.

ART. 298. There shall be a national institute for the whole Republic, the duty of which shall be to collect discoveries, and to perfect the arts and sciences.

ART. 299. The different institutions for public instruction have, between themselves, no relation of subordination, nor of administrative correspondence.

ART. 300. Citizens have the right to form special institutions for education and instruction, as well as free societies for the promotion of science, letters, and arts.

ART. 301. National festivals shall be maintained to encourage a feeling of brotherhood among citizens, and a love of the Constitution, of the country, and the laws.

TITLE XI.

TAXATION.

ART. 302. The public taxes are considered and established annually by the Legislative Body. It alone belongs to this body to levy taxes. They can not exist longer than a year unless they are expressly renewed.

ART. 303. The Legislative Body may create any kind of taxes it may believe necessary; but it must lay annually a tax on real and personal estate.

ART. 304. Every individual not included in Articles 12 and 13 of the Constitution, and not on the roll of direct taxes, has the right to appear before the municipal administration of his commune and to have himself inscribed for a personal tax equal to the local value of three days' agricultural labor.

ART. 305. The registration mentioned in the preceding article can only be done in the month of *Messidor* of every year (from the 19th of June to the 18th of July).

ART. 306. Taxes of every description are distributed among all taxable persons in proportion to their property.

ART. 307. The Executive Directory directs and superintends the collection and payment of taxes, and to this effect issues all necessary orders.

ART. 308. The detailed account of the expenses of the ministers, signed and ratified by them, are made public at the commencement of each year. The same rule applies to the accounts of the income of the different taxes and of all public revenues.

ART. 309. The accounts of these receipts and expenditures are stated separately, according to their nature; they explain the money received and expended every year in each part of the general administration.

ART. 310. In like manner the special expenditures of the departments are published, and those which relate to the courts, to the administrations, to the progress of science, and to all public works and institutions.

ART. 311. The departmental administrations and municipalities can make no change regarding the sums determined upon by the Legislative body, nor, without being authorized by it, negotiate or allow any local loan on the citizens of the department, or of the communes, or of the cantons.

ART. 312. The Legislative Body has alone the right to regulate the coining and the circulation of all kinds of coins, and to fix their value, weight, and impress.

ART. 313. The Directory superintends the coining of money, and appoints the officers who have the immediate exercise of this superintendence.

ART. 314. The Legislative Body establishes the taxes of the colonies and their commercial relations to the mother State.

ART. 315. There shall be five commissioners of the National Treasury, appointed by the Council of the Ancients from a threefold list presented by the Council of the Five Hundred.

ART. 316. Their term of office is five years; one of them is removed every year, and may indefinitely and without interval be re-elected.

ART. 317. The Commissioners of the Treasury are compelled to superintend the receipts of all national moneys, to regulate the application and the payment of all public expenses of which the Legislative Body shall approve; to keep an open account of disbursements and income with the receiver of direct taxes of each department, with the different national excisemen, and with the paymasters of the departments; to carry on the necessary correspondence with the said receivers, paymasters, excisemen, and administrators, in order to insure the exact and regular return of the moneys.

ART. 318. They can, without rendering themselves guilty of a misdemeanor, allow no payment to be made except by virtue of: 1. By a decree of the Legislative Body, and to the amount specified by the same for every object. 2. A decree of the Directory. 3. The signature of the minister who orders the expense.

ART. 319. Nor can they, without rendering themselves guilty of a misdemeanor, approve of any payment, unless the order, signed by the minister to whose department the expenditure belongs, bear the date both of the decision of the Executive Directory and the decree of the Legislative Body which authorized the payment.

ART. 320. The receivers of the direct taxes in each department, the different national excisemen and paymasters in the departments, deliver over their respective accounts to the National Treasury, which shall verify and approve of them.

ART. 321. There shall be five commissioners of the national accounts, who are chosen by the Legislative Body, at the same time, according to the same forms and conditions as the Commissioners of the Treasury.

ART. 322. The general account of receipts and expenditures of the Republic, supported by special accounts and vouchers, are laid before the Commissioners of Accounts by the Commissioners of the Treasury, who examine and certify the same.

ART. 323. The Commissioners of Accounts must give to the Legislative Body information of the abuses, defalcations, and all cases of responsibility which they discover in the course of their operations. They propose, on their part, measures advantageous to the Republic.

ART. 324. The result of the accounts, approved by the Commissioners of Accounts, is printed and published.

ART. 325. The Commissioners, both of the National Treasury and of Accounts, can only be suspended and removed by the Legislative Body. But during the adjournment of the Legislative Body, the Executive Directory may provisionally suspend and replace the Commissioners of the National Treasury, to the number of two, at most, on condition that the Executive Directory report the fact to both councils of the Legislative Body as soon as they convene.

TITLE XII.
FOREIGN RELATIONS.

ART. 326. War can only be declared by a decree of the Legislative Body, on the formal and urgent request of the Executive Directory.

ART. 327. The two legislative councils concur in the form of the decree by which war is declared.

ART. 328. In cases of imminent or actual hostilities, threats, or preparations of war against the French Republic, the Executive Directory must employ, for the defense of the State, the means in its power, on condition of informing the Legislative Body thereof without delay. It may, in this case, point out the increase of force and the new legislative provisions which circumstances might require.

ART. 329. The Directory can alone maintain foreign political relations, carry on negotiations, distribute the land and sea forces, as it may seem proper, and, in case of war, determine their movements.

ART. 330. It is authorized to make preliminary agreements of armistice, of neutrality; it may also enter into secret compacts.

ART. 331. The Executive Directory concludes and signs, or causes to be signed, with foreign powers, all treaties of peace, of alliance, of truce, of neutrality, of commerce, and other compacts which it may deem necessary for the welfare of the State. These treaties and compacts are negotiated in the name of the French Republic, through diplomatic agents appointed with instructions by the Executive Directory.

ART. 332. In case that a treaty contains secret articles, the provisions of these articles can not be destructive of patents, nor contain any alienation of the territory of the Republic.

ART. 333. Treaties are only valid after they have been examined and ratified by the Legislative Body; nevertheless, the secret agreements may provisionally be executed as soon as they have been decreed by the Directory.

ART. 334. Neither of the legislative councils shall deliberate on war or peace except in committee of the whole.

ART. 335. Foreigners, whether they be domiciled in France or not, inherit the estates of their relations, whether they be foreigners or Frenchmen; they may enter into contracts, buy and take estates situated in France, and dispose of them like French citizens in any way authorized by law.

TITLE XIII.

REVISION OF THE CONSTITUTION.

ART. 336. If experience should show objections to any of the articles of this Constitution, the Council of the Ancients shall propose a revision of them.

ART. 337. The proposition of the Council of the Ancients, in this case, is submitted for ratification to the Council of the Five Hundred.

ART. 338. If, in the space of nine years, the proposition of the Council of the Ancients, ratified by the Council of the Five Hundred, has been made at three different periods, being at an interval of three years, at least, an assembly of revision shall be convoked.

ART. 339. This assembly is formed of two members from each department, who are chosen in the same manner as members of the Legislative Body, and must conform with the same conditions which are required for the Council of the Ancients.

ART. 340. The Council of the Ancients appoints, for the meeting of the Assembly of Revision, a place which must be at least twenty myriameters removed from the one where the Legislative Body sits.

ART. 341. The Assembly of Revision has the right to change its place of meeting if it observe the distance prescribed in the foregoing article.

ART. 342. The Assembly of Revision exercises no legislative or governmental function, but confines itself to the articles of the Constitution specified by the Legislative Body.

ART. 343. All the articles of the Constitution, without exception, retain their force until the changes proposed by the Assembly of Revision have been adopted by the people.

ART. 344. The members of the Assembly of Revision deliberate together.

ART. 345. Citizens who are members of the Legislative Body, at the time the Assembly of Revision is being called together, can not be chosen members of the former.

ART. 346. The Assembly of Revision sends the proposition of the reform which it has agreed upon immediately to the primary assemblies. It is dissolved as soon as the project has been forwarded to the latter.

ART. 347. In no case may the duration of the Assembly of Revision exceed three months.

ART. 348. The members of the Assembly of Revision can at no time be made responsible, accused, or judged on account of what they have said or written in the exercise of their duties. During the time of their official duties they can not be summoned into court except by a decision of the Assembly of Revision.

ART. 349. The Assembly of Revision shall not attend any public ceremony; its members receive the same salary as the members of the Legislative Body.

ART. 350. The Assembly of Revision has the right, in the commune where it sits, to exercise or have exercised police regulations.

TITLE XIV.

GENERAL PROVISIONS.

ART. 351. There is among citizens no other kind of superiors than the public functionaries, and these are only so in regard to the exercise of their duties.

ART. 352. The law recognizes no religious vows, nor any other obligation conflicting with the natural rights of man.

ART. 353. No one can be hindered from speaking, writing, printing, and publishing his thoughts. Writings may not be submitted to any censorship before publication. No one can be made responsible for what he has written or published, except in cases provided for by law.

ART. 354. No one can be hindered from exercising the religion he may choose, if he conforms himself to the law. No one can be forced to contribute toward the support of any religious worship. The Republic pays nothing toward it.

ART. 355. There are neither privileges nor wardens of corporations, nor restrictions of the liberty of the press, of commerce, and of the exercise of trade and arts of all kinds. Every prohibitive law of this kind, if circumstances make it necessary, is to be regarded as temporary, and has force only for one year at the longest, unless it be formally renewed.

ART. 356. The law watches especially over the professions which take interest in public morals, the security and health of citizens, but the admittance to the exercise of such trades can not depend on the payment of money.

ART. 357. The law must reward inventors and maintain the exclusive property in their discoveries and in their productions.

ART. 358. The Constitution guarantees the inviolability of all property, and reasonable compensation for that the sacrifice of which is required by public necessity legally approved of.

ART. 359. The house of every citizen is an inviolable place of refuge. During the night no person has the right to enter it, except in case of fire, inundation, or a call proceeding from the interior of the house. During the day the orders of the legitimate authorities may be executed in it. No house search can be had except by virtue of the law, and only for the person or object expressly named in the warrant ordering the search.

ART. 360. No corporation or association can be established which is opposed to public order.

ART. 361. No assembly of citizens can regard itself a society of the people.

ART. 362. No special society which is occupied with political questions can correspond with any other, nor affiliate with it, nor hold public sessions which consist of members and associates different from one another, nor impose conditions of admission and eligibility, nor arrogate exclusive rights, nor allow its members to wear any external mark of their association.

ART. 363. Citizens can only exercise their political rights in the primary and communal assemblies.

ART. 364. All citizens have the right to address petitions to the public authorities, but they must be made only by single individuals, and no leagued association can present them in their general and collective name, except the existing authorities, and these only on questions which relate to them as such. Petitioners must never forget the respect due to the constituted authorities.

ART. 365. Every armed mob is an attack upon the Constitution, and ought to be dispersed immediately by force.

ART. 366. Every unarmed congregation of people ought likewise to be dispersed: first, by verbal order, and, if necessary, by the use of the armed force.

ART. 367. Several constituted boards can never unite to deliberate together; no act emanating from such a union can be executed.

ART. 368. No person is allowed to wear badges of distinction which commemorate past offices or services performed.

ART. 369. The members of the Legislative Body, and all public officers, when exercising the functions of office, must wear the costume or marks of power with which they are invested; the law specifies the form.

ART. 370. No citizen can wholly or in part refuse compensation or a salary which is given him by law, by virtue of his office.

ART. 371. There shall be a uniformity of weights and measures in the Republic.

ART. 372. The French time of counting commences with the 22d of September, 1792, the day of the foundation of the Republic.

ART. 373. The French nation declares that it will in no way suffer the return of those Frenchmen who, having abandoned their country since July 15, 1789, are not included in the exceptions which are contained in the laws against emigrants; and it interdicts the Legislative Body to make new exceptions in this respect. The estates of the emigrants are irrevocably confiscated for the benefit of the Republic.

ART. 374. The French nation declares likewise, as a guarantee of the public faith, that, after a legal appropriation of national property, whatever its origin may have been, the legal purchaser shall never be dispossessed of the same, provided, however, that if any claimant's application is well founded, he shall be indemnified from the National Treasury.

ART. 375. None of the powers instituted by the Constitution has the right to change them in whole or in part, except the amendments which may be made by revision, in accordance with the provisions of Title XIII.

ART. 376. Citizens must ever bear in mind that the duration, preservation, and prosperity of the Republic, will principally depend upon the wisdom of the elections in the primary and electoral assemblies.

ART. 377. The French nation intrusts the safe-keeping of this Constitution to the fidelity of the Legislative Body; of the Executive Directory; of the administrators and judges; to the vigilance of fathers of families; to the wives and mothers; to the love of the young citizens, and to the courage of all Frenchmen.

APPENDIX IV.

CONSTITUTION OF THE FRENCH REPUBLIC, DECEMBER 13, 1799 (22d FRIMAIRE, YEAR VIII).

TITLE I.
OF THE EXERCISE OF THE RIGHTS OF CITIZENSHIP.

ARTICLE 1. The French Republic is one and indivisible. Its European territory is divided into departments and communal districts.

2. Every man born and residing in France, who is twenty-one years old, has his name inscribed on the civic register of his communal district, and who has lived for a year on the territory of the Republic, is a French citizen.

3. An alien becomes a French citizen when he has attained the age of twenty-one years, and having declared his intention to settle in France, he has resided there for ten consecutive years.

4. The rights of a French citizen are lost: By naturalization in a foreign country; by accepting office or a pension granted by a foreign government; by affiliation with a foreign corporation which is based upon distinctions of birth; by being condemned to inflictive or infamous punishments.

5. The exercise of the rights of French citizenship is suspended: By bankruptcy; if a person becomes the direct successor to an estate of an insolvent; by judicial decree, indictment, or contempt of court.

6. In order to be able to exercise the rights of citizenship in a communal district, it is necessary to have acquired there a residence of one year, and not to have lost it by an absence of one year.

7. The citizens of each communal district select, by election, from themselves those whom they believe best fitted to manage public affairs.

A list of citizens is thus made who have the public confidence, which list shall consist of one-tenth of the citizens of the district. The public officers of the district are then taken from this list.

8. The citizens named in the communal lists of a department then select a second list of one-tenth of their own number. It is from this departmental list of notables that the public officers of the department must be taken.

9. The citizens named in the department list likewise select one-tenth of their number; from this election a third list of citizens, who are eligible to the national offices, is formed.

10. Citizens who have the right to co-operate in the formation of one of the lists mentioned in the preceding three articles, must assemble every three years to fill vacancies caused by death, or on account of absence from other cause than the exercise of public functions.

11. They can, at the same time, strike off the name of any person inscribed on the list whom they do not judge proper to retain, and to fill the vacancies thus created by other persons in whom they have greater confidence.

12. No one can be stricken from the lists except by an absolute majority of those who have the right to co-operate in its formation.

13. A citizen is not made ineligible for selection on a list of notables because he may have been retired from a list of higher or lower degree.

14. Registration is only requisite in regard to those public offices for which this condition is expressly required by the Constitution or by the law. The lists of eligible persons are elected for the first time during the ninth year. Citizens who shall be named for the first formation of the constituted authorities, shall form a necessary part of the first lists of eligible persons.

TITLE II.

OF THE CONSERVATIVE SENATE.

15. The Conservative Senate shall consist of eighty members, who are not removable, and are appointed for life; they must be at least forty years old. In order to form the Senate, there shall first be nominated sixty members; in the eighth year the number shall be increased to sixty-two, in the ninth year to sixty-four, and thus gradually increasing until the number of eighty is reached, by the addition of two members each year in the first ten years.

16. The nomination of senator is made by the Senate, which chooses between three candidates, of whom the first is presented by the Legislative Body, the second by the Tribunate, and the third by the First Consul. It only chooses between two candidates if one of them is proposed by two of the presenting authorities. It is compelled to accept the candidate whom the three powers present at the same time.

17. When the First Consul vacates his place, either by resignation or expiration of the term of office, he becomes a senator with full and absolute powers. The other two Consuls may, during the month which follows the expiration of their functions, take a seat in the Senate, but they are not compelled to make use of this right. If they resign their office they have no claim to this right.

18. A senator is forever ineligible for any other public office.

19. All the lists made in the departments, by virtue of Article 9, are forwarded to the Senate; they form a national register.

20. It chooses from this list the legislators, the tribunes, the consuls, judges of *cassation*, and commissioners of accounts.

21. It confirms or annuls all acts which the Tribunate or the government refer to it as unconstitutional; the registers of eligible persons are comprised among these acts.

22. A fixed income, drawn from the national domains, is appropriated for the expenses of the Senate. The annual salary of each of its members is paid out of these revenues, and is equal to the twentieth part of the salary of the First Consul.

23. The sessions of the Senate are not public.

24. Citizens Siéyès and Roger Ducos, who are withdrawing, are named members of the Conservative Senate; they shall unite with the Second and Third Consuls who are named by the present Constitution. These four citizens nominate the majority of the Senate, which henceforth completes itself, and proceeds to the elections which are confided to it.

Title III.

OF THE LEGISLATIVE POWER.

25. No new laws shall be promulgated except the bills proposing them shall have been presented by the government, communicated to the Tribunate, and decreed by the Legislative Body.

26. The propositions which the government proposes shall be drawn up in articles. At any time during their passage the government can withdraw them, and bring them forward in a modified form.

27. The Tribunate is composed of 100 members, who shall be at least twenty-five years of age; one-fifth of them is renewed annually, and they are indefinitely re eligible so long as they remain on the national lists.

28. The Tribunate deliberates on the bills; it votes on the adoption and rejection of the same. It sends three orators from its own body by whom the motives which it has already expressed upon each of these propositions are laid before the Legislative Body and defended. It refers to the Senate only questions of constitutionality affecting the lists of eligibility, the acts of the Legislative Body, and those of the government.

29. It expresses its wishes upon laws already made and to be made, upon abuses to be corrected, upon improvements to be undertaken in all parts of the public administration, but never upon civil and criminal matters pending before the courts. The wish which it expresses by virtue of this article has no necessary consequence, and compels no constituted authority to deliberate on the subject suggested.

30. When the Tribunate adjourns, it may nominate a committee of ten to fifteen of its members, charged with the duty of convoking it in case it should deem such action expedient.

31. The Legislative Body is composed of 300 members, who shall be at least thirty years of age; one-fifth of them is renewed annually. There must be at least one citizen from each department of the Republic who is a member of this body.

32. A member leaving the Legislative Body can not re-enter it until after an interval of one year; but he may immediately be re-elected to any other public function, including that of tribune, if he be otherwise eligible.

33. The sessions of the Legislative Body commence every year on the 1st of *Frimaire* (November 21), and last only four months. The government may, during the other eight months, convoke it in extraordinary session.

34. The Legislative Body passes the laws by secret ballot, and without any discussion of the proposed laws by its own members, which laws have been discussed before it by the orators of the government.

35. The sessions of the Tribunate and those of the Legislative Body are public, but the number of those present who are not members must in neither body exceed 200.

36. The annual salary of a tribune is 15,000, and that of a legislator 10,000 francs.

37. Every decree of the Legislative Body shall be promulgated the tenth day after its issuance, provided, in this delay, it has not been referred to the Senate on the ground of unconstitutionality. This appeal can not be taken against laws which have been promulgated.

38. The first renewal of the Legislative Body and of the Tribunate shall not take place until the tenth year.

Title IV.

Of the Government.

39. The government is confided to three consuls, nominated for ten years, and indefinitely re-eligible. Each of them is elected individually, with the distinguishing title of the First, Second, or Third Consul.

The Constitution appoints Citizen Bonaparte, former Provisional Consul, to the office of First Consul; Citizen Cambacérès, former Minister of Justice, Second Consul; and Citizen Lebrun, former member of the Commission of the Council of the Ancients, as Third Consul. For this time the Third Consul is only appointed for five years.

40. The First Consul has special duties and rights, in which he may, if the occasion arises, be at once supplied by one of his colleagues.

41. The First Consul promulgates the laws; he nominates and revokes, at pleasure, the members of the Council of State, the ministers, the ambassadors, and other high foreign official agents, the officers of the land and sea forces, the members of the local administrations, and the governmental commissioners in the courts. He nominates all the criminal and civil judges other than the justices of the peace, the judges of *cassation*, without power to revoke their appointments.

42. In all other governmental acts, the Second and Third Consuls have the right to give their opinion, but not to vote; they sign the records of these acts in order to verify their presence, and may, if they so desire, append their opinion thereon, after which the decision of the First Consul is sufficient.

43. The salary of the First Consul, for the eighth year, shall be 500,000 francs. The salary of each of the other two shall be equal to three-tenths of that of the First Consul.

44. The government proposes the laws, and makes the necessary arrangements to secure their execution.

45. The government regulates the revenue and the expenditures of the State according to the law which determines annually the amount of both. It superintends the coining of money, which the law not only orders the issuance of, but fixes its denomination, weight, and impress.

46. If the government is informed that a conspiracy exists against the State, it may issue summonses and orders of arrest against the persons who are supposed to be the authors of or accessory to the same; but, if within ten days after their arrest, they are not either set at liberty or delivered to the courts, then the minister who signed the order shall be guilty of the crime of arbitrary arrest.

47. The government provides for the interior safety and the exterior defense of the State, distributes the land and sea forces, and regulates their movements.

48. The active National Guard is subject to administrative regulations; the inactive National Guard is only subject to law.

49. The government conducts foreign political relations and negotiations; enters into preliminary stipulations; signs, or causes to be signed and concluded all treaties of peace or alliance, truce, neutrality, commerce, and other agreements.

50. Declarations of peace, alliance, and commerce are, like the laws, proposed, discussed, and promulgated. Only the discussions and deliberations upon these subjects, in the Tribunate as well as in the Legislative Body, take place in secret committee of the whole when the government demands such action.

51. The secret articles of a treaty must not be destructive of the existing acts enacted in public.

52. The Council of State is charged, under the direction of the Consuls, with drawing up projects of law, provisions of public administration, and the settlement of contentions that arise in administrative matters.

53. The orators who debate in the name of the government before the Legislative Body are always taken from the members of the Council of State. No more than three of these orators are sent to defend a single proposition of law.

54. The ministers procure the execution of the laws and the decrees of the public administrations.

55. No act of the government can have effect unless it is signed by a minister.

56. One of the ministers is specially charged with the administration of the public treasury; he verifies the receipts, orders the application of moneys and payments authorized by law. He can only make payments by virtue of: 1. Of a law, and to the amount of the appropriation for its objects. 2. A decree of the government. 3. Of an order signed by a minister.

57. The detailed accounts of the expenses of each minister, signed and certified by him, must be published.

58. The government can only elect and retain such councilor and ministers, citizens whose names are inscribed on the national register.

59. The local administrations, established either for each communal district, or for more extended portions of territory, are subordinated to the ministers. No one can become or remain a member of these administrations, unless his name is inscribed and retained on one of the national lists mentioned in Articles 7 and 8.

Title V.

OF THE COURTS.

60. Each communal district has one or several justices of the peace, elected directly by the citizens for three years. Their principal duty shall be to advise parties to a settlement, and in case this can not be effected, to submit their differences to arbitration.

61. In civil matters there are courts of primary jurisdiction and appeal. The law determines the organization of both, their rights, and the territory forming the jurisdiction of each.

62. In matters of crimes calling for afflictive and infamous punishments, a first jury admits or rejects the accusation; if it be admitted, a second jury passes upon the facts, and the judges forming a criminal court award the sentences. Their judgment is without appeal.

63. The position of a public prosecutor in a criminal court is filled by the commissioner of the government.

64. Crimes which do not carry corporal or infamous punishments are passed upon by the courts of correctional police, subject to appeal to the criminal court.

65. There is a Court of *Cassation* for the whole Republic; it has jurisdiction on applications for *cassation* of judgments passed by courts in the last resort; on applications for removal of cases from one court to another, by reason of legal prejudice or of the public safety; on orders of judges, or on complaints against a whole court.

66. The Court of *Cassation* does not take cognizance of the facts, but it reverses judgments in which the forms of procedure have been violated, and which contain an express contravention of the law, and refers the facts upon which the case is brought to a court which has jurisdiction over it.

67. The judges of the courts of the first instance, and the commissioners of the government established in these courts are taken from the communal or departmental lists. The judges forming the court of appeal, and the commissioners associated with them, are taken from the departmental list. The judges composing the Court of *Cassation*, and the commissioners associated with them, are taken from the national list.

68. The judges, other than the justices of the peace, are appointed for life, at least until they are condemned for malfeasance in office, or they are not retained upon the lists of eligible persons.

Title VI.

OF THE RESPONSIBILITY OF PUBLIC OFFICERS.

69. The functions of the members of the Senate, of the Legislative Body, of the Tribunate, of the Consuls, and the councilors of State do not include responsibility.

70. Personal crimes liable to corporal and infamous punishments committed by a member of the Senate, of the Tribunate, of the Legislative Body, or Council of State, are prosecuted before the ordinary courts after a deliberation of the body to which the accused belongs, and that body has authorized the prosecution.

71. Those ministers who are accused of a private crime, liable to corporal or infamous punishments, are considered as members of the Council of State.

72. The ministers are responsible: 1. For all acts of the government signed by them, and declared unconstitutional by the Senate. 2. For non-execution of the laws, and public administrative decrees. 3. For special orders they have given, if they are in violation of the Constitution, the laws, or the decrees.

73 In cases mentioned in the preceding article, the Tribunate sets forth the complaint against the minister by an act on which the Legislative Body deliberates in the ordinary forms. After having summoned and heard the accused, the minister who is placed in judgment by a decree of the Legislative Body is judged by a high court of justice, without appeal and without recourse to *cassation*. The High Court is

composed of judges and a jury. The judges are chosen by the Tribunal of *Cassation* from its own members; the jurymen are taken from the national lists, in all respects as the law determines.

74. The civil and criminal judges are, for crimes relating to the violation of their duties, prosecuted before the courts to which the Court of *Cassation* shall send them, after having annulled their acts.

75. The agents of the government, other than the ministers, can only be prosecuted for acts relating to their duties, by virtue of a decision of the Council of State; and in this case the prosecution takes place before the ordinary courts.

Title VII.

General Provisions.

76. The house of every person living on French territory is an inviolable place of refuge. During the night no one can enter it, except in case of fire, inundation, or a call proceeding from the interior of the house. During the day, it may be entered in a special case determined, or by a law, or by an order emanating from a public authority.

77. In order that the warrant which authorizes the arrest of a person can be executed, it is required: 1. That it formally express the ground of the arrest, and the law for the execution of which it is ordered. 2. That it emanate from an officer to whom the law has given this right. 3. That the accused is fully notified of the ground of arrest and that the accused be served with a copy of the charge.

78. No jailor can receive or detain any person, unless the act which orders the arrest is transcribed on his register, and the order must be in the form prescribed in the preceding article for an order for the detention of a person, a decree of accusation, or a final sentence.

79. Every jailor is compelled, and no order can release him, to bring the arrested person before the civil officer who has the police of the jail under his control, at all times the officer shall require it.

80. Access to the arrested person can not be denied to his relations and his friends, if they produce an order of the civil officer, who is always compelled to give the same unless the jailor produce an order of the judge to keep the person in close custody.

81. All those whom the law does not give the right of arrest shall issue, sign, execute, or cause to be executed, a warrant of arrest; or if

any person, even in the case of an authorized arrest, shall receive or detain the arrested person at a place of detention which is not properly and publicly assigned as such, and all jailors who shall act contrary to the three preceding articles, shall be guilty of the crime of arbitrary arrest.

82. All severities employed in arrests, detentions, or executions other than those authorized by law, are crimes.

83. All persons have the right to address individual petitions to the constituted authorities, and especially to the Tribunate.

84. The public force is essentially obedient; no armed body can deliberate.

85. Crimes committed by persons in the military service are submitted to special courts, which have special forms of sentence.

86. The French nation declares that it will accord pensions to all soldiers and officers wounded in the defense of their country; also to widows and children of all military persons who die on the battle field, or from their wounds.

87. National rewards shall be given to all soldiers who shall render distinguished service in battles for the Republic.

88. A national institute is charged with collecting discoveries relating to science and art.

89. A commission of national accounts regulates and verifies the receipts and expenses of the Republic. This commission is composed of seven members chosen by the Senate from the national list.

90. A constituted body can only deliberate at a session thereof where at least two-thirds of its members are present.

91. The French colonies are governed by special laws.

92. In case of armed rebellion, or of troubles which menace the safety of the State, the law may suspend the authority of the Constitution in the places and for the times it may determine. This suspension may provisionally be declared, in similar cases, by a decree of the government, when the Legislative Body is in recess, provided that in the same decree this body shall be convoked within the shortest possible time.

93. The French nation declares that in no case will it allow Frenchmen to return, who, having abandoned their country since July 14, 1789, are not comprised in the exceptions of the laws against emigrants; and it interdicts all new exceptions on this subject. The estates of the emigrants are irrevocably confiscated to the use of the Republic.

94. The French nation declares that after a legally consummated sale of the national estates, whatever may have been the grounds of the sale, the legal purchasers can not be dispossessed of the same, except in the case of a justly founded claim, and indemnity shall be paid by the public treasury.

95. The present Constitution shall forthwith be offered for adoption to the French nation.

Done at Paris, the 22d *Frimaire* (December 13, 1799), in the eighth year of the Republic, one and indivisible.

APPENDIX V.

CONSTITUTIONAL CHARTER OF 1814.

ARTICLE 1. Frenchmen are equal before the law, whatever may be their rank and title.

2. They contribute, without distinction, and in proportion to their fortunes, to the expenses of the State.

3. They are, without distinction, admissible to all civil and military employment.

4. Their individual liberty is equally guaranteed. No one can be arrested or prosecuted, except in the cases provided for by law, and according to the forms which it prescribes.

5. Every one may exercise his religion with equal freedom and receive for his religious worship the same protection.

6. However, the Catholic, Apostolic, and Roman religion is the religion of the State.

7. The ministers of the Catholic, Apostolic, and Roman religion, and those of other Christian worship, alone receive salaries or stipends from the royal treasury.

8. Frenchmen have the right to publish their opinions and cause them to be printed, if they conform to the laws, which may correct abuses against this liberty.

9. All property, without exception as to that which is called national property, is inviolable, the law making no difference between them.

10. The State may exact a sacrifice of property in the public interest, but only with a previous indemnity.

11. All investigations as to opinions and votes expressed or given before the restoration, are interdicted. The same secrecy is required of the courts and of all citizens.

12. Conscription is abolished. The method of recruiting for the army and for the marine is to be determined by law.

OF THE FORM OF THE GOVERNMENT OF THE KING.

13. The person of the King is inviolable and sacred. His ministers are responsible. To the King alone belongs executive power.

14. The King is the supreme head of the State; commands the land and marine forces; declares war; makes treaties of peace, alliance, and commerce; appoints to all offices of public administration, and makes the rules and orders for the execution of the laws and the safety of the State.

15. The legislative power is exercised in common by the King, the Chamber of Peers, and the Chamber of Deputies of the departments.

16. The King proposes the laws.

17. The proposition of a law is, at the pleasure of the King, presented either to the Chamber of Peers or that of the deputies, except the law in respect to taxes, which must first be addressed to the Chamber of Deputies.

18. All laws must be freely discussed and voted by a majority of each of the two Chambers.

19. The Chambers have the right to petition the King to propose a law on any subject, and to indicate what appears to them to be expedient that the law should contain.

20. This petition may be made by either of the two Chambers, but after it has been discussed in secret committee it can only be sent to the other Chamber by the one which shall have proposed it, after a lapse of ten days.

21. If the petition is adopted by the other Chamber, it shall be laid before the King, and if rejected by him, it can not be brought up again in the same session.

22. The King alone sanctions and promulgates the laws.

23. The civil list is fixed for the duration of the reign, by the first legislature after the accession of the King.

OF THE CHAMBER OF PEERS.

24. The Chamber of Peers is an essential part of the legislative power.

25. It is convoked by the King at the same time with the Chamber of Deputies of the Departments. The sessions of both chambers begin and end at the same time.

26. Every assembly of the Chamber of Peers, which should be held when the Chamber of Deputies is not in session, or which is not ordered by the King, is illicit and null of full right.

27. The nomination of the peers of France belongs to the King. Their number is unlimited. He may, at his pleasure, vary their dignities, name them for life, or make them hereditary.

28. The peers have access to the chamber at their twenty-fifth year of age, but only a deliberative voice at the age of thirty years.

29. The Chamber of Peers is presided over by the Chancelor of France, and in his absence, by a peer named by the King.

30. The members of the royal family, and the princes of the blood are peers by right of birth; they sit immediately behind the president, but they have no deliberative voice until they attain their twenty-fifth year of age.

31. The princes can only take their seats in the Chamber by the order of the King, expressed for each session by a message, under penalty of rendering everything null which has been done in their presence.

32. All deliberations of the Chamber of Peers are secret.

33. The Chamber of Peers has cognizance of the crimes of high treason and of attempts against the safety of the State, which the law will determine.

34. No peer can be arrested or judged on a criminal charge, except by the authority of the Chamber.

OF THE CHAMBER OF DEPUTIES OF THE DEPARTMENTS.

35. The Chamber of Deputies shall be composed of the deputies elected by the electoral colleges, the organization of which shall be determined by law.

36. Each department shall have the same number of deputies which it has previously had.

37. The deputies shall be elected for five years, and in such a manner that the Chamber is renewed each year by a fifth.

38. No deputy can be admitted to the Chamber unless he has attained the age of forty years, and pays a direct tax of 1,000 francs.

39. If, nevertheless, there are not to be found in the department fifty persons of the age indicated paying at least 1,000 francs of direct taxes, their number shall be completed by those who pay the highest taxes under 1,000 francs, and these may be elected concurrently with the first named.

40. The electors who nominate the deputies can not vote if they do not pay a direct tax of 300 francs, and if they are less than thirty years of age.

41. The presidents of the electoral colleges shall be named by the King and be legally members of the college.

42. At least one-half of the deputies shall be chosen from among those who are eligible and who have their political residence in the department.

43. The president of the Chamber is named by the King from a list of five members presented by the Chamber.

44. The sessions of the Chamber are public, but the demand of five members is sufficient to form it into a secret committee of the whole.

45. The Chamber divides itself into committees to consider the propositions which have been presented to it by the King.

46. No amendment can be made to the law, unless it has been proposed and consented to by the King, and it has also been sent back to, and discussed in the committees.

47. The Chamber of Deputies receives all propositions concerning taxes, and it is only after they have been approved by that body that they may be forwarded to the Chamber of Peers.

48. No tax can be raised or collected unless it has been consented to by the two Chambers and by the King.

49. The tax on real estate can only be raised for one year. Indirect taxes may be levied for several years.

50. The King convokes the two Chambers annually; he prorogues them, and can dissolve that of the deputies of the departments, but, in this case, he must convoke a new Chamber within three months.

51. No bodily restraint can be exercised against a member of the Chamber during the session, nor within six weeks which shall precede or follow the sessions.

52. No member of the Chamber can, during the session, be arrested or prosecuted in a criminal proceeding, except if he be taken in the act, and after the Chamber has permitted his prosecution.

53. All petitions to both Chambers can only be made and presented in writing. The law interdicts their being presented personally to the bar.

OF THE MINISTERS.

54. Ministers may be members, either of the Chamber of Peers or of the Chamber of Deputies. They have, moreover, their entrance to both Chambers, and must be heard when they demand it.

55. The Chamber of Deputies has the right to impeach the ministers, and to compel them to appear before the Chamber of Peers, which body only has the right to judge them.

56. They can only be impeached for treason and peculation. Special laws shall determine the nature of these crimes and the mode of their prosecution.

OF JUDICIAL REGULATIONS.

57. All justice emanates from the King. It is administered in his name by the judges whom he nominates and whom he institutes.

58. The judges appointed by the King can not be removed.

59. The existing ordinary courts and tribunals are continued. They can only be changed by virtue of a law.

60. The existing commercial court is conserved.

61. The justices of the peace are likewise retained. The justices of the peace, although named by the King, are removable.

62. No one can be removed from the jurisdiction of his legal judges.

63. Consequently, there can not be established any extraordinary commissions or tribunals, but under this denomination the provostal courts are not included in so far as their reinstitution may be deemed necessary.

64. The debates in criminal matters shall be public, at least when publicity shall not be dangerous to public order and morals; and in this case the tribunal shall so declare by a judicial order.

65. The juries are retained. Changes which experience may suggest can only be effected by law.

66. The punishment of confiscation of property is abolished, and can never be re-established

67. The King has the right to pardon and commute punishment.

68. The Civil Code and the existing laws which do not conflict with the present Charter remain in full force until they may be abrogated.

OF SPECIAL RIGHTS GUARANTEED BY THE STATE.

69. Persons in active military service, officers and soldiers retired, widows, officers, and soldiers pensioned, retain their rank, honors, and pensions.

70. The public debt is guaranteed. Every kind of engagement entered into by the State with its creditors is inviolable.

71. The old nobility retake their titles. The new nobility retain theirs. The King may create nobles at pleasure, but he only accords to them rank and honors, without any release from the burdens and duties of society.

72. The Legion of Honor is retained. The King shall determine its internal regulations and the nature of the decorations.

73. The colonies are governed by special laws and regulations.

74. The King and his successors shall, at the time of the coronation, swear faithfully to observe the present Constitutional Charter.

OF ARTICLES OF TEMPORARY EFFECT.

75. The deputies of the departments of France who sat in the Legislative Body at the last adjournment shall continue to sit in the Chamber of Deputies until replaced.

76. The first renewal of the fifth of the Chamber of Deputies shall take place, at the latest, in the year 1816, according to the established order.

We command that the present Constitutional Charter, by virtue of our proclamation of May 2d, be laid before the Senate and the Legislative Body, and be immediately communicated to the Chambers of Peers and Deputies.

Done at Paris, in the year of grace 1814, and of our reign the 19th.

LOUIS.

APPENDIX VI.

ADDITIONAL ACT TO THE CONSTITUTIONS OF THE EMPIRE (APRIL 22, 1815).

Napoleon, etc.

Since we were called, fifteen years ago, by the vote of France, to the government of the State, we have sought, following the needs and the desires of the nation, and profiting by the lessons of experience, to perfect, at different times, the constitutional forms. The Constitutions of the Empire were formed by a series of acts, which have been accepted by the people. Our object was to organize a grand system of European confederation, that we had adopted in conformity with the spirit of the time, and as favorable to the progress of civilization. In order to complete it, and to give it full extension, and all the stability of which it was susceptible, we had postponed the establishment of several interior institutions, more especially designed to protect the liberty of citizens.

Our object henceforth shall be to increase the prosperity of France by giving support to public liberty. For this reason a necessity arises for several important modifications in the Constitutions, *Senatûs consulta*, and other acts, which now constitute the laws of the Empire.

Wishing, for these motives, on the one side, to conserve that which is good and salutary in the past, and, on the other, to make the Constitutions of our Empire conform to all the national desires and needs, as well as to maintain peace with Europe, we have resolved to propose to the people a series of provisions tending to modify and to perfect the Constitutional Acts, to encompass the rights of citizens with every guarantee, to give a representative system in its full extension, to invest the intermediary corps with consideration and desirable power; in a word, to combine the highest condition of public liberty and individual security with power and necessary centralization, in order to make the foreigner respect the independence of the French people and the dignity of our crown. Therefore, the following articles, forming a supplementary act to the Constitutions of the Empire, shall be submitted to the free and solemn acceptance of all citizens throughout the extent of France.

TITLE I.

GENERAL PROVISIONS.

ARTICLE 1. The Constitutions of the Empire, called the Constitutional Act of 22d *Frimaire*, year VIII, the *Senatûs consulta* of the 14th and 16th *Thermidor*, year X, and that of the 28th *Floréal*, year XII, are modified by the following provisions. All other provisions are confirmed and maintained.

2. The legislative power shall be exercised by the Emperor, and by the two Chambers.

3. The first Chamber, called the Chamber of Peers, is hereditary.

4. The Emperor names its members, who are irrevocable, they, and their male descendants, from eldest to eldest in direct line. The number of peers is unlimited. Adoption does not transmit the rank and dignity of peers. The peers take their seats at the age of twenty-one years, but they do not have a deliberative voice until they are twenty-five years.

5. The Chamber of Peers shall be presided over by the Chief Chancellor of the Empire, or, in the case provided for by Article 51 of the *Senatûs consultum* of 28th *Floréal*, year XII, by one of the members of this Chamber, specially designated by the Emperor.

6. The members of the imperial family, in the order of succession, are peers by right. They take their seats after the president. They take their seats at eighteen years, but have not a deliberative voice until they are twenty-one years of age.

7. The second Chamber, called the Chamber of Representatives, shall be elected by the people.

8. This Chamber shall have 629 members. They must be at least twenty-five years of age.

9. The president of the Chamber of Representatives shall be chosen by the Chamber, on the opening of the first session. He remains in office until the renewal of the Chamber. His nomination shall be submitted to the approval of the Emperor.

10. The Chamber of Representatives verifies the powers of its members, and decides upon the validity of contested elections.

11. The members of the Chamber of Representatives shall receive an indemnity, during the session, for traveling expenses, to be decreed by the Constituent Assembly.

12. They are indefinitely re-eligible.

13. The Chamber of Representatives shall be wholly renewed every five years.

14. No member of either Chamber can be arrested, except he is taken in the act, nor prosecuted in a criminal or correctional way, during the sessions, except by virtue of a resolution of the Chamber of which he is a member.

15. No one can be arrested, nor detained for debt, from the time of the convocation until forty days after the session.

16. The peers are tried by their own Chamber, in criminal and correctional matters, under the forms which shall be regulated by law.

17. The obligations and attributes of peer and representative must be consistent with every public duty and law—with the exception of the privileges already mentioned. The prefects and the sub-prefects are not eligible to the electoral colleges of the departments or of the arrondissements which they administer.

18. The Emperor sends the ministers of State and councilors of State before the Chambers, where they have seats and take part in the discussions, but they only vote when they are members of the Chamber either as peers or representatives of the people.

19. Ministers who are members of the Chamber of Peers, or that of the Representatives, or who have a seat by direction of the government, give to the Chambers any information which is deemed expedient, when its publicity does not compromise the interest of the State.

20. The sessions of the two Chambers are public. They may, nevertheless, form themselves into a secret committee of the whole; the Chamber of Peers upon the demand of ten members; that of the representatives upon the demand of twenty-five members. The government may also demand the formation of secret committees in order to send communications to them. In all cases, however, the resolutions or the votes shall take place in public session.

21. The Emperor can prorogue, adjourn, or dissolve the Chamber of Representatives. The proclamation which announces the dissolution convokes the electoral colleges for a new election, and indicates a date within six months, at the latest, when the representatives shall assemble.

22. During the recess of the Chamber of Representatives, or in case of the dissolution of this Chamber, the Chamber of Peers can not assemble.

23. The government has the proposition of the law; the Chambers may propose amendments to the same; if these amendments are not approved of by the government, the Chambers are compelled to vote upon the law as it has been proposed.

24. The Chambers may invite the government to propose a law upon a defined subject, and to draw up what may appear to them expedient to insert in the law. This request may be made by either of the two Chambers.

25. When a bill is passed by one of the two Chambers it is transmitted to the other; and if it is approved by it, it is transmitted to the Emperor.

26. No written speech, except the reports of the committees, or reports of ministers upon the laws which have been presented, and the accounts rendered, can be read in either of the Chambers.

Title II.
OF THE ELECTORAL COLLEGES AND THE MODE OF ELECTION.

27. The electoral colleges of the departments and of the arrondissements are retained, in accordance with the *Senatûs consultum* of the 16th *Thermidor*, year X, except the following modifications.

28. The canton assemblies shall fill, by annual elections, all the vacancies in the electoral colleges.

29. Dating from 1816 a member of the Chamber of Peers, designated by the Emperor, shall be president (for life and unremovable) of each electoral college of the department.

30. Dating from the same time, the electoral college of each department shall nominate, from the members of each college of arrondissement, a president and two vice-presidents. For this purpose, the assembly of the departmental college shall precede that of the college arrondissement fifteen days.

31. The department and arrondissement colleges shall nominate the representatives established by the act and table herewith annexed.

32. The representatives may be chosen without regard to residence, throughout the extent of France. Each department or arrondissement college which shall choose a representative outside of the department or arrondissement, shall elect a substitute, who shall necessarily be taken from the department or arrondissement in which he lives.

33. Industry, and manufacturing and commercial property shall have a special representation. The election of commercial and manufacturing representatives shall be conducted by the electoral college of the department, upon a special list drawn up at a joint meeting of the commercial and consultative chambers, according to the act and table herewith annexed.

TITLE III.

OF THE LAW OF TAXATION.

34. General direct taxes, either land or personal, are only voted for one year; the indirect taxes can be voted for several years. In the case of the dissolution of the Chamber of Representatives, the taxes voted in the preceding session shall be continued until the new meeting of the Chamber.

35. No direct or indirect tax in money or in kind can be collected, no loan can take place, no inscription of credit on the ledger of the public debt can be made, no domain can be alienated or exchanged, no levy of men for the army ordered, no portion of the territory can be exchanged, except by virtue of a law.

36. Every proposition as to taxes, loans, or levy of men, can only be made by the Chamber of Representatives.

37. The following bills shall originate in the Chamber of Representatives: 1. The general budget of the State, containing the statement of receipts and estimate of funds assigned for the year to each department of the ministry. 2. The account of the receipts and expenses of the year or of preceding years.

TITLE IV.

OF THE MINISTERS AND THEIR RESPONSIBILITY.

38. All acts of the government must be countersigned by a minister having a department.

39. Ministers are responsible for the acts of the government signed by them, as well as for the execution of the laws.

40. They may be impeached by the Chamber of Representatives and tried by that of the peers.

41. Every minister, every commander of the army by land or sea, may be impeached by the Chamber of Representatives and tried by the Chamber of Peers, for having compromised the safety or honor of the nation.

42. The Chamber of Peers, in this case, exercises, either to characterize the misdemeanor or crime, or to inflict the penalty, a discretionary power.

43. Before voting an impeachment of a minister, the Chamber of Representatives must declare that there is cause to investigate the charges.

44. This declaration can only be made after a report of a committee of sixty members chosen by lot. This committee shall not make its report any sooner than ten days after its nomination.

45. When the Chamber has declared that there are grounds for the examination, it may call the minister within its body to demand explanations of him. This summons can only be made ten days after the report of the committee.

46. In no other case may ministers having a department be called or summoned by the Chambers.

47. When the Chamber of representatives has declared that there are grounds for an examination against a minister, a new committee of sixty members is formed, selected by lot, as in the case of the first, and this committee makes a new report upon the accusation in question. This committee must make its report within ten days after its nomination.

48. The accusation can only be announced within ten days after the reading and distribution of the report.

49. The accusation being pronounced, the Chamber of Representatives names five commissioners, taken from its body, to prosecute the charge before the Chamber of Peers.

50. Article 75 of Title VIII, of the Constitutional Act of the 22d *Frimaire*, year VIII, providing that the agents of the government can only be prosecuted by virtue of a decision of the Council of State, shall be modified by a law.

Title V.

OF THE JUDICIAL POWER.

51. The Emperor names all the judges. They are appointed for life and unremovable from the time of their nomination, except the nomination of the justices of the peace and commercial judges, which shall take place according to existing law. The present judges named by the Emperor by virtue of the terms of the *Senatûs consultum* of October 12, 1807, and whom he shall judge proper to retain, shall have allowances made for them for life before January 1 next.

52. The institution of juries is retained.

53. The debates on criminal matters are public.

54. The military tribunals alone have jurisdiction of military misdemeanors.

55. All other misdemeanors, even when committed by members of military organizations, are tried by the civil tribunals.

56. All crimes and misdemeanors over which the Imperial High Court had jurisdiction, and whose trial is not reserved by the present act for the Chamber of Peers, shall be taken before the ordinary tribunals.

57. The Emperor has the right to grant pardons, even in correctional matters, and accord amnesties.

58. The interpretations of law made by the Court of *Cassation* shall be granted in the form of a law.

TITLE VI.
OF THE RIGHTS OF CITIZENS.

59. All Frenchmen are equal before the law, either in their contribution by taxes and public charges, or for admission to civil and military employment.

60. No one can, under any pretext, be taken from the jurisdiction of the judges assigned by law.

61. No one can be prosecuted, arrested, detained, nor exiled, except in the cases provided by law, and according to the prescribed forms.

62. Liberty of worship is guaranteed to all.

63. All property possessed or acquired by law, and all credits assumed by the State, are inviolable.

64. Every citizen has the right to print and to publish his thoughts, by signing them without any previous censorship, except legal responsibility, after publication, by trial by jury, even if there are only grounds for the application of a correctional penalty.

65. The right of petition is assured to all citizens. Every petition must be made individually. These petitions must be addressed either to the government or to the two Chambers. Nevertheless, they must be entitled: "To His Majesty the Emperor." They are presented to the Chambers under the guarantee of a member who recommends the petition. They are read publicly. If the Chamber take them into consideration, they are transmitted to the Emperor by the president.

66. No division, no part of the territory, can be declared in a state of siege, except in the event of invasion by a foreign force or of civil

disturbance or insurrection. In the first case, the declaration is made by an act of the government; in the second, by virtue of law. In all cases, if the Chambers are not in session, the act of the government declaring the state of siege must be converted into a proposition of law within the first fifteen days after the Chambers assemble.

67. The French people declare that by the delegation of powers which it has made and now makes, it has not intended nor intends to give the right to propose the re-establishment of the Bourbons, or any prince of that family, upon the throne, even in the event of the extinction of the imperial dynasty, or the right to re-establish either the ancient feudal nobility or the feudal and manorial rights, or the tithes, or any privileged and ruling worship, or the right to attack the irrevocability of the sale of national domains; and the government, the Chambers, and all citizens are specially forbidden to make any proposition of this nature.

Here follows a decree and a table fixing the number of deputies to be elected, and a second decree and table regulating the number of deputies to represent property and industry.

APPENDIX VII.

CONSTITUTIONAL CHARTER OF 1830.

Louis Philippe, King of the French, to all to whom these presents shall come, greeting:

We have ordered and ordained that the Constitutional Charter of 1814, as amended by the two Chambers on August 7th, and accepted by us on the 9th, be republished in the following terms:

OF THE PUBLIC LAW OF THE FRENCH.

ARTICLE 1. Frenchmen are equal before the law, whatever may be their rank and title.

2. They contribute, without distinction, and in proportion to their fortunes, to the expenses of the State.

3. They are, without distinction, admissible to all civil and military employment.

4. Their individual liberty is equally guaranteed. No one can be arrested or prosecuted, except in the cases provided for by law, and according to the forms which it prescribes.

5. Every one may exercise his religion with equal freedom, and receive for his religious worship the same protection.

6. The ministers of the Catholic, Apostolic, and Roman religion, professed by the majority of the French, and those of other Christian worship, receive salaries and stipends from the public treasury.

7. Frenchmen have the right to publish their opinions and cause them to be printed, if they conform to the laws. The censorship can never be re-established.

8. All property, without exception as to that which is called national property, is inviolable, the law making no difference between them.

9. The State may exact a sacrifice of property in the public interest, but only with a previous indemnity.

10. All investigations as to opinions and votes, expressed or given before the restoration, are interdicted. The same oblivion is required of the courts and of all citizens.

11. Conscription is abolished. The method of recruiting for the army and for the marine is to be determined by law.

OF THE FORM OF THE KING'S GOVERNMENT.

12. The person of the King is inviolable and sacred. His ministers are responsible. To the King alone belongs executive power.

13. The King is the supreme head of the State; commands the land and marine forces, declares war, makes treaties of peace, alliance, and commerce; appoints to all offices of public administration, and makes the rules and orders for the execution of the laws, without ever having power either to suspend the laws themselves, or dispense with their execution. Nevertheless, no foreign troops can be admitted into the service of the State except by virtue of a law.

14. The legislative power is exercised in common by the King, the Chamber of Peers, and the Chamber of Deputies.

15. The proposition of the laws belongs to the King, to the Chamber of Peers, and to the Chamber of Deputies. Nevertheless, all laws regarding taxes must first be voted by the Chamber of Deputies.

16. All laws must be freely discussed and voted by the majority of each of the two Chambers.

17. If a project of law be rejected by one of the three powers, it can not be brought forward again in the same session.

18. The King alone sanctions and promulgates the law.

19. The civil list is determined for the duration of the reign by the first legislative assembly after the accession of the King.

OF THE CHAMBER OF PEERS.

20. The Chamber of Peers is an essential part of the legislative power.

21. It is convoked by the King, at the same time with the Chamber of Deputies. The sessions of both Chambers begin and end at the same time.

22. Every assembly of the Chamber of Peers which may be held when the Chamber of Deputies is not in session, is illicit, and null of full right, except only in such cases when it is assembled as a court of justice, and then it can only exercise judicial functions.

23. The nomination of the peers of France belongs to the King. Their number is unlimited. He may, at his pleasure, vary their dignities, name them for life, or make them hereditary.

24. The peers have access to the Chamber at their twenty-fifth year of age, but they shall only have a deliberate voice at the age of thirty years.

25. The Chamber of Peers is presided over by the Chancellor of France, and in his absence, by a peer named by the King.

26. The princes of the blood are peers by right of birth; they sit immediately behind the president.

27. The sessions of the Chamber of Peers are public, as those of the Chamber of Deputies.

28. The Chamber of Peers has cognizance of the crimes of high treason and of attempts against the safety of the State, which the laws will determine.

29. No peer can be arrested or judged on a criminal charge, except by the authority of the Chamber.

OF THE CHAMBER OF DEPUTIES.

30. The Chamber of Deputies shall be composed of deputies elected by the electoral colleges, the organization of which shall be determined by law.

31. The deputies are elected for five years.

32. No deputy can be admitted into the Chamber if he has not attained the age of thirty years, and if he does not unite in himself the other qualifications determined by law.

33. If, nevertheless, there are not to be found in the department fifty persons of the age indicated paying the amount of taxes fixed by law, their number shall be completed from the persons who pay the greatest amount of taxes under the amount fixed by law; and these may be elected concurrently with the first named.

34. No person can be an elector if he is under twenty-five years of age, and if he does not unite the other qualifications determined by law.

35. The presidents of the electoral colleges are named by the electors.

36. One-half, at least, of the deputies shall be chosen from among those who are eligible and have their political residence in the department.

37. The president of the Chamber of Deputies is elected by the Chamber itself at the opening of each session.

38. The sessions of the Chamber are public, but on the request of five members it may be formed into secret committee of the whole.

39. The Chamber divides itself into committees to consider the propositions of law which may have been presented to it by the King.

40. No tax can be raised or collected unless it has been consented to by the two Chambers, and sanctioned by the King.

41. The tax on real estate can only be raised for one year. Indirect taxes may be levied for several years.

42. The King convokes the two Chambers annually. He prorogues them, and can dissolve that of the deputies, but in this case he must convoke a new Chamber within three months.

43. No bodily restraint can be exercised against a member of the Chamber during the session, nor within six weeks which shall precede or follow the session.

44. No member of the Chamber can, during the session, be arrested or prosecuted in a criminal proceeding, except he be taken in the act, and after the Chamber has allowed his prosecution.

45. All petitions to both Chambers can only be made and presented in writing. The law interdicts their being presented personally at the bar.

OF THE MINISTERS.

46. Ministers may be members, either of the Chamber of Peers or of the Chamber of Deputies. They have, moreover, their entrance to both Chambers, and must be heard when they demand it.

47. The Chamber of Deputies has the right to impeach the ministers, and to compel them to appear before the Chamber of Peers, which body only has the right to judge them.

OF JUDICIAL REGULATIONS.

48. All justice emanates from the King. It is administered in his name by the judges whom he nominates and whom he institutes.

49. The judges appointed by the King can not be removed.

50. The existing ordinary courts and tribunals are continued. They can only be changed by virtue of a law.

51. The existing commercial court is retained.

52. The justices of the peace are likewise retained. The justices of the peace, although named by the King, are removable.

53. No one can be removed from the jurisdiction of his legal judges.

54. Consequently, there can not be established any extraordinary commissions or tribunals, under whatever title or denomination this ever might be.

55. The debates in criminal matters shall be public, at least when publicity shall not be dangerous to public order and morals, and, in this case, the tribunal shall so declare by a judicial order.

56. The juries are retained. Changes which experience may suggest can only be effected by law.

57. The punishment of confiscation of property is abolished, and can never be re-established.

58. The King has the right to pardon and commute punishment.

59. The civil code and the existing laws which do not conflict with the present Charter remain in full force until they may be abrogated.

OF SPECIAL RIGHTS GUARANTEED BY THE STATE.

60. Persons in active military service, officers and soldiers retired, widows, officers, and soldiers pensioned, retain their rank, honors, and pensions.

61. The public debt is guaranteed. Every kind of engagement entered into by the State with its creditors, is inviolable.

62. The old nobility retain their titles. The new nobility retain theirs. The King creates nobles at pleasure; but he only accords to them rank and honors, without any release from the burdens and duties of society.

63. The Legion of Honor is retained. The King shall determine its internal regulations, and the nature of its decorations.

64. The colonies are governed by laws and regulations.

65. The King and his successors shall swear, at their accession, in presence of the two Chambers, to observe faithfully the present Constitutional Charter.

66. The present Charter and the rights it consecrates, are intrusted to the patriotism and to the courage of the National Guard, and to all French citizens.

67. France resumes her colors. For the future there shall be no other cockade than the tricolored cockade.

OF SPECIAL PROVISIONS.

68. All the nominations of new peers made during the reign of Charles X. are declared null and void.

Article 23 of the Charter shall be submitted to a new examination during the session of 1831.

69. There shall, successively, be provided by separate laws, and that with the shortest possible delay, for the following subjects: 1. Application of the trial by jury to misdemeanors of the press and political offenses. 2. The responsibility of ministers and of other executive agents. 3. The re-election of deputies appointed to public functions with salaries. 4. The annual vote of the army estimates. 5. The organization of the National Guard, with the intervention of the National Guards in the choice of their officers. 6. Provisions which would insure, in a legal manner, the position and condition of officers of all grades by land and sea. 7. Departmental and municipal institutions founded upon an elective system. 8. Public instruction and the liberty of instruction. 9. The abolition of the double vote, and the settlement of electoral conditions and of eligibility.

70. All laws and ordinances, in so far as they may conflict with the provisions adopted for the amendment of the Charter, are hereby annulled and abrogated.

We command all our courts and tribunals, and administrative bodies, that they guard and maintain the present Constitutional Charter, cause it to be guarded, observed, and maintained, and in order to render it known to all, they cause it to be published in all the municipalities of the kingdom, and everywhere it need be, that this instrument may be firm and stable forever, and we have, therefore, caused our seal to be affixed thereto.

Done at the Palais Royal, at Paris, the 14th day of August, 1830.

LOUIS PHILIPPE.

APPENDIX VIII.

CONSTITUTION OF 1848.

CHAPTER I.
OF SOVEREIGNTY.

ARTICLE 1. Sovereignty exists in the whole body of French citizens. It is inalienable and imprescriptible. No individual, no part of the people can assume its exercise.

CHAPTER II.
OF THE RIGHTS OF CITIZENS GUARANTEED BY THE CONSTITUTION.

2. No person can be arrested or detained, except according to law.

3. The habitation of every person living on French territory is inviolable, and can not be entered except according to the forms, and the cases provided for by law.

4. No one shall be removed from the jurisdiction of his judges. No extraordinary commissions or tribunals can be formed, of whatever title or by any denomination.

5. The penalty of death for political offenses is abolished.

6. Slavery can not exist on French territory.

7. Every person may freely profess his own religion, and receive equal protection from the State in its exercise. The ministers now recognized by law, or who may hereafter be acknowledged, have the right to receive a stipend from the State.

8. Citizens have the right of associating together, and of assembling peaceably and unarmed; of petitioning, and of manifesting their opinions through the press or otherwise. The exercise of these rights is only limited by the liberty of others and the public safety. The press can in no case be subjected to censorship.

9. Education is free. The liberty of instruction is exercised according to capacity and morality as expressed by the law, and under the

superintendence of the State. This surveillance extends to all establishments of education and instruction, without any exception.

10. All citizens are equally admissible to public employment, without any other grounds for preference than their own merit, and according to the conditions that shall be prescribed by law. All titles of nobility, all distinctions of birth, of class, and of caste, are abolished forever.

11. All property is inviolable. Nevertheless, the State may demand the sacrifice of property on public grounds, legally established, and for a just indemnity.

12. Confiscation of estates can never be re-established

13. The Constitution guarantees to citizens the freedom of labor and industry. Society favors and encourages the development of labor by gratuitous primary instruction, by professional education, by equality of rights between employer and workman, by savings institutions, and those of credit, by agricultural institutions, by voluntary associations; and the establishment by the State, the departments, and the communes, of proper public works for the employment of laborers without work; abandoned children, the infirm, and the aged without resources, and whose families can not aid them, must have aid given them.

14. The public debt is guaranteed. All contracts entered into by the State with its creditors are inviolable.

15. Taxes are imposed for the common welfare. Every one contributes in proportion to his means and fortunes.

16. No tax can be raised or collected except by virtue of law.

17. Direct taxation is only levied for one year. Indirect taxation may be awarded for several years.

CHAPTER III.

OF THE PUBLIC POWERS.

18. All public powers, whatever they may be, emanate from the people. They can not be inherited.

19. The separation of powers is the first principle of free government.

CHAPTER IV.

OF THE LEGISLATIVE POWER.

20. The French people delegate the legislative power to one assembly.

21. The total number of the representatives of the people shall be 750, including those from Algeria and the French colonies.

22. This number shall be increased to 900 for assemblies which shall be convoked to amend the Constitution.

23. Population is the basis for elections.

24. Suffrage is direct and universal. Voting is by secret ballot.

25. All Frenchmen twenty-one years of age, and who are in the enjoyment of their civil and political rights, are electors without property qualifications.

26. All electors are eligible to be elected to office, without reference to place of abode, who are twenty-five years of age.

27. The electoral law shall determine the causes which may deprive a French citizen of the right to elect or of being elected. It shall designate the citizens who, exercising, or having exercised official duties in a department or territory, can not be elected there.

28. The holding of any salaried public position is incompatible with the mandate of representative of the people. No member of the National Assembly can, during the continuance of the legislature, be named or promoted to a salaried public position, the appointment of which is in the gift of the executive power. Exceptions to the two preceding paragraphs shall be determined by the organic electoral law.

29. The provisions of the preceding article are not applicable to assemblies elected for the revision of the Constitution.

30. The election of representatives shall be by departments and by ballot on a general ticket. The electors shall vote in the chief place of the canton; nevertheless, by reason of local circumstances, the canton may be divided into several sub-divisions, in the form and upon the conditions which shall be determined by the electoral law.

31. The National Assembly is elected for three years, and then it is wholly renewed. Forty-five days, at least, before the end of the legislature, a law shall determine the date of the new elections. If no law intervenes within the time fixed by the preceding article, the electors shall unite with full power on the thirtieth day which precedes the close of the legislature. The new Assembly is convoked with full power on the day following that on which the mandate of the preceding expires.

32. The Assembly is permanent. Nevertheless, it may adjourn for a period which it shall fix. During the prorogation, a commission, composed of members of committees, and twenty-five representatives named by the Assembly by ballot, and having an absolute majority,

has the right, in cases of urgency, to convoke the Assembly. The President of the Assembly has, also, the right to convoke the Assembly. The National Assembly determines the place of its sessions. It controls the military forces established for its security and disposes of the same.

33. Representatives may be re-elected.

34. Members of the National Assembly are the representatives, not of the department which elects them, but of the whole of France.

35. They can not receive imperative instructions.

36. The persons of the representatives are inviolable. They can not be pursued, arrested, or judged, at any time, for opinions expressed in the body of the National Assembly.

37. They can not be arrested criminally, except in case they are taken in the act, nor prosecuted until after the Assembly has sanctioned the prosecution. In case of an arrest in the act, the matter shall immediately be referred to the Assembly, which shall authorize or forbid the continuation of the prosecution. This provision applies to a citizen who is under arrest at the time of his election.

38. Each representative of the people is to receive a salary which he can not refuse.

39. The sessions of the Assembly are public. Nevertheless, the Assembly may form itself into a secret committee of the whole, upon a demand of a number of representatives to be fixed by the rules. Each representative has the right of initiating parliamentary measures, which right shall be exercised according to the regulations.

40. The presence of an absolute majority is necessary to vote on any law.

41. No bill, except in cases of urgency, shall definitively be voted until after three readings, at intervals of not less than five days.

42. Every proposition, the object of which is to declare a vote of urgency, must be preceded by an explanation of the grounds on which it is based. If the Assembly is of the opinion to accede to the project, it orders the matter to be sent to the committees, and fixes the time when the report on the question of urgency shall be presented to it. Upon the report, if the Assembly admit the urgency, it shall then fix the time of the debate. If it decides against the proposition of urgency, the motions shall take their usual course.

CHAPTER V.
OF THE EXECUTIVE POWER.

43. The French people delegates the executive power to a citizen, who shall receive the title of President of the Republic.

44. The president must be born a Frenchman; at least thirty years of age, and must never have lost his citizenship.

45. The President of the Republic is elected for four years, and is not eligible for re-election, until after an interval of four years. Neither shall the vice-president, nor any of his relations or kindred of the president, to the sixth degree inclusive, be eligible for re-election after him, within the same interval of time.

46. The election shall take place on the second Sunday in the month of May. In the event of death, resignation, or from other cause, a president should be elected at another time, his power shall expire on the second Sunday of the month of May of the fourth year which follows his election. The president shall be elected by ballot, and by an absolute majority of votes, by the direct votes of all the electors of the French departments, and of Algeria.

47. The minutes of the electoral returns shall immediately be transmitted to the National Assembly, which shall determine, without delay, upon the validity of the election, and proclaim the President of the Republic. If no candidate shall have obtained more than one half of the votes cast, and at least 2,000,000 of votes, or if the conditions required by Article 44 have not been complied with, the National Assembly shall elect the President of the Republic by an absolute majority, and by ballot from among the five eligible candidates, who have received the greatest number of votes.

48. The President of the Republic, before entering upon his duties, shall, in the presence of the Assembly, take the following oath: "*In presence of God, and before the French people, represented by the National Assembly, I swear to remain faithful to the Democratic Republic, one and indivisible, and to fulfill all the duties which the Constitution imposes upon me.*"

49. He shall have the right, through his ministers, of presenting bills to the National Assembly. He shall supervise and secure the execution of the laws.

50. He disposes of the armed force, without power ever to command in person.

51. He can not cede any portion of the territory, nor dissolve or prorogue the National Assembly, nor suspend the operation of the Constitution and the laws.

52. He shall present annually, by a message, to the National Assembly, a statement of the general state of affairs of the Republic.

53. He negotiates and ratifies treaties. No treaty is definitive until it has been approved by the National Assembly.

54. He shall watch over the defense of the State, but he shall not commence any war without the consent of the National Assembly.

55. He shall have the right of pardon, but he shall not exercise this right until he has taken the advice of the Council of State. Amnesties shall only be accorded by law. The President of the Republic, the ministers, as well as all other persons condemned by the High Court of Justice, can only be pardoned by the National Assembly.

56. The President of the Republic shall promulgate the laws in the name of the French people.

57. Laws of urgency shall be promulgated within three days, and all other laws within one month, estimating the time from the day when they shall have been passed by the National Assembly.

58. During the time fixed for the promulgation of the laws, the President of the Republic may, by a message containing the grounds therefor, demand a reconsideration of the law. The Assembly shall deliberate, and if it passes the law again, it shall be definitive, and shall be transmitted to the President of the Republic. In such an event, the promulgation of the law shall be made within the time fixed for laws of urgency.

59. In default of promulgation of the law by the President of the Republic, within the time determined by the preceding articles, the President of the National Assembly shall provide for the promulgation.

60. Envoys and ambassadors from foreign powers are accredited to the President of the Republic.

61. He shall preside at all national solemnities.

62. He shall be furnished with a residence at the expense of the Republic, and shall receive an annual allowance of 600,000 francs.

63. He shall reside in the place where the National Assembly sits, and can not leave the continental territory of the Republic without authority of law.

64. The President of the Republic shall appoint and revoke the appointment of the ministers. He shall appoint and revoke, in a council of ministers, the diplomatic agents, the commanders-in-chief

of the armies by land and sea, the prefects, the chief commandant of the National Guards of the Seine, the Governors of Algeria and of the colonies, the attorneys-general, and other functionaries of high rank. He shall appoint and dismiss, upon the request of a competent minister, according to the conditions determined by law, the governmental agents of secondary rank.

65. He has the right to suspend agents of the executive power elected by the people, for a period not exceeding three months. He shall only be able to dismiss them on the advice of the Council of State. The law will determine the case in which agents who have been dismissed are ineligible to any office. This declaration of ineligibility can only be pronounced by a judgment.

66. The number of ministers and their powers shall be decreed by the legislative power.

67. The acts of the President of the Republic, other than those by which he appoints and dismisses the ministers, have no effect unless countersigned by a minister.

68. The President of the Republic, the ministers, the agents, and the depositaries of public authority, are responsible, each in that which concerns him, for all governmental or administrative acts: Every measure the President of the Republic may take to dissolve or prorogue the National Assembly, or place any obstacle to the exercise of its powers, shall constitute the crime of high treason. By this single act, the president is stripped of his functions; citizens are compelled to refuse obedience to him, and the executive power passes with full right to the National Assembly. The judges of the High Court of Justice shall immediately assemble, on pain of forfeiture of their offices. They convene a jury at a place they shall designate, in order to proceed to the trial of the president and his accomplices; they shall themselves appoint an officer who shall act as attorney-general. A law shall determine the other cases of responsibility, and the forms and the conditions of the prosecution.

69. Ministers shall have admission to the National Assembly; they shall be heard whenever they demand it, and they cause the commissioners appointed by the President of the Republic to assist them.

70. There shall be a Vice President of the Republic named by the National Assembly, upon the presentation of three candidates made by the president within the month which follows his election. The vice-president shall take the same oath as the president. The vice-president shall not be appointed from among the kindred of the

president in the sixth degree inclusive. In case of the impeachment of the president, the vice-president shall replace him. If the presidency become vacant by death, resignation, or otherwise, an election for president shall take place within a month.

CHAPTER VI.
OF THE COUNCIL OF STATE.

71. There shall be a Council of State, of which the vice-president shall, by virtue of his office, be the president.

72. The members of this council are named for six years by the National Assembly. One-half of its members shall be renewed within the first two months of each legislature, by secret ballot and by absolute majority. They are indefinitely re-eligible.

73. Such members of the Council of State who shall have been taken from the body of the National Assembly, shall immediately be replaced by a representative of the people.

74. Members of the Council of State can only be dismissed by the Assembly, and upon the proposition of the President of the Republic.

75. The Council of State shall be consulted upon the bills of the government, which, according to law, must be presented for their previous examination; and also upon parliamentary bills which the Assembly shall have sent to it. It shall prepare the rules of public administration; it alone makes those regulations in regard to which the National Assembly has given it a special commission. It shall exercise all the powers of control and of superintendence which have been deferred to it by the law, in regard to the public administrations. The law will determine the other powers of the council.

CHAPTER VII.
OF THE INTERIOR ADMINISTRATION.

76. The division of the territory into departments, arrondissements, cantons, and communes shall be sustained. Their present circumscriptions shall not be changed except by law.

77. There shall be: 1. In each department an administration composed of a prefect, a general council, and a council of prefecture. 2. In each arrondissement, a sub-prefect. 3. In each canton, a canton council; nevertheless, only a single canton council shall be established in cities divided into several cantons. 4. In each commune, an administration, composed of a mayor, his assistants, and a municipal council.

78. A law shall determine the formation and duties of the general councils, the cantonal councils, the municipal councils, and the mode of nomination of the mayor and his assistants.

79. The general councils and the municipal councils shall be elected by a direct vote of all citizens living in the department or in the commune. Each canton shall elect a member of the general council. A special law shall regulate the mode of election in the Department of the Seine, in the City of Paris, and in cities of more than 20,000 persons.

80. The general councils, the cantonal councils, and the municipal councils may be dissolved by the President of the Republic, upon the advice of the Council of State. The law will fix the period within which a new election shall be had.

CHAPTER VIII.
OF THE JUDICIARY POWER.

81. Justice shall be awarded gratuitously, in the name of the French people. The debates shall be public, except in cases where publicity may be detrimental either to order or to morals, and in this case, the tribunal shall declare the same by a decree.

82. The jury shall be continued in criminal cases.

83. The jurisdiction of all political misdemeanors and of all misdemeanors committed by the press, belongs to the jury. The organic laws shall determine the jurisdiction in criminal libels and defamation against private individuals.

84. The jury alone shall decide upon the question of damages claimed on account of misdemeanors of the press.

85. The justices of the peace and their substitutes, the judges of the first instance and of appeal, the members of the Court of *Cassation*, and the Court of Accounts, shall be appointed by the President of the Republic, according to an order of candidateship, or conditions which shall be regulated by the organic laws.

86. The magistrates shall be appointed by the President of the Republic.

87. The judges of the first instance and of appeal, the members of the Court of *Cassation*, and the Court of Accounts, shall be appointed for life. They can only be dismissed or suspended by a judgment, nor retired except for cause, and according to the forms of law.

88. The councils of war and revision of the armies by land and sea, the maritime tribunals, the courts of commerce, the *prud' hommes*,

and other special tribunals, shall retain their organization and their present jurisdiction until the laws regulating the same are repealed.

89. Conflicts of jurisdiction and privilege between administrative and judicial authority shall be regulated by a special tribunal of members of the Court of *Cassation* and of the Council of State appointed every three years, in equal number, by their respective bodies. This tribunal shall be presided over by a minister of justice.

90. Appeals for incompetence or excess of power against the decrees of the Court of Accounts shall be carried before the special tribunal organized to decide such cases of conflictive jurisdiction.

91. A High Court of Justice shall decide, without appeal or recourse of *cassation* or demurrer, the accusations made by the National Assembly against the President of the Republic and his ministers. It shall likewise, in the same way, try all cases of persons accused of crimes, attempts, or conspiracies against the internal and external safety of the State, which the Assembly may have sent before it. Except the case provided for in Article 68, it shall not be called together except by virtue of a decree of the National Assembly which names the city in which the court shall hold its sittings.

92. The High Court shall be composed of five judges and thirty-six jurymen. Every year, in the first fifteen days of the month of November, the Court of *Cassation* shall appoint from among its members, by secret ballot and by absolute majority, the judges of the High Court, the number to be five judges and supplemental judges. These five judges shall select their president. The magistrates filling the functions of the public ministry shall be designated by the President of the Republic, and in case of accusation of the president or his ministers, by the National Assembly. The jurymen, to the number of thirty-six, and four supplemental jurymen, shall be taken from among the members of the general councils of the departments. Representatives elected by the people can not form part of these juries.

93. When a decree of the National Assembly has ordered the formation of the High Court of Justice, and in the case provided for in Article 68, on the requisition of the president or of one of the judges, the president of the Court of Appeal, and, in default of that court, the president of the tribunal of the first instance of the chief judicial place of the department, shall draw lots in public for the name of a member of the general council.

94. On the day appointed for the trial, if there are less than sixty jurymen present, the number shall be filled by supplemental jurymen,

drawn by lot, by the President of the High Court of Justice, from among the members of the general council of the department in which the court sits.

95. The jurymen who shall not have produced an adequate excuse for absence, shall be condemned to pay a fine of not less than 1,000 francs, and not more than 10,000, and to be deprived of their political rights for five years at the utmost.

96. Both the accused and the public prosecutor shall have the right of challenge, as in ordinary cases.

97. The verdict of guilty by the jury can only be rendered by a two-thirds vote.

98. In all cases of the responsibility of ministers, the National Assembly may, according to circumstances, send the accused minister either before the High Court of Justice or before the ordinary tribunals for civil damages.

99. The National Assembly and the President of the Republic may, in all cases, transmit the examination of the acts of any functionary (other than the President of the Republic) to the Council of State whose report shall be made public.

100. The President of the Republic can only be brought to trial before the High Court of Justice. Except as provided for in Article 68, he can only be prosecuted upon an accusation made by the National Assembly, and for crimes and misdemeanors which shall be determined by law.

CHAPTER IX.
OF THE PUBLIC FORCES.

101. The public force is instituted for the defense of the State against foreign enemies, and to insure, at home, the maintenance of order, and the execution of the laws. It is composed of the National Guard, and the army by sea and land.

102. Every Frenchman, except the cases provided for by law, owes his services to the army and to the National Guard. The privilege of every citizen to be exempted from personal military service shall be regulated by the law of the recruiting service.

103. The organization of the National Guard, and the formation of the army shall be regulated by law.

104. The public force is essentially obedient, and can not deliberate.

105. The public force employed to maintain order in the interior only acts on the requisition of the constituted authorities, according to the law prescribed by the legislative power.

106. A law shall determine the cases in which the state of siege shall be declared, and shall regulate the forms and the effects of this measure.

107. No foreign troops can be introduced into French territory without the previous consent of the National Assembly.

CHAPTER X.
OF SPECIAL REGULATIONS.

108. The Legion of Honor is retained; its statutes shall be revised and placed in harmony with the Constitution.

109. The territory of Algeria, and of the colonies, is declared to be French territory, and shall be governed by their separate laws, until a special law places them under the provisions of the present Constitution.

110. The National Assembly confides the trust of the Constitution and the rights it consecrates, to the guardianship and patriotism of all Frenchmen.

CHAPTER XI.
OF THE REVISION OF THE CONSTITUTION.

111. Whenever, in the last year of a legislature, the National Assembly shall have expressed a wish that the Constitution be amended in whole or in part, it shall proceed with the revision in the following manner: The intention expressed by the Assembly shall only take the form of a final decree after three successive deliberations shall have been held, at an interval of one month between each reading, and after a vote of three-fourths of the Assembly. The number of votes must be at least 500. The Assembly for Revision shall only be convened for three months. It shall only engage in the special revision for which it was assembled. Nevertheless, it may, in cases of urgency, provide for legislative necessities.

CHAPTER XII.
OF TRANSITORY ARRANGEMENTS.

112. The provisions of the codes, laws, and regulations, now in force, and which are not in conflict with the present Constitution, shall remain in full force, until they are amended or repealed.

113. All the authorities constituted by the existing law shall remain in the exercise of their duties until the organic laws shall be passed concerning them.

114. The law of the judiciary organization will determine the particular mode for the appointment and first composition of the new tribunals.

115. After the vote upon the Constitution, the Constituent National Assembly shall proceed to frame the organic laws, which shall be decreed by a special law.

116. The first election of the President of the Republic shall be proceeded with in conformity with the special law passed by the National Assembly on October 28, 1848.

APPENDIX IX.

THE CONSTITUTION OF 1852.

The President of the Republic, considering that the French people has been called upon to express its opinion on the following resolution: "The people desire the maintenance of the authority of Louis Napoleon Bonaparte, and give him the necessary power to frame a Constitution according to the bases laid down in his proclamation of December 2d." Considering that the bases submitted for acceptation to the people were: " 1. A responsible chief elected for ten years. 2. Ministers dependent on the executive power alone. 3. A Council of State composed of the most distinguished men, to prepare the laws, and to advocate them before the Legislative Body. 4. A Legislative Body to discuss and pass the laws, elected by universal suffrage, without *scrutin de liste*, which falsify the election. 5. A second Assembly composed of the most illustrious men of the country, as an equipoising power, guardian of the fundamental compact, and of the public liberties."

Considering that the people have replied affirmatively by 7,500,000 votes, the Constitution is hereby promulgated, the tenor of which is as follows:

TITLE I.

ARTICLE 1. The Constitution recognizes, confirms, and guarantees the great principles of 1789, which constitute the ground-work of the public rights of the French.

TITLE II.

FORMS OF THE GOVERNMENT OF THE REPUBLIC.

2. The government of the French Republic is confided for ten years to Prince Louis Napoleon Bonaparte, now President of the Republic.

3. The President of the Republic governs by means of ministers, of the Council of State, of the Senate, and of the Legislative Body.

4. The legislative power is exercised jointly by the President of the Republic, the Senate, and the Legislative Body.

TITLE III.
OF THE PRESIDENT OF THE REPUBLIC.

5. The President of the Republic is responsible to the French people, to whom he has always the right to appeal.

6. The President of the Republic is the Chief of State; he commands the land and sea forces, declares war, makes treaties of peace, of alliance and commerce, appoints employés, and makes the necessary regulations and decrees for the execution of the laws.

7. Justice is rendered in his name.

8. He alone has the initiative of the laws.

9. He has the right to grant pardons.

10. He sanctions and promulgates the laws and the *Senatûs consulta*.

11. He presents, annually, by a message to the Senate and to the Legislative Body, the state of the affairs of the Republic.

12. He has the right to declare the state of siege in one or several departments, on the condition that he report the fact to the Senate within the shortest possible time. The effect of the state of siege shall be regular by law.

13. The ministers are only subject to the Chief of State; they are only responsible for the acts of the government in so far as they are individually concerned; there is no joint responsibility among them; and they can only be impeached by the Senate.

14. The ministers, the members of the Senate, of the Legislative Body, of the Council of State; the officers of the land and marine forces, the magistrates, and the public functionaries, take the following oath: *I swear obedience to the Constitution and fidelity to the President.*

15. A *Senatûs consultum* shall determine the sum annually allowed to the President of the Republic, and for the duration of his functions.

16. If the President of the Republic dies before the expiration of his term of office, the Senate shall call upon the nation to proceed to a new election.

17. The Chief of State has the right, by a secret act deposited in the archives of the Senate, to designate to the French people the names of the citizens whom he appoints, in the interests of France, to the confidence of the people and to their suffrages.

18. Until the election of the new President of the Republic the president of the Senate governs, with the concurrence of the ministers in office, who organize themselves into a Council of Government, and decide by a majority of votes.

TITLE IV.

OF THE SENATE.

19. The number of senators shall not exceed 150; the number for the first year is fixed at eighty.

20. The Senate is composed: 1. Of cardinals, marshals, and admirals; 2. Of citizens whom the President of the Republic may think proper to raise to the dignity of senators.

21. The senators can not be removed, and are appointed for life.

22. The functions of senators are gratuitous; nevertheless, the President of the Republic may grant to senators, on account of services rendered, and their fortune, a personal income, which can not exceed 30,000 francs annually.

23. The president and vice-presidents of the Senate are appointed by the President of the Republic, and chosen from among the senators. They are named for one year. The salary of the president of the Senate is fixed by a decree.

24. The President of the Republic convokes and prorogues the Senate. He fixes the duration of its sessions by a decree. The sessions of the Senate are not public.

25. The Senate is the guardian of the fundamental compact and of the public liberties. No law can be promulgated until it shall have submitted to it.

26. The Senate may oppose the promulgation: 1. Of laws which may be contrary to, or constitute an attack on, the Constitution, on religion, on morals, on freedom of worship, on individual liberty, on the equality of citizens before the law, on the inviolability of property, and on the unremovability of the magistracy; those who may compromise the defense of the territory.

27. The Senate regulates by *Senatûs consulta:* 1. The Constitution of the colonies and of Algeria. 2. All that has not been provided for by the Constitution, and is necessary for its working. 3. The interpretation of the Constitution in case of conflict of opinion.

28. These *Senatûs consulta* shall be submitted, for his approval, to the President of the Republic, and promulgated by him.

29. The Senate approves or annuls all acts which have been transmitted to it as unconstitutional by the government, or denounced for the same cause by petitions of citizens.

30. The Senate may, by an address to the President of the Republic, set forth the ground-work of laws of great national interest.

31. It may also propose amendments to the Constitution. If the proposition is adopted by the executive power, it must be decreed by a *Senatûs consultum*.

32. Nevertheless, all amendments to the fundamental ground-work of the Constitution, as laid down in the proclamation of December 2, and adopted by the French people, shall be submitted to universal suffrage.

33. In case of the dissolution of the Legislative Body, the Senate, upon the proposition of the President of the Republic, shall provide by measures of urgency for all that is necessary for the working of the government.

TITLE V.

OF THE LEGISLATIVE BODY.

34. Population shall be the basis of all elections.

35. There shall be one deputy to the Legislative Body for every 35,000 electors.

36. Deputies are elected by universal suffrage, without *scrutin de liste*.

37. They receive no salary.

38. They are elected for six years.

39. The Legislative Body votes upon bills and taxes.

40. Any amendment adopted by the commission charged to examine bills shall be sent back without discussion to the Council of State, by the president of the Legislative Body. If the amendment is not approved by the Council of State, it can not be submitted to the discussion of the Legislative Body.

41. The ordinary sessions of the Legislative Body lasts three months; its sessions are public, but, on the demand of five members, it may form itself into a secret committee of the whole.

42. The accounts of the sittings of the Legislative Body by the journals, or by other means of publication, shall only consist in the reproduction of the minutes of the sittings, drawn up at the conclusion of each session, under the direction of the president of the Legislative Body.

43. The president and the vice presidents of the Legislative Body shall be named by the President of the Republic for one year; they are chosen from the deputies. The salary of the legislative president will be fixed by a decree.

44. Ministers can not be members of the Legislative Body.

45. The right of petition is exercised before the Senate. No petition can be addressed to the Legislative Body.

46. The President of the Republic convokes, adjourns, prorogues, and dissolves the Legislative Body. In the event of its being dissolved, the President of the Republic must convoke a new one within the period of six months.

Title VI.

OF THE COUNCIL OF STATE.

47. The number of councilors of State in ordinary service is from forty to fifty.

48. The councilors of State are named by the President of the Republic, and are removable by him.

49. The Council of State is presided over by the President of the Republic, and, in his absence, by the person whom he appoints as vice-president of the Council of State.

50. The Council of State is charged, under the direction of the President of the Republic, to draw up bills, and regulations of the public administration, and to decide differences which may arise in matters of administration.

51. It supports, in the name of the government, the discussion of bills before the Senate and the Legislative Body. The councilors of State charged to speak in the name of the government are nominated by the President of the Republic.

52. The salary of each councilor of State is 25,000 francs.

53. The ministers have rank, sitting, and deliberative voice in the Council of State.

Title VII.

OF THE HIGH COURT OF JUSTICE.

54. A high court of justice shall try, without appeal, or without recourse to *cassation*, all persons who shall have been sent before it charged with crime *attentats*, or conspiracies against the President of the Republic, and against the internal or external safety of the State. It can only be formed by virtue of a decree of the President of the Republic.

55. A *Senatûs consultum* shall determine the organization of this high court.

TITLE VIII.
GENERAL AND TEMPORARY PROVISIONS.

56. The existing provisions of the codes, laws, and regulations, which are not in conflict with this Constitution, remain in force until they shall have been legally repealed.

57. The municipal organization shall be determined by law. The mayors shall be appointed by the executive power, and may be chosen from persons who are not members of the municipal council.

58. The present Constitution shall be in force from the day on which the great bodies of the State shall have been constituted. The decrees issued by the President of the Republic from December 2 until that period shall have the force of law.

Done at the Palace of the Tuileries, the 14th of January, 1852.

                (Signed)   LOUIS NAPOLEON.

APPENDIX X.

CONSTITUTIONAL LAWS OF 1875.

LAW UPON THE ORGANIZATION OF THE SENATE, FEBRUARY 24, 1875.

ARTICLE 1. The Senate is composed of 300 members, 225 of whom are elected by the departments and colonies, and seventy-five by the National Assembly.

ART. 2. The departments of the Seine and du Nord elect each five senators. The departments of the Seine-Inférieure, Pas-de-Calais, Gironde, Rhône, Finistère, Côtes-du-Nord, each four senators. The departments of the Loire-Inférieure, Saône-et-Loire, Ille-et-Vilaine, Seine-et-Oise, Isère, Puy-de-Dôme, Somme, Bouches-du-Rhône, Aisne, Loire, Manche, Maine-et-Loire, Morbihan, Dordogne, Haute-Garonne, Charente-Inférieure, Calvados, Sarthe, Hérault, Basses-Pyrénées, Gard, Aveyron, Vendée, Orne, Oise, Vosges, Allier, each three senators. All the other departments, each two senators.

The territory of Belfort, the three departments of Algérie, the four colonies of Martinique, of Guadeloupe, of Réunion, and French India elect each one senator.

ART. 3. No one can be a senator unless he is a Frenchman, and is at least forty years of age, and vested with civil and political rights.

ART. 4. The senators of the departments and of the colonies shall be elected on a general ticket by an absolute majority, by an electoral college assembled in the capital of the department or colony, and composed of the following members: 1. Of the deputies. 2. The councilors-general. 3. The councilors of arrondissement. 4. The delegates elected by the electors of the commune, one by each municipal council.

In French India, the members of the colonial council or of the local councils shall be substituted for the councilors-general, the councilors of arrondissement, and for the delegates of the municipal councils. They vote in the capital of each settlement.

ART. 5. The senators named by the Assembly shall be elected by *scrutin de liste*, and by an absolute majority of votes.

ART. 6. The senators of the departments and of the colonies shall be elected for nine years, and renewable by one-third every three years. At the end of the first session, the departments shall be divided into three series, containing each an equal number of senators. It shall then proceed by lot to designate the series which shall be renewed at the expiration of the first and second triennial periods.

ART. 7. The senators elected by the Assembly are unremovable. In the event of a vacancy by death, resignation, or other cause, it shall, within two months, be filled by the Senate itself.

ART. 8. The Senate has, concurrently with the Chamber of Deputies, the initiation and the making of the laws. The laws relating to the finances, however, must, in the first instance, be presented to and voted by the Chamber of Deputies.

ART. 9. The Senate can be constituted a court of justice to try either the President of the Republic or the ministers, and to take cognizance of attempts (*attentats*) committed against the safety of the State.

ART. 10. The election of the Senate shall be proceeded with one month before the time fixed by the National Assembly for its adjournment. The Senate shall enter upon its duties and organize the same day the National Assembly adjourns.

ART. 11. The present law shall not be promulgated until after the law upon the public powers shall have been definitely voted.

CONSTITUTIONAL LAW UPON THE ORGANIZATION OF THE PUBLIC POWERS, FEBRUARY 25, 1875.

ARTICLE 1. The legislative power shall be exercised by two assemblies, the Chamber of Deputies and the Senate. The Chamber of Deputies shall be chosen by universal suffrage, under the conditions determined by the electoral law. The composition and the mode of choosing, and the power and privileges of the Senate, shall be regulated by a special law.

ART. 2. The President of the Republic shall be elected by an absolute majority of votes, by the Senate and by the Chamber of

Deputies, united in National Assembly. He shall be elected for seven years, and be re-eligible.

ART. 3. The President of the Republic has the initiative of the laws, concurrently with the members of the two Chambers; he promulgates the laws when they shall have been voted by the two Chambers, and he superintends and assures the execution of the laws. He has the power to grant pardons, but amnesties can only be accorded by law. He disposes of the armed forces. He appoints all the civil and military employés. He presides on all occasions of national solemnity; envoys and ambassadors from foreign powers are accredited to him. Each of the acts of the President of the Republic shall be countersigned by a minister.

ART. 4. As soon as vacancies shall be produced after the promulgation of the present law, the President of the Republic shall appoint, in council of ministers, the councilors of State in ordinary service. The appointment of the councilors of State thus named can only be revoked by a decree passed in council of ministers. The councilors of State, appointed by virtue of the law of May 24, 1872, can not be removed until the expiration of their office, and according to the forms determined by that law. After the adjournment of the National Assembly, the revocation can only be pronounced by a resolution of the Senate.

ART. 5. The President of the Republic can, with the advice of the Senate, dissolve the Chamber of Deputies before the legal expiration of its mandate. In this event, the electoral colleges shall, within three months, be convoked for a new election.

ART. 6. The ministers are responsible, as a whole, before the Chambers for the general policy of the government, and individually for their personal acts. The President of the Republic is only responsible for high treason.

ART. 7. In the event of a vacancy by reason of his death, or from other cause, the two assemblies, in joint session, shall immediately proceed to the election of a new President. The Council of Ministers, during the interval, shall be invested with executive power.

ART 8. The Chambers shall have the right, by separate deliberations taken in each Chamber, by an absolute majority of votes, either voluntarily, or on the demand of the President of the Republic, to declare that there are substantial reasons for the revision of the constitutional laws. After each of the two Chambers shall have passed this resolution, they shall reunite in National Assembly and proceed to the revision. The laws enacting a revision of the constitutional laws, in whole or in part, shall be passed by an absolute majority of the members composing the National Assembly. During the period for which the law of November 20, 1873, confers power upon Marshal McMahon, this revision can only take place on the proposition of the President of the Republic.

Art. 9. The seat of the executive power and of the two Chambers shall be at Versailles.

CONSTITUTIONAL LAW UPON THE RELATIONS OF THE PUBLIC POWERS, JULY 16, 1875.

Article 1. The Senate and the Chamber of Deputies shall assemble annually on the second Tuesday of January, unless they are sooner called together by the President of the Republic. The two Chambers must remain annually in session at least five months. The session of one commences and terminates at the same time as the other. Public prayers shall, on the Sunday which shall follow the opening, be addressed to God, in the churches and temples, beseeching His aid in the labors of the assemblies.

Art. 2. The President of the Republic shall pronounce the closing of the session. On extraordinary occasions he has the right to convoke the Chambers. He must convoke them if, during the recess, a demand is made for a convocation by an absolute majority of the members composing each Chamber. The President can adjourn the Chambers; however, the adjournment can not exceed the term of one month, or take place more than twice during the same session.

Art. 3. At least one month before the legal term of the powers of the President of the Republic shall terminate, the Chambers shall be united in National Assembly in order to proceed to the election of a new President. In default of convocation, this meeting shall take place, by its own right, on the fifteenth day before the expiration of the executive term. In the event of the death or resignation of the President of the Republic, the two Chambers shall immediately reassemble by their own right. In the event that, by application of Article 5 of the law of February 25, 1875, the Chamber of Deputies should be dissolved at the time the presidency of the Republic should become vacant, the electoral colleges shall immediately be convoked, and the Senate shall reassemble by its own right.

Art. 4. All sessions of either of the two Chambers which shall be held out of the time of the regular session are illegal and void, except in the case provided for in the preceding article and that where the Senate is assembled as a court of justice, and in this last case it can only exercise judicial functions.

ART. 5. The sessions of the Senate and those of the Chamber of Deputies are public. Nevertheless, each Chamber can form itself into a secret committee, upon the demand of a certain number of its members, fixed by the rules. It then decides, by an absolute majority, if the session should be resumed in public upon the same subject.

ART. 6. The President of the Republic communicates with the Chambers by messages, which are read on the tribune by a minister. The ministers have a seat in the two Chambers, and must be heard when they demand it. They may be assisted in the discussion of a bill by commissioners appointed by a decree of the President of the Republic.

ART. 7. The President of the Republic promulgates the laws within the month which follows the transmission to the government of a regularly enacted law. He must, within three days, promulgate the laws whose promulgation shall have been declared urgent by an express vote of one or the other Chamber. In the interim fixed for the promulgation, the President of the Republic may, by a message which shall state his motives therefor, demand of the two Chambers a new deliberation, which can not be refused.

ART. 8. The President of the Republic negotiates and ratifies treaties. As soon as the interest and safety of the State shall permit, he shall give information of their contents to the Chambers. Treaties of peace, of commerce, treaties which involve the finances of the State, those which refer to the condition of persons, and to the rights of property of Frenchmen in foreign countries, are not final until voted by the two Chambers. No cession, no exchange, no annexation of territory can take place except by virtue of law.

ART. 9. The President of the Republic can not declare war except with the previous consent of the two Chambers.

ART. 10. Each of the Chambers is judge of the eligibility of its members and of the regularity of their election; it alone can accept their resignation.

ART. 11. The bureau of each of the two Chambers shall be elected annually for the duration of the session, and for all extraordinary sessions which shall take place before the ordinary session of the following year. When the two assemblies shall unite in National Assembly, their bureau shall be composed of the president, vice-presidents, and secretaries of the Senate.

ART. 12. The President of the Republic can not be impeached except by the Chamber of Deputies, and can not be tried except by the Senate. The ministers can be impeached by the Chamber of Deputies for crimes committed in the exercise of their functions. In this case they are tried by the Senate.

The Senate may be constituted a court of justice by a decree of the President of the Republic, made in council of ministers, to try all persons charged with attempts *(attentat)* against the safety of the State. If the examination of the case has already been commenced in the ordinary courts of justice, the decree convening the Senate may be issued at any time before indictment. A law shall determine the mode of procedure in the matter of the complaint, examination, and trial in such cases.

ART. 13. No member of either Chamber can, during its session, be prosecuted or arrested in any correctional or criminal matter except with the authorization of the Chamber of which he is a member, or in case he is taken in the act. The detention or the prosecution of a member of either Chamber is suspended during the session, and for the whole of its duration, if the Chamber so require.

INDEX.

A.
	PAGE
Additional Act of 1815, text of, Appendix VI	309
" " vote on	113
" " fashioned after British Constitution	112
" " its annulment	114
" " description of	109-112
Address, right of	216
" discussion of	212
Administration, local, Constitution of 1791	27
" " Constitution of 1793	41
" " Constitution of 1795	52, 53
" " Constitution of 1799	74, 77, 84
" " of present France	246-256
Administrative Law	246-256
Alexander, Emperor of Russia	115, 117
" army of	99
Albert	164
Alembert, D'	16
Allison, on crimes of the Convention	37
Alsace ceded	226
Amendment to Constitution of 1795	55
America compared with France and England	268
Americans, criticism of	258
Angoulême, Duke of	115
Arrondissement, government of	248
Arago, member of Provisional Government, 1848	164, 165
" member of Commission of 1848	172, 224
Argenson, D', the Marquis, his Reflections of the Government of France	17
" aim of	26, 65
Artois, Count of, return to Paris	115, 129, 143, 144
Austria and Prussia, treaty between	29

B.
Babœuf executed	60
Bank of France organized	78
Barbaroux of Marseilles accuses Robespierre	30
Barodet, his proposition to revise Constitution of 1875	239
Barrot, Ferdinand, Minister of Interior	189

(409)

			PAGE
Benoist, as to **Revolution**			138
Berry, Duke of			115
Berton, General, plot of			141, 151
Berthier, as to property of Church			119, 143
Bigot de Preamenen, as to Civic Code			80, 81
Billault, death of			212
Bineau, Minister of Public Works			189
Bismarck, opinion of Napoleon			214, 215
Blackstone, as to separation of powers			27, 56
Blanc, Louis, quoted			151
"	"	as to Socialism	169
"	"	as to the Presidency	180-182, 229
"	"	as to hereditary peerage	159, 160
"	"	as member of Provisional Government of 1848	164
Bonald, de			120
Bonaparte, Madame, establishment of			84
"	Jerome		100
"	Joseph		100
Bordeaux, compact entered into at			230
Bories			151
Bourbons, the, Siéyès' opinion of			70
"	"	their rule unpopular	108
"	"	pretentions of	122
"	"	return to France	127
Boulanger, General, his case stated by Naquet			259-262
"	opposed by Pelletan		262-265
Boulay, de la Meurthe, as to Constitution of 1799			71
Bourdon quoted			48
Bourrienne, de			79
Bouvier, Dumolard, his petition to the King			129
Bright likened to Babœuf			11
Brissot executed			45
Broglie, Duke of			150, 229
Brumaire, 18th, Revolution of			63
Bugeaud			165

C.

		PAGE
Cabinet, government in England		205
Cambacérès		79, 80
Cambon, as to objects of Revolution		34, 35
Camille-Desmoullus executed		45
Campo Formio, Treaty of		61
Canton, the Government of		249
Carbonari, plot of		141
Carnot, his opinion as to monarchy		94, 129, 130
"	the right of address not exercised by	259
Caron, Colonel, plot of		141
Carrel, Armand, on ordinances of Charles X		146
Cassation, Tribunal of, established		23

INDEX.

	PAGE
Catholicism, establishment of	86, 154
Cavaignac, as candidate for Presidency	184-186
Cayla, Madame, negotiations of	141
" " influence of	143
Chabot	28
Chambord, Count of, his refusal to negotiate	220
Changarnier, his ambition	165, 231
Charette shot	60
Charlemagne	97
" the Concordat of	110
Charles X, accession of	144, 145
" five ordinances of	145, 146
" at St. Cloud	147
" abdication of	149-151
" movement against, effect of	165
Charter of 1814, preamble of	122
" " provisions of	115-128
" " executive power	123-125
" " legislative power	125, 126
" " judicial power	126
" 1830, provisions of	152-157
" " executive power	155, 156
Chaumette	12
Chénier, as to subjects	86
Church and State	15
Civil Code, origin of	57, 58, 80, 81
" completed	92
" called Code Napoleon	103
Clubs, Cordeliers and Jacobin	12
Clootz, Anacharsis	12
Cobden likened to Babœuf	11
Cochin China, conquest of	211
Code Napoleon	57
Commission, as to Charter of 1814	115, 117
Commons, the House of, power of	267
Commune, the government of	248
Concordat, the, terms of Napoleon's	82, 83
" of Charlemagne	110
Condorcet, life and work of, his life of Turgot, etc	18, 65
Congress of Vienna	107
Considérant, as to the election of President	176
Constant, Benjamin, asked to frame a Constitution	109, 138
" " Commissioner 1830	154
Constituent Assembly, declarations of	22, 23
" " last sitting of	28
" " action of	31
" "	59, 63
Constituent National Assembly of 1848, members of, Commissioners by	172
" " " " Proclamation of	171

INDEX.

		PAGE
Constitution of 1791, text of, Appendix I		273-303
"	" principal features of, its legislative, executive and judicial power	24-28
"	1793, text of, Appendix II	305-313
"	" provisions of	38-42
"	" guarantees of	41, 42
"	" suspended	44
"	1795, text of, Appendix III	315-349
"	" provisions of	49-57
"	1799, text of, Appendix IV	351-361
"	" described	72-79
"	1814, text of, Appendix V	363
"	" description of	115-128
"	" executive power	123-125
"	" legislative power	125, 126
"	" judicial power	126
"	1815, text of, Appendix VI	369
"	" description of	109-112
"	1830, text of, Appendix VII	377
"	" provisions of	152-160
"	1848, text of, Appendix VIII	383
"	" provisions of	173-184
"	" as to executive power	175-177
"	" legislative power	178
"	" judicial power	178, 179
"	" amendment of	183, 193
"	" adoption of	184
"	" organized, conflicts of	194
"	1852, text of, Appendix IX	397
"	" provisions of	198-204
"	" Council of State	199
"	" Ministry	200
"	" Senate	201
"	" Legislative Body	201
"	" remarks on	203, 204
"	" modifications of	224
"	" of Rivet	228, 229
"	1875, provisions	233-248
"	" amendments to	237
"	" text, Appendix X	403
"	" practical working of	256-258
Constitutional Act of 1804, making Napoleon Emperor		94-96
Constitutional Charter of 1814, text of, Appendix V		363-368
"	" of 1830, text of, Appendix VII	377
Constitutional Laws of 1875, text of, Appendix X		403
Consular Government, the, amendments to		89-91
Consulate, the Provisional		67
"	" powers of	68, 69
"	the, and the First Empire	67

INDEX. 413

	PAGE
Contrat, Social	16
Convention, the National	50, 63
" legislation of	38, 57, 58
" as to the inviolability of law	32
" declared war against Holland and Spain	37
" suppresses the Executive Council	43
" Thiers on	59
Conway, Moncure D., as to the Presidency	181, 182
Corcelles, de, on public tumults	139
Cordeliers, the	19, 80
Council of the Five Hundred	51
" " " " resistance of	62
" " Ancients, Constitution of 1795	51
Counter Revolution, reflections on	49
Cousin-Montauban, General, decorated	211
Cremieux, member of Provisional Government of 1848	164, 224
Cromwell	13

D

Danton	12, 19
" disaffected	36
" executed	45
Daunou on the word "subject"	86
Decazes sent to England	136
Delessert, Benjamin, as Commissioner, 1830	154
Democracy, growth of	38
" the French Manifesto of	243-245
Department, voting by, discussed	240, 245
" government of	247, 248
Deputies, the Chamber of, 1814	125, 126
" election of, laws of, 1875	238
" the Chamber of, powers of	256-258
Dicey, A. V., quoted	251
Diderot, life and work of	17
"	65, 151
Directory, the	56, 57, 60
" revolutionary powers of	61, 62, 63
" finances of	68
District voting	245
Dufaure, as to labor question	174
Dumouriez quoted	29
"	132
Dupanloup, as to education	180
Dupin	150, 151
Dupont, De l'Eure, member of Provisional Government	164
Duprat, Pascal	229
Duruy, Minister of Public Instruction of	214

E

	PAGE
Education, system of, First Consul	88
" controlled by Church	135, 136
" Thiers prepares a law on	189, 190
Electoral law of 1820	137, 139
Emile	16
Empire, the First	67
" the Second	205
" the Constitutional, of Napoleon	220, 221
" the Second, closing scenes of	222
Empress of Russia, the	17
Encyclopédie, the	16
Enghein, Duc D'	92
England compared with America and France	268
" blockade against	104
English system advocated	44
" Government, the, referred to	129
Espinasse, General, circular of	210
Europe, coalition against France	85
Evolution in Government	11, 120, 121, 270, 271
" reflections on	63-66
Executive and Legislative, the, separation of	267
Executive Council, reflections on	40
" " of 1793 suppressed	43
Executive Power	123-125
" " of Constitution of 1791	24-28
" " of Constitution of 1793	40
" " in Constitution of 1795	51, 52, 56, 57
" " Charter, 1830	155-157
" " Constitution, 1848	178, 179
" " the Ventavon Bill	231
" " of Constitution of 1875	234, 234

F

Favre, Jules, elected Deputy	210, 224
Ferry, Jules	224
Feuillants, the	20
Finances of the Directory	67, 68
First Consul, see Napoleon Bonaparte	
" " powers of	73, 74
" " proposed legislation of	78
" " character of	80
" " agreement as to Concordat	82, 83
" " ability of	84
" " his opinions	87
" " his opinion of public men	85
" " proposed a system of education	88
" " made Consul for life	89
" " power of	91

INDEX. 415

	PAGE
First Consul, as to Revolution	91
" " proposition to proclaim him Emperor	92, 93
Flocon	164
Fouché, the head of police	130
Fould, Minister of Finance	189
Fouquier, Tinville, executed	49
Foy, General, opinions of	138
" speech of	142
France, divisions and local government of, prior to 1789	26
" success of armies of	31
" divisions of, under Constitution of 1793	39
" armies of, in 1796	61
" Bank of, organized	78
" compared with England and America	268
" plans of revision in	271, 272
" divisions of	247
Francis I. of Austria	104
Frederick of Prussia	16
Fronde, opinions of	268

G

Gambetta, member of Provisional Government of 1870	224-229
" his argument in favor of *scrutin de liste*	240
" defeat of	241
" his opinions and ambition	268
Garnier-Pagés, member of Provisional Government 1848	164
" " member of Commission of 1848	172
" " member of Government of 1870	224
Girondists, the, charges against	30, 36, 37
" " execution of	45
Gladstone on the Irish question	208
Glais-Bizoin	225
Government, reflections on	31, 32
" of 1793, declared revolutionary	44
" reflections on	63-66
" Constitutional, reflections on	120, 121
" evolution in	246
" local, present France, provisions of	246-250
" Provisional, of 1870	224
Grand Elector, the	70, 71
Great Britain, government of	85
" " peace with	88
" " treaty with	211
Grévy, as to election of President	176, 177
" his opinion of National Assembly	231
" forced to resign	258
" his inertia	259
" accession of	266
Guizot as a conservative	162
" ridiculed the Left	150, 163

H

	PAGE
Harrison, Frederick, quoted	18
Haussmann, threats of	212
Hautpoul, D', Minister of War	189
Hazlitt, as to Marat's zeal	43
Héloïse, La Nouvelle	16
Henry IV	63
Hératry, as Commissioner, 1830	154
Herbert executed	45
Herbois, D', Collot, quoted	46
History, continuity in	12
Hugo, Victor, deserts the Right	188
" " on State education	189
Hume, David	17, 65
Hungary and Bohemia make war	20

I

Italy, democracy in	13

J

Jacobins, the	19, 30, 80
" discontent of	62
" attack of the Gilded Youth on	49
Jacobin Clubs, the	60
Josephine, Empress, the divorce	104
Judicial power of Constitution of 1791	24-28
" " " 1793	41
" " " 1795	53, 54
" " 1814	126
" " Constitution of 1848	178, 179
" " 1852	202
Judicial system of France	249, 250
Justinian	108

K

King, the, powers of, under Charter of 1814	123-125

L

Laboulaye, his entreaty	232
Lafayette, Marquis of	19
" flight of	30
" disapproves of Additional Act	112
" on Government of 1820	140
" at Hotel de Ville	148, 154
Laflitte	147, 150
Lagrange	82
Lamartine, member of Commission of 1848	172
" as to election of President	176
La Place	82
Lebrun	79

INDEX.

	PAGE
Ledru, Rollin, as to Provisional Government of 1848	161
" " as candidate for Presidency	184–186
" " member of Commission of 1848	172
Legion of Honor, the, origin of	78
" " " created	87–88
Legislative Assembly, first sitting of	28
" " closed, its legislation	30
Legislative Body, the, of 1799	73, 74
" " resistance to First Consul, its members stricken off the list	86
" " the, declares the Second Empire	207
" " " powers increased under Second Empire	216, 217, 219
Legislative Power of Constitution of 1791	24–28
" " " 1793	39, 40
" " " 1795	50, 51
" " " 1799	72–74
" " " 1848	178
" " " 1852	201, 202
" " " 1875	231, 235–237
Lenglé, proposition of, to amend Constitution of 1875	239
Leroux, Pierre, on ordinances of Charles X	146
Locke	65
Lolme, de	56
Lorraine, ceded	226
Louis XI	63
Louis XII	11
Louis XIV	63, 64
" silenced his Parliament	11
Louis XV	64
Louis XVI, accession to throne	18
" flight of	23, 24
" Constitution of 1792 accepted by	23
" vetoed bills	28
" separated from family	31
" execution of	33
" as to power of Convention to put him on trial	32, 33
" reflections on execution of	33, 34
Louis XVIII, placed on throne	106
" fled from France	108
" reception in London	118
" as to proposed Constitution; entry into Paris	119
" his declaration	119
" as to English Constitution	120
" the title of	127
" reign of	143
Louis Philippe, called to the throne	153
" errors of	160, 161, 162
" mistakes of	163
" abdication of	164

	PAGE
Louis Philippe embarks for England	165
Louisiana, purchase of, by the United States	91

M

Mabli, aim of	26
MacMahon, opinion of	209
" nominated President	230
" elected for seven years	231
" dissolution of Chamber by	256, 257
" resignation of	257
" the fall of	256
Maine, Henry S., opinion of Government in England	268
Malesherbes, aim of	26
" executed	45
Manuel, de, expulsion of	142
Marat quoted	31
" assassination of	42
Maria Louisa, her marriage with Napoleon	104
Marie, member of Provisional Government of 1848	164
" member of Commission of 1848	172
Marie Antoinette executed	45
Marmount commands forces of Charles X	117
Marrast	164
Mexico, expedition to	212
" French troops withdrawn from	215
Mignet, his opinion of Robespierre	48
Ministry without portfolio	211
" of 1814	126
" Liberal, members of	219
Mirabeau	18
" quoted	22
Molé refused to form Ministry	163
Monarchies of 1814 and 1830	63
Monarchists, cabals of	177
" the, rely on MacMahon	231
Monarchy, discussion as to	93, 94
" the restoration of	115
Moncey, Marshal	117
Montalembert, de, as to education	182
Montesquieu, as to separation of powers	27
"	58, 65
Morley, John, compared to Saint Just	12
Morny, his death	214
Mortemart	147
Monnier, his school	110
Mountaineers, the, methods of	37

N

Nantes, the Edict of, revocation	23
Napoleon I., see First Consul	

INDEX. 419

		PAGE
Napoleon I., commands troops of Convention		59
"	victories in Italy	61
"	other battles	62
"	as Consul	67
"	as to specialists	69
"	regarded as a Cæsar or Cromwell	69, 70
"	his oath to support Constitution of the Empire	96, 97
"	coronation of	98
"	his energies	99
"	power of	100
"	as to manufacturers	100
"	legislation	100
"	as to peace and war	101
"	finances and internal improvements	102
"	his character	103
"	marriage with Maria Louisa	104
"	his blockade against England	104
"	his ambition	104
"	dissolution of marriage with Empress Josephine	104
"	his invasion of Russia	105
"	deposition of	106
"	his return to France	107
"	changes proposed by him	109
"	a new government favored by him	110
"	as to Constitution of 1815	111
"	signs the Act at Champ de Mai	113
"	his second abdication	114, 131
"	return to France	130
"	influence of his name	140, 141
Napoleon III		160
"	returns to France	168
"	his election as President	184, 186
"	the commencement of *coup d'état*	168
"	seeks Presidency for life	188
"	conspiracies of	191-194
"	his Cabinet, members of	192
"	speech of	193
"	dissolves National Assembly	195
"	power to form Constitution delegated	196
"	Empire of, established	206
"	as to Regency	208
"	amnesty of	210
"	on Constitutional changes	215, 216
"	forfeiture of his throne	223, 226
Naquet, Alfred, quoted		259
National Assembly of 1848		171
"	" " dissolved, 1851	195
"	" of Bordeaux	226
"	" opinion of Grévy	231

420 INDEX.

	PAGE
Necker	18
Nelson	99
Nemours, Duke of	164
Netherlands, Democracy in	13
New Year's Day, ceremony of, abolished	29

O.

Odilon Barrot	150, 163
" " as to election of President	176
Ollivier, Emile, on extension of prerogatives	215
Orléanist, the monarchy of	152
" party of, and its objects	269
Orleans, Duke of, executed	45
" " as Lieutenant General	152
" "	147, 151
Oudinot, Marshal	117

P.

Paley, opinions of	56
Parieu, Minister of Education	189
Paris, defense of the city of	227, 228
" Count of, his negotiations at Frohsdorf	230
Parliamentarism, contradictions of	235
Parliamentary government in England	266
Parties, combinations of	228
Pasquier, views of	138
Peel, Sir Robert, as to corn laws	11
Peerage, discussion as to abolition of	157-160
Peers, the Chamber of, 1814	125
" Chamber of, 1830	153
Pelletan, Camille, quoted	262
Périer, Casimir	147, 150
" " as to hereditary peerage	157
Persigny, circular of	212
Petion	30
Peyronnet, de, declaration of	145
Philip le Bel	63
Philosophical Dictionary, the	16
Picard, member of Provisional Government of 1870	225
Pilnitz, treaty of	29
Pitt, designs of	44
Pope, the, Encyclical of	44
Portalis, as to Civil Code	80, 81
Portal, attendance on King	143, 144
Presidency of Republic of 1848	175-178
President, Constitution 1848, election of	176, 177, 184-186
" " " powers of	177
" powers of, Constitution of 1875	234, 235, 236
" election of, in United States (see executive power)	258

INDEX. 421

	PAGE
Press, rights of	123
" the, restrictive measures	187
Prince Imperial, the Society of	220
Property, National	123
Provisional Government of 1848	166, 173
" " " Proclamation of	171
Prussia and Austria, treaty between	29
Public Powers, laws of, proposed by Thiers	231
" " laws organizing	233
" " provisions of	233, 234
Public Safety, Committee of	35
" " Committee of, placed above Executive Committee	43
" " powers of, curtailed	49

Q.

Quinet, Edgar, on State instruction.................. 189

R.

Radical party, the, its demands	270-272
Reign of Terror over	45, 49
Rémusat on ordinances of Charles X.	146
Republic, the First	11
" of 1848	64
" the Second	166
" the Third	223
" " proclamation of	224, 225
Republican party, the, its objects, how conditioned	270
Revision proposed	239-242
" " by Ferry	241
" of August 14, 1884	242, 243
" in France	259
" various plans of	271, 272
Revolution, the	11
" " Cromwellian, American and French compared	13
" " its character	23
" " French, a reformation	34
" " French, objects of	34, 35
" "	63-66
" " indestructible of	98
Revolutionary Tribunal, jurisdiction of	35
" Commission of Twelve, the	36
" Committees established	45
Revolutions, reflections on	20
Richelieu, de, treaty signed by	132
" Ministry of	141
Robespierre	12, 19, 30
" on Pitt	44
" as to burgher aristocracy and the Girondists	36
" as to Constitution of 1793	42
" oration at Marat's funeral	43

422 INDEX.

	PAGE
Robespierre, as to belief in Supreme Being......47,	48
" executed......	48
Rœderer, as to Constitution of 1799	71
Roger-Ducos, as Consul....	67
Roland, Madame, executed	45
Roman Catholic Religion......	123
Roman Expedition, the......	190
Rome, siege of....	187
Rouher, Minister of Justice......	189
" policy of......	218
Rousseau, life and work of 16, 57,	65
Royalists, the, intention of......	232

S.

	PAGE
Saint Vincent Society suppressed......	212
Saint Just quoted...... 23,	45
" opinions of......	37
Savoy and Nice, annexation of....	211
Sébastiani as Commissioner, 1830	154
Séchelles, Herault de, author of Constitution of 1793....	38
Second Republic, the......	166
Senate, the, of 1799	70
" Conservative......73,	74
" resistance to Concordat......	84
" powers of, extended......	216
Senators, election of, laws of 1875......	238
Septenate, the......	232
Siéyès, Abbé......18,	62
" as Consul......	67
" as to Constitution of 1799......	69–72
" efforts of......	85
" liked the British Constitution......	109
" as to Additional Act......	110
Simon, Jules......	225
Sismondi, de, his opinion of Additional Act......	112
Staël, Madame de, approves Additional Act	112
State and Church, combination between......	14
States-general, the......20,	21
Suffrage, universal, of 1848	175
" restrictions of......	235–237
Supreme Being, the worship of, and festivals to......46,	47
Suwarrow......	62
Switzerland, democracy in......	13

T

	PAGE
Talleyrand, his sympathy with the people......	19
" as to Constitution of 1799......	71
" negotiates evacuation......	118
" conspiracies of......	133

INDEX.   423

	PAGE
Tennis Court, the meeting in	21
Thiers, as to Constitution of 1793	42
" on the Convention	59
" on Bonaparte	79, 80
" on ordinances of Charles X	146
" declaration in favor of Duke Orleans	147, 148
" as to peerage	159, 160
" maxim of	162
" as to banquet	163
" as to labor question	174
" as to election of President	176
" on parliamentarism	214
" opinions of	215
" offered the premiership by the Empress	223
" right of speech as President limited	229
" his resignation accepted	230
Tiers état, the	21
Tilsit, peace of	99
Tocqueville, de, as to French functionaries	75-77
Tolleron	151
Tracy, as Commissioner, 1830	154
Tribunals Extraordinary, opinion of M. Grévy	188
" " " Dufaure	188
Tribunate, the, of Siéyès Constitution	70
" " action of	80
" " of 1799	73, 74
" " resistance to Concordat	81
" " agitated political and social questions	85
Trochu, proclamations of	224
Tronchet, as to Civil Code	80, 81
" his opinion of First Consul	91
Tuileries attached	30
Turgot, aim of	18, 26
Twelve Committees, the, established	46

U

United States, Constitution of, as to separation of powers	27
" " as to amendment	82
" " referred to	74
" Government of	84
" Presidential system compared with that of France	259
" the Constitution of, comment upon	267, 268

V

Vann, de, Bertin, as Commissioner, 1830	154
Vendée, la, subdued	60, 62
Ventavon, as to executive power	231
Vergniaud, his speech	29
" executed	45
Versailles, government removed from	238

	PAGE
Villafranca, peace of	10
Villèle, de, ministry of	141, 143, 144
Villemain, commission in 1830	154
Vincennes, conspiracy of	140
Voltaire, life and work of	16, 65
Voting by department and district	268, 269

W

Washington, want of semblance to Cromwell	13
Wallon, his amendment	232, 233
Wallonnat, the	233
Wellington, Duke of, the British army under	104, 105
" " quoted	132
Workmen, association of	214

X

Xavier, Louis Stanislaus	115

www.ingramcontent.com/pod-product-compliance
Lightning Source LLC
Chambersburg PA
CBHW020834020526
44114CB00040B/781